BRITAIN AND THE
AUSTRALIAN COLONIES
1818-1831

BRITAIN
AND THE
AUSTRALIAN
COLONIES
1818–1831
The Technique of Government

BY

J. J. EDDY

CLARENDON PRESS · OXFORD
1969

Oxford University Press, Ely House, London W. 1

GLASGOW NEW YORK TORONTO MELBOURNE WELLINGTON
CAPE TOWN SALISBURY IBADAN NAIROBI LUSAKA ADDIS ABABA
BOMBAY CALCUTTA MADRAS KARACHI LAHORE DACCA
KUALA LUMPUR SINGAPORE HONG KONG TOKYO

PRINTED IN GREAT BRITAIN
BY W. & J. MACKAY & CO LTD, CHATHAM

FOREWORD

T HIS study is an attempt to site—within the wider context of Imperial government between Waterloo and the Reform Bill—the history and development of the emerging Australian colonies. In its preparation I have been helped and encouraged by many institutions and people, chiefly in Britain and Australia. I should like to acknowledge my great debt to the Australian and English Provinces of the Society of Jesus, the Association of Commonwealth Universities, and the Universities of Oxford and Melbourne, who made my research possible.

In particular I am grateful to those with whom I have discussed the work either in part or in full: Dr. A. F. Madden, Professor H. J. Habakkuk, Professor J. A. Gallagher, Dr. R. M. Hartwell, Mr. D. K. Fieldhouse, and Dr. C. W. Newbury of Oxford: Professor J. A. La Nauze of the Australian National University: Dr. G. Serle of Monash University: Professor A. W. Martin of La Trobe University: and Professors R. M. Crawford and W. Macmahon Ball of Melbourne University.

I also acknowledge with thanks the assistance I have received from many librarians and archivists, especially at the Public Record Office, the British Museum, the Institute of Historical Research, London; the Bodleian Library and Rhodes House Library, Oxford; the Public Library of Victoria and the Mitchell Library in Sydney.

J. J. EDDY, S.J.

The Australian National University,
Canberra

ABBREVIATIONS

Adm.	Admiralty Papers in the Public Record Office
A.O.	Audit Office Papers in the Public Record Office
B.M. Add. MSS.	British Museum, Additional Manuscripts
B.M.	*British Monthly*
B.T.	Board of Trade Papers in the Public Record Office
C.H.R.	*Canadian Historical Review*
C.O.	Colonial Office Papers in the Public Record Office
Ec.R.	*Eclectic Review*
E.R.	*Edinburgh Review*
F.O.	Foreign Office Papers in the Public Record Office
G.M.	*Gentleman's Magazine*
H.O.	Home Office Papers in the Public Record Office
H.R.A.	*Historical Records of Australia*
H.S. A.N.Z.	*Historical Studies, Australia and New Zealand*
M.C.	*Morning Chronicle*
M.L.	Mitchell Library
M.R.	*Monthly Review*
N.M.M.	*New Monthly Magazine*
P.D.	Parliamentary Debates
P.P.	Parliamentary Papers
P.R.O.	Public Record Office
Q.R.	*Quarterly Review*
R.A.H.S.	Royal Australian Historical Society
S.C.	Select Committee
W.R.	*Westminster Review*

CONTENTS

INTRODUCTORY: A COLONIAL HYBRID

ON 23 April 1817 Lord Bathurst, Secretary of State for War and the Colonies, informed Lord Sidmouth at the Home Department that he had 'for some time past had under consideration the present state of the settlements in New South Wales'. He had grave doubts whether they were fulfilling the purpose 'for which they were originally established'. Transportation of convicts, he felt, was not viewed with proper apprehension at home, and had not proved an effective means of reformation. Besides, the colony was now looked on as 'an object of anxious solicitude to all, who were desirous of leaving their Native Country and had Capital to apply to the Improvement of Land': and the nature of penal government had materially curtailed the exercise by settlers of 'those rights which they enjoyed in this country, and to which as British subjects they conceive themselves entitled in every part of His Majesty's Dominions'. A Commissioner of Inquiry must be appointed. Unless the whole system could be thoroughly overhauled, it might have to be abandoned.[1] Here, after thirty years, was formal and explicit recognition of the unique colonial dilemma which had always been implied in Britain's penal experiment at the Antipodes.

In the augmented colonial galaxy of 1815, the West Indies, though entering on an era of decline, were important for strategic as well as commercial and traditional reasons. Problems connected with slavery continued to assure the plantation colonies of a paramount place in the concern of humanitarian and reforming groups as well as administrators.[2] British North America, with its complicated regional and racial structure, and its challenging proximity to a Republican neighbour still so painfully remembered, had long provided scope for imperial experiment and executive improvisation.[3] But what the Colonial Office later regularly termed 'the progressive and rapid increase of the Australian Colonies and of the colony of the Cape of Good Hope' was a relatively new element in colonial government.[4]

---

[1] *Historical Records of Australia*, Series I, Vol. x, p. 807, Bathurst–Sidmouth, 23 Apr. 1817.

[2] D. J. Murray, *The West Indies and the Development of Colonial Government 1801–1834* (Oxford, 1965).

[3] H. T. Manning, *The Revolt of French Canada, 1800–1835* (London, 1962).

[4] C.O. 323/213/97, Draft of Memorandum, Goderich–Spring Rice, 28 Jan. 1831.

And although the concluding years of the war and early days of the peace witnessed in the Antipodes a civilizing burst of activity, exploration, construction of public works and a certain maturing of the convict system, it was clear that a cross-roads had been reached and a time for second thoughts.

The settlements in New Holland, 'not having been established with any view to territorial or commercial advantage . . . must chiefly be considered as Receptacles for offenders', Bathurst officially informed his Commissioner of Inquiry.[1] They were, therefore, peculiar in themselves and could not be administered with 'the usual Reference to those General Principles of Colonial Policy, which are applicable to other Foreign Possessions of His Majesty'. So long as they continued to be 'destined by the Legislature of the Country to these purposes, their Growth as Colonies must be a Secondary Consideration, and the leading Duty of those, to whom their Administration is entrusted, will be to keep up in them such a system of just discipline, as may render transportation an object of serious apprehension'. Yet the course of free expansion had to be balanced against the demands of authority, and he warned the Commissioner to bear in mind the possibility of a cessation of transportation to the existing settlements if, as he suspected, they had already become incapable of 'undergoing any efficient change'. 'The problem is—', minuted an under-secretary over five years later, '—(and it is no easy one)—to blend Colonial Policy with Punishment, . . . and all arguments which have no reference to the situation of New South Wales as a penal Colony can have no weight with the Government.'[2]

The period of the early naval governors had been in practice a struggle for existence against long odds. The immense distance from home and the harsh character of the land would themselves have created formidable difficulties for the authorities; and to them were added the special complications which arose from the convict establishment. Once the pioneering phase ended, however, the ambiguity of the whole enterprise had made itself felt. An example of 'long-range administration carried to its utmost extreme',[3] there was no aspect of the colony's life which was not the concern of some department of the central government. But when survival was guaranteed and an adequate routine established in communication and penal

---

[1] *H.R.A.* I/x/4, Bathurst–Bigge, 6 Jan. 1819.   [2] C.O. 201/155/305.
[3] D. M. Young, *The Colonial Office in the Early Nineteenth Century* (London, 1961), p. 249.

discipline, British statesmen could afford to pay less systematic attention to what could, of course, only be regarded as a political as well as a strategic backwater. The powers of the British official representative, the autocratic governor, were in any case so all-embracing that, from the beginning, the complaint was rather of over-government than of neglect.

Critics like Adam Smith and Bentham might oppose all colonies because of their expense, or MacKintosh, Romilly's successor as a constitutional gadfly and spokesman for New South Wales, might insist in 1816 when the war-machine was being dismantled that Great Britain would eventually break down under the strain of providing for the defence of her rapidly grown empire. But colonies, and particularly colonies of settlement, had become, and were acknowledged to have become, so much part and parcel of a shared national experience that their retention and growth was at least as natural and acceptable as the disturbing and somewhat startling evolution of the new industrial cities of the north. Lord Liverpool, speaking in the Lords to one of Huskisson's consolidation bills in 1825, took it that colonies 'must be considered as integral parts of Great Britain, as much as London, or Liverpool'.[1] The next year in the Sydney *Australian* the correspondent 'John Bull' quoted the *Quarterly Review* with approval to the effect that Sydney was now a town equal to Yarmouth, Hull, Leith, Aberdeen, or Belfast, and would soon stand comparison with Portsmouth, Bristol, and Liverpool. Adam Smith, he commented, did not write or think for New South Wales, but for an old and powerful kingdom, deep in debt, maintaining vast armies and navies, and swarming like a beehive with an abundant and industrious population. His principles and the government's pettiness must not be allowed to tease, worry, perplex, and ruin men who had made the colony 'the shrewdest, cleverest, and most independent under the British crown'; men who 'left in a desert island, at the Antipodes of our father land, . . . wonderful to say, are rapidly converting it into English parks, and erecting English palaces'.[2]

Most of the social elements of nineteenth-century England proved to be exportable to Australia, from cricket to the common law, and there is really a difference rather of scale than of kind between the feelings which impelled Wilberforce to chair meetings of the Society for Destitute Seamen and the contemporary Benevolent Society in Parramatta. Telford and Macadam, Lancaster and Bell, these were

[1] P.D. new series, xiii/1134, 14 June 1825.   [2] 13 Dec. 1826.

signs of the times, not prerogatives of the heartland. The *Birmingham Spectator* complained in 1824 about the bad state of the roads; a world away the newly independent Australian Press reported in 1826 that 'not a road in the colony was in a decent state of repair.'[1] Much later, when the third Earl Grey wanted to describe the character of colonial assemblies, he avoided any flattering reference to the mother of parliaments at Westminster and chose a more homely comparison. 'The town councils of English boroughs are not very unlike these assemblies, either in the number of their members, or in the general character of the business with which they have to deal.'[2]

Apart from the common 'style' of living and the links of origin which bound Britain to her colonies, external challenge had heightened the sense of Empire. The organization of Napoleon's final defeat itself had entailed new levels of planning and imagination. Crude though some of the results were, and at times inept, the long years of military effort and the changing geographical focus had forced upon most British ministers a practical consciousness which, even if it remained instinctive, inchoate, or rudimentary, was effectively global. Britain, rhapsodized the *Quarterly Review*, had 'entered the conflict poor and feeble. She came out of it rich and invincible'.[3]

It was coming to be recognized, by some reluctantly, by others more enthusiastically, that in the expansion of England at least the administrators would be forced to embark on what was in essence a civilizing task. In 1819, a year of political crisis and near violence, MacKintosh, speaking in support of the claims of New South Wales to share in the benefits of the Constitution, lamented that the colonies under George III had not been granted all those benefits 'which seemed to be considered as indispensable to the happiness of the people as light and air' even where they had been introduced into places little adapted for their reception. He trusted that the lack of 'circumspection' which had deprived the Empire of such a blessing would not lead to any diminution at home of 'that love of liberty, on which the good government, the glory, and the prosperity of the country depended'. Canning in reply satirically painted MacKintosh as 'even in the present most liberal day . . . probably the single philosopher who, standing on the pier at Sheerness during the lading

[1] A. Briggs, *Press and Public Opinion in Early 19th Century Birmingham* (Oxford, 1949), p. 4; T. A. Coghlan, *Labour and Industry in Australia* (Oxford, 1918), ii, 176.
[2] *Parliamentary Reform*, etc. (London, 1864), p. 336.
[3] *Q.R.*, xxviii (1822), 197.

of a ship-full of convicts, would point it out to some foreign friend as freighted with a cargo of materials for building up a British constitution'.[1] Yet it was Canning's followers and subordinates who came to accept just such a civilizing mission in the better years of Liberal Toryism shortly to come. In 1828 Huskisson, introducing the New South Wales Act of that year, took for granted the eventual 'establishment of institutions in these colonies similar to those of the people from whom the inhabitants have sprung'.[2] By 1832 the parliamentary under-secretary could declare unequivocally in favour of the ultimate extension to the Australian colonies of a full range of civil liberties including representative assembly;[3] and the Secretary of State 'avow . . . without reserve . . . that the firmest bond of union between the parent state and its Dependencies, will be found in maintaining a general harmony between the respective Institutions, and it is becoming the British name, thus to transfer to distant regions the greatest possible amount both of the spirit of civil liberty and of the forms of Social Order, to which Great Britain is chiefly indebted for the rank she holds among civilized nations'.[4]

There were no infallible precedents or grand-scale recipes to guide them, but the administrators were enabled to call upon living analogies from various sectors of government experience and on observations made over long periods in many parts of the parent and colonial world. Chance played its part along with human design, but even by 1815 the course of 'improvement' in the overseas Empire was, if chaotic, predictably more smooth and hopeful than in places nearer at hand, Britain's other island, for example, the distressful 'cloud in the West'.

As a public issue, New South Wales was naturally far from the forefront, where Currency, Corn, and Catholics vied for attention with deeper questions of Reform and Retrenchment or more ephemeral ones like the Queen's Divorce and party manoeuvres. But the Antipodes already had in 1818 a precarious life of their own, for 'Botany Bay' had become a byword for human degradation, and rumours of sullen and troublesome brutalities and authoritarian high-handedness had seeped into the awareness of many ranks of a people primarily occupied with more immediate concerns. Brougham, presenting to the House of Commons a petition from the free men

[1] P.D. xxxix/496 ff. 18 Feb. 1819.   [2] P.D. n.s. xviii/1430, 2 Apr. 1828.
[3] P.D. 3rd series, xiii, Howick—28 June 1832.
[4] C.O. 296/10/333, Goderich–Grant, 30 Jan. 1832.

who had been summarily flogged under Governor Macquarie, thought New South Wales 'extremely important', soon perhaps to become 'the most so of all our foreign colonies'.[1] Castlereagh, leading for the government in the major full-dress debate on Transportation, declared that 'one of the great advantages of the peace was that it enabled the house to devote more of their time to enquiries into subjects of this nature'.[2]

To the reputation for crime and despair was opposed an obverse report of natural beauties, great material potential and the dream of a better society in a new and British land. When Henry Lytton Bulwer reflected on the change that had taken place by 1832, his words were little more than an epitome of widely held views about the hopeful future of a once 'insignificant and guilty spot, without wealth, capability or importance', but now possessing 'vast and daily increasing resources' and 'a large population of free Englishmen', to which might profitably be directed 'the stream of our stifled and dammed up state of civilization'.[3]

During the years 1818 to 1831 the British penetration of Australia became more varied, broader, and more perceptive. This transition period clearly brought about a metamorphosis in the penal experiment. Despite the ironies and handicaps of origin and geography, disappointment and personal tragedy, temporary failure to produce workable policies, and many apparent paradoxes, advances were consolidated in most directions. Necessity was the source of much of the activity. It was not safe or wise, especially during a time of post-war maladjustment and social unrest, to rely on distance, martial law, the military virtues of Scots martinets, or sheer luck, to eliminate abuses and iron out anomalies, even in the Antipodes. A new diagnosis and assessment based on detailed, reliable and up-to-date information would have to be made about the 'technique' of government, and the possible future direction to be taken by the colonies, always under the fostering care of a central administration itself undergoing a series of changes in the course of post-war reconstruction.

Evidence became increasingly available that both as an instrument of retributive justice and a method of colonial government transportation was irremediably erratic and unreliable. It was, as a system, confusing, and it led to confusions. In matters of expense, it was open-ended. Slipshod justice at home inevitably led to haphazard

---

[1] P.D. xxxix/1124, 23 Mar. 1819.   [2] P.D. xxxix/479, 18 Feb. 1819.
[3] P.D. 3rd S. xiii/1089, 28 June 1832.

results in distant Australia. The dumping of convicts could lead to inhumanity, cruelty, and might even sow disaster. Analogous to slavery, transportation, and the assignment system, was a gamble. It could be unmitigated horror; or a form of constructive improvement, giving the hopeless and helpless of the metropolitan power an un-dreamt-of chance of redemption and the roots of a strong and satisfy-ing life not altogether divorced from the customs, traditions and, increasingly, the free institutions of a beloved homeland.[1] It certainly proved to be no tidy short-hand for obliteration, for nowhere in the colonial empire was the machine of government so deeply involved in detail, or so intimately meshed with the structure and texture of society as in the penal colonies.

Despite the widest differences of geographical context, habit, and background, there was taking place in each of the colonies a process of development where the same sort of problems arose and the same or similar interests were at stake. More often than not, the colonial and metropolitan movements of legal, constitutional, economic and social change form a continuous pattern and can only be understood as various manifestations or reflections of a common civilization. It sometimes happened that the field for adaptation would be wider and freer at the periphery than in the restricted, tradition-bound home districts. More often, perhaps, resources of talent and material avail-able at home were found lacking in the far-flung empire. But common problems, many of them 'much too vast, too new, and too unexpec-ted' for statesmanship to cope with adequately, faced administrators at home and in Britain's post-war colonies.[2] Administrators, especi-ally in a time of great social and economic transition, are a necessary buffer between the people and their problems. The intricate needs of new areas and populations demanded for their satisfaction not only inexorable industry in office work, but painstaking planning, broad courage, and imagination. At the very least business brains and constant care were required to prevent minor crises blowing up into major political storms. In New South Wales, and the new colonies in Australia founded in the 1820s, no less than in Canada, the Cape, and the industrial complexes of England, the period between the end of the great war with Napoleon and the passing of the Reform Bill in 1832 saw the age of 'improvement' well introduced. These linked

[1] A. G. L. Shaw, *Convicts and the Colonies* (London, 1966), pp. 358–60.
[2] *Select Documents on British Colonial Policy 1830–60*, ed. K. N. Bell and W. P. Morell (Oxford, 1928), p. xiii.

societies had lives of their own, specific histories, some unique institutions, and a separate rhythm of success or failure. But at bottom they were organically connected societies, explicable only in terms of each other.

The Australian colonies, so far away, so pathetic in origin, so neglected and so negligible, so harsh by nature and so problematical in conception, yet provide a faithful mirror to the metropolitan power. In addition to the normal imperial links of commerce and strategy there were legal, financial, religious, material and social factors which distinguished Australia from many other troublesome dominions where executive function and detailed control were not so inherently involved. A footnote to British history perhaps, the Australian chapter is nevertheless a test case of Britain's adaptability and of social and administrative adjustment in a time of relatively unchartered change. Its ironies, hopes, upheavals, fears, disappointments and triumphs illustrate at once some of the strangest features of the founding country and the resilient powers of a proud and confident civilization acting in very peculiar and ambiguous local circumstances indeed.

It was an age of facile generalizations, iron laws, and panaceas. But it was also, as Hazlitt warned, 'an age of talkers, and not of doers'.[1] New South Wales and its satellite communities, like so many other contemporary social groupings, looked to the British Government if not for vivid and imaginative new blue-prints at least for effective and empirical administration. To have made distinguishable and quite rapid forward steps in that direction was no mean achievement, especially as there clearly existed among those who had to make them a distrust of panaceas. 'Believe me', wrote Walter Scott, an admirer of Lord Bathurst and a stout defender of Tory government, to his friend Ballantyne in 1819, 'there is nothing which can be proposed of a sweeping or dashing nature in religion, politics or public economy which is not therefore radically wrong.'[2]

Detailed dictation of policy from above by autocratic statesmen was in the 1820s, given the global scale of Britain's overseas possessions, not possible. Bathurst for one was the last to be inspired by a Grand Design of imperial strategy. 'There is nothing so fatal to investigation of truth, as the having a preconceived system', he minuted on one of Major Moody's 'sensible' observations in 1826.[3]

---

[1] *The Spirit of the Age* (London, 1825), p. 57.
[2] *The Letters of Sir Walter Scott*, ed. H. Grierson (Edinburgh, 1932), vi, 35.
[3] C.O. 324/75/65.

Yet he and his under-secretaries came to realize that efficiency, good sense, and business diligence were necessary prerequisites for turning away wrath and offering even tentative and interim solutions to a host of problems which presented themselves in a piecemeal and often painful procession. Huskisson, when he launched his programme of fiscal reform, positively disclaimed any anxiety 'to give effect to new principles', and declared that 'in the vast and complex interests of this country, all general theories, however incontrovertible in the abstract, require to be weighed with a calm circumspection . . . and to be adapted to all the existing relations of society, with a careful hand, and a due regard to the establishments and institutions which have grown up under those relations'.[1]

Undramatic and unspectacular as such Tory scepticism was in contrast with the Benthamite verve of later 'systematic' colonizers, its effects were considerable. At the time it alone was politically feasible and it continued to influence deeply the character of life and institutions as the Australian colonies began to change irreversibly in the early 1830s.

A great number of British organizations and individuals, and most of the statesmen of the period 1818–31 were engaged in questions concerning, and problems raised by, the Australian colonies, both in their penal and settlement aspects. The attention of many men including Liverpool, Castlereagh, Canning, Peel, Huskisson, Brougham, Grey, Wilberforce, Hume, Wellington and MacKintosh, some of whom had connections spanning the course of their official lives, was constructive and vital to the development of those colonies. The advancement, neglect, or stagnation of Australia was recognized to depend upon changes taking place in the colonies themselves. But the future depended also, as had the past, upon the course of politics and events at home; for these colonies were entirely British in origin and aspiration. The deepest, most continuous and systematic official influence was undoubtedly that of the Third Secretariat, itself undergoing development as an increasingly sensitive and responsible instrument of policy and civilization.

[1] *Speeches* (London, 1831), ii, 304, 21 Mar. 1824.

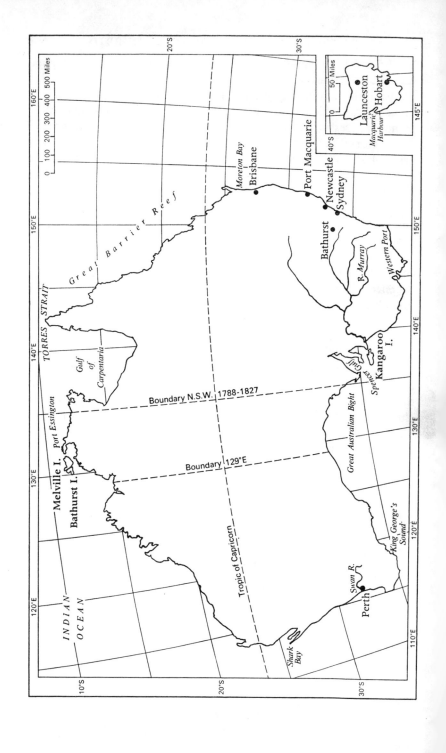

I

THE COLONIAL OFFICE: SECRETARIES AND UNDER-SECRETARIES OF STATE 1818–31

'THERE is an ample field for you to range in extending from Botany Bay to Prince Edward's Island', wrote Robert Peel in August 1812 when he was advising his friend and successor Henry Goulburn about the duties of an under-secretary at the colonial department. 'You will of course have the superintendence of the correspondence of all the British colonies on the face of the globe on all subjects military and civil, but when you are master of the routine which I am sure that *you* will be in a month you will find it go on very smoothly.' Two years in the office (10 June 1810–4 August 1812) had convinced Peel that: 'There is no occasion in most cases for immediate decision and in many it does not much signify if it is deferred for some time . . . The quantity of writing which you have bears no proportion to the quantity of reading.'[1]

After the conduct of colonial business had been transferred to the Third Secretariat of State by a departmental reshuffle in August 1801, there had followed a decade of comparative neglect.[2] The chief object of ministers at a time of continental war was naturally to avoid trouble in imperial affairs and make only urgent decisions. Some colonial problems could wait. Others could not be allowed to. Not all neglect of colonial government was 'salutary' in Burke's sense.

When the maps were needed again after Napoleon's eclipse in 1815, it was obvious that the bewildering array of overseas responsibilities confronting Goulburn and Lord Bathurst (Secretary of State for War and the Colonies 10 June 1812 to 30 April 1827) called for a higher level of activity from the central authorities. Many years later it was generally allowed that the 'functions of the Colonial Office are remarkable for their variety, importance, and difficulty'.[3] Even by 1831 the permanent officials could with confidence prepare a draft

---

[1] Goulburn Papers, 11/13, Peel-Goulburn, 12, 15 Aug. 1812.
[2] D. M. Young, op. cit., pp. 12 ff.
[3] P.P. 1854 xxvii (1715), p. 82, Committee of Enquiry into the C.O., 15 Dec. 1849.

letter for Goderich (Secretary of State 30 April 1827–3 September 1827 and 22 November 1830–3 April 1833) to send to the Treasury, asserting that: 'Since the conclusion of the Peace various circumstances have occurred to increase beyond all former precedent the amount, variety, and importance of the business connected with the administration of Colonial affairs in this Department.'[1] But in 1815 the burden of office was not appreciated by any but those who had to bear it. 'Work as I may I make no progress', Goulburn lamented to his wife[2] shortly before a Whig attack on the very existence of the department created still more work for him by forcing Bathurst to dispense with his second under-secretary, Major-General Sir Henry Bunbury, who had hitherto been employed on the military side.

*   *   *   *   *

Bathurst had succeeded Lord Liverpool (Secretary of State 31 October 1809–10 June 1812) when the latter formed a government which defied all predictions and probability to survive until 1827. The Tories could not expect to produce another Pitt to galvanize England, and the 'caretaker' Liverpool Government was in fact only stabilized by a combination of good management, good fortune and the absence of a serious alternative. But Liverpool was a shrewd and competent statesman with a flair for the blending of volatile elements in time to avert crises: and it was under his presidency, unable and disinclined as he was to accomplish any radical solution to post-war problems, that room was made for the admission to the ministry of 'a new school of abler, more enlightened, more progressive men like Canning, Peel and Huskisson'.[3] 'The accession of Mr. Canning to the Cabinet, in a position too of surpassing influence, soon led to a further weeding of the mediocrities', wrote Disraeli,[4] 'and among other introductions to the memorable entrance of Mr. Huskisson. In this wise did that Cabinet once notable only for the absence of all those qualities which authorize the possession of power, come to be generally esteemed as a body of men who for parliamentary eloquence, official practice, political information, sagacity in council, and a due understanding of their epoch, were inferior to none that had directed the policy of the empire since the Revolution.'

---

[1] C.O. 323/213/96, 28 Jan. 1831.   [2] Goulburn Papers, 11/7, 13 Feb. 1816.
[3] A. Aspinall, *Lord Brougham and the Whig Party* (London, 1927), p. 100.
[4] *Coningsby*, Bk. II, Ch. I.

Bathurst, a High Tory, presided over colonial affairs for nearly fifteen years, weathered the restless years after victory, and took more than a permissive share in the rationalization of the Colonial Office under Goulburn's more volatile successor, Wilmot Horton (under-secretary 11 December 1821–5 January 1828). He and his under-secretaries can safely be said to have laid the working foundations of a great government department. 'For the six years from 1815 to 1821', Goulburn wrote in his Memoirs, 'I was never absent from the office for more than seven consecutive days and only that time on two or three occasions. I must in justice say for the Gentlemen in the office that whether stimulated by my example or not I will say they willingly made a sacrifice of their own time and enabled me to carry on the Colonial business with an Establishment far below what was either before or afterwards deemed absolutely necessary. There was indeed a strong motive for economy, for so little understood at that time was the importance of colonial administration that the House of Commons was more than once moved by no less a man than Mr. Tierney to abolish the office altogether, and in the impatience of expenditure then prevalent the project strange to say found numerous supporters.'[1]

Faced with a vast growth in correspondence, increasing pressure from a Treasury engaged in post-war reductions, and the review of colonial and metropolitan critics, Goulburn had nevertheless gone far to justify his defence of the Third Secretariat as an indispensable Cabinet agency responsible to a Parliament showing more concern with the *minutiae* of departmental administration by the time he left the office. He had, he felt, come to terms with the duties of his depart-ment and found it disagreeable to move away from his connection with Lord Bathurst, of whom he had grown fond, when in 1821 he was chosen to go to Ireland as Chief Secretary, again succeeding Peel.[2] Of vital significance for the colonies was his establishment of a regular tradition by which routine chores were delegated to area clerks, consultant experts, and sub-agencies. On the whole, however, he managed to see all the correspondence which came in and almost always minuted his brief reflections overleaf.

Bathurst, no innovator, rarely considered that colonial situations called for a drastic change in institutions or the working of govern-ment in an entirely new direction. It was foolish, as Wilmot Horton

---

[1] Goulburn Papers, IV/6; for Tierney's attack, P.D. xxxiii/892–921 and xxxvi/51–82.
[2] Goulburn Papers IV/6/14/2.

found in the middle twenties, to go out of the way to seek broad principles. Bathurst was certainly not interested in reform as such, nor did he initiate any new evaluations of colonial rule or its place and influence on British statecraft. The changes he wrought were piecemeal, by adapting and improving if necessary what was already established to be workable. Reforms had, therefore, to be promoted from within the colonies or prompted by Parliamentary agitation, which was, he realized, as often as not spasmodic, trivial, or inspired by *parti pris*. He was, however, intelligent and very shrewd, and trusted his practical and wide experience to guide him in making the many adjustments time and circumstances forced upon him.

Problems came up from below, in the colonies as elsewhere, and demanded business-like efficiency at some stage of the government process. Bathurst fully realized that, as the various colonial requirements had a certain similarity about them, he would be able in practice to apply consistent expedients: e.g. supporting the authority of the governor *vis-à-vis* the colonists, while at the same time building up the constitutional checks against the arbitrary exercise of authority by the governor; the formation of legal and executive branches upon which the business of administration 'for the public advantage' could be devolved. Even under the pressure of parliamentary opponents, colonial complaint, or the urging of expert opinion, Bathurst was slow to act in any definitive way. This may have been due to some degree to his 'indolence'; but there is much evidence to suggest that it reflects far more than has been supposed his positive conviction that 'quieta non movere' was a wise maxim in colonial government. It is no accident that Mrs. Arbuthnot wrote of him that 'he hates all innovations and wᵈ have done perfectly and been considered a very upright minister in the time of Sir Robert Walpole'.[1] The very quest for a suitable arrangement was a delicate one and, he knew from long expertise, an eternal one. No item seemed too small for it to be raised for his comment and appraised in some form or other, and gradually, as his department evolved an *esprit de corps* under his parliamentary under-secretaries, he allowed responsibilities to descend almost imperceptibly upon the clerical staff and its assistant specialists, commissioners, and agents, whether these last were appointed by the Colonial Office, the Treasury, the colonists themselves, or other groups. It was perhaps first in his office that the political head

<hr>

[1] *The Journal of Mrs Arbuthnot 1820–1832*, ed. F. Bamford and the Duke of Wellington (London, 1950), i, 158–9.

admitted his inability to cope personally with the flow of regular business.[1] This reluctance to become involved in complicated minutiae was quite characteristic of Bathurst. When he felt he had to assimilate the details of some more than usually troublesome case, he almost always did so economically, concisely and with great sophistication. There was, too, the simple fact that it had become physically impossible to keep up with the mail of the whole department. In 1806, fifteen clerks had handled 2,555 letters; in 1816, eleven handled 7,648; in 1824, seventeen handled 12,450.[2]

* * * * *

Administrative action, when it is piecemeal and performed anonymously by civil servants, is rarely accounted a vivid contribution to progress. But competent attention to the round of paper work which was entailed in the effective administration of government departments such as the Home Office, the Colonial Office, or the Board of Control should neither be despised nor taken as read. Nor should the notorious and real failures of a panic-stricken 'guardian' post-war régime be allowed to obscure the no less real advances which were taking place in executive method and 'carry-through'; or the liberalization in style and technique which occurred in many fields about this time, often forged in the course of lengthy and complicated series of interdepartmental communications or detailed correspondence stretching over many months or even years. The daily necessity for consultation, from the Cabinet down, and the habit of intelligent implementation under review of policies practically arrived at, undoubtedly smoothed the way for peaceful evolution and fostered initiative at the periphery. It called for a reasoned and regular response at the centre to a complex circle of issues now being raised more or less urgently both at home and in the colonies. 'What happened in the Cabinet and in the Colonial Office are points on this circle; but so are the happenings in some squalid Jamaica work-house and the rough justice of a special magistrate's court.'[3] So were convict rations at Port Dalrymple and the new road to Parramatta.

---

[1] Young, op. cit., p. 3.

[2] C.O. 854/1: q. in Young, op. cit., p. 245, and pp. 282-4. 'The most striking increase in correspondence was with New South Wales. Fifteen letters were sent in 1806; in 1824 there were 1104, almost a third of the despatches sent overseas that year;' p. 249. Many of these were, of course, short routine letters.

[3] W. L. Burn, *Emancipation and Apprenticeship in the British West Indies* (London, 1937), p. 8.

Few of the men who dealt with the affairs of Empire during the period between 1815 and 1832 were primarily inspired with a coherent and positive vision of colonial policy. Horton, who has been roundly if not justly condemned as an idealist 'policy-maker', was 'in his faith in the efficacy of immediate government planning based on a study of statistics . . . an anachronism in the administrative machine of his day'.[1] Huskisson, whose seminal period at the Board of Trade effected a great movement towards imperial reciprocity and freer trade, was, at the Colonial Office in 1827–8, too immersed in political and parliamentary questions to initiate and administer any definite shift in government method: and his tour of duty was short and disturbed by ill-health. Goderich, experienced in Treasury matters, did see through or at least encourage a series of financial rationalizations, and wept when he had to leave office. Sir George Murray, Wellington's choice for Third Secretary, looked well but was far too vague to make much mark, especially as his coming coincided with rapid movements among the department's under-secretaries. Yet each of these men, and particularly Bathurst, had an effect on the development of colonial government for better or for worse. Regarding their work as the necessary concomitant of high office, a drudgery performed in the King's service, and an obligation of duty rather than an exciting field for imaginative or constructive statesmanship, they were not and cannot be dismissed as altogether uncreative. Their aims were not perhaps high or magnanimous, and in some cases their notions were neither liberal nor distinguished, but in the event their official achievements were manifold and formative. By building 'a central machinery which could furnish information for the ministry and parliament on colonial affairs'[2] and by allowing it to be run with painstaking attention to detail by departmental experts such as Stephen, Taylor, and Hay, they inaugurated a new and underestimated stage of State policy—progress in disguise by statesmen in disguise.

Later a myth would arise, in which 1830 became a magic dividing line in British colonial history. From the time of hurt recoil after the loss of America in 1783, it was maintained, all was darkness. An imperial remnant was controlled by an obscurantist Colonial Office. Public interest in the overseas possessions was negligible. Then a new era dawned as the Colonial Office was goaded into rational activity

[1] Young, op. cit., p. 52.
[2] H. T. Manning, *British Colonial Government after the American Revolution* (New Haven, 1933), p. 483.

by vital and far-seeing men, through whose influence Britain at last realized the potential of her colonies as fields for enterprise—a new world to be called in to redress the balance of the old. Such a legend foreshortens history. In fact, interest in colonial affairs never flagged among important groups such as the missionary societies, foreign traders, investors, and the radicals. The changing colonies themselves demanded and received attention long before the arrival of 'systematic colonization'.

In the end, even Bathurst had to act, in the West Indies for example, where, he told the Lords, reforms 'would best be obtained by giving time to the colonial legislatures to mature the measures they were disposed to adopt',[1] though it was not until after the collapse of Liverpool's heirs that the Government was cajoled, manoeuvred and pushed into more direct intervention in the affairs of abolition and confiscation. Canning himself, *beau idéal* of Liberal Toryism, declared that he favoured the 'slow and silent course of temperate but authoritative admonition'.[2] Australian governors, after the peace, often complained desolately of apathy and lack of direction from home. When the Colonial Office had matured its habit and style, however, dilatoriness, though perhaps occasionally due to oversight, forgetfulness, or sheer stress of work, would almost always be explicable in terms of the need for reflection, deeper consultation, or the inherent and ineradicable difficulty of making long-distance decisions about intricate local problems involving unknown personalities and consequences. Certainly there would be no simple repetition, except during the years of political change and administrative 'torpor' of 1828–30, of the kind of plea made in 1816 and repeated in 1817 by Lachlan Macquarie when he wrote to Henry Goulburn that 'a great number of very interesting and important Points relative to this Colony as contained in my Despatches of the years 1813, 1814, and 1815 have never yet been noticed at all by his His Lordship'.[3]

Jobbery and corruption had survived the reforming movement of the 1780s, and Mrs. Arbuthnot, the wife of an experienced Patronage Secretary, thought Bathurst 'a very bad minister for present times'. He wanted everything 'to go in the old way, likes a job for the sake of a job', but 'not to get money into his own pocket for there cannot be a more disinterested man'.[4] Yet patronage books were of course no

---

[1] P.D. xxxix/852, 4 Mar. 1819.   [2] P.D. n.s. x/1105.
[3] H.R.A. I/ix/98, Macquarie–Goulburn, 22 Mar. 1816; /409, 17 May 1817.
[4] *Journal*, i, 158–9.

prerogative of the Tories. 'Lord Goderich will of course have abundance of Candidates on his List for all the desirable offices which may fall vacant in his Department', wrote Robert Hay, the first permanent under-secretary at the Colonial Office to a protégé in 1831.[1]

Personality, temperament, and the drive of ambition continued to play their parts along with background and connection in the evolution of civil service for British institutions at home and abroad. It cannot be argued that a modern, stable, and mature administrative élite began immediately after 1815 to hammer out systematic and satisfactory solutions to the multifarious felt needs of many publics. There were consistent failures to understand the nature of the new problems and no finally effective answers were provided by those Tory or Whig statesmen whose political duty it was to attempt to deal with them. But already mistakes and inadequacies had a tendency to become high-lighted, and under the criticisms of Utilitarian, Radical, and other groups concerned, administrators learnt that care, discretion and diligence were of the essence of peaceful government action in a time of rapid and almost unprecedented change. They did not as a rule value ideals divorced from practical utility: to do so was to risk alienation from the political power which was the 'unum necessarium'. Nevertheless they had to be active, intelligent, and substantially humane as they attempted to meet day-to-day problems with a developing set of general principles in mind. In this sense a multitude of decisions and a wealth of experience do, taken together, constitute a policy, a style, or a 'technique'. The quest for a workable and regular system might be disguised in Bathurst's alleged farewell to governors, 'joy be with you and let us hear as little of you as possible':[2] or in the Treasury's attempt to initiate an Imperial currency:[3] or in the bustling activities of young lions like E. G. Stanley and Lord Howick. Yet evidence from many parts of the Empire refutes Carlyle's later and savage indictment of the Colonial Office as a world-wide jungle of red tape, inhabited by doleful creatures, deaf or nearly so, to human reason or entreaty.

Treasury attempts to control and reduce the expenditure of all departments, and continual probings into ministerial budgets by Whigs and Radicals meant that the offices were forced to advance

[1] C.O. 324/87/28, Hay–Riddell, 16 Sept. 1831.
[2] S. S. Bell, *The Colonial Administration of Great Britain* (London, 1859), p. 460 n.
[3] C.O. 323/202/31, Harrison–Horton, 12 Feb. 1825.

cautiously and against the grain. Sometimes retrenchment had the effect of confining the development of colonial government when circumstances in colonies really demanded more generous policies of expenditure to keep pace with local demands. Often, however, retrenchment movements had healthy side-effects. In 1818 Goulburn was able to superannuate some of his more inefficient clerks and adjust the pensions and classification of office personnel.[1] Together with other under-secretaries he was called in January 1818 on Liverpool's advice, to prepare joint statements on salaries.[2] Later in the year, Treasury minutes were issued insisting on the 'reduction of Establishment and Expense', on the lines of the reforming committees of the 1780s. It was simple enough to lay down the norm that 'no offices should be upheld which are unnecessary',[3] but particularly in the Colonial Office, with its growing overseas responsibilities and vast increase of business, the practice was difficult. Plans for dividing the affairs of the empire between two 'regional' under-secretaries had to be shelved for eight years until Robert Hay was appointed by Order-in-Council in 1825.[4] Such penny-pinching was exportable, and Australian governors were perpetually being reprimanded for expanding their establishments.

The search for regularity of system in civil service appointments was carried out zealously by the Treasury, but even at home there were disappointments. The Treasury was forced to admit the impossibility of introducing 'any uniform system . . . for the payment of persons in Public Offices' and allow that the 'Establishment of every Public Office must be modelled with reference to its own extent and its peculiar Duties', when the Colonial Office protested that proposed reforms would prevent it offering 'suitable encouragement to persons of diligence and ability to engage in the public service'.[5]

From 1818 Herries and others had begun the long campaign to rationalize the military and revenue departments in order to render them both more efficient and amenable to Treasury control, and by 1819 their attention was turned again to the overseas establishments. The Colonial Audit Office, a Treasury sub-branch, was already harrying Goulburn. Now the Treasury sought full estimates and demanded 'in detail the whole of the salaries, pay or allowances to

---

[1] Young, op. cit., p. 62, 162.
[2] C.O. 323/188/162, Lushington–Goulburn, 18 Jan. 1818.
[3] C.O. 323/188/201, Treasury Minute, 15 July 1818.
[4] C.O. 324/145/148, Bathurst–Lord President, 1 July 1825.
[5] C.O. 323/188/217, Harrison–Goulburn, 6 Nov. 1818.

officers or clerks upon those Establishments', with an eye 'that every office which may be unnecessary or the duties of which can be more efficiently executed at less expense to the public should be abolished'.[1] The Treasury, confused by the variety of colonial conditions and itself proceeding hesitantly and by fits and starts, often wearied Lord Bathurst; and his quasi-permanence in office enabled him to take a superior line with the most earnest Treasury suggestions. In 1821 for example, when asked for statements of colonial revenue required for the House of Commons, he minuted: 'refer the Treasury to the Audit Office who have the only means of furnishing the complete account'.[2]

Again in 1821 the Government was forced by economic stress to suspend salary loadings and review all Civil Service emoluments.[3] It so happened that just when embryo civil services were being set up in many of the overseas colonies of settlement, the Colonial Office itself was expected, most unrealistically, to revert to the salary scales of 1797 and to reduce its staff to the numbers current at that date. A Treasury Minute of 10 August 1821[4] ordered, among other reductions, a cut of 5 per cent in the salaries of officers receiving more than £100 per annum. Bathurst, suspicious of Treasury interference and jealous of his departmental independence or at least mobility, resented this decision which seemed based on the supposition that the civil service was on the same footing as the military forces, expendable according to a systematic or emergency programme of economy. He interpreted the instruction benignly, sensibly governing the reorganization of his office with 'a due regard to the interests of those who are at present in the office and whose faithful services entitle them to every possible consideration.' Goulburn pointed out 'that, independently of other considerations, the great increase of the Colonial Possessions of the Crown has thrown upon this Department an addition of correspondence and labour beyond what has occurred in most other Departments of the State'.[5] Shortly after, when Goulburn had handed over to Wilmot Horton and the subject was taken up again by a persistent Treasury, Bathurst took the opportunity to defend his staff even more firmly. 'Lord Bathurst does not conceive that his office can be

[1] C.O. 323/190/210, 20 July 1818.
[2] C.O. 323/194/191, and 324/143/245–6, Goulburn–Harrison, 15 Aug. 1821.
[3] *Bathurst Papers*, pp. 493–4, Liverpool–Bathurst, 7 Jan. 1821 and C.O. 323/194/163 ff.
[4] C.O. 324/194/169.
[5] C.O. 324/143/364, Goulburn–Lushington, 30 Nov. 1821.

compared with that of the Treasury, either with regard to the number of Persons employed, the nature of the duties in which its several members are occupied, or the advantages to be obtained by Service and Promotion.'[1] He noted that Treasury clerks had higher wages and greater expectations, while Colonial Office clerks had longer hours and more important duties. In 1822 he wrote of the long service and good quality of work given by the clerks;[2] yet he was of course no spendthrift either in Downing St. or elsewhere and promised 'that all appointments which may henceforth be made by this Department of persons to situations in which it may be necessary that any Public Monies should pass through their hands will be at the time of their appointment communicated to the Treasury for their Lordships' information'.[3]

Bathurst, on balance a strong Minister, remains a somewhat enigmatic figure. A man of good humour about whom Sydney Smith wrote: 'I know nobody who has more fun and wit',[4] he was also judged widely as 'a man of business, attentive to the duties of his important office'.[5] A continuous member of the inner Cabinet since his appointment as Secretary of State in June 1812, he was considered at various times as a possible alternative to Liverpool.[6] This powerful position, enhanced by the respect he commanded as a leading and popular member of the highest aristocratic society, enabled him to forward any particular project upon which he set his heart. But he was unambitious and not altogether in sympathy with many of the developments he saw taking place. Wynn told Buckingham on 10 September 1823 that he thought the 'only real and efficient Cabinet upon all matters consists of Lords Liverpool, Bathurst, the Duke of Wellington, and Canning, and that the others are only more or less consulted upon difficult business by these four'.[7] Not at all Palmerston's 'old stumped-up Tory',[8] he was, like Wellington, suspicious of the new men, one of whom was in his very office making a stir. In

[1] C.O. 324/144/8, Wilmot–Lushington, 14 Jan. 1822.

[2] C.O. 324/144/15, Bathurst–Harrowby, 31 Jan. 1822.

[3] C.O. 324/144/39, Wilmot–Harrison, 26 Feb. 1822.

[4] *The Letters of Sydney Smith*, ed. N. C. Smith (Oxford, 1952), ii. 476.

[5] *The Times*, 29 July 1834.

[6] e.g. A. Aspinall, *The Formation of Canning's Ministry—February–August 1827* (Camden Soc., 3rd Series, lix, 1937), 38.

[7] Duke of Buckingham and Chandos, *Memoirs of the Court of George IV* (London, 1859), i, 494.

[8] H. L. Bulwer, *The Life of Henry John Temple, Viscount Palmerston* (London, 1870), i, 179.

1823, when he wished to speak to the conservative patronage secretary, he told him it was safe to 'come to his office because Mr. Wilmot (the under-secretary) was gone'.[1]

Horton wrote of him later that 'his general politics did not respond to the movement of the latter days in which he lived; yet in all cases where first rate practical good sense, and a rapid yet discreet view of intricate subjects was essentially required, Lord Bathurst possessed a mind far more able to grapple with difficulties than many of those persons who underrated his political efficiency'.[2] Greville, his private secretary, wrote that he was 'greatly averse to changes but unwillingly acquiescing in many'.[3]

Bathurst came to delegate the ordinary business of the department to his under-secretaries, while he maintained an overall view of events, personalities, and the course of policy in almost all the colonial dependencies. He often complained about being inundated at Cirencester by avalanches of overseas dispatches, yet frequently showed a grasp of detail and memory for administrative complexities which startled and occasionally embarrassed subordinate officials and area clerks. Certainly he remained the last court of appeal; and Australian governors in their dispatches showed their appreciation of his intelligence and power. His action, if once fully elicited, was convincing and decisive. But he was never favourable to dynamic change and was, like the King, uneasy about the 'dreadful liberal taint' introduced into the Cabinet by Canning.[4] His urbanity was not at all the same thing as the systematic *laissez-faire* cultivated by Huskisson and the Whigs. He was naturally of Wellington's camp, and Mrs. Arbuthnot describes him in 1823 as saying that 'he was excessively uneasy at the way in which Canning was managing our foreign concerns and that nothing would save us but the Duke's authority and his excessive good temper'.[5] By March he was 'in a great fuss at Mr. Canning's goings on and his mode of doing business'.[6] Though he had now to deal with Huskisson at the Board of Trade, he doubtless shared the opinion of the King who had his reservations about Canning's chief lieutenant and friend: 'no doubt . . . a very clever man, but he is

[1] Mrs. Arbuthnot, *Journal*, i, 210, 3 Feb. 1823.

[2] In his apologia, *Exposition and Defence of Earl Bathurst's Administration, etc.* (London, 1838), pp. 39–40.

[3] Quoted in D. J. Murray, op. cit., p. 118.

[4] F. Cathcart to Bagot of the Foreign Office, 9 Mar. 1825, q. in J. Bagot, *George Canning and His Friends* (London, 1909), ii, 279.

[5] *Journal*, i, 210.   [6] ibid., p. 220.

not always a prudent one'.[1] Like the King too, who in 1824 lamented that 'the opinions of the Opposition and liberals are uniformly acted upon',[2] he doubtless found Liverpool's support of Spanish American independence alarming. 'Lord Liverpool', he told the Arbuthnots, 'had completely and entirely changed his politics and was become quite a liberal.'[3] Nothing could contrast more with his reticence than Canning's use of the platform, 'going round the country speechifying and discussing the acts and intentions of the Government. This is quite a new system among us and excites great indignation'.[4]

In January 1825 the King quoted Bathurst's uneasiness with the 'new political liberalism' in a long and excited letter to Liverpool.[5] He warned the Prime Minister that recognition of the independence of Spanish America smacked of that 'anarchy produced throughout the world by the French Revolution'; that the revolutionary spirit was not extinguished, especially in Ireland; that 'the liberalism now adopted by the King's Government' was inconsonant with the heritage of Mr. Pitt; and that the whole unhappy business might lead to the application of democracy and liberal principles, in opposition to a monarchical aristocracy, 'to the emancipation of our eastern possessions or to any other of the remote settlements, at present under the dominion of the British Crown'. It was part of the irony of a kaleidoscopic imperial scene that by this time Lord Bathurst's own department was busily engaged in setting up in Australia social, legal and constitutional institutions which could only develop eventually in a liberal direction.

Henry Goulburn's thoroughness enabled Bathurst to devolve upon the under-secretary all the regular business of the department; but he certainly saw all the important documents, minuting many of them for action or reference, and never signed anything he was not prepared to stand by. The consistency of the Secretariat as expressing in its decisions the King's commands sometimes proved painful to maintain, especially as the materials for those decisions began to be moulded by many hands and concerned increasingly delicate or debatable topics. Thus James Stephen in 1825 prepared at Lord Bathurst's directions a fairly casual dispatch to Governor Darling proposing the licensing of newspapers and the imposition on the colonial press of restrictions similar to those imposed at home. This

---

[1] *Letters of George IV*, ed. A. Aspinall (London, 1938), iii, 39.
[2] ibid., p. 97.   [3] *Journal*, i, 328, 19 July 1824.
[4] ibid., p. 275, 18 Nov. 1823.   [5] *Letters* iii, 98.

led indirectly to years of confusion, disputes and recriminations. It was sometimes neither clear nor remembered during times of rapid turn-over in secretaries exactly what had been decided and for what reasons.[1]

* * * * *

Goulburn was succeeded at the Office by Robert John Wilmot, a protégé of Lord Harrowby, whose appointment coincided with the arrival of the Canningites. He was under-secretary from 11 December 1821 to 5 January 1828: succeeded in reorganizing the work of the department in a way more suited to the growing demands made upon it; and perhaps by excess of zeal in the causes of Emigration and Catholic Emancipation rendered himself unsuitable for higher office.[2] Huskisson wrote of his appointment: 'Goulburn's vacancy makes room for Wilmot which is a good appointment and at which I rejoice. It is the only comfortable thing I have had to mention.'[3] Horton thought very highly of Huskisson and got on well with Robinson; but Canning thought him imprudent. Unlike Goulburn, he had no experience of administration, and he succeeded to office in the middle of a retrenchment drive. Greville warned him that 'you will receive no active assistance in getting through your business, which is beyond belief, lonesome and laborious—nothing can equal the stupidity and prolixity of your colonial correspondents and you will be assailed with documents of bulk immeasurable without one interval of repose'.[4] Less meticulous than Goulburn, he was forced to make wider use of the existing talents in the department and to 're-model' it, by introducing new men among whom were Henry Taylor, T. F. Elliott and Hyde Villiers.

Above all Horton made more use of Goulburn's most outstanding and influential import into the office—James Stephen, who began his remarkable career in 1813 when the under-secretary had required his assistance 'on some legal questions'.[5] Broadly humanitarian, flexible, open to new ideas, often sceptical, always realistic, Stephen from the

[1] H.R.A. IV/i/613, Stephen–Hay, 16 July 1825; I/xii/16, Bathurst–Darling, 12 July 1825; IV/i/720, Forbes–Horton, 27 May 1827.
[2] E. G. Jones, 'Sir R. J. Wilmot Horton' (Bristol University M.A. Thesis 1936), pp. 74–6.
[3] B.M. Add. MSS. 38743 (Huskisson Papers), f. 61: Huskisson–Binning, 6 Dec. 1821.
[4] Greville–Wilmot, 4 Dec. 1821, q. in E. J. Jones, op. cit., p. 39.
[5] C.O. 323/197/162, Stephen–Wilmot, 21 Apr. 1923.

first played a very important part in the development of colonial government, and continued to do so for nearly forty years. Sensitive to a fault and astoundingly industrious, he extended his role considerably under Goulburn's successor. He was trusted and consulted by his superiors and his opinion on most subjects was pivotal, if not invariably final. Thousands of facts, cases and problems were brought to him in the course of his service, passed through his synthetizing mind and were filed away for future use. Apart from his reports on colonial laws, which he made also as legal adviser to the Board of Trade, he was invariably consulted on legal problems which did not need the attention of the Attorney- and Solicitor-General. He was required to 'unravel and write a coherent report on involved problems' of all description, prepare drafts for letters to officials at home and in the colonies, dispatches for Governors and Bills for Parliament. Much of his work bore 'but a faint and fictitious relation to his profession as a lawyer'.[1] The 'Australian' activities of Stephen were probably quite as troublesome as his West Indian and Canadian duties. Horton seized upon him for guidance and there can have been few important items concerning the colonies which did not receive Horton's minute 'Send this to Mr. Stephen'.[2]

As the Bigge correspondence grew and the reports came in, both secretary and under-secretary relied on Stephen more and more. Typical of his involvement was the minute on Bigge's report on New Zealand and the prevention of outrages perpetrated in the Pacific by escaped convicts; 'send this immediately to Mr. Stephen, requesting him to read it and then return it to me himself for the purpose of my having some conversation with him upon it'.[3] He was thoroughly immersed in the affairs of the Australian colonies in the years from 1823 and, with Francis Forbes, and a host of interested or influential people consulted by Horton, contributed to the New South Wales Act (4. G. IV. c. 96). Indeed he had to sort out some of the confusion which resulted from the use of 'too many cooks' and the last-minute inclusion of a section setting up a Legislative Council.[4]

Horton's discursive method of administration involved Stephen much more deeply than before in the field of decision-making. Even in his own chosen field, the law, this could be acutely embarrassing.

[1] Stephen–Howick 10 Feb. 1832. q. in Murray, op. cit., p. 121.
[2] e.g. C.O. 201/109/372, Sorell–Bathurst, 16 Nov. 1832, enc. the Port regulations for Hobart.
[3] C.O. 201/142/486, on Bigge–Bathurst, 27 Feb. 1823.
[4] H.R.A. IV/i/746, Forbes–Hay, 12 Nov. 1827.

Thus when the newly-appointed Attorney-General of New South Wales, Saxe Bannister, was about to leave England, he asked Horton to be allowed to see and take copies of the legal opinions Stephen and his predecessors had given the colonial department. Bannister, also a member of Lincoln's Inn, had 'found advantage in consulting the papers relating to colonial legislation, preserved in the books of the Board of Trade', and now wanted to consult more recent documents, as well as those kept in the Colonial Office 'relative to the Government at Quebec before 1791 when under a Legislative Council, and afterwards when under an Assembly'.[1] Stephen told Horton that he had in this subject a 'peculiar personal Interest'. Whereas his predecessors had confined themselves 'to a very short expression of their opinions whether particular Acts were objectionable in point of Law or not', he had thought it better 'to explain at length the reasons for every opinion, which I have had the honor to submit to Lord Bathurst or yourself'. He therefore felt himself 'responsible for almost every legal opinion recorded in your office, in which any discussion of Colonial Law occur', and as a barrister he was unwilling 'to expose to the criticism of the Public every legal opinion he may have had occasion to write'. Ten years of detailed reports, once disclosed to over thirty colonial Attorney-Generals, would only be the source of mischief. Some of his numerous opinions had been adopted by Lord Bathurst, while others had not. 'I cannot conceive', he wrote, 'that his Lordship would think it expedient that the various parties, who may have been affected by his decisions, should have the opportunity of tracing in my written Reports the History of a part of those private deliberations, which have more or less influenced his Judgment.' Consequent revelations might include extremely controversial matters relating, for example, to Slavery. Lord Bathurst had promised him that such communications would always be received as strictly confidential. What Bannister wanted, therefore, amounted to 'a complete History of my Official Life and proceedings, and of this branch of the Administration'. Such an application could be reasonably made only by a member of the Cabinet.[2]

*   *   *   *   *

Bathurst resigned in April 1827, though he returned to Cabinet office as Lord President of the Council from January 1828 to November

[1] H.R.A. IV/i/492, Bannister–Horton, 9 Aug. 1823.
[2] H.R.A. IV/i/504, Stephen–Horton, 22 Sept. 1823.

1830 and hence did not lose contact with the conduct of imperial affairs.[1] Goderich, who had been briefly under-secretary in 1809, President of the Board of Trade (1818–23) and Chancellor of the Exchequer (1823–7), was Secretary of State for a brief time on his way to a disastrous term as Prime Minister (August 1827–January 1828). He was not a strong minister and obviously distracted by the political changes taking place around him; but his interest in financial matters was important because decisions had to be taken at this time about the rearrangement of colonial accounts and revenues in the Australian colonies. He returned with the Whigs in 1830.

During the Goderich ministry Huskisson was Third Secretary (3 September 1827–30 May 1828). Stephen's statesman of 'dominant understanding' found himself increasingly ill at ease within the Wellington Cabinet. His period in office was one of promise and unfulfilled potential rather than solid achievement. But his indirect contribution to the department and to colonial government was of long standing, and in the session of January to May his leadership of the minority group in the Cabinet gave him considerable authority. Peel, long acquainted with Australian realities, was the Government leader in the Commons; and Henry Goulburn was Chancellor of the Exchequer. For the Australian colonies, therefore, 1828 was a memorable year. The preparations of two years past led to Huskisson's introduction of the 1828 New South Wales Bill, later 9. G. IV c. 83, intended to give a more permanent and improved constitutional and legal structure to the colonies, and in fact prolonged in its essentials until 1842. Huskisson replaced Horton with E. G. Stanley (15 October 1827–5 February 1828), a young Whig of 28, even then supported for leadership of the majority Whig faction, but in the course of events twice Colonial Secretary (1833–4, 1841–5) and three times Prime Minister (1852, 1858–9, 1866–8). Huskisson owed it to the Lansdowne group to appoint the future Lord Derby.[2] Goderich had suggested that 'either Francis Leveson or young Stanley would suit you admirably and be very creditable and useful appointments'.[3] Huskisson was able to make use of them both, for after the Duke

[1] H. T. Manning, 'Colonial Crises before the Cabinet, 1829–1835', *Bull. Inst. Hist. Res.*, XXX (1957), 41–61.

[2] B.M. Add. MSS. 38750, f. 180; Huskisson–Lansdowne, 1 Sept. 1827, Private and Confidential.

[3] ibid., f. 23; Goderich–Huskisson, 14 Aug. 1827.

became Prime Minister, Stanley resigned with the other Goderich Whigs, and Lord Francis Leveson Gower was appointed under-secretary (5 February–30 May 1828).

The two young under-secretaries were very different men. Both had charge of the details concerning the Australian colonies, but Hay maintained a paternal supervision of their work. Stanley was a doubter and took little for granted. When various colonial boards recommended protective duties to help their infant products, he cast scorn on their painfully elaborated reasons. 'Surely encouragement should rather be given to the cultivation of articles *not* produced in the mother country, which may be profitably exported thither, and enable the Colony to pay in produce for the imports she receives.' He was very confident of his own opinions,[1] and his advice, if sometimes abrasive, was capable and direct. It was a good introduction to a remarkable career.

Lord Francis, a brother-in-law of Greville, son of the family through whom Huskisson owed his early introduction to Pitt, was a more leisurely person. He had been a junior Commissioner of the Treasury, where he found that 'the great mass of its business is now in the hands of the clerks, gentlemen whose time and talents are exclusively devoted to its details'.[2] It would not be much different at the Colonial Office. 'I have deferred looking over these for the present and should wish for Mr. Short's opinion how far they demand attention', he minuted one of General Darling's dispatches which enclosed six months' Executive Council Minutes for New South Wales. 'All matters of importance to which these Minutes of Council refer have been brought before the Secretary of State in separate despatches', Short assured him: 'It does not therefore appear necessary that Lord Francis Leveson Gower should give himself the trouble of looking over these minutes.'[3] Still, there were routine chores to perform within his bailiwick, the Eastern Department, and when he moved on to become Chief Secretary in Ireland, some of them followed him.[4] A poet and contributor to the *Quarterly*, Lord Francis does not seem to have escaped the strictures he applied to the Treasury Commissioners for 'affixing their signatures to a quantity of the documents by which much of the business of the empire is transacted

---

[1] C.O. 201/186/317, Minute on Frankland Lewis–Hay, 7 Dec. 1827.
[2] B.M. Add. MSS. 38749, f. 200: Gower–Huskisson, 5 May 1827.
[3] C.O. 201/183/396, M. on Darling–Goderich, 10 Oct. 1827.
[4] H.R.A. I/xiv/660, Hay–Darling, 20 Feb. 1829.

. . . the contents of which are also unknown to those who sign them'
by a very wide margin.[1] But he was a pleasant man, 'well-connected',
and a favourite of Wellington's.[2] There must have been some executive quality in him to satisfy the diligent Peel.

On Huskisson's departure, Wellington chose his old Quarter-
master-General and Chief of Staff, Sir George Murray, to be Third
Secretary. He had been for six weeks in 1815 Lieutenant-Governor
of Upper Canada, and was regarded as an upright, popular soldier.
Peel, who hoped he would assist to carry the burden of the administration in the Commons, was horrified to discover how inarticulate he
could be; and he tended to be unreliably liberal. Murray has been
judged by some, including Greville, who quoted Hay's opinion that
'he had never met with any public officer so totally inefficient as he',
to have been totally incapable of grasping administrative detail or
keeping the department in order. He appears as a kind of bewildered
senior clerk to Wellington, who relied on Bathurst and Goulburn for
advice in imperial crises.[3] It is certainly hard to take his comment in
the House shortly after his period of office as a reasoned defence of
positive *laissez-faire*: 'I have always supposed until this moment, that
to abstain from any extraordinary activity in the measures to be
carried into effect with respect to the colonies was a merit rather than
a defect.'[4] Yet, although he was a weak Minister and relied utterly
on Hay and the office staff, his dealings with the Australian colonies
were kindly and reasonably attentive.

Under Murray, the political under-secretary should have had an
opportunity to work wonders, but Horace Twiss (30 May 1828–22
November 1830) had been rejected for Horton as Goulburn's successor in 1821, and succeeded to an office as yet unformed in its
organization and increasingly drawn into heavier responsibilities.
Henry Taylor says he was indecisive, and so occupied with detail that
he became 'incapable of coming to a conclusion'; whereas Hay,
'obtuse but bold' was accustomed to go 'straight to a decision, which
was right or wrong as might happen'.[5] In fact, the parliamentary
work crushed his spirit. Misunderstandings abounded under Twiss,
and both Stephen and Hay often had to come to his rescue. In 1830

[1] B.M. Add. MSS. 38749, f. 251: Gower–Huskisson, 5 May 1827.
[2] N. Gash, *Mr. Secretary Peel* (London, 1961), p. 517.
[3] Young, op. cit., p. 110; Murray, op. cit., p. 148.
[4] P.D. 3rd series, I/1060, 13 Dec. 1830.
[5] *Autobiography* (London, 1885), i, 117–8.

there existed a sort of dyarchy, with Hay and Twiss both minuting Australian dispatches.[1]

When the Whigs came in at the end of 1830 they may have had no coherent plan of procedure, but there was an increased insistence on conscious control exercised by an administration acting upon firm principles of retrenchment and reform. The climate was sympathetic for change, and with the end of Governor Darling's flinty reign and Richard Bourke's appointment there occurred in New South Wales at least a notable liberal opportunity. The continuities, however, remained. Goderich, talkative, inactive, with 'truly . . . no will or opinion of his own'[2] was back; and the office now had traditions and habits which were, if not invulnerable to the vigorous assault of Lord Howick and the Treasury, at least well entrenched. Permissive, procrastinating, confused, under scrutiny from parliamentary and radical utilitarian critics, the Office had weathered out many storms. Even General Murray, however, had had to promise a colonial 'budget', and the Whigs considered themselves obliged to give more than lip service to the principle of retrenchment.

Above all, the Whigs had in the parliamentary under-secretary, Lord Howick, son of the Prime Minister, an 'able, unassuming', 'honest and ardent' activist.[3] He was, as a new broom, anxious to examine all dark corners of a long Tory rule, and eager to snatch at fresh ideas for the more efficient government of the empire. He had for his own special field the West Indies, but he was not impressed by geographical limitations. Hay, back in charge of Australian affairs briefly,[4] surrendered them to Howick, and he immediately made upon their conduct an impact which made it clear that a new and major influence had emerged. Interested in the reorganization of the Office and its departments, optimistic about the possibility of evolving a system of authoritative colonial government at once efficient and liberal, he set himself and his subordinates a task which, if acknowledged by his Tory predecessors, had never been quite so vigorously pursued. Much of the foundation for an 'improving' government of the Empire had been laid. But it was apt that the Era of Reform should be introduced in the colonies of settlement with a renewed sense of administrative purpose and executive confidence.

[1] C.O. 324/86/144, Hay–Stirling, 8 June 1830.
[2] Howick–Grey, 29 May 1832, q. in Murray, op. cit., p. 166.
[3] Taylor–Miss Fenwick, 1831, q. in Murray, op. cit., p. 166.
[4] C.O. 324/87/10, Hay–Dumaresq, 17 Jan. 1831.

II

ADMINISTRATORS, LAWYERS AND THE DEVELOPMENT OF COLONIAL GOVERNMENT

In 1824, Wilmot Horton wrote somewhat hopefully to the colonial secretary of New South Wales: 'It is scarcely possible to supply by specific instructions all the details that are necessary to carry on any measure of considerable magnitude; but nothing can be more easy, when the spirit and object of such a measure be distinctly detailed, than to supply on the spot such facilities as will carry it into practical effect.'[1] Vigorous and improving activity by colonial officials was the *sine qua non* of progress, but Horton envisaged practical and enlightened schemes for imperial advancement and human prosperity emanating from a colonial department replete with advisory bodies, and boards of consulting experts. Such constructive long-range administration, though eminently worth-while as an ideal, was difficult to set up. The practice proved to be fitful, vague and uncoordinated, due at least in part to the limitations and ambiguities which existed in the organization of the central machinery of government.

Horton's methods necessarily resulted in the office clerks becoming involved in departmental decisions and negotiations, some of them quite delicate. He was not as thorough in executive supervision as Henry Goulburn, and the remodelling failed to extend far enough. Arrangements concerning legal appointments in the aftermath of the New South Wales Act were conducted at various stages between Horton and Stephen, not yet completely absorbed by the colonial department; by Adam Gordon, senior clerk, who was employed frequently to verify credentials;[2] by James Chapman, the chief clerk,[3] and George Baillie.[4]

Stephen gave interviews to lawyers going out to the colonies, but he was handicapped in his efforts to obtain better service by his unofficial

[1] C.O. 201/155/506, Horton–F. Goulburn, 7 July 1824.
[2] H.R.A. IV/i/528, Stephen–Horton, 8 Dec. 1823; H.R.A. IV/i/639, Stephen–Gordon, 28 Mar. 1826.
[3] H.R.A. IV/i/498, W. Dealty–Chapman, 1 Sept. 1823.
[4] H.R.A. IV/i/524, Stephen–Baillie, 22 Nov. 1823.

status in the department. The question of salaries was central.[1] He had no power to decide what amounts were suitable, but pressed for reasonably high emoluments, suggesting sums which were 'certainly not higher than corresponding functionaries receive in many of our West Indian Islands, . . . far less able to afford such an expenditure'; and was clear that it would be 'a real economy to make an adequate provision for effective servants of the Public'.[2]

In 1823 Stephen prepared drafts of the Letters Patent for erecting the new Courts and the Order in Council for 'regulating the mode of proceeding, the duties of the various officers attached to the Courts, the duties of Advocates and Attornies, and the fees and emoluments of the various officers'.[3] Stephen clearly foresaw the key role to be played in the reconstituted legal and colonial framework by these officials, who would not only have to proceed against all criminals by information, and hence discharge the functions performed in England by the Grand Jury; but would also, under the Act, be called on to prepare and advise the Governor upon the drafts of all legislative measures if ever they were to pass the Chief Justice as not being repugnant to the law of England. They would also have to become advisers to the Governor on all legal questions and institute necessary proceedings for the protection of the revenue and rights of the Crown. Such services must obviously be well remunerated, as lawyers in the Australian colonies were now receiving large incomes.[4]

When J. T. Gellibrand, first Attorney-General of Van Diemen's Land, claimed Stephen's sanction for his engaging in private practice, in the course of which he had become involved in some very shady transactions, Stephen tartly denied the allegation. 'It appears to me perfectly inadmissible', he wrote[5] 'for any man to prefer a demand of this nature upon no other authority than that of a verbal communication with a very subordinate Member of Lord Bathurst's office.'

This case, in which Alfred Stephen, his first cousin, emerged as the chief antagonist of the Attorney-General, forced Stephen to decline 'interfering, directly or indirectly' in its investigation.[6] In fact, though he never ceased from playing a crucial part in almost all decisions

[1] H.R.A. IV/i/568, Bannister–Horton, 1 Oct. 1824.
[2] H.R.A. IV/i/525, Stephen–Baillie, 22 Nov. 1823.
[3] H.R.A. IV/i/500, Stephen–Horton, 1 Sept. 1823.
[4] H.R.A. IV/i/503, Horton–Stephen, 8 Sept. 1823.
[5] C.O. 280/8/105, Stephen–Hay, 11 July 1826.
[6] C.O. 280/8/111, Stephen–Bathurst, 17 July 1826.

made in the Colonial Office concerning the Australian colonies, the presence there of his numerous and prominent cousins and his uncle, John Stephen, was at least as potentially embarrassing to him as was his father's reputation as an opponent of slavery. In a long report on controversies among the colonial lawyers, Stephen assured Sir George Murray that he had, in his official dealings with his uncle, now Puisne Judge at New South Wales, behaved 'as though he were an entire stranger to me'. Yet he was aware of his five cousins in the colonies: the eldest who had acted as Solicitor-General in Sydney; John Jn., at that time a troublesome Registrar of the Supreme Court; Alfred, Solicitor-General and Crown Solicitor of Van Diemen's Land; Francis, recently favoured by Governor Darling with the Clerkship of the Supreme Court in New South Wales; and a fifth brother working as a clerk in the Commissariat.[1] Darling, with whom Stephen had conferred exhaustively in London, was in correspondence with Stephen about his relatives, and accused the younger John Stephen of being as 'arrogant an Intriguant as ever embarrassed any Government' and of wishing to abuse his cousin's influence at the Colonial Office.[2]

The arrival of trained lawyers, the initiative of the Colonial Office in the wake of the Bigge Reports, the growing interest of home groups and the increasing complexity of colonial demand all eventually had a liberalizing effect. The last-minute addition to the 1823 Act of provision for a Legislative Council is testimony to the devolutionary intentions of the home Government. Hay noted on Stephen's important memorandum about the needs of the Australian colonies in 1828: 'We should not legislate too much in detail for any of these Colonies. It is a fault into which this Country has often fallen, and never with impunity.' Yet, as Stephen pointed out, there could not be a simple surrender by a government department of the details of colonial administration to local administrators. 'New South Wales, not being a conquered colony, but having been acquired by the mere occupation of a vacant territory, the King, according to the settled rule of law, could not, in the mere exercise of his prerogative, create any Judicial or Legislative Institutions there, deviating in any essential circumstances from the corresponding Institutions of the Mother Country. It became necessary therefore to resort to Parliament to supply this defect in the Royal authority.' 'It being thought necessary',

[1] C.O. 201/195/400, Stephen–Murray, 15 Aug. 1828.
[2] H.R.A. I/xiii/651, Darling–Stephen, 16 Dec. 1827.

he wrote, 'to establish courts without trial by jury, and a Legislature without Representation, those invasions upon the first principles of English law require a direct Parliamentary sanction.' Many changes had been found necessary; but to bring them about both legislative and administrative authority was required.[1]

Vigilance and painstaking attention to detail were now the only refuge of administrators, for official correspondence no longer echoed authoritatively in a sullen void, but was caught up in a tense dialogue among men who were determined to gain recognition and the redress of grievances. The laws of a great nation might be, in many respects, as Stephen wrote, 'utterly inapplicable to the condition of an infant settlement', but the law of England remained 'the birthright of English Subjects, which they carry with them when they quit their native land, to make settlements on waste or unoccupied territories'.[2] It would be, and had been long debated how much of the 'English Code is thus supplied', but the answer 'so much as is applicable to their circumstances' contained in itself the seeds of many an administrator's nightmare. For the dutiful military governors, Macquarie, Brisbane, Sorell, Arthur and Darling it implied anxiety, toil, and disappointment. For the Colonial Office, even under the urbane Bathurst it meant considerable trouble from all sides, usually ending in unsatisfactory compromise. Thus, for example, Bathurst had to tell the King that, because of dissensions between Sir Thomas Brisbane and his Colonial Secretary Major Frederick Goulburn, it had become 'expedient that they both should be recalled'.[3] So too James Stephen, after a long examination of unsavoury scandals in New South Wales dispatches, found that he would have to recommend a censure of the colonial veteran Samuel Marsden. He realized that this would have serious results and would excite that 'numerous body with whom that Gentleman is connected in this Country'; but above all he lamented the necessity of humiliating the old chaplain. 'I feel it is a species of impiety to be, in any manner, accessory to his public disgrace.'[4]

General Darling, bustling with optimistic activity and energetic plans for a reform of all departments was certainly no exception to the harsh rule. Nor would a civilian like Commissioner Bigge have fared much better had he been appointed governor, as it was rumoured he would be: for the problem was not a transitory one but a dilemma

[1] C.O. 201/195/345.   [2] C.O. 201/195/351 ff.   [3] *Bathurst Papers*, p. 575.
[4] C.O. 201/175/294, Stephen–Hay, 14 July 1826.

as old as colonization, as government itself. 'Power and importance rank very high with us male fools', Darling's secretary wrote home to his mother, high in expectation as he rode through the 'mysterious light forests' of the Australian bush. 'There is a vast scope here which, I confess, has more charm for me than the narrow compass of your snug little island.'[1] He had been in the Peninsula, in Canada, Belgium, fought at Waterloo, but all this could be little guarantee of administrative prowess. 'There are many brave men who are not fit to govern colonies', Wellington wrote to Bathurst about Governor Brisbane.[2] That statesman, pondering his letter of recall to Sir Thomas could only add the final word: 'I cannot say I like it, but I do not know how to mend it, without making it more complimentary, or more severe. As it is, it is unmeaning enough, which is perhaps the best thing it could be.'[3]

Stephen alone, then, could hardly hope to do more than trim the jungle growth of confusion which was springing up around government as the Australian colonies expanded. That Australian governors recognized his position is shown by Darling's letter to the permanent under-secretary enclosing his 'Remarks on the proposed New South Wales Bill' of 1827–8: 'It is, however, unnecessary for me to trouble you further on the subject, as I have written fully to Mr. Stephen.'[4] These remarks included a strong attack on the idea of a legislative assembly, which the Governor was sure would in the present circumstances be 'absurd in the extreme', would retard rather than advance the colony, and would unsettle the people by 'diverting them from the necessary attention to their business'.[5]

In fact of course, with the appointment of Hay in July 1825 another level was introduced into the machinery of decision-making in Downing Street, and a very important one, for Hay became a most faithful friend of Australian advancement, in almost continual supervision of its colonial government for ten vital years. Colonial officials looked towards the central government for regularity of response, guidance and support. Francis Forbes, Chief Justice of New South Wales and a copious correspondent of Horton's, in 1827 set forth in an extraordinary letter the vision of a liberal official. Governments,

<hr>

[1] Dumaresq Papers, Mitchell Library, A/2571, 6 Mar. 1826.
[2] *Bathurst Papers*, p. 576.
[3] M.L. A/73/158, Letters of Lord Bathurst to R. W. Horton 1825–7.
[4] H.R.A. I/xiii/652, Darling–Hay, 17 Dec. 1827.
[5] H.R.A. I/xiii/657, Darling–Stephen, 17 Dec. 1827.

he felt, 'are founded in opinion, and formed by events'. A wide colonial experience had taught him that all changes, except those wrought by time, were revolutionary and mischievous. Whoever abruptly attempted to make violent alterations, merely because they seemed better in the abstract, was 'a traitor and a maniac'. But he found himself forced to make an exception for colonies such as New South Wales 'where the people are not of the production of the place, but for the most part emigrants from England and Ireland, and annually bring with them the opinions and habits of the countries from which they come'.

New South Wales, beginning as a patriarchal penal farm with the government of 'everything necessarily centred in the Governor as the *primum mobile* of the machine' must, he thought, move forward under the care of England. With all its peculiarities, New South Wales must enjoy all English laws and an English government. 'I am led to believe that the great policy of England towards this second giantess of her begetting is to educate her in principles strictly English; it is her interest, it is her duty; she owes it to her own glory, and to the happiness of all Asia.' Transportation was in essence a method of improving the British realm, of which the colonies 'were only a more remote portion'. The Australian colonies differed from all others. The two peoples, sprung from a common stock, would be 'united by identity of laws and institutions, similarity of habits and feelings . . . those enduring ties between people sprung from one common ancestry, which the worst policy cannot wholly eradicate, and the best may render eternal'.[1]

Yet what Stephen later described as the 'pragmatic' spirit of the British Government was of the greatest importance in the history of imperial development. So multifarious were the objects of Colonial Office solicitude that he would later complain bitterly of the impossibility of careful thought or the maturing of a consistent and well-considered policy. 'What should be the aim of Government? We should have studious and speculative men, standing aloof from mere despatch-writing and projecting schemes of comprehensive and remote good. But . . . I do not know my alphabet better than I know that this is not the spirit of British Government and that the ambition of every Secretary of State and his operations will be bounded by the great ultimate object of getting off the mails.'[2] His famous criticism of

[1] H.R.A. IV/i/688, Forbes–Horton, 6 Mar. 1827.
[2] C. E. Stephen, *The First Sir James Stephen* (London, 1906), p. 42.

the department and its members, the majority of whom, he told the Northcote-Trevelyan Committee, had in his time 'possessed only in a low degree, and some of them in a degree almost incredibly low, either the talents or the habits of men of business, or the industry, zeal, or the knowledge required for the effective performance of their appropriate functions',[1] was probably too harsh. It must be set against Hay's defence of the senior clerks in 1831 without whose 'general talents and capacity for business . . . this branch of the public service must have been involved in a state of inextricable confusion'.[2]

In the years 1823–7 the administration came to accept that it had the duty of taking the initiative in directing how colonial affairs should be conducted, yet at the same time it was seeking to disown the role that it had come to have in colonial government.[3] Just as the Office was leaving the colonists to make moves towards amelioration in the West Indies, but was forced into a more active role to encourage them, so in the Australian colonies the home departments were forced into greater activity in order to lay down the foundations of future autonomy in various fields. Of course in the Australian colonies there were no intractable legislative assemblies; but the nature of transportation provided an analogous challenge. The year 1824 was an *annus mirabilis* during which the department was increased from 1 under-secretary, 1 private secretary, 10 clerks, 1 librarian and 1 part-time counsel to 2 under-secretaries, 3 private secretaries, 15 clerks, 2 librarians, 2 registrars, 1 précis writer, and a full-time counsel, Stephen, shared with the Board of Trade.[4] Separate agencies and specialists were set up; and the business of the Empire was divided into four convenient geographical areas.[5] But not all complexity in organization leads to simplification of function and operation.

Delay, procrastination and lack of coherence on the part of the Colonial Office were not always explicable by mere obtuseness or neglect. Horton's minute on a trade memorandum raising some important questions about the effect of the East India Company Charter on the trade of New South Wales: 'The first part of this letter should be sent to the Treasury, the second to the Board of Trade, and the third

[1] P.D. H.C. 1854–5, XX (1870), p. 75.
[2] C.O. 324/146/303, Hay–Spring Rice, 21 July 1831.
[3] Murray, op. cit., p. 145.   [4] At £1500 p.a. C.O. 324/145/76, 31 Jan. 1825.
[5] Order in Council of 19 Mar. 1824; cf. Young, op. cit., p. 68.

to the Post Office', tells its own story.[1] The process could be nerve-racking to the distant and dependent governors. In 1823 Bathurst acknowledged to Brisbane that proclamations, the old form of administration in New South Wales, were invalid; but until the Bill which later became 4 G. IV c. 96, establishing a Legislative Council, was passed, the proclamations must 'remain on their present footing'.[2] It was not, however, until 19 January 1824, after much consultation in London[3] and the near-collapse of Brisbane's administration, that Bathurst sent a dispatch enclosing the Warrant 'nominating the five principal officers of the colony to seats in the Council'.[4]

Hand-to-mouth administration was accompanied by attempts at more systematic reforms in government method. Thus Stephen was asked in 1822 to confer with Bigge and prepare a Bill to continue until 1824 the indemnity for the levying of duties which had been hastily extended to the Governor of New South Wales when it had become clear that the whole basis of the colony's taxes was arbitrary and illegal.[5] Very simple administrative directions could have far-reaching results. In 1824 Stephen and Moody began to revise the Instructions to colonial governors.[6] Henceforth the Office, in which Stephen's stature and importance was growing rapidly, found itself being inexorably drawn into a more active role in the investigation and supervision of the official conduct of colonial administrators. The next year Stephen protested that 'it makes my head ache even now to think of the incessant talkings and interviews' he held with General Darling, about to sail for New South Wales;[7] and he submitted to Horton an exhaustive review of the detailed new Commission and Instructions that would be needed to replace the old instruments, so often transcribed, and now no longer applicable 'in any part'. The decision to issue a distinct Commission for Van Diemen's Land 'as a separate and independent colony' set formal seal on an arrangement already resulting in the arrival at the department of a subtly different series of administrative documents which soon swelled in volume and complexity under Governor Arthur to rival that of the parent colony.[8]

[1] C.O. 201/147/564, Whiston and Hewett–Bathurst, 1 Aug. 1823.
[2] H.R.A. I/xi/65, Bathurst–Brisbane, 30 Mar. 1823.
[3] e.g. C.O. 201/147/334, T. H. Scott–Horton, 22 Aug. 1823.
[4] H.R.A. I/xi/195, Bathurst–Brisbane, 19 Jan. 1824.
[5] 59, G. III c. 114 (1819); renewed in 1. G. IV c. 62 (1820), 1 and 2 G. IV c. 8 (1821), and 3. G. IV c. 96 (1822).
[6] C.O. 324/145/18, Horton–Moody, 31 July 1824.
[7] H.R.A. IV/i/622, 19 Aug. 1825.
[8] Files at C.O. 280; and H.R.A. IV/i/612, Stephen–Horton, 27 Mar. 1825.

Stephen's opinion that 'it would seem highly convenient to render the Instructions a comprehensive Code of Regulations for the Governor's Guide, and upon all the more important branches of his administration' led him to suggest a battery of new instructions under the headings of Executive Government, Legislative, Revenue, Crown lands, Judicial affairs, Ecclesiastical affairs and Education, Police, Convicts, Native inhabitants, and New Settlements. He framed his recommendations both with an eye to general imperial precedent and the practice of the old colonies, and Canada, as well as to the special requirements of Australia. Among his proposals was the formation of an Executive Council to assist, or rather to 'control' the Governor, like those found in the Empire 'in former times, and . . . recently in the Cape of Good Hope and Mauritius'.[1] Thus the Colonial Office through the acceptance of such opinions came to treat the governor as their agent, who would obtain information for imperial purposes, help form decisions on the conduct of affairs and carry them out once made. This supervisory function could be very onerous in the case of the Australian colonies. But it was not necessarily adopted in a fit of absence of mind.

As departments multiplied, the central authorities were called upon to send out greater numbers of civil servants and officials, and to select better men. 'The reputation of your office is involved in the proper administration of this Government', wrote Darling. Though he was inclined to count vulgarity and popularity as almost as dangerous in subordinate officers as inefficiency, he was surely not far from the mark when he bewailed that 'there is no Colony under His Majesty's Government, where attention to the selection of Individuals, is so important as here and in Van Diemen's Land— not only the character of the Government but the moral improvement of the people mainly depend on it'.[2] The Office took long to learn its lesson. 'They will *job* colonial appointments at Downing St., in spite of all the failures, . . .' wrote Barron Field to Marsden about the same men of whose appointments Darling, no friend of his, had complained.[3] But, through the bitter experience of mistake after mistake, the lesson gradually went home.

Stephen, though in favour of a unified imperial system, was very conscious of the differences between colonial backgrounds, and the

[1] ibid., pp. 606, 594.
[2] C.O. 323/146/244 Darling–Horton, Private and confidential, 11 Dec. 1826.
[3] M.L. A/1992 (Marsden Papers), f. 458 Field–Marsden, 28 July 1826.

need for adaptation. While engaged in extending British laws and institutions even to the penal colonies he realized that the doctrine of non-repugnancy could be fanatically and over-scrupulously maintained. 'A perfect parallelism between the law of England and that of Van Diemen's Land is, in the nature of things, impossible', he minuted. 'It is quite enough if there be that general correspondence between the two which is necessary for perpetuating in the colony Institutions substantially the same with those of England.'[1] For the Australian colonies, he perceived, the pertinent question was not so much what kind of institutions should be fostered, but at what pace it was safe to go.

Colonial Office clerks played, and were known by those concerned with Australian affairs to play, an influential role in the conduct of official business during the 1820s. Edward Barnard, who superintended the routine work of the penal colonies until he was appointed Agent for New South Wales and Van Diemen's Land in 1822[2] on Bigge's advice, was a capable man whose interest in the colonies became more rather than less active as the duties of his agency multiplied. John Macarthur, Jr., who kept a very close eye on such matters, reported to his father in 1822 that he must expect some delays. 'In the Colonial Office, the quantity of business, and the disputes referred home from almost every settlement, afford some excuse for the Under-secretary. The effects of the system on Barnard, who is of an anxious temper, were very visible, and the apprehension of sinking under it has induced him to retire from the office on the salary of agent and the half pay to which he was entitled by length of services— in all about £700 per annum.'[3] Barnard was only 36 years of age, and had served eighteen years in the department. He had been 'much dissatisfied with the inattention of Mr. Goulburn and Lord Bathurst to the affairs of the colony' during the interval of Bigge's Commission which those two statesmen had employed as a breathing-space.[4] Despite Walter Buchanan's verdict on the agent: 'Barnard enjoys a kind of *otium cum dignitate*',[5] he eventually became much more deeply immersed in Australian affairs, having to respond to the hugely increased demands of the expanding colonial departments. Field told Marsden that 'the surest channel for the complaints of the colony is

[1] C.O. 280/22/118, M. on Arthur–Huskisson, 19 Apr. 1828.
[2] H.R.A. I/x/728, Bathurst–Brisbane, 1 Sept. 1822.
[3] M.L. A/2911 (Macarthur Papers), f. 190: 8 Dec. 1822.
[4] ibid., f. 124: 1 June 1821.
[5] M.L. A/4267, Buchanan–Bowman, 12 Feb. 1824.

through Barnard to Lord Bathurst, and not through Wilmot Horton, where everything is made to square with MacArthur's views'.[1]

Barnard was succeeded at the New South Wales desk by one of the Baillie brothers, probably Thomas who became a very controversial Commissioner of Crown Lands in New Brunswick in 1824, when Henry Trevor Short took over: 'a friend of mine . . . a most gentlemanly fellow', Buchanan described him.[2] Short was a thorough but unoriginal man who was trusted by successive Secretaries and Under-secretaries of State. Sir George Murray especially came to rely on his knowledge and memory of Australian affairs. By 1828 Gordon Gairdner, very influential during the next decade, dealt with New South Wales affairs, while H. S. Kelsey coped neatly with Colonel Arthur's voluminous dispatches from Van Diemen's Land. T. F. Elliott, later a major administrator of the Government emigration schemes, was engaged at various times to check colonial revenues and as a précis-writer.[3]

* * * * *

Hay's appointment as Permanent Under-secretary on 5 July 1825 by Order in Council[4] began a new era for the Colonial Office.

It was probably intended, as Stephen later stated, that the Permanent Under-secretary was to be the 'depository of all that knowledge of which the Secretary of State must daily avail himself',[5] and to be the key figure who seemed to be essential in securing unity of action, continuity of policy, the centre of contact with other departments, and the end to that fragmentation which was plaguing Horton's new-fashioned office. Horton had soon found that his parliamentary life, social activities, and interest in questions connected with political economy, education and emigration were an intolerable burden when combined with the consultations and business necessary for a more lively direction of colonial affairs. His health had suffered and Henry Taylor, when he entered the Office, thought its condition was one of 'utter confusion'.[6] The gradual assimilation of Stephen into the department from 1823 to 1825, when he became full-time,[7] did much

---

[1] M.L. A/1992, f. 413: 28 June 1824.
[2] M.L. A/4267, Buchanan–Bowman, 12 Feb. 1824.
[3] e.g. C.O. 280/16/240, M. on Arthur–Huskisson, 14 Apr. 1828.
[4] C.O. 324/145/148, Bathurst–Harrowby, 1 July 1825.
[5] C.O. 537/22, Memo. of Stephen, 30 Mar. 1832.   [6] *Autobiography*, I, 64.
[7] C.O. 324/145/76, Bathurst–Harrowby, 31 Jan. 1825.

to assist, but the devolution of work upon the regional clerks and the establishment of special bodies still left great problems of co-ordination. Lord Bathurst was too old and perhaps too shrewd to attempt a close supervisory role, though he retained of course full responsibility for the Office and was capable of initiative in an emergency. Stephen himself would have been a controversial choice as permanent under-secretary, as Hume's attack on him in the House proved.[1] But Horton finally by 're-itererated application',[2] and with Bathurst's support obtained his second under-secretary by an Order in Council of 5 July 1825.[3] Liverpool had hesitated over the appointment, fearing that it would lead in the House of Commons to the old proposals by which the Third Secretariat would be either eliminated or absorbed in 'the India Board, Board of Trade or some other office'.[4]

Hay, a Christ Church man like Canning, Peel, and Horton himself, had been in 1812 private secretary to Lord Melville, First Lord of the Admiralty, and before coming to the Colonial Office was a Commissioner at the Victualling office.[5] He maintained a close connection with the Admiralty through his friendship with John Barrow, and this friendship, extending more deeply than the merely official, was to have a powerful effect on the course of several Australian initiatives by the British authorities. Barrow's son, George, was Hay's private secretary. Henry Taylor's verdict on Hay, 'certainly not equal to the office he held'[6] has given Hay a bad reputation, and his administrative style was dilettante compared with the professional standards of a Stephen. But it has to be remembered that there was still much room for debate about what the duties of the new office were, and how they should be carried out. There is, for example, much criticism of Hay's encouragement of unofficial correspondence to supplement official dispatches and reports. At a time when the Office was trying to discourage the growth of its responsibilities, Hay doubtless appeared to be adding a heavy and awkward burden. The practice certainly led to dissension and recriminations when it became obvious to his colonial correspondents that their 'Private and Confidential' lines to Downing Street were not exclusive. On balance the system was invidious and subversive of the trust traditionally reposed in responsible colonial officers, and encouraged the reporting

[1] P.D. n.s. XIV/1081, 3 Mar. 1826.
[2] Horton–Lushington, confidential, 3 June 1826; q. in Jones, op. cit., p. 42.
[3] C.O. 324/145/148, Bathurst–Harrowby, 1 July 1825.
[4] B.M. Add. MSS. 38299 (Liverpool Papers) Liverpool–Bathurst, 5 Oct. 1824.
[5] c.f. Young, op. cit., p. 85 ff.   [6] *Autobiography*, i, 232.

of gossip which was often unfounded. But it must be recognized that the men who took advantage of Hay's offer to unburden themselves to the home authorities were very grateful for this sign of favour and opportunity to release upon their official superiors a host of ideas, hopes, and fears, as well as their troubles. Horton had initiated the practice, and the series of Colonial Office volumes containing these semi-official papers came in fact to be treated as almost a routine departmental record. They are needed frequently to supplement an accurate historical understanding of events in various colonies, particularly in the effects upon policy-formation brought about by persistent personal pressure and representation. Governors, judges, officials, and many private individuals believed that their confidential links with Downing Street effectively brought them into contact with the centre of power and movement. Governor Arthur wrote to Huskisson to thank him for his invitation to write privately. 'Under any circumstances, and in the Administration of the best-established and most organized colony, I should feel sensible of the honor, and privilege, and advantage, thus so considerately and kindly proferred, but, under the weight of responsibility incident to a new, rising, distant, and most perplexing Government,—with Lands to grant, —Emigrants to settle,—Institutions to form,—the Instructions of H.M.G. to observe,—and the Colonists, if possible, to conciliate . . .' he was overwhelmed with gratitude.[1] Pathetically, when the letter arrived, Huskisson was already out of office and beyond encouraging Arthur and his vision of convict discipline.

Some of the results of this 'unofficial' traffic could and did lead to the introduction and implementation of colonial schemes. More often, however, though Hay was very fascinated by the personal side of imperial government, it is probable that he hoped to exercise through the correspondence a vague, 'non-political', persuasive system of improvement and advancement. While he continued to assure the colonial officials of his devotion to Antipodean affairs,[2] he was not in the late twenties in immediate control of the details of their administration. There is, therefore, during the tours of duty which brought Edward Stanley, Francis Leveson Gower, Horace Twiss, and Lord Howick to administer the Australian department an eerie, almost ghostly presence. Hay usually contented himself with supplementing or underlining decisions already taken in the course

[1] C.O. 280/16/150, Arthur–Huskisson, 10 Mar. 1828.
[2] e.g. C.O. 324/86/45, Hay–Burnett, 10 July 1828.

of official business. But, where the Parliamentary Secretaries and Secretaries of State moved on, Hay remained, hoping, perhaps, by maintaining the flow of such correspondence, to exercise some benign supervisory role. Perhaps Stephen was right in stamping out such correspondence when he succeeded Hay; but there can be no doubt that the first permanent head of the Office thought it was his duty to cushion the effect of hard colonial realities for the increasing number of colonial officials being appointed, by offering them his friendship and interest. The experiment may not have been successful, and was probably the source of much confusion, duplication, and labour; but it was in purpose clearly humane.

In 1827 Bathurst, wishing to provide Hay with a protective testimonial, left on record the history of his appointment as a 'stationary' under-secretary in line with Treasury, Home and Foreign Office precedents. He strongly advised Hay against any partisan display of his political opinions, and the next year dissuaded him from standing for parliament during a period of rapid and confused change.[1]

By 1832, when Hay was failing in health and the personal relationships between the men most influential in the Office had become strained, the weaknesses of a geographical division between the Permanent and Parliamentary Under-secretary had become obvious. In that year Stephen, Hay, and Taylor all presented their views on the workings of the office, which Lord Howick was determined would be more efficient, and, in the Whig manner, operate more economically.[2] Certainly the internal structure of the Office had come to have serious weaknesses, and one of the most serious lay in the lack of co-ordination consequent upon misunderstandings about the role of the Permanent Under-secretary.

Before he resigned hurt and not a little disillusioned Horton tried to have Stephen made assistant under-secretary to fill up what was lacking in Hay; but Huskisson wrote that while he admitted Stephen's 'indispensable importance' he could not see his way clear to support such an appointment.[3] So the Permanent Under-secretary survived the frequent changes of government which took place after Liverpool's ministry collapsed, without any authoritative statement of his duties; and he gradually came to play a central but idiosyncratic role

---

[1] B.M. Add. MSS. Loan 57 (*Bathurst Papers*)/18/2237, Minute of 20 Apr. 1827; /2314, Hay–Bathurst, 22 Oct. 1828; 57/59, Bathurst–Hay, 23 Oct. 1828.

[2] Murray, op. cit., pp. 220–9.

[3] B.M. Add. MSS. 38751, f. 267–70: Huskisson–Horton, 18 Oct. 1827.

in the work of the office. His own amateur temperament combined with what he called the 'diversity of opinions which have prevailed among the different individuals to whom the management of Colonial affairs has been entrusted' to force him into a humble estimation of his duties.[1] Of necessity Stephen and the senior clerks found themselves engaged in more and more responsible tasks, but the manner of devolution proved to be infuriatingly haphazard under weak Ministers, and Taylor, looking back, called the years 1828–30 years of 'torpor' because of the lack of initiative at the top and the boredom and sense of frustration in the lower ranks. The department's routine was, in fact, well enough established.

* * * * *

Many of the problems which confronted the Colonial Office were politically as well as administratively intractable. Retrenchment cabined and confined some efforts towards advancement; interdepartmental relations could drag out interminably and raise new and significant questions. In most colonial issues there was room for debate. Amelioration, emancipation, transportation, emigration and civil administration were all complex and delicate political fields. 'It is not so easy . . . as it may at first appear for the Secretary of State . . . to find candidates free from objections for distant appointments', Hay lectured Arthur.[2] Colonial needs cried out for more and better appointments; the home public imagined that the Office was conducting a vast 'job'. Trial and error could prove painful at a remove of twelve thousand miles. Yet Hay was sincere in his insistence that the governor should not shrink from representing failures to the 'Government at home, in order that prompt measures may be adopted for remedying the evil'. There was no fear that overworked colonial administrators would not protest and do it vociferously; but promptness is a relative thing. It was not always in the power of the Colonial Office to decide whether the correct status of the home government was that of '*servus servorum*' or universal provider.

Henry Taylor, foreshadowing his *The Statesman*, in 1832 wrote in favour of constructive administration by a professional and permanent civil service élite, with the transitory Ministers attending to the parliamentary side of government in accordance with the principles

---

[1] C.O. 537/22/17 Hay, Memo., 2 Apr. 1832.
[2] C.O. 324/86/55, Hay–Arthur, 14 Aug. 1828.

of responsibility. Stephen devoted his attention to the more prag-matic task of organizing an efficient service to eliminate the 'critical and alarming state in which the affairs of almost all our colonial possessions are at present placed'.[1] He pointed to the lack of a proper division of labour in the Office, by which the Parliamentary Under-secretary was caught up with political and parliamentary business as well as having to administer the details of half the Empire, whereas the Permanent Under-secretary in his half of the globe had been able to conduct affairs on a personal rather than a systematic imperial approach. The department was 'justly obnoxious to the charge of frequent procrastination—of much incertainty of purpose—self-contradiction—and neglect of many urgent interests.' He was in-clined to place his confidence in an increased bureaucracy, but he recognized that problems of expansion had created for the personnel of the office a real dilemma. Too much responsibility for the senior clerks would result, and had in fact resulted, in unpunctuality, instability, and lack of co-ordination in the imperial machinery; too little for the junior clerks would lead to boredom and make them unsuitable for useful work. The Secretary of State and the Parlia-mentary Under-secretary should, he thought, take the decisions more boldly and accept responsibility; but the Permanent Under-secretary should provide them with all the necessary information and guidance necessary for ensuring a basic continuity in principle and practice.

Hay, however, laid less stress on the failure in executive function. In 1828 when Horace Twiss was overwhelmed with House of Commons business, he had unsuccessfully attempted to take charge of all Office business. He still thought the political heads of the depart-ment were the key to administrative consistency and executive efficiency. The shortcomings of recent years, he maintained—un-sympathetic as a Tory to many of the reforming notions now at large —were due to frequent changes of ministry rather than the structure of the Office.[2] In the event, he was discarded as Stephen stepped into the post for which he seemed created. It was ironical that, though Hay seems to have underestimated the disorganization which had resulted from his own failure to establish a firmly controlled and co-ordinated machine for dealing with imperial problems, and was castigated by Howick for being 'illiberal and narrow in the extreme',[3] it was Stephen who underestimated the bitterness which could be generated

[1] C.O. 537/22/3 Memo., 30 Mar. 1832.
[2] C.O. 537/22/17, Memo., Hay, 2 Apr. 1832.   [3] Murray, op. cit., p. 226.

by difference of opinion about colonial affairs. Later, he was to experience its full force.

Inevitably those caught up in the official process became increasingly aware of manifold bureaucratic inadequacies. But it is also clear that the years under review witnessed noteworthy administrative reforms and a remarkably rapid development of a technique of imperial government.

III

PARLIAMENT, THE EXECUTIVES
AND AUSTRALIA

HENRY TAYLOR, writing in his *The Statesman* (1836) from over ten years' experience in the Colonial department, judged that the 'far greater proportion of the duties which are performed in the office of a minister are and must be performed under no effective responsibility'.[1] Where politics and parties were not at stake, and there was no flagrant neglect or glaring injustice to individuals which a party could exploit, responsibility to parliament was 'merely nominal'. Brougham declared in 1818 that the only issues which could attract members to the House in any number were 'party and personal questions, the conduct of the Royal family, breach of privileges, or the preservation or pursuit of place'.[2] Serious debates on colonial policy could only occasionally provide such attractions, and Taylor advised his would-be Machiavelli that, if he wished to reduce his worries and avoid public scandal, he could do so by shifting responsibilities to other departments, making snap decisions without bothering to give explanations, and deferring questions, 'till, as Lord Bacon says "they resolve themselves"'. While conceding that public opinion must be assuaged, the 'safe man' could attend rather to loud and energetic clients than devote time and attention to anticipating such public interests as were dumb, feeble, or obscure.

In contradistinction, Taylor's alert official would be sensitive to all the suggestions of circumstance, would encourage and turn to account the stirrings of popular protest against abuse, and would work towards an ideal of strong, intelligent and continuous government under constructive parliamentary control. Parliament should supervise the executive but not descend to pettifogging attacks on individuals, based on unreliable information or hearsay: and the administrators should work effectively towards new legislation based on knowledge and experience. In this way 'what was superfluous in the legislation in question might be abrogated; what was amiss might be amended; what was insufficient, enlarged; what was doubtful, determined; what

[1] ed. H. J. Laski (Cambridge, 1927), p. 109 ff.   [2] P.D. xxxvii, 8 May 1818.

was wanting, added'.[1] Despite much painstaking effort on the part of officials and a spate of parliamentary activities, Britain's government of her Australian colonies before 1832 did not and could not conform to this ideal.

Britain was, in fact, engaged in a piecemeal process of re-discovering Australia and setting up alongside the existing penal framework all the working parts and institutions of a free society as then understood. When Joseph Hume in 1830 pointed to the scandalous and terrible numerical inequality of the sexes arising from the system of penal transportation, Sir Robert Peel acknowledged the question as one of great social moment. But, despite Hume's optimistic assertion that 'women who were old here were made young there', Peel knew from experience that there were practical and speculative objections to wholesale female transportation. It was 'obvious . . . that New South Wales had long outgrown all the objects for which it was chosen as a a place of transportation'. Yet real dilemmas existed. 'The situation of a Secretary of State amidst such conflicting opinions was not a very agreeable one', he confessed.[2]

Even had intelligent administrators been free from traditional or doctrinaire limitations in their attitudes towards crime and its punishment, the novel and often intractable character of problems raised by colonial growth would have prevented them from acting in an orderly, preordained or consistent fashion. It was certainly impossible for the departments concerned with the government of the Australian colonies to act as though they were altogether independent of parliament, which was beginning to exercise greater influence and to exert more pressure upon the executive.

By 1815 that 'continued course of successive improvement in the general order of the world' proclaimed by Pitt in 1792 had suffered some notable set-backs, and the necessary reconstruction after a long period of war took place against a background of violence, smouldering in agrarian agitations and occasionally bursting into sharp flame in the insanitary urban conglomerations growing up unscheduled in the wake of economic change. Colonel T. P. Macqueen, M.P. for Bedfordshire, writing to John Macarthur in New South Wales, thought revolution was near. As a magistrate and landowner, he was concerned about the 'bad spirit among the lower classes and the idle poor'. Yet he hoped that the rising would be 'as little sanguinary as possible'. If he survived any serious disturbance, he gave fair notice

[1] op. cit., p. 149; and cf. Chs. 25, 26, 27.   [2] P.D. xxiv/943-4, 21 May 1830.

that he would 'try to reach Sydney and apply to your advice in the character of a rural settler'.[1]

The penal colonies, in the nature of things, were not regarded by the ministry as a minor and separate issue, but as a small section of that large dramatic issue of the 'State of the Nation'. In their penal character they played the part of a safety-valve; as settlements they shared in the 'improving' spirit of the age. When Sir George Murray sent Governors Darling and Arthur the New South Wales Act (4 G. IV c. 96), for example, he explained that it had been enacted that the Statutes of the realm were, in so far as possible, in force in the colony, including those 'of the present session . . . in order that the inhabitants may have the benefit of the great improvements which have recently been made by Parliament in the Criminal Law of England'.[2]

All government, reactionary or reforming, claimed to uphold the timeless, honoured Constitution. But that constitution was in practice undergoing adjustments and modifications. The Whigs were routed, and the Radicals distrusted. The Tories, therefore, had to carry on the business of government. Hazlitt, trying to distinguish Whig from Tory, remarked that the Tory was 'governed by sense and habit alone', but that the 'modern Whig is but the fag-end of a Tory'.[3] In 1819, Brougham, who on 23 March had presented a petition against the arbitrary government of Governor Macquarie,[4] was writing to Grey that 'we must abstain from Reform as a Party, exactly as we have always done'.[5] A clear liberal and a consistent friend of Australian aspirations, Sir James MacKintosh, writing to John Russell about Peterloo in 1819, made his first insistent point 'irreconcilable war' against the Radicals.[6] The Radicals, in their turn, tended to despise the Whigs for their lack of idealism and fragmentation into small groups around powerful personalities.[7] Traditional advocates of strong administration, Pitt's heirs found themselves saddled with responsibilities which led then sometimes to act in ways which might

[1] M.L. A/2900, Macqueen–Macarthur, 4 Nov. 1819.
[2] H.R.A. I/xiv/269, Murray–Darling, 31 July 1828.
[3] The Collected Works of W. Hazlitt, ed. A. R. Waller and A. Glover (London, 1906), iii, 41.
[4] P.D. xxxix/1124.
[5] The Life and Times of Henry Lord Brougham, written by Himself (London, 1871), ii, 340.
[6] P. A. Brown, The French Revolution in English History (London, 1918), p.177.
[7] A. Mitchell, 'The Whigs in Opposition 1815–1830' (Oxford Univ. D.Phil. thesis, 1964), p. 12 ff.; P. Fraser, 'The Conduct of Public Business in the House of Commons 1812–1827 (London Univ. Ph.D. thesis, 1957), p. 14 ff.

have surprised the Utilitarians. In 1820 Liverpool would not have hesitated to strengthen his government by the support of both Brougham and MacKintosh.[1] Robert Owen was consulted by the elder Peel about factory legislation and the Prime Minister accepted his advice.[2] Fresh ideas were not always welcomed by ministers, of course, and when George Mudie, editor of *The Economist*, wrote to Bathurst warmly recommending the application of New Lanark ideas to the colonies, 'particularly to the Canadas, New Holland, and Van Diemen's Land', so as to make them 'of immense value to Great Britain', Bathurst replied that he did not consider that the 'projects of Mr. Owen' could be applied to the colonies with advantage, and told Mudie to save himself the trouble of coming round for discussions.[3] Yet his new under-secretary Horton would consult the Mills, Francis Place, Malthus, and McCulloch, and take advice from many quarters.

Liverpool recognized that the emergency actions of 1819 offered no permanent solutions, and took advantage of the breathing space offered by economic recovery to enlarge the basis of his support. Already, in the accomplishment of victory in war, the Tories had learnt by experience 'to adopt capacity from whatever quarter it appeared'.[4] By means of exhaustive consultations, persuasions and reasonings, Liverpool evolved a reasonably effective method of controlling men divided by political and personal allegiance. He was perpetually threatened with the major rifts which overwhelmed the ministries of his successors, and compromise frequently led to unsatisfactory results. But though great social questions could frequently be shelved or neutralized, he could never afford to neglect or despise efficient administration. 'The misfortune of this Government is that it is a Government of departments', commented the King in 1823, after the admission of the Grenvilles and return of the Canningites.[5] Such a government, increasingly based on hard work and intelligent appreciation of complex new realities at home and abroad, was by no means unhealthy.[6]

The liberalization of the ministry did not result in the emergence of a consistent programme of reforming legislation either in Britain

[1] Mrs. Arbuthnot, op. cit., p. 18.
[2] L. Stephen, *The English Utilitarians* (London, 1900), ii, 120.
[3] C.O. 323/195/276, Mudie–Bathurst, 30 June 1821.
[4] G. M. Young, *Portrait of an Age* (Oxford, ed. 1957), p. 30.
[5] *Letters*, p. lxxvii.
[6] *The Diary of Henry Hobhouse*, ed. A. Aspinall (London, 1947), ix.

or in her colonies. The issues at stake were numerous and intricate; periodical political crises brought matured plans to a standstill; and die-hard conservative elements sometimes blocked attempts at adaptation and experimentation. Peel succeeded Sidmouth at the Home Office in January 1822; Canning became leader in the Commons after Castlereagh's death in the same year. In 1823 F. J. Robinson succeeded Vansittart as Chancellor of the Exchequer, thus making room for Huskisson at the Board of Trade. All these men, or their subordinates, brought about rationalizations and improvements in their departments. Old piecemeal legislation was consolidated. Peel declared that 'Parliament had legislated too frequently on particular instances, instead of proceeding on general principles'.[1] Lord Colchester became alarmed that the liberality of the day would seriously threaten 'the British Empire with the overthrow of all its ancient institutions by which it has been nourished'.[2] Brougham, sarcastically, marvelled in 1825 at the change which had taken place, and thanked God that the nation was 'never more likely to be troubled even with the visions of those old, mean, absurd, senseless, inconsistent, shopkeeper-like, huckster-like, beggar-like doctrines, which had at last given way before the manly, generous, and philosophical principles, which the King's ministers had been compelled to adopt, by the almost unanimous sense of the country'.[3] It is clear that lack of political cohesion within the ministry did not prevent considerable administrative reform and legislative readjustment. Many of these developments had imperial repercussions.

Canning himself was no special friend of the colonies, emigration, or Botany Bay, though he wrote the usual letters of commendation for respectable would-be settlers in the Antipodes. He came to discount Horton, who considered himself Canning's faithful follower, and ruled out promotion for the under-secretary on the grounds that Horton had 'spoilt himself for Ireland' by issuing pamphlets.[4] Granville told Horton that Canning was so strongly prejudiced against Government aid for emigration that 'it was hopeless to urge him to take your Report upon it into his serious consideration'.[5] With Hay, who had sent him some inquiries about encouragement for emigration, Canning was crusty, replying that such considerations 'might,

---

[1] *The Times*, 10 Mar. 1826.   [2] *Diary* (London, 1861), iii, 300.
[3] P.D. n.s. xii/54, 3 Feb. 1825.
[4] Littleton–Horton, 20 Oct. 1827, in Jones, op. cit., p. 78.
[5] Granville–Horton, 20 Nov. 1826, ibid., p. 75.

with greater propriety, have been addressed to any other Department in the State than the Foreign Office'.[1] But his accession to the ministry enabled it to present a much more confident front to its enemies. Even in March 1822 he had intervened conclusively against Tierney's move to consolidate offices along the lines of his former attempt in 1816. In this consolidation New South Wales would have gone to the Home Office, already involved in the workings of the convict system. The motive for this unsettling suggestion was partly retrenchment, but the Whigs also hoped to embarrass C. W. Wynn, who had in the course of the Grenville alliance and reshuffle that followed, taken Bragge Bathurst's place as President of the India Board of Control. Creevey, who had been, as Secretary of that Board fifteen years before, in a position analogous to that of the under-secretary at the Colonial department, supported the reform, describing how languidly he had spent his time, 'sometimes reading the newspapers; at others, looking out my window'.[2] Courtenay, the current Secretary, answered him indignantly in a cry, frequently and fervently echoed by Horton, for greater assistance to deal with the mass of papers now mounting at the office. Canning, no doubt attentively observed by Horton who was then engaged in remodelling his own department, rose to give the House a lesson in administrative method and a description of government at work. The papers received were drawn up increasingly well, he said, and the 'actual business of the board, in point of extent, delicacy, and difficulty', contrasted with what it had been when Tierney himself was President, had increased a hundredfold.[3] As at the Colonial Office, the India Board produced its decisions and dispatches by a process of consultation, reference, delegation, correction, supervision, and verbal as well as written communications with all persons concerned. There, too, reading was proliferating, with 'enclosures accompanying the despatch with a proud and portly importance of its own which often threw its principal in the shade'. He described military dispatches, one of which was accompanied by 199 papers, in all 13,511 pages; a judicial dispatch with an appendage of 1,937 pages; and a financial statement with 2,588 pages by its side.

The 'real mode of doing business', Canning declared, was to distribute the business among different hands, and then have the results brought in for decision: and the heads of the department were

---

[1] C.O. 323/205/172, Planta–Hay, 2 Oct. 1826.
[2] P.D. n.s. vi/1123, 14 Mar. 1822.   [3] ibid., /1147 ff.

forced by self-respect to keep pace with their subordinates. Parliamentary publicity was an added security for the faithful discharge of departmental responsibilities.

Liverpool and Canning circularized government offices requesting ministers to send in statements of any legislative measures intended for presentation, so that the ministry could rally a majority.[1] Colonial affairs were part and parcel of this expanding parliamentary business. Horton's reply[2] is a somewhat despairing list of projected legislation. It was drawn up by James Stephen and included such matters as 'the regulation of the Judicial system of Newfoundland and other general measures connected with the government of that settlement— measures of the same nature with regard to New South Wales' (thus heralding the important legislative consequences of the Bigge Commission). He promised to send drafts of 'such bills as Earl Bathurst may consider necessary for carrying these measures into effect' before the meeting of Parliament.

In 1824 Canning and the Prime Minister sent a joint circular[3] strongly pleading the 'greatest importance' of introducing into Parliament every government bill as soon as possible after the opening of the session. The experience of past sessions had shown that the Government might be compelled to abandon bills already through half their stages, or to continue the sitting inconveniently, without being able to maintain attendances. They threatened that no bill would be supported if introduced by a department after Easter. Horton minuted this 'Shew this to Mr. Stephen as no time must be lost in considering what Bills must be brought in.' Canning repeated his request[4] and next year wrote personally to Bathurst, commending the departments' alacrity in bringing forward 'all the Public business'. He begged for a 'continuance of the same exertion' for the general convenience of the government and Parliament.[5]

Items of business were multiplying, five-fold from 1760–1820,[6] and colonial legislation, especially in puzzling and controverted fields such as the penal and slave colonies, required more consultation and preparation than most if it was to go through without hitch. Greville noticed the growing role of departmental advisers engaged in anonymous labours for their parliamentary superiors. During Wellington's

---

[1] e.g. C.O. 323/196/188, Arbuthnot-Bathurst, 27 Dec. 1822.
[2] C.O. 323/196/197, 21 Jan. 1823.   [3] C.O. 323/199/188, 15 Jan. 1824.
[4] C.O. 323/199/200, Canning and Liverpool–Horton, 20 Feb. 1824.
[5] C.O. 323/203/15, 2 Jan. 1825.   [6] Fraser, op. cit., p. 20.

ministry he wrote that 'in every department of Government' there could be found a 'few obscure men of industry and ability who do the business and supply the knowledge requsite', despite ignorance and incompetence on the part of the chiefs.[1] Greville describes both Deacon Hume, Robinson's secretary at the Board of Trade, and Stephen as 'very clever' and judged that Stephen was responsible for all the preparations and business of the Colonial Office.[2] Both men provided, seated in their 'separate apartments in Downing St., and Whitehall, the unseen source of many a splendid reputation'.[3]

There was taking place a political development whereby the ministry, containing liberal elements, and seeking to find wider support, became permeable to the pressure of public opinion. Canning, Peel, Huskisson, and others showed, despite initial reluctance and occasional uncomfortable feelings, an appreciation of the influence of popular sentiment and the need to gauge and satisfy it. The *Westminster Review*, in a remarkable article in October 1826 on the 'State of the Nation',[4] noticed that it had become essential for statesmen to 'have the good opinion of the people of England'. The knowledge that what was said in Parliament or done by departments would come before the public was an influential factor in determining government policy. This had produced a great change in the practical workings of the House of Commons, 'a change amounting in reality, to a great revolution'. The Ministry now must heed public opinion if it was to be stable and powerful. 'Formerly the House of Commons was considered the check upon the King's ministers. Now it is the King's ministers who are the check upon the House of Commons.' The ministry had, in fact, under the glare of newspaper reporting, radical criticism, and its own reforming momentum, become 'the conspicuous mark', and this amounted already to 'something of a real responsibility; it carries punishment and reward along with it'. Such was the liberalizing impetus that opposition groups, not having full access to the departmental documents, tended to view the ministry statically, and accused them of being arrogant and reactionary; while the government, making painful efforts to keep up with changing needs, was hindered from passing essential reforms by irrelevant or destructive criticism. 'Common sense requires an improvement', commented the *Edinburgh Review*,[5] unfriendly to the Liverpool

[1] i, 306, 8 Aug. 1829.   [2] i, 337, 1 Dec. 1829.
[3] C. Badham, *The Life of J. D. Hume* (London, 1859), i, 18; Huskisson, *Speeches*, i, 106 ff.   [4] vi, 266.   [5] Mar. 1824.

government now well into its liberal phase. 'An opposition member brings it forward and . . . public opinion decides at once in its favour . . . till the scale is turned and independent men of all parties become anxious to see the alteration effected. Suddenly the minister proposes the reprobate project as a government measure . . .' The situation was paradoxical. Parliament was playing an increasing part in the formation of policies and in the supervision of a more liberal executive; and ministers were becoming more accountable to the House of Commons, now much more influential because of the shift in Cabinet strength in its direction. Whereas in 1812 there had been three Cabinet members in the Commons, and ten in the Lords, by 1818 there were six in the Commons. This changed little for the rest of the century. Parliament was in process of becoming a more powerful and increasingly engaged legislative assembly at a time of political change and party divisions. It was also providing a more readily available court of appeal and review body for the investigation of government methods both at home and in the colonies. But there were complications.

There was in the House a large non-party element, perhaps one-quarter,[1] and many members attended only casually. It was rare for more than half the members to appear for a debate or a division—perhaps twice or three times in a session. Some regular supporters were accustomed to abstain on issues which they thought too controversial or unpopular. It is therefore not true to say that bills were not important because they were brought down late at night, or at the end of a session, at this period. Many significant questions were decided by votes involving less than a hundred members. The ministry had a delicate task to rally lax and unpredictable supporters. The power of the opposition lay in its ability to arouse popular outcry and to harass anxious and often overworked ministers in the House. Especially when the ministry seemed weak or vulnerable, the opposition Whigs coalesced sufficiently to mount regular attacks. Tierney's attempt at systematic opposition to government measures *qua* government measures never lost sight of the great objective of putting ministers out of office. The nucleus of support for ministers comprised only about forty members and though strong in many of its departments, was weak in parliamentary *esprit de corps*. Palmerston, Secretary at War, whose sympathies were Canningite and in favour of Catholic emancipation, stood against Henry Goulburn, Chief Secretary for Ireland and a Peelite, in an election at Cambridge in

[1] Fraser, op. cit., p. 14.

1826. Horton's career of active policy-making was hampered by his failure or refusal to adapt his methods to a party 'system' consisting in essence of small bands grouped around outstanding leaders.

Robinson, 'lazy' by Liverpool's standards[1] and 'timid' by Greville's,[2] earned his sobriquet of 'Prosperity' from his liberal budgets of the early twenties. Yet, a 'fair and candid man, and an excellent minister in days of calm and sunshine', he had to rely on Huskisson during the panic of 1825–6, and failed to show sufficient stamina or to rally enough support to establish a durable ministry in 1827.

Huskisson himself found that the death of Canning exposed him to political isolation. He linked a practical knowledge of economics and administration with a liberal vision, and sought both as President of the Board of Trade and as Colonial Secretary to encourage imperial aspirations by the introduction of parliamentary legislation. In March 1824 he had declared his intention of sweeping away the 'old system of exclusion and monopoly which had cramped and impeded the prosperity of the Empire'[3] and in May 1828 he looked back proudly on Acts which must redound gloriously to a 'nation that has laid the foundation of similar happiness and prosperity to other nations, kindred in blood, in habits, and in feelings to ourselves'.[4] His own career had always had an imperial connection. A member of Pitt's own kindergarten, chief clerk at the old Colonial Office in 1795, agent for the Cape, and later for Ceylon, member for the shipping port of Liverpool from 1823, he could not but be concerned with Britain's global role. His reforms were aimed at seeking 'all the commercial benefits of our continuing parts of one great Empire, and enjoying alike, under the sway and protection of the same Sovereign all the rights and privileges of British subjects'.[5] His anxiety to have his reforms understood and popular as well as effective was relevant to the administration of Australia, yet both at the Board of Trade and at the Third Secretariat he admitted himself puzzled by the Antipodean colonies. Political circumstances brought it about that he would be out of office by the time the 1828 New South Wales Bill, which he introduced, became law. His earlier rationalization of the Navigation Laws undoubtedly had a liberating effect on the general development of colonial government, comparable perhaps to the later concession of responsible government. But he too was greatly hampered by the state of 'clan' politics. Herries, whose reforming

---

[1] *Bathurst Papers*, p. 553.   [2] Greville, i, 156.   [3] *Speeches*, i, 313.
[4] ibid., ii, 287.   [5] ibid., ii, 313.

career as Financial Secretary of the Treasury was in many ways as sympathetic, as his politics were antipathetic, to Huskisson's, characterized his rival's consolidation of the endless tangle of Customs laws as 'indecent presumption and haste'.[1] In fact, Huskisson was no hothead. 'The government and legislature must keep pace with the spirit of the age. They should neither be behind it, nor before it', he declared in defence of Russell's Bill to enfranchise Manchester, Leeds, and Birmingham.[2] He thought the spirit of the age called for the population of New South Wales to enjoy in the future 'the advantages resulting from trial by jury, and an elective assembly, on the same principle as that which was so successful in its operation in England'.[3]

* * * * *

Pressures on the ministry came from a wide variety of sources, most of which had imperial views to air. Criticism, not always informed or constructive, came from the Press, theorists of Political Economy, utilitarians, special lobbies for humanitarian or evangelical causes, private interests, and colonial representatives. The parliamentary radicals included Burdett, Cochrane, Alderman Wood, and Joseph Hume, who was back in Parliament from 1818 and acted as 'the night-watchman of the House of Commons who lives upon petty abuses'.[4] Radical Whigs, numbering about thirty, included the aristocratic Bedford connection, Lord Ossulton and his brother Henry Grey Bennet, and 'new men' including Edward Ellice and J. G. Lambton. These saw their role as a 'bridge-party' between the responsible radicals and the Whig majority and aimed at discrediting the more violent of the radicals while providing a respectable Whig leadership for popular demands. They acted as a pressure group pulling the party to the left just as the Grenvilles had tended to moor it to the right.[5] In the middle were Grey, Tierney, Holland, Lansdowne and MacKintosh.

When John Macarthur wrote to his father to explain the events which led to the end of Tory rule in 1830, he noted that relaxed discipline, diminished patronage, and the 'fear of offending the constituents, amongst whom the prevailing spirit of the age for inquiry

---

[1] Mrs. Arbuthnot, *Journal*, i, 390, 30 Apr. 1825; cf. A. Brady, *William Huskisson and Liberal Reform* (Oxford, 1928), Ch. V.
[2] *Speeches*, iii, 495. [3] P.D. n.s. xix/1459, 20 June 1828.
[4] Walter Scott, q. in C. B. R. Kent, *The English Radicals* (London, 1899), p. 210.
[5] Mitchell, op. cit., p. 10.

and Reform had made silent but Marked progress', had resulted in members 'tendering only a qualified support, or . . . altogether absenting themselves from the House'.[1] He might also have added that certain Tories, some of them playing leading roles in harrying the ministry over alleged abuses or neglect of the Antipodes, had long opposed the very notion of party organization. Wilberforce declared himself 'decidedly convinced that Party is one of the chief evils which in politics we have now reason to regret' and in 1820 attacked party as 'a grand excuse for governing by influence, which is but a softer term for governing by corruption'.[2] His 'successor' Fowell Buxton, an avid student of 'The Criminal law, the Prisons, the Police, Botany Bay, the Slave Trade, etc', was accustomed to vote as he liked, 'sometimes pro, and sometimes con.'[3] Any issue which could unite Hume, Brougham, Bennet, MacKintosh, Buxton, and Wilberforce had to be handled with care by the ministry. 'New South Wales' in which many of these men took quite a direct interest, and with which they kept up personal contacts, could under some circumstances do this.

While it is noticeable, therefore, that 'interest' and party politics were volatile in the pre-Reform Parliament, the House of Commons was, in the fifteen years before the 1832 Act being transformed both in its internal functions *vis-à-vis* the ministry, and in its relationship with the public outside. The publication of debates, the growth of newspapers, the influence of periodicals, and its own reforming spirit exercised pressures on the ministry. Colonists were not slow to take advantage of the opportunities offered them by the changing role of Parliament and hastened to exploit the vulnerability of various executive departments to adverse public comment. Most local disputes from the Australian colonies found their way home both to the Offices concerned, chiefly the Colonial department, and to parliamentary spokesmen. Wentworth, writing to Bathurst about Governor Darling's brutality in the case of the soldiers Sudds and Thompson threatened to write, as he did, 'also to several members of the House of Commons who sit on the Opposition Benches of that House'.[4] Father Therry, excluded from the colonial hospitals, informed Colonial Secretary MacLeay that 'the humblest individual in a free British society had an inherent privilege to send a representation

[1] i.e. M.L. A/2911/424, John Macarthur Jr , 6 Jan. 1831.
[2] *The Life of Wilberforce by his Sons* (London, 1838), v, 151; and Fraser, op. cit., p. 30.
[3] *Memoirs of Sir T. F. Buxton*, ed. C. Buxton (London, 1848), pp. 76, 95.
[4] C.O. 201/179/516, W. C. Wentworth–Bathurst, 15 Dec. 1826.

. . . not only to the Governor but to the King-in-Council or H.M. Parliament'.[1] Edward Eagar, introduced to Bathurst as the delegate of the 'Emancipated Convicts of New South Wales and its Dependencies to carry Home their Petition to His Majesty and Parliament',[2] set himself up as an active parliamentary consultant, wrote against his opponents Barron Field, Marsden, and de Mestre, criticized the Bigge Reports effectively, and was able to influence Horton, Stephen, and Forbes during the preparations for the 1823 Bill.[3] James Bowman, the 'exclusive' colonial surgeon, was so alarmed about the effects which those 'vagabond rascal representatives' Redfern and Eagar might have, that he asked Walter Buchanan of the shipping firm Buckle, Bagster and Buchanan to insert notices in the English press to discredit the emancipists.[4] John Macarthur himself considered taking a seat in Parliament in order to have more easy access to the source of political power.[5]

Parliamentary interest in colonial matters as such was fitful, intermittent, and secondary; but the Empire was not limited to a separate compartment among the affairs of State. There were directly relevant exchanges on the Slave Trade, Widow-burning in India, Canada, and Transportation; constitutional enactments, such as those which advanced crown colony government in the Australian colonies 1823–8; Royal Commissions and Select Committees whose recommendations changed the course of colonial history. British politics in the round provided the strong basis for debate about derivative societies overseas. For ministers and opposition at home, colonial affairs were an integral part of the experience and dialogue of government. Though the state of England provided the most exciting field for parliamentary conflict, Goulburn and his successors as spokesmen for the Colonial Office found themselves increasingly under attack. Some of the criticism was formidably specialist, organized, and effective; much was frantic or inaccurate. All was potentially destructive. Thus Henry Grey Bennet, active in a search to make himself a career and to rally opposition, found in New South Wales a perfect stick with which to beat the ministry in 1819. Marryat, attacking Ralph Woodford's régime in Trinidad in 1822, referred to the Rum Rebellion and argued that arbitrary power in the colonies

[1] Therry Papers, 26 Jan. 1828.
[2] H.R.A. I/x/557, Macquarie–Bathurst, 22 Oct. 1821.
[3] C.O. 201/111/219, 1 July 1822; /231, 6 Nov. 1822; C.O. 201/146 *passim*, e.g. /379 Eagar–Horton, 9 May 1823.
[4] M.L. A/4266, 13 July 1821.   [5] i.e. M.L. A/2911, 20 Nov. 1825.

would soon 'like their other productions, be imported here'. He quoted Franklin's: 'Our slavery would have brought on yours', and declared that 'great delegated powers, exercised at a distance from the seat of government, ever have been and ever will be abused'. Goulburn, rising to oppose his demand for representative government in Trinidad, pointed out that the effect of the British constitution in slave colonies was to throw the whole power into the hands of a white oligarchy. The same argument would be used six years later by Huskisson to delay the establishment of assembly in the Australian colonies. It would throw the power to a small minority and render Crown colony government mild and liberal by comparison.[1]

It was often an uphill and courageous fight for ministers to maintain their prepared positions against powerful special lobbies, particularly when the correct policies demanded expenditure which could be attacked as unnecessary or wasteful. The Colonial Office spokesmen often found themselves caught in a cross-fire from the radicals, the Treasury, colonial representatives, and its own divided mind. Public criticism became more specific and immediate. The number of petitions and public meetings during the twenties grew.[2] But whereas public opinion and parliamentary activity tended to go in waves and according to issues and events, administration had to be continuous. Much of the criticism of Hume, Ricardo, and other radicals was bounded by the legislative horizons of *laissez-faire*, retrenchment, and 'systematic' reform. The problems of administrators were often pell-mell, unsystematic, and required for their solution expensive paternalist plans to aid the common people which *laissez-faire* ruled out.

* * * * *

Grey Bennet, who played a prominent part in bringing forward New South Wales as an issue in Parliament, was the sort of humanitarian activist who followed up his interests outside the House. The 1818 election had been a very lively one, the most active till 1830, and the Whigs were, at least until Peterloo, looking around for issues on which to attack the Government. Bennet's use of 'free speech, free press, and free meeting' was not altogether in line with the generally conservative attitude of the middle group of Whigs, who, though not as averse as Sidmouth to tampering with the *status quo*, were ready

[1] P.D. vii/1834 ff. 25 July 1822.   [2] Fraser, op. cit., Ch. 5, and p. 140 ff.

to support only those changes which were aimed at bringing institutions up to date so that they might be the more effectively preserved.[1] But, in times of political excitement, Bennet, M.P. for Westminster, and a leading protagonist of the 'platform', could bring together widely diverse groups—theoretical Benthamites, Brougham, the radical retrenchers, and the practical men of the anti-ministry right. He was a natural ally of Joseph Hume, and together they launched a concentrated attack on a discredited and battered administration.

By 1822 it was clear that the ministry would survive, and some of the Whigs had joined the government. Yet, though Hume and his friends became cut off from the main body of the Whigs, the ministry remained sensitive to their criticisms. Strong in debate, Bennet presented his case against the abuse of authority in the Australian colonies in two important pamphlets, *Letter to Lord Sidmouth* (1819) and *Letter to Earl Bathurst* (1820). Much of his information was prejudiced and out of date, but the impact of his arguments was felt and remembered. Sir Thomas Brisbane, who succeeded Macquarie, was very anxious not to come under Bennet's formidable censure, and he begged his friend, the Deputy Paymaster-General, to let him know if Bennet ever spoke of him or his doings. Somewhat unfairly to Macquarie, he commented: 'It is quite wonderful to think how Mr. Bennett could at such a distance obtain such accurate information for this pamphlet'; and he asked his correspondent to send the newspapers 'one at least from both sides of politics'.[2]

In February 1819 Bennet earned Wilberforce's commendation for his campaign against cruelty to chimney sweeps; in September he was in 'revolutionary' Manchester collecting material for a radical protest petition, and in December calling for a Committee of Inquiry into the State of the Manufacturing Districts.[3] On 25 January, he described how he had visited a convict ship and told of his horror at the sight. MacKintosh joined in, uniting Bennet's single question to the wider one of penal reform. Buxton rose to support them, and the House returned to the debate the next day.[4] When Bathurst decided on his Commissioner, it was not too remarkable that he should choose John Thomas Bigge, an approved friend of Bennet's.[5] But concessions could not easily put off such an opponent. 'It did not follow', he declared, 'because his majesty's government had done their duty, that

[1] Mitchell, op. cit., p. 197 ff.
[2] P.M.G. 1/1, Brisbane–Craufurd, 14 Feb. 1822.   [3] Mitchell, op. cit., p. 214.
[4] P.D. xxxix/88 ff., 96, and 115 ff.   [5] P.D. xxxix/462, 18 Feb. 1819.

the House of Commons were to abstain from performing theirs.'[1] Certainly he had established in 1819 that the issue of the Australian colonies could be usefully employed by radicals at home and discontented colonials to disturb Colonial Office complacency and harass the Government in the House.[2]

James MacKintosh was at the height of his powers as a political force when he adopted the cause of the Australian colonies in 1819. He had taken over Romilly's leadership of the law reformers and Scarlett told James Losh in August that MacKintosh was the ablest speaker in the House and, should Tierney's health fade, the fittest leader for the opposition.[3] As early as 1807 he had from India formed the ambition of being a law-giver in Botany Bay where his life's work might be to test his theories, and 'rescue at least the children of the convicts from brutality and barbarism by education'. He had by then already 'read, heard, and thought so much about this extraordinary colony', that he was very confident of his general opinions, and declared that if an enlightened governor did not soon go out, success would be impossible. The hope of a liberal society in the Antipodes never ceased to fire his imagination. In 1807 he had vowed that if he were appointed Governor and Chief Justice, he would consult Bentham 'and Miss Edgworth', and, if supported from home with a sufficient military force, 'a store of schoolmasters from Lancaster, with some good Irish priests for their countrymen, and good Methodists for the rest', he would 'joyfully endeavour to introduce law and morality into that wretched country, and give it (what never was yet given to any plantation) the fit constitution for a penal colony, which was to grow into a great and prosperous community'. Otherwise, he feared, the Australians would become in fifty years the greatest nuisance on the face of the earth—an unmixed community of ruffians who 'will shake off the yoke of England, and, placed at a distance which makes them inaccessible to conquest, will become a republic of pirates the most formidable that ever roamed the seas . . .'[4] It was a thought to which MacKintosh often returned, and when in 1828 he rose, tired and old, to oppose Huskisson's

[1] ibid.

[2] On Bennet, cf. Wentworth *N.S.W.* (London, 3rd ed. 1820), p. 387; L. Radzinowicz, *A History of English Criminal Law and its Administration from 1750* (London, 1948–), i, Chs. 18, 19; ii, 74; iii, Ch. 11, p. 357 ff.

[3] *Diary of James Losh*, ed. E. Hughes (Surtees Society, clxxi, 1962), i, 95.

[4] *Memoirs of the Life of the Rt. Hon. Sir James MacKintosh*, ed. R. J. MacKintosh (London, 1836), i, 342–3.

N.S.W. Bill for its failure to institute trial by jury and an elective council, he argued strongly that the 'only way to wipe out the foul stain cast upon these colonies would be, to show their inhabitants that they were placed upon the same footing and enjoyed the same privileges as other parts of his majesty's possessions'.[1] It was a sign of the times that Huskisson could argue forcibly that he had himself, as MacKintosh had conceded, no reserves in wanting to assimilate the Australian colonies to all free British ways of life, that his legislation was a necessary step along a clear road, and that he had carefully investigated all allegations of arbitrary and despotic government. The state of society, however, in those colonies was raw and immature, with most of its inhabitants scattered over a vast area. Two-thirds of them arose not from some monastery, but from Newgate, 'condemned to fourteen years of punishment for their aggressions against the civil and moral interests of their fellow subjects'. Huskisson understood the personal bitterness and class warfare which the emancipist-exclusive division caused, and he had good grounds for doubting MacKintosh's claim that a representative assembly containing such disparate elements would really blend men together and soften asperities. But he, too, was anxious that the customs of England be not forgotten. Though he had hoped to make some more permanent arrangement for future development in the colonies, he granted that the Bill would be temporary in its duration, until, as he felt sure, a time would come when 'new settlers of wealth, intelligence, and reputation' would cause a constant infusion of British principles amongst the population. Even at that time, he went on hopefully, there was a free press 'which had a due influence and control over public affairs'; and he noted that the population 'on all occasions, manifested a jealousy with respect to their rights'.[2]

On 2 May 1828 MacKintosh told the House that he believed in a colonial policy of 'full and efficient protection from all foreign influence; full permission to conduct the whole of their own internal affairs; compelling them to pay all the reasonable expenses of their own government, and giving them at the same time, a perfect control over the expenditure of the money; and imposing no restrictions of any kind upon the industry or traffic of the people'.[3] Such 'few and simple maxims' may have received at that time no widespread support, but his constant affirmation that 'the administration of justice

[1] P.D. n.s. xix/1456 ff., 20 June 1828.   [2] P.D. loc. cit. /1459 ff.
[3] P.D. n.s. xix/320.

in the colonies ought to be subject to parliamentary vigilance' was certainly generally accepted.[1] Jephson, stressing that full discussion of colonial scandals like Darling's alleged cruelty was essential, declared that 'the House had not a more important duty to perform than that of watching the conduct of governors of colonies'.[2] MacKintosh's contribution to bringing about the recognition of this supervisory function was considerable.

* * * * *

It is possible to exaggerate the efforts of the Colonial administrators to avoid parliamentary publicity. It is true that under-secretaries had often to be rescued in debates by the government leaders; and that the accepted way of turning away wrath on the subject of the Australian colonies was an affirmation of goodwill towards high-minded ciritics, the hurried shelving of prepared measures, or a promise to inquire further through Select Committee or Royal Commission. Bathurst may have done all he could to avoid and discourage parliamentary interest because it posed a threat to the internal order of the colonies:[3] but of course that kind of statement was never made publicly. Indeed, as the Colonial Office found itself being drawn towards authoritative intervention in colonial affairs, even if this authority was directed towards the establishment of more liberal institutions, it had to depend on parliamentary action. Sometimes this was politically dangerous; and not all of Bathurst's discreet actions can be summed up as 'Legislative quiescence'.

The under-secretaries, however, were Commons men, and all were proud of their parliamentary candour. Goulburn, fully concurring that the 'chief control of colonies must be looked for in the influence of public opinion', pointed out that he had, with that object in view, laid more papers on the table of the House than had ever before been submitted to Parliament'.[4] Horton, chosen for his speaking ability, lashed out at Hume in the same month, repudiating the suggestion that the government 'liable as they were to public opinion, and the opinion of Parliament' would wish to support a governor who had behaved badly. As always, he defended a distant administrator's right to be heard in defence. But he was proud of the colonial department's record in laying papers relating to the colonies before the House. In 1806, fourteen folio pages had been presented; in 1825 over 2,000, at

[1] P.D. n.s. v/1125, 6 June 1821.   [2] P.D. n.s. xxv/450, 17 June 1830.
[3] Young, op. cit., pp. 178, 201.   [4] P.D. n.s. xiv/1061, 1 Mar. 1826.

a cost for printing of £4,000. He was always disposed to furnish any information required by any honourable member. Any generalized suspicions of surreptitious extravagance and abuse were utterly false.[1] Sir George Murray always made a point of welcoming parliamentary inquiry, though he reasonably pointed out that there was danger of 'abuse of power by a Member' rather more often than in the administration of the colonies, if members were content to get their information from 'some of the most violent and prejudiced persons' interested.[2] His goodwill in presenting documentation to the House, specifically on Australian matters, was praised several times.[3] Attacks on colonial governors, Arthur, Macquarie, Maitland, Charles Somerset, Darling, and Woodford for example, were commonplace events. Colonial under-secretaries, Huskisson, and Murray, were immersed in parliamentary work and, with the increase of communication between members and Australian correspondents, nothing could long remain without airing. The decade saw the department arguing for fair play on behalf of its local representatives against a series of 'exposures', some of them unjust and of dubious origin, others carefully launched with accurate information and a determination to curb the power of the executive. So intense could parliamentary criticism become that in times of 'torpor' or internal party strife, the ministry seemed almost to be 'responsible without power'.[4]

There were, of course, some salutary parliamentary checks which during times of lax or confused administration led to improvements. One such was the suggestion of Sir M. W. Ridley that, in order to make colonial appointments more equitable and uncontroversial, they should first be 'published in the *London Gazette*, that the public might have an opportunity of judging the character of the individuals selected to fill such situations'.[5] Horton, now out of office, applauded this suggestion and called for the 'utmost publicity to all transactions in the colonies'.[6] In the same speech he raised objections to what was now become almost an 'improving' orthodoxy—colonial retrenchment. At a time when statistics were replacing the trope, and factual returns being used rather than oratory as a means of persuasion, he

[1] P.D. n.s. xiv/1290 f., 10 Mar. 1826.
[2] P.D. n.s. xxv/1129, 9 July 1830 on Governor Darling.
[3] e.g. P.D. n.s. xxiv/437, John Stewart, 17 June 1830; /450 Jephson ibid.
[4] Fraser, op. cit., p. 40.
[5] P.D. n.s. xix/1463, 20 June 1828, on the New South Wales Bill.
[6] P.D. n.s. xxv/287, 11 June 1830.

opposed the proposal that all colonies should pay for themselves. Bathurst had realized the inevitability of preparing colonial accounts for Parliament, and the Treasury under Goulburn became enthusiastic about such returns, even though Sir George Murray confessed himself generally sympathetic towards giving assistance to infant colonies in the hope that eventually they would stand on their own feet.[1] Horton, relating how Bathurst had urged the colonies on the way to self-sufficiency in 1825, explained that the Secretary of State had hoped that Huskisson's liberal concessions would lead them to accept financial responsibilities. It would now be deplorable if the British Parliament intervened too heavily in matters of expenditure. It might end, as Hay wrote to Goderich, alarmed about Howick's forward policy of presenting the House with an overdose of official documents, in 'placing the government of the colonies practically in the hands of Mr. Hume and his associates'.[2] There had been some danger of that for several years.

* * * * *

Joseph Hume, whose influence as an apostle of retrenchment and financial rationalization affected many government departments, had naturally lost little time after his election in 1818 in turning his interest to expensive colonial schemes, among the chief of which he accounted the Australian colonies. A man of means, whose fortunes had been made during a short career overseas as a civil servant in India, he impressed both Ricardo and Brougham with his tenacity and thoroughness. Especially at times of political stress, the ministry was forced to regard him with great caution. His speech of 27 June 1821[3] for example, a classic 'anti-budget' packed with statistics, led to a hasty review of government establishments. Just at a time when the business of the Colonial Office was multiplying, and its responsibilities in the Antipodes indefinitely extended, the department became vulnerable to effective and fundamental onslaughts maintained from without by retrenching members and presided over within the ministry by a Treasury inexorably bent on stringent economizing measures. In 1830 Hume, after a characteristic attack on Bathurst's

---

[1] C.O. 323/203/360, G. W. Brande–Horton, 25 Feb. 1825; P.D. xxv/330, 14 June 1830.

[2] q. in D. J. Murray, op. cit., p. 168. Cf. also C.O. 324/93/256, Hay–Goderich, 4 Jan. 1832; 323/169/5, Howick–Hay, 2, 4 Jan. 1832; 202/28/141, Hay–Stewart, 25 Apr. 1832.   [3] P.D. n.s. v/1345 f.

illiberal system of misrule, and the 'vast increase in judicial and all public establishments in the colonies' made it clear that he considered that 'the expenses of the colonial governments were deserving of as much care and attention from that House as any expenses incurred at Home'.[1]

Hume was never frightened of inconsistency. He attacked the Canadian Waste Lands Bill, designed, as Horton explained, on the precedent of the Australian Agricultural Company. The government, he alleged, had created colonial *débâcles* at the Cape and Botany Bay, and if there were a reformed House of Commons he would impeach Lord Bathurst for breach of duty.[2] Yet he and Bennet allowed their names to appear on the prospectus of the Australian Agricultural Company. Bathurst wrote to Huskisson that Hume seemed 'a prodigious Puppy',[3] but he asked Horton whether any Colonial Office clerks had taken shares in the Canada Company or the Australian Company. In fact they had; and the full list of proprietors, including fifteen M.P.s, showed the names of Adam Gordon, Henry Short, Hyde Villiers, and Bigge, as well as Hume, Bennet, John and Abel Smith, Larpent, Hart Davis, Baring, Torrens, Tooke and John Stephen.[4] When he criticized the rising expenses of the New South Wales Pension list as 'enough to frighten one', Murray had to remind him that one at least of these pensions was paid at Hume's own repeated request.[5]

Both Hume and Brougham kept a close eye on Governor Arthur. Brougham had defended Bradley successfully against Arthur in a case arising from his West Indian administration, and Arthur protested bitterly against Hume's raising the subject in the House when he could present no defence. Hume, he thought, 'seems always to disregard the anxious, and frequently distressing situation of an officer in command, and to anticipate that he must ever be overbearing because he is vested with some power, although that power is controlled by the most heavy responsibility'.[6] Shortly afterwards Hume wrote to Sir George Murray enclosing letters he had received from convicts at Macquarie Harbour and their petition to the House of Commons.

---

[1] P.D. n.s. xxiv/1166, 27 May 1830.   [2] P.D. n.s. xii/1033 ff., 15 Mar. 1825.
[3] M.L. A/73 Bathurst–Huskisson, 12 Oct. 1825.
[4] C.O. 280/2/5, 16, 115, Australian Agricultural Company, 1824–5; M.L. A/4315, A.A.Co. Letter-book.
[5] P.D. n.s. xxv/285, 287, 11 June 1830; C.O. 201/156/48 ff. and /202, Horton–Hume, 11 Nov. 1824.
[6] C.O. 280/17/131, Arthur–Hay, 11 Aug. 1828.

The convicts called upon his 'generous and disinterested feelings in the cause of liberty and the punishment of oppression'. They claimed the Governor had withheld their complaints and appeal, and Hume demanded that Murray correct such misrule and injustice.[1] A few days later he wrote to Hay to assure the convicts that he would support their case.[2] Murray questioned Arthur on the matter and the Governor disclaimed that he had ever seen the letter. He deplored Hume's inconsistency, at one moment criticizing the alleged relaxation of convict discipline in the House, and then writing inflammatory letters to convicts 'scarcely calculated to promote the submission of their depraved characters to the constituted authorities, or to make them feel the disgrace and ignominy of being transported'.[3] (In fact, the Tasmanian colonial secretary *had* received the convicts' petition and failed to pass it on; and Arthur *was* reluctant to forward petitions, destructive of authority and time-consuming.)[4] The Home Office firmly instructed Arthur to send petitions as usual;[5] but it is easy to see how unpleasant threats could be, to send 'documents to the other side of the House as will astound the Parliament for I can and will procure them'.[6] Nevertheless, despite Hume's hostility, Stephen could write to Arthur towards the end of his long administration that 'of all the Governors whom this department has employed in my time, you have enjoyed the most uninterrupted Reputation for all the qualities which a Governor ought to possess and the strongest hold upon the favourable opinion of your official superiors'.[7] Sir George Murray was sympathetic to Arthur's application for an extension of his governorship, accompanied as it was with a reference to 'Bear' Ellice his patron, and waived Huskisson's newly instituted six-year appointment rule in the governor's favour.[8]

Hume became a post-box for colonial complaints, and busied himself about issues as varied as liberty of the Press in India, distress among the Cape settlers, extravagance in the Church of Ireland, and judicial arrangements in British North America. Many of the contacts he made in dealing with one colonial issue served him in others also.

[1] C.O. 280/18/362, Hume–Murray, 9 Dec. 1828.
[2] C.O. 280/18/375, 15 Dec. 1828.
[3] C.O. 280/21/342, Arthur–Hay, 12 Sept. 1829.
[4] C.O. 280/25/104, Arthur–Murray, 12 Aug. 1830; /21/389, Arthur–Hay, 31 Oct. 1829.
[5] C.O. 280/26/37, Phillipps–Hay, 19 Mar. 1830.
[6] C.O. 280/4/94, ἀληθης (Kemp?)–Bathurst, 12 July 1825.
[7] q. in A. G. L. Shaw, *Convicts and the Colonies*, p. 194.
[8] C.O. 280/17/403, Arthur–Murray, 5 Nov. 1828.

Thus he was in contact with Francis Forbes, ex-Chief Justice of Newfoundland, about to proceed, after a period of intense work at the Colonial Office on the 1823 New South Wales Bill, to become first Chief Justice under that Bill.[1] He kept up a regular correspondence with Wentworth.[2] Assisted by a staff of secretaries and frequently supported in his campaigns by Brougham and MacKintosh, his appeals against jobbery and extravagance could be particularly damaging. There was doubtless something attractive to a frustrated Opposition in seeing James Stephen as a kind of *éminence grise*, the Empire as a great job, the Colonial department as an expensive incubus, and vast sums being spent to 'keep pampered minions in power, over whose conduct no salutary check was exercised'.[3]

Like many another M.P. Hume was not averse to seeking favours from the Colonial Office. He conducted quite a campaign to obtain land for the Lawrences, finally obtaining for them a grant of 10,000 acres;[4] though he was not quite as regular a client as Wilberforce, who had many contacts with Marsden and other colonial clergymen and was continually called in by them to perform little favours of patronage.[5] Buxton, of course, was involved in his capacity as humanitarian and country gentleman, and was the 'Parliamentary Agent of the Agricultural Society' of New South Wales, sending out stock and arranging finance.[6] His invitation to Horton to come and shoot pheasants while they discussed a questionnaire on the state of Colonial gaols, Van Diemen's Land, etc., Bathurst thought was a trap.[7]

* * * * *

Potter Macqueen did not have to sail for an Australian refuge in 1819, but he, too, invited the under-secretary to come and shoot pheasants.[8] He wrote of the applications he constantly received from artisans and labourers desirous of emigrating to New South Wales; and in 1824

---

[1] P.D. n.s. viii/247, 14 May 1823.   [2] *Australian*, 31 May 1833.

[3] P.D. n.s. xiv/61, 2 Feb. 1826; cf. also P.D. n.s. xiv/1081, 3 Mar. 1826, vs. Stephen; /1126, 6 Mar. vs. colonial expenditure; /1290, 10 Mar. Horton vs. Hume.

[4] C.O. 201/107/62, Hume–Vansittart, 8 Feb. 1821; Young, op. cit., p. 287.

[5] e.g. C.O. 201/96/460, Wilberforce–Goulburn, 25 Oct. 1819, about Rev. Cartwright's female relatives; C.O. 201/113/592, Wilberforce–Horton, backing Rev. MacArthur, the first official Presbyterian chaplain; M.L. A/1992, Marsden Papers *passim*.

[6] C.O. 201/155/146, Buxton–Horton, 2 Oct. 1824.

[7] C.O. 323/200/94, Buxton–Horton, 29 July 1824.

[8] C.O. 201/102/269, Macqueen–Goulburn, 5 Nov. 1820.

sent out Peter Macintyre as his agent. Eventually he obtained a handsome land grant and reserve, and by 1827 could state that he had invested over £23,000 in the colony.[1] His contacts with the Macarthurs were close, and in 1819 he assured old John that he had 'been doing all in my power to promote the interest of the Colony in the House last session'.[2] His ambitions to see a 'legion of respectable settlers from England and Scotland' emigrating to Australia was eventually realized; John Macarthur helped him fight the 1826 election against the Russell family in Bedfordshire; and his commercial and personal interest in Australia developed.[3]

Other M.P.s whose interest in the Antipodes was more than casual included the Torrens family, Bootle Wilbraham, John Pearse of the Van Diemen's Land Company, E. J. Curtcis, and the bankers M. W. Ridley, Marjoribanks, Hart Davis and John Smith. John Gladstone, Huskisson's Liverpool manager and the father of William, wrote in 1825 to tell Horton that the Liverpool merchants were interested in obtaining a charter and land grant of 500,000 acres in New South Wales on the same conditions that the London Australian Company had obtained,[4] and he maintained his correspondence on trade, flax, etc., in New Zealand. E. J. Littleton and Lambton approached Lord Bathurst during the boom of 1825 and, disclaiming all projects of conquests in New Zealand, declared themselves ready to launch a commercial venture in that distant land.[5] Bathurst interviewed them and wrote to warn them that no military assistance would be given them from New South Wales for the 'occupation of the Territory', but merely to protect them if they found it impossible to carry on their proposed commerce and needed to withdraw.[6] By May they were offering Horton a hundred shares, but in March 1826 Littleton was writing sadly that 'in the present state of the Money Market in England I see no hope of success for our project'. Without an exclusive privilege or monopoly the plan must fail, though he considered it 'of real national importance'.[7] Hart Davis did obtain 30,000 acres

[1] C.O. 201/156/336, Macqueen–Horton, 12 Apr. 1824; /397, 2 Oct. 1824; /427, suggesting the emigration of pensioners; H.R.A. I/xiii/632, Macqueen–Horton, 3 Nov. 1827, in Stanley–Darling, 7 Dec. 1827.

[2] M.L. A/2900, Macqueen–Macarthur, 4 Nov. 1819.

[3] M.L. A/2900, 5 Feb. 1822; A/2911, 18 July 1826.

[4] C.O. 201/166/426, Gladstone–Horton, 13 Apr. 1825.

[5] C.O. 201/167/229, Littleton–Bathurst, 30 Mar. 1825.

[6] C.O. 201/167/231, Bathurst–Littleton, 29 Mar. 1825.

[7] C.O. 201/167/233, Stamped 28 May 1825; C.O. 201/179/91, Littleton–Horton, 22 Mar. 1826.

in Australia for his sons.[1] But the Marjoribanks, Gibbs, Keate, and Elphinstone Stock Association, which started bravely in 1825 with a promise of 20,000 acres, went through some very lean times in Van Diemen's Land and by 1830 were pressing the Colonial Office to treat them as colonial benefactors because of their £30,000 outlay.[2]

A curious parliamentary episode occurred in 1826, when, among a series of exposures of discredited commercial ventures, there was an attempt by Sir Charles Forbes to characterize the Australian Agricultural Company as a 'monopoly' of one family, an obvious reference to the powerful Macarthur interest.[3] The banker John Smith, Governor of the Company and a regular correspondent of the Colonial Office, denied the charge. The 'whole business of the company was managed at home', he asserted, and he was supported by R. Hart Davis, another director. Horton defended the Company, saying that although, like the Canadian and V.D.L. Companies, it had been formed 'under the auspices of the colonial department, yet not a single share in any of these companies was possessed by any individual connected with that department'. Perhaps the clerks and Edward Barnard had disposed of their shares by that time. Young John Macarthur immediately went into action. By December he was writing to his mother that Sir Charles Forbes had 'engaged to retract, in his place, in the House of Commons, the observations he made against the Company, and has expressed his regret to me . . . for any offence he may have given me from his supposed allusion to my family . . . This was all that could be desired'. Forbes, he wrote, was a 'very indiscreet and absurd old man to whom no one pays attention in the House'. He had got his prompting from a letter, probably sent by Wentworth in Sydney.[4]

The young lawyer could hardly have been a better representative of his family in the affairs of the Company. John Smith wrote to him in 1824, relating how he had approached Baring and Wilberforce about 'the Company's projects and plans'. Wilberforce was pleased, and 'as he is in direct communication with Lord Bathurst' Smith wanted to introduce him to Macarthur. 'Let me say', he went on about the great humanitarian, 'that though strong in his religious

[1] C.O. 201/166/311, 11 July 1825.

[2] C.O. 280/27/81, 90, Aug. 1830. The Van Diemen's Land Company had, by comparison, they claimed, spent only £50,000 for their 250,000 acres.

[3] P.D. n.s. xvi/280 ff., 5 Dec. 1826

[4] M.L. A/2911/385 Jno. Macarthur Jn–Elizabeth, Dec. 1826.

feelings and opinions there is not a greater mistake than to suppose that he is not a man of the highest liberality. He deplores the bad policy of Government in sending out military Governors, and is disposed with a little encouragement to take measures to prevent it'. Baring, on the other hand, 'has no opinion of our Company, and tells me that he has two millions of acres in N. America with which he can do little or nothing'.[1] The Company was able to capture such people as Brogden, the Chairman of Ways and Means; Marjoribanks, brother of the Deputy Chairman of the East India Company; and George Brown, a West India banker.[2] James Macarthur successfully offered shares to the Chief Justice, Francis Forbes, in New South Wales:[3] and according to the same plan, his brother advised him to give twenty shares to Colonel Dumaresq and Colonial Secretary MacLeay.[4] At Marjoribank's house near Watford, Herts., John Macarthur met 'Mr. Loch, an East Indian and Australian Director'.[5] The directors and auditors of the Company resolved 'to give Lord Bathurst a grand dinner on Saturday the 18th of June' at which the new Governor, General Darling, and Mr. MacLeay, could meet ministers, several of whom, Huskisson, Wynn, and others, were expected. The entertainment was 'to promote good will and friendly feelings amongst the parties, and to increase the attention paid to the affairs of the Colony'.[6] By 12 June he was writing that the party would include Bathurst, Huskisson, Wynn, Horton, Henry Torrens, Sir Byam Martin, the Attorney- and Solicitor-Generals, Sir M. W. Ridley, Mr. Ord, Mr. Ridley Colborne, Mr. Abercromby, etc; and that Peel, Canning and Robinson had sent apologies. 'Our object in this dinner is to impress the new Governor, and also the public, *with our strength*, and the growing importance of the Colony.' All the directors would attend except Grey Bennet, whose only remaining child was dying, and who, in his wretchedness, had been forced to neglect all public business.[7] Macarthur thought that the time had come to use the 'Parliamentary weight and influence of the Company' to repress the 'Convict Faction'.

* * * * *

Perhaps in no other section of the colonial Empire were the tasks of statesman, parliamentarian, or administrator so puzzling or at first

---

[1] A/2911/459, J. Smith, M.P.–Macarthur, 11 Nov. 1824.
[2] A/4315.   [3] A/4319, 1 Nov. 1824.
[4] A/2911, Jno–Jas. Macarthur, 3 Aug. 1826.   [5] ibid., 24 May 1825.
[6] ibid., 5 June 1825.   [7] ibid., 12 June 1825.

sight so distasteful as in Australia. The character of the colonies in 1818 was such that the Government was forced to play an active role at every stage of social and economic life, yet from its foundation as an 'official' colony *par excellence*, it was open to attack on legal, financial, and constitutional grounds. Jeremy Bentham, whose final conversion to Australian colonization heartened the Wakefieldians after the founding of Western Australia in 1829, had vigorously condemned the experiment in penal migration in his *Letters to Lord Pelham giving a comparative view of the system of penal colonization in New South Wales and the Home Penitentiary System* (1802), and in his *Plea for the Constitution* (1803) had developed his attack against the right of the Crown to legislate without reference to Parliament. It was to be the cry of all parliamentary critics from Romilly to Daniel O'Connell; but it proved more simple for the ministry to recognize the existence of a basic flaw in the system than to provide an immediately viable solution. Bentham and the critics conceded that the governors of a penal farm would often be forced into making absolute proclamations which would in fact be 'original acts of legislation', but they condemned root and branch the permanent establishment of a system under British rule which could oppress British subjects, innocent as well as guilty, by the breach of 'Magna Carta, the Petition of Right, the Habeas Corpus Act, and the Bill of Rights', as well as the very Transportation Acts under which the colony was supposed to operate.

The episode of the 'Rum Rebellion' of 1808 and the deposition of Governor Bligh by the soldiers had created a scandal in England, but it ended satisfactorily enough in the appointment of Lachlan Macquarie, a reliable and effective Scots military administrator, who brought his own regiment with him from India. He proceeded with dignity, confidence and enthusiasm, to mould and administer a peculiarly mixed society whose development was dependent upon infusions from the home country and whose success or failure was bound to cause inquiry and disquiet there. The 'Old Viceroy', as he was later popularly remembered, grasped the initiative firmly, and his autocratic zeal and thorough integrity of purpose were welcome to Liverpool and Peel at the Colonial Office. His independent spirit, paternal care, and readiness to accept responsibility were agreeable at a time when little creative vision or administrative ingenuity could be brought to bear on any of the overseas colonies. But even in 1810 a parliamentary select committee had cast a long shadow before it when it admittted itself puzzled by a project which had cost so much.[1] It discussed Bentham's plans for reducing expenditure on criminal administration and the limitations and inconveniences of the Australian settlements. 'The greater the distance the greater the Difficulty of auditing and checking the Expense; while at the same time, the greater the Distance, the greater the Difficulty, not to say Impossibility, of disallowing the Practice.' The Committee inquired shrewdly whether 'the advantages looked for from this Establishment may not be dependent upon its Weakness . . . the more thriving, the less terrible': and confessed to the conviction that 'while to some the Emigration remains a punishment, to others it may become an adventure'.

Romilly in that year several times spoke of the Australian experiment as perhaps 'the boldest and most unpromising project which was ever held out to any administration, to establish a new colony which should consist entirely of the outcasts of society, and the refuse of mankind', a project never tried 'in any former age or by any other nation'.[2]

In 1812, another Finance Committee had recoiled at the huge sums involved and shown themselves rightly uncomfortable about accounting procedures, the disbursing of parliamentary grants to an Agent under no proper supervision, and the neglect of officials to submit bills to audit.[3] The same year, a select Committee of the Commons, conceded by the Government in order to satisfy Romilly's demand for full investigation, formally examined the workings of transportation during the previous twenty-five years, and declared itself broadly satisfied with the progress Macquarie had made and the direction he was taking.[4] It recommended, however, the formation of a council, to temper the Governor's monopoly of authority, thus recognizing that the erstwhile penal farm now had at least some of the characteristics of a colony of settlement. This proposal, much to Macquarie's relief and approval, was rejected as 'untimely' by Lord Bathurst, who had just succeeded Liverpool at the Colonial department.[5] The Committee

---

[1] P.P. 1810 iv (348), p. 375 ff., 28th Report from the Select Committee on Finance, etc.

[2] P.D. xvi/945, 9 May 1810; xvii/326, 5 June 1810.

[3] P.P. 1812 ii (339), 489 ff., Twelfth Report from the Committee on the Public Expenditure, etc.

[4] P.D. xix/186, 4 Mar. 1811; P.P. 1812 ii, p. 573 ff.

[5] H.R.A. I/vii/669, Bathurst–Macquarie, 23 Nov. 1812; /771, Macquarie–Bathurst, 28 June 1813.

affirmed that, no matter how justly or benignly exercised, so great a monopoly of power by the Governor or any other would create opposition and discontent among men unused to such a system 'in their own country'. It showed a great deal of interest in the natural and commercial advantages held out by the colonies, and in any restrictions which had been imposed on its free development. These 'unwholesome' regulations the Committee suggested should be abolished, because 'improvement in wealth, and the means of properly employing and reforming the convicts, are essential to the progress of each other'. They pointed with pride to what had been accomplished in humanizing the 'freight' aspect of convictism, an interest taken up again in 1816.[1] The Committee also suggested that women-folk be allowed to rejoin convicts, who on emancipation were to be respectably settled. Witnesses included ex-Governors Hunter and Bligh and many connected with the colony in both its capacities of gaol and settlement. The Government's encouragement, by land and other assistance, to settlers of capital was noticed. Maurice Margarot, one of the Scottish 'exiles', gave as the leading obstacles to improvement the poor selection of officials by the Government, and the arbitrary habits of governors who had 'no rule to go by but one Act of Parliament, which enjoins them to keep as near to the laws of England as they can'.

By the time the 1819 Committee turned its attention to the administration of those 'singular and extensive' Establishments,[2] considered as colonies, 'as well as in its more immediate connection with the system of criminal jurisprudence', Parliament was really examining a greatly changed situation. Macquarie in New South Wales and Sorell in Van Diemen's Land had consolidated the foundations of a society predicated on emancipation, and they claimed both executive and parliamentary support for their 'clean-slate' policy towards freed convicts. Yet the sudden influx of convicts after 1814 put a great strain upon all their arrangements; and the inevitable confrontation between the aspirations of a 'respectable' settler society and a 'freed' community which formed the colonial majority was already causing unrest. At one extreme the administration was blamed for its leniency to convicts, some of whom were undoubtedly dangerous criminals who would stop at no excess, violence, or savagery. At the other, Macquarie was blamed for his neglect of the free sector, and his

[1] P.P. 1816 xviii (314), p. 291 ff., Account of Convicts dying since 1810, etc.
[2] P.P. 1819 vii (579).

harshness towards the colonial officials, particularly the legal men. Despite the colonies' isolation and allowances which could be made for a certain modicum of military autocracy, complaints persisted in being heard at home, and governors could not altogether be screened from criticism in the press or in parliament. Lord Castlereagh, echoing Bathurst's instructions to Commissioner Bigge, declared that it had become 'necessary to enquire even in justice to that colony whether the period had not arrived when it might be relieved from being the resort of such characters as had hitherto been sent to it',[1] and continual and successful challenges to the exercise of financial and legislative autocracy made parliamentary intervention necessary.

The lack of power to legislate had long embarrassed the Governor,[2] but, though John Macarthur had challenged the validity of the Governor's orders as early as January 1806, on the grounds that 'no order or regulation given by a Governor could be binding or legal unless sanctioned by Act of Parliament',[3] the governors had usually protected themselves by submitting their regulations in some form for the approval of the Secretary of State. J. W. Plummer, the Government's legal adviser about affairs connected with the Bligh rebellion, had warned Macquarie of the defects in his powers, especially those resulting from 'the absolute omission of parliamentary sanction to the greater part of the Colonial government'.[4] Plummer thought parliamentary action was urgently required in order to set up a new system combining 'strong and energetic executive power with as great a portion of private liberty and public privilege as the nature of the colony and its peculiar circumstances will admit', and, foreshadowing future developments, recommended a council on the Indian precedent, and the appointment of an agent at home, whose duties he was himself prepared to perform.

The complex way in which parliamentary activity, the colonial interpretation of existing legislation, departmental response, and personal delegation in London could interact is illustrated by the 'Vale' case. Lachlan Macquarie had allowed the *Traveller*, a United States ship from Canton, into Sydney harbour in April 1816, thinking this was legally justified after the end of the war. Benjamin Vale, an assistant chaplain, challenged this decision and with the government

[1] P.D. xxxix/750.
[2] A.C.V. Melbourne, *Early Constitutional Developments in Australia* (ed. Brisbane, 1963), Ch. IV.
[3] H.R.A. IV/i/44, Memorial of Gov. King, 2 Jan. 1806.
[4] H.R.A. I/vii/197, 4 May 1809.

solicitor Moore seized the *Traveller* as a 'lawful prize' under the Navigation Act. Macquarie, already under attack in the colony for issuing General Orders with the 'force and validity of law . . . unexampled in any other part of his Majesty's Dominions', punished and court-martialled Vale, and discontinued Moore's salary. He then wrote to the Colonial Office, asking for allowances to be made for his motives. Bathurst, however, had already heard of the incident and wrote to reprove Macquarie for his 'illegal' actions and to order him to reinstate Vale, which Macquarie refused to do. Vale had in the meantime brought home a petition levelling charges against the Governor, which was signed in some instances by forged signatures. Macquarie, explaining the fraud to the Secretary of State, stated that he had punished those who signed the petition by withholding land grants and other signs of favour. Bathurst refused to sanction this, and unhesitatingly told the Governor that, by punishing as an act of sedition such signatories, he had attempted 'to interfere with the right, which all His Majesty's subjects possess, of addressing their petitions upon every subject to the House of Commons'. By making the exercise of that right prejudicial to their interest, Macquarie had been guilty of 'a most serious offence'. In any case, nothing had been able to prevent Grey Bennet from presenting the petition to the House on 10 March 1817.[1]

*   *   *   *   *

For New South Wales, 1819 was a parliamentary *annus mirabilis*. Grey Bennet managed to combine three Whig interests into his powerful speech of 18 February: the arbitrariness of Government, its financial extravagance, and its religious intolerance in expelling Jeremiah O'Flynn, the unauthorized Franciscan priest who had anticipated Bathurst's plans for providing the Irish Catholics of the colony with an official chaplain. Bennet, like Wilberforce who supported him, was well primed by Samuel Marsden; and he invoked the 1812 Committee's support for his demand that a governor's council be set up.[2] Castlereagh, replying as 'an ally rather than an opponent', was able to announce the creation of the Commission of Enquiry.

[1] H.R.A. I/ix/24, Enc. 2 Oct. 1815 in Macquarie–Bathurst, 20 Feb. 1816; I/ix/206, Macquarie–Bathurst, 6 Feb. 1817; I/ix/385, Bathurst–Macquarie, 22 Apr. 1817; I/ix/493, Macquarie–Bathurst, 24 Nov. 1817; I/ix/822, Macquarie–Bathurst, 24 July 1818; I/ix/732, Macquarie–Goulburn, 15 Dec. 1817; I/ix/761, Bathurst–Macquarie, 12 May 1818; P.D. xxxv/920, 10 Mar. 1817.
[2] P.D. xxxix/464 f.

This did not deflect Wilberforce who declared himself 'possessed of so much information respecting the state of New South Wales as to form the ground of considerable enquiry', and criticized Castlereagh for stifling investigation. MacKintosh, who claimed to have great personal respect for Macquarie 'with whom he had long ago an intimate acquaintance', condemned the administration for its neglect of civil and religious liberty. His rather high-flying plea for the constitution earned him colonial gratitude, but was ridiculed by Canning. Tierney and Buxton, however, made strong speeches against the Government; and on 1 March[1] Castlereagh announced a Committee to take evidence and report to the House on the state of gaols and other prisons, including New South Wales. Australia was again to be treated as part of a British problem; though Henry Goulburn managed to have accepted two necessary colonial measures, 59 G. III c. 114, which indemnified the Governor for his independent levying of duties on trade, and 59 G. III c. 122, which opened the trade of the colony to ships of every size.

On 23 March, Brougham presented the petition of Blake and Williams, whom Macquarie had ordered to be flogged.[2] Wilberforce, who knew the Governor, defended him as an 'able, active, and disinterested man', but was critical of the system, and a fortnight later turned his attention to the question of female convicts.[3] Goulburn, speaking for the administration, consistently begged critics to leave over their complaints until Bigge had reported.

The 1819 Select Committee sat through April to July. In the meantime there had been a great Catholic debate, Joseph Hume's attack on colonial expenditure, and inquiries about the Red River settlement. The same day that the Committee's report was published saw £50,000 granted for emigration to the Cape. Hume somewhat inconsistently applauded this last measure, and hoped that ministries would go even further.[4] It is clear that the colonies were not forgotten. The state of England, of course, was of paramount concern to the members of the Committee, but they took a great amount of valuable evidence on 'the state and natural resources of the country itself, considered as a colony, as well as in its more immediate connection with the system of criminal jurisprudence'.[5] The Janus nature of the settlements was fully grasped, and the inquiry turned its attention naturally to the condition of the free settlers, the texture of society,

[1] ibid., /740 ff. [2] ibid., /1124 ff. [3] ibid., /1433. [4] P.D. xl/1549 f.
[5] P.P. 1819 vii (579).

schools, chaplains, natives, agriculture, commerce, and colonial aspirations. Chief Justice Bent, John Macarthur Jr, Alexander Riley, and many other first-class witnesses were heard, though the appointment of the Bigge Commission undoubtedly removed the edge from the Committee's recommendations. It seemed unjust to judge Macquarie *in absentia*, and the Report remained inconclusive on this issue also. But the members of the Committee showed interest, intelligent briefing by colonial consultants, and a good knowledge of official documents.[1] The questions asked were those which would exercise the minds and executive talents of administrators for many years—settlement, commerce, government economy, duties and regulations, labour conditions, law and religion. Riley's evidence alone amounted to a colonial almanac. 'By an ideal line parallel with the 135th degree of longitude (dividing the continent in half)', he stated, Great Britain had taken possession of a unique colonial territory, 'commanding within itself a breadth of latitude exceeding the acquisition of any power in the world, extending from the 10th to the 45th degree', with a range of climate and capabilities unknown in those parts of America, Africa, Asia or Europe controlled by one nation.[2] He undoubtedly communicated to some members the enthusiasm which fifteen years as a leading shipper and merchant in New South Wales and Van Diemen's Land had generated in him.

Whereas several years before Romilly and Wilberforce could complain of neglect and lack of information, the Australian colonies were now surrounded by a glare of publicity. 'It seems upon the whole that tho' New South Wales does not appear to promise such a boundless field for colonization as was at one time expected', wrote James Losh after reading Oxley's 'tedious and ill-digested' Journals, yet it 'has many and great advantages for an industrious settler with a moderate capital'.[3] A friend of Grey, Lambton, Attwood, Brougham and MacKintosh, he thought that Wentworth's book, dedicated to MacKintosh, was important and informative, though strongly partisan.[4] The Bigge Reports, when they came, he found too dull and heavy, but a 'most valuable addition to our stock of colonial information'. Bigge, a close friend and neighbour, had often discussed Australian affairs with him, and he thought his observations 'calm, dispassionate and generally sensible'.[5]

---

[1] e.g. C.O. 201/97/268, 12 July 1819, clerk to Select Cᵉᵉ re C.O. dispatches.
[2] op. cit., p. 63, 22 Apr. 1819.   [3] *Diary*, I, 122, 30 Oct. 1820.
[4] ibid., p. 183, 29 June 1823.   [5] ibid., pp. 157, 173, 183.

John Macarthur described to the Committee the high hopes raised by the development of the wool industry. Richard Jones, Riley's partner, gave a clear account of the effects of transportation and military government. The Committee may have been puzzled to learn that, despite the convict quality of society, a Sydney stranger would 'regard himself as in some country town in England; it is as well-ordered and as well regulated' with over 1,000 houses and 7,000 people.[1]

Behind all the evidence of hope, however, there lay the sad problems of juvenile delinquency, Capper's Hulks, Grattan's doleful Ireland. It is obvious that the same humanitarian interest which had inspired the anti-slavery movement was now turning to the question of social stress in England, its corollary—crime; and eventually to the distant penal settlements and their government. The members of the Committee, like so many other British officials and administrators, were alarmed at the overcrowding of the prisons, the expanding crime-rate in the cities, and the failure of local government bodies to effect sound and inexpensive remedies. Unlike the doctrinaires of the thirties, they kept an open mind about the efficacy of transportation as a method of retributive punishment and social redemption; but they were gradually forced by mounting evidence to take into account the rising costs of the system and the changes which time had already wrought on the nature of the Australian settlements and which the near future seemed bound to accelerate. It was implicitly felt that, though no powerful group was whole-heartedly enthusiastic about transportation in itself, the system had advantages both for a new country which awaited exploitation and for a home country facing acute problems involving a 'redundant population' of criminal, delinquent, and distressed classes. It was also agreed that constitutional and administrative changes would be necessary. The ministry was not necessarily avoiding basic decisions or acting defensively against a boisterous Opposition when it demanded more and accurate information before committing itself to positive changes in the framework and 'style' of government.[2]

Bigge's Reports, printed by order of the House, 25 June 1822, 21 February 1823, and 13 March 1823[3] provided Parliament with

---

[1] op. supra. cit., pp. 135, 147.
[2] H.R.A. I/x/4, Bathurst–Bigge, 5 Jan. 1819; C.O. 201/142/1, Bigge–Bathurst, 4 Oct. 1819.
[3] P.P. 1822 x (448), p. 539 ff.; 1823 x (33), p. 515 ff.; 1823 x (136), p. 607 ff.

another fuller and first-hand review of the past experience and a set of detailed proposals for an unambitious future development. Circumscribed to a certain extent by their terms of reference, they were, with recommendations and submissions from many other sources, to provide the matter for the New South Wales Bill of 1823, prepared at the Colonial Office by Francis Forbes and James Stephen; and indeed they became the groundwork of much of the administration and planning for the next decade.[1]

MacKintosh, who had been partly instrumental in preventing Horton from uniting the Canadas in 1822 on the ground that his Bill was a last minute aristocratic 'job' got up without consultation of the colonists,[2] presented the lawyer-emancipist Edward Eagar's petition against military jurors and the Governor's power of arbitrary deportation on 2 July 1823. The Bill was already before the House, and Eagar had seen it in draft. In fact the Colonial Office had tried to satisfy all parties from the governor to the emancipists, to establish the rule of law, to maintain strong executive authority, and to iron out anomalies. But MacKintosh attacked it, claiming that it perpetuated an illiberal system of government which inflicted 'unnecessary degradation and ignominy' on the emancipists while it encouraged 'the insolence of other orders in society'. New South Wales had ceased to be a mere receptacle for convicts and had 'latterly grown into considerable importance, and was rich in all the capacities which promised eventually a high destination'. The House would be unworthy of a people 'whose glory, and whose principal source of national greatness sprang from the love and enjoyment of popular securities' if it sanctioned the liberty and comforts of thousands of English subjects to be placed at the will of a governor 'whose fatuity or whose malice might be manipulated by powerful anonymous interests'.[3] A few days later the Bill was read a second time. Peel, who had a proprietory interest in the affair,[4] confessed that because of the great press of other important business it had been impossible for ministers to consider fully all the details of the Bill. Despite dissension over the expediency of trial by jury and other similar issues, the inclusion of a clause establishing a legislative council seemed to render immediate reconsideration unnecessary. Horton assured the House that the Bill

[1] Melbourne, op. cit., Part I, Ch. 9.
[2] P.D. n.s. vii/1199 f., 20 June 1822; /1731, 23 July 1822.
[3] P.D. n.s. ix/1401 ff., 2 July 1823.
[4] C.O. 201/144/105, Hobhouse–Wilmot, 21 Feb. 1823; /134, Hobhouse–Horton, 19 May 1823.

related to New South Wales more as a British colony than in the light of transportation, and Canning proposed that the whole question could be reviewed after five years. The amended Bill passed 41/30, and the minority included Bennet, Hume, Hobhouse, Maberly, Bright, Attwood, Ricardo, Wilberforce, MacKintosh, Spring Rice, John Smith and Marjoribanks.[1]

*　*　*　*　*

During the next few years a continual but confusing series of Parliamentary Papers were printed about the Australian colonies, often at Hume's request. Expenditure and revenue accounts, lists of landgrants, military expenses, dispatches on the conduct of magistrates, and of course the regular publication of the laws and ordinances of the new Legislative Council, all provided Parliament with more or less useful information. The growth of the colonies' commerce and trade, and the expenses of the transportation system were more accurately recorded as the departmental Blue Books improved. Horton's Emigration Committees always included Australian evidence and the colonies' need for labour and capital was fully expressed.[2] It is obvious that the great distance and heavy expense of Antipodean emigration prejudiced Horton towards British North America, but his inquiries indirectly disclosed a great deal of detail about Australian life and social conditions which became available to the House of Commons. The drive towards retrenchment and Treasury control, too, elicited much perplexing information about the colonies. Peter Smith, a senior clerk of the Colonial Office, related in 1837 how, on application from Hume, copies of the Colonial Blue Books were sent to the library of the House of Commons; and by 1827 they were printed for the use of the Finance Committee.[3] Governor Darling's embroilment with Wentworth, Arthur's native policy, Swan River, the Ripon Land Regulations and the inconclusive Select Committee on Secondary Punishment[4] all caused a spate of printings and contributed to Parliament's view of the course of Australian development. Later, the Molesworth Committee on

---

[1] P.D. n.s. ix/1447 ff., 7 July 1823.

[2] e.g. Eagar's ambitious plan for a Board of Emigration and mass migration in P.P. 1826 IV (404), p. 237 ff.; P.P. 1826–7 V (88), (237), (550)—Australian evidence.

[3] P.P. 1837 vii (516), p. 349 and e.g. H.R.A. I/xiv/221, Murray–Darling, 5 June 1828 asking him henceforward to have thirty copies printed each year.

[4] P.P. 1831 vii (276), p. 519 ff.

Transportation of 1837 was of decisive importance, but its members, in addition to the Wakefieldian reformers, included some familiar names. Peel, after many years' connection with the fortunes of the Australian settlements, was still strangely fascinated by the thought of a felon society where gentle Englishwomen did not fear to dwell and large colonial fortunes could be made. He ought perhaps from long experience to have been able to answer his question: 'How can a man beginning with nothing acquire £20,000 a year, without being an industrious, well-conducted man?'[1]

When Huskisson came to introduce the New South Wales Bill in 1828, there had intervened a period of full-scale preparation which had involved the Colonial Office in a series of negotiations with governors, lawyers, colonial delegations, correspondents, and a host of interested parties at home and in the colony.[2] Stephen had drafted a Bill aimed at making the colonial government as normal as possible, but it was realized that the political jealousy between emancipists and exclusives and the need to find a correct balance between executive and judiciary imposed limitations on what was practicable. Huskisson did, however, intend that the enlarged Council would vote freely 'on all matters connected with their expenditure, and, indeed, concerning their affairs generally'. The great object was to 'meddle as little with details as possible, which were always much better arranged upon the spot'. MacKintosh rejected this opinion on the ground that the bill made no allowance for even part-elective representation or for trial by jury. Spring Rice agreed with other critics that the Bill could never be accepted as permanent, and that it should be at most a temporary arrangement till that time when the colonies 'could no longer be considered as penal' and the whole course of government must therefore be changed.[3]

Huskisson was out of office by the time the bill became law,[4] and when Sir George Murray sent instructions to Governor Darling, he admitted that the Act, though liberal, was vague. In general the British Government was hoping that detailed legislation by Parliament or by the Colonial Office would become less and less necessary; though by retaining the power to create institutions and review legislation in the colonies the mother country could assert ultimate control. Murray hoped that the devolution of legislative power on a

---

[1] P.P. 1837 xix (518), p. 107.   [2] Cf. Melbourne, op. cit., II/Ch. V.
[3] P.D. n.s. xviii/1430 f., 1 Apr. 1828: /1559 ff., 18 Apr. 1828: xix/1456 ff., 20 June 1828.   [4] 9 G. IV c. 83, 25 July 1828.

Council enlarged by the 'more intelligent, wealthy and respectable members of the Commercial, Agricultural, and Professional Bodies of the Colony' would more adequately represent the various interests of the colony and both 'receive a salutary influence from Public Opinion, and . . . exercise a wholesome control over it'.[1] The Governor, in fact, was now understood to be reliant on his council. The theory hitherto had been that the Australian colonies constituted a special case, where autocratic power was a necessary means to peaceful government. Now, wrote Murray, 'it was thought . . . inexpedient to suppose or make provision for extreme cases, because in truth such cases, when they occur, will usually be found to make an adequate provision for themselves, and because evils of this nature may sometimes be excited by the express anticipation of them'.[2] Such optimism could only in the long term lead to eventual colonial self-government. But it is doubtful whether mere liberal intentions really saved the home authorities much trouble. They certainly infinitely complicated life for Darling and Arthur who were both already feeling the full force of virulent colonial criticism, and nascent political debate. They could not, in the peculiar state and constitution of the colonies, silence parliamentary critics.

Francis Forbes, writing to Horton in 1827, pointed out that petitions and addresses would arrive in England from the Australian colonies just as long as there was no house of assembly. No attempt to curb public opinion could succeed. If suppressed in the colonies by the silencing of the Press, it would 'seek such other channels of proclaiming itself, as cannot be closed, the English press, and the British Parliament'. It was impossible to govern a people, 'newly sprung from intellectual and enterprizing England', as Indians or Mauritians. They were more 'intelligent, active and determined', bringing improved knowledge and enlarged opinions with them. Correctly anticipating the results which followed the unwise attempts made in the thirties to reverse Huskisson's promise of financial autonomy, Forbes thought it would not be long before the cry of 'no taxation without representation' would be heard.[3] But, as Howick later pointed out, a colonial assembly, though desirable in principle, could become the instrument of a dominant faction.[4] The colonial government, therefore, was essentially immature; and the representative role of

---

[1] H.R.A. I/xiv/260, Murray–Darling, 31 July 1828. [2] ibid., /269.
[3] H.R.A. IV/i/679, Forbes–Horton, 6 Feb. 1827.
[4] P.D. 3rd s. xiii/1089 ff., 28 June 1832.

the British Parliament became all the more important. No Australian spokesman would have laughed with the House at Joseph Hume's suggestion, in the debate on the Reform Bill of 16 August 1831, that seats be given to the colonies.

* * * * *

The last years of Tory rule saw Australian affairs frequently discussed at Westminster. The founding of the Swan River settlement brought an attack on Murray and Peel for alleged jobbery and illiberal administration.[1] Murray found himself, though friendly to most of the Whigs and a general favourite, frequently face to face with Hume, whose retrenchment campaign was now more formidable because Goulburn at the Treasury was engaged on a radical programme of investigation and economy. The special Commission of Colonial inquiry was, said Goulburn, 'appointed by a Government desirous of concealing no abuses, and of producing, by every practicable means, additional resources for the service of the country'.[2] Hume remained unconvinced, and claimed that the waste of resources spent on colonial misrule would eventually ruin the country.[3] The colonies should be left more to themselves and not kept in leading-strings. James Stephen was an extravagant luxury. Spring Rice defended the colonial department's 'standing counsel', however; though Sir John Newport, a leading Irish Whig, reminded the House that when Parliament was granting large sums for expenses of New South Wales, the agent Chinnery had defaulted to the tune of £18–£20,000.[4] When Peel's brother-in-law Dawson moved for the customary £120,000 grant for New South Wales–Van Diemen's Land expenses on 11 June 1830, Hume declared it was 'too bad to be called on to vote £270,000 without knowing how it was to be expended', and urged that the colonies pay their way from local revenues. The governor had unbridled access to the colonial revenues, Treasury bills, and Commisariat funds for the military; and rendered no account to the Secretary of State. Pensions were, like salaries, proliferating. Murray's bewilderment was no adequate answer. Darling, already under a cloud for using convict labour as a bribe for political support, should be recalled.[5]

Sir George Murray was no match for Hume, yet he never refused

---

[1] P.D. n.s. xxi/463 ff., 6 Apr. 1829; /712, 13 Apr.; /913, 1 May; /1736, 4 June.
[2] P.D. n.s. xxiii/324–5, 15 Mar. 1830.   [3] P.D. n.s. xxiv/1166 f., 27 May 1830.
[4] P.D. n.s. xxiv/711 ff., 14 May 1830.   [5] P.D. n.s. xxv/283 ff., 11 June 1830.

the House an explanation. The Swan River colony was run by one man because the radicals insisted on retrenchment; allegations of Colonial Office jobbery could be discredited as artful propaganda when the full history of the department's dealings was accurately told; Peel was incapable of corruption, as Brougham admitted; there were bound to be disgruntled colonists attracted by the readiness of the member for Aberdeen to lodge complaints against Darling's system of patronage; he himself had refused the Governor's relation Dumaresq an appointment because of the strong feeling aroused in the colony both for and against the General and because it was necessary that true impartiality should be shown.[1] It was all to no avail.

Peel, the Government's best speaker, was willing to concede that the time might have come for a strict re-examination of the merits of transportation and had no objections to a new Select Committee. 'It was, indeed', he stated, foreshadowing the doctrinaire emphasis soon to be placed on retributive and vindictive punishment, 'in the contemplation of Government to endeavour to make the punishment of transportation, when had recourse to, much more severe than at present.' Even now it was dreaded in Ireland, though the English town criminals tended to view it with equanimity. He thought secondary punishments at home were preferable to transportation, and the hulks cheapest of all the proposed systems. But he welcomed inquiry. Next session would be a good time; by then documents could be collected and the subject minutely examined.[2] Where were the reports of Goulburn's Commission? Had not Darling suppressed the free colonial newspapers which had been announced as the bulwarks of civil liberty? To Hume's continual inquiries Murray could offer only amiable, and true, apologies about the difficulty of distant administration, delays in obtaining returns, the great labour and amount of time spent in compiling accounts and consulting other departments, and the achievements of a government which had raised a thriving community of sixty thousand souls from penal isolation, and rendered help to all religious denominations according to the Spirit of the Age.[3] In the end he promised to lay a regular colonial budget before the House. Peel, too, defending the practice of allocating colonial funds without reference to the House, emphasized that more

[1] P.D. n.s. xxi/712, 12 Apr. 1829; /913, 1 May 1829; /1738–9, 4 June 1829; C.O. 397/1/131 Twiss–Joseph Hume, 20 Apr. 1829; P.D. n.s. xxiv/948, 21 May 1830.
[2] P.D. n.s. xxiv/941 ff., 21 May 1830; xxv/284, 11 June 1830.
[3] P.D. n.s. xxv/285 f., 11 June 1830.

information would soon be made available to explain the details of colonial estimates. 'The House could not expect more than a new practice, conformable to its present feelings and wishes. His right hon. friend could not say, "I will compel the colonial legislatures to receive the reductions of the House of Commons", merely because the House of Commons thought they ought to be made'.[1]

A notable addition to the critics of the ministry on Australian affairs, as on so much else, was Daniel O'Connell. He spoke often against Governor Darling's suppression of the press and arbitrary habits; criticized the careless habits of the Irish Criminal Jurisdiction, and thought that Darling's unpopularity, evidence for his unfitness and want of management, disqualified the Governor from office. It was ironical that Colonel Arthur should be writing to the Permanent Under-secretary at much the same time to the effect that, though conscious of the need for good relations with his people, public opinion in Van Diemen's Land was altogether too violent and vola- tile. 'I shall suspect myself, and you may therefore well suspect me also, if my Administration be ever a more popular one.'[2] O'Connell and Hume persisted in proposing Wentworth's case against Darling. The Liberator declared that 'unless the Governors of our distant colonies were kept under proper control, there was no extent of despotism which they would not practise'. Murray, willingly granting that the House had a 'perfect right to the production of any docu- ments with regard to any charge which might be preferred against any Governor', nevertheless felt that it was an abuse of privilege to condemn any man unheard. Hume might say that 'the press and that House were the only guardians of the colonists from the tyranny of local governments', but the Colonial Office had nothing to hide on this subject or on any other connected with convict discipline, administration, or the expenses of the Australian colonies. Peel, agreeing with Sir Michael Ridley, felt that Sir George Murray could be trusted to check abuses. He was convinced that educated convicts had caused much of the trouble emanating from the penal settlements which were now hardly penal in character at all. But the Committee he promised would, as it turned out, not take place under Tory auspices.[3]

*   *   *   *   *

[1] P.D. n.s. xxv/294 ff., 11 June 1830; /337, 14 June 1830.
[2] P.D. n.s. xxv/288, 11 June 1830; /445, 17 June 1830; /1110, 8 July 1830; C.O. 280/19/26, Arthur–Hay, Private and confidential, 26 Jan. 1829.
[3] P.D. n.s. xxv/1114, 8 July 1830; /1127 ff., 9 July 1830; /254, 11 June 1830.

When the Whigs came to deal with the Australian colonies, they found that they had to carry on most of the parliamentary chores which Horace Twiss and George Murray found so hard. The colonial budget had been promised, and the Committee on Secondary Punishments was in preparation. Swan River had to be defended, and the problem of General Darling remained, at least until Richard Bourke could take over as Governor in New South Wales. But Howick had some very definite advantages. He could expect Tory understanding in questions concerning the continuity of departmental policy. Thus when he confronted Hume about Darling, he knew that Twiss would support his reference to the 'great degree of excitement and party spirit in the colony' by a little lecture on the danger of accepting information tendered by colonial correspondents indiscriminately.[1] It was possible for him to approach Hume outside the House:[2] or he could, if necessary, rally radical support by abuse of the old ministers. 'The colonial administration of the country had . . . been for years one system of jobbery', he declared on one occasion.[3]

Above all, Howick ceased to adopt the apologetic posture towards Parliament. He soon realized, as had the Tories, that liberal intentions and attempts to institute a general system of colonial government had practical limitations. The Emigration Bill which delighted Horton had to be shelved.[4] But whereas the Tories under attack had sometimes seemed evasive if not reactionary, Howick was confident that he could guide the Commons toward that positive action which experience had shown to be a component part of imperial administration. Unlike Henry Taylor's 'safe man' he did not welcome obscurity or shun parliamentary publicity. By releasing a deluge of dispatches and complex official documents he hoped to silence uninformed critics. There was 'much safety in a multitude of papers' he told Goderich.[5]

For the Australian colonies, it was the commencement of a connection with a man destined, both as Howick of the Ripon Regulations and as Grey of self-government, to become a central figure in the course of their political history. The dissensions between exclusive and emancipist had been well aired at Westminster in the discussions about the series of addresses to Darling which followed Wentworth's

[1] P.D. 3rd series ii/88, 23 Dec. 1830.
[2] e.g. C.O. 408/8/22, Goderich–Hume, 12 Jan. 1832.
[3] P.D. 3rd series ii/691, 18 Feb. 1831.
[4] P.D. 3rd series ii/875 ff., 22 Feb. 1831.   [5] q. in Murray, op. cit., p. 169.

attempt to impeach the Governor.[1] Howick, and Huskisson before him, knew that these destructive social divisions imposed restrictions on any immediate prospect of representative government. But his own ministerial zeal, the accession of doctrinaire 'systematic' colonizers with the advent of Reform, and the recognition by commercial and banking members, some of them already long engaged in Australian affairs, of the emerging potential of the colonies, precluded all possibility of parliamentary neglect. It was quite certain that colonial dissatisfaction at the 'failure of the efforts of Parliament to keep pace with the advancement of society' expressed in the general petition of 1830 in the aftermath of the inconclusive 1828 Act,[2] could only grow as the population, wealth, and diversity of the colonial communities developed. Colonists as well as government departments had become convinced of the ultimate and determining power of the Commons, and this realization forced interested parties both in Britain and Australia to husband their influence in a more organized and sophisticated way.

[1] P.D. n.s. xxv/1110 ff., 8 July 1830; /1125 ff., 9 July 1830.
[2] *Australian*, 10 Feb. 1830.

IV

PUBLIC OPINION, POLITICS AND THE PRESS

IMPERIAL government in the years immediately before 1832 was a complicated process in the course of which administrators at home and in the colonies were called upon to exercise great and fundamental powers impartially and yet could never be insulated from real political pressures of increasing variety and intensity. Parliamentary inquiries, debates, and comment contributed in a special way to the formulation of policies, but perhaps of equal significance was the continuous and often tedious dialogue which officials found themselves conducting with wider small publics, more demanding, more insistent on receiving satisfaction for real or alleged grievance, and more capable of rallying influential support. 'Public opinion never had such influence on public measures', Peel wrote to Croker, 'and yet never was so dissatisfied with the share which it possessed. It is growing too large for the channels that it has been accustomed to run through.'[1] The period 1818–31 was notable for the rapid multiplication of departmental correspondence with groups and individuals, for organized petitions seeking detailed improvement or expressing protest and criticism, and for the effective role played by opposition, independent and government Press.[2] The Australian colonies participated fully in all these developments.

The Press was recognized, at a time when elementary education was becoming more widespread, both as a means of disseminating information and as an important forum for political and social discussion. The impact of radical journalism had led in Britain to an initial reaction of harsh legislation and even suppression, but gradually the Tory ministry found it wiser to allow the Press a growing measure of free expression.[3] In the proliferation of reviews, journals,

---

[1] Peel–Croker, 23 Mar. 1820, *Croker*, ed. L. J. Jennings (London, 1885), i, 170.

[2] P. Fraser, 'Public Petitioning of Parliament before 1832', *History*, Oct. 1961, p. 199 ff.

[3] e.g. W. H. Wickwar, *The Struggle for the Freedom of the Press, 1819–1832* (London, 1928); A. Aspinall, *Politics and the Press 1780–1850* (London, 1949); A. Briggs, *Press and Public Opinion in Early 19th Century Birmingham* (Oxford, 1949); E. Halévy, *The Liberal Awakening 1815–30* (ed. London, 1961), p. 66 ff.

and periodicals, most points of view gained more or less literate representation, and, although the initiative was frequently claimed by radical prints, ministerialists and Whigs alike realized the importance of obtaining regular publicity for the exposition of their views on public affairs. Brougham wrote for the liberal, usually pro-government *Times*, and for the opposition, free-trade *Morning Chronicle*; Lambton, MacKintosh, Tierney, and Romilly for the dailies; while Colonel Torrens bought the *Globe, Nation, Evening Chronicle, Argus,* and *Traveller*.[1] The *Edinburgh Review*, founded by Brougham, Jeffrey, and Sydney Smith in 1802, was at its classical apogee by 1818, with a circulation of about 14,000. 'After a long period of half-starvation on the *Annual Register* and the *Gentleman's Magazine'*, wrote the *Westminster Review*, the *Edinburgh* had given 'tolerably substantial food to the middle classes'.[2] Its rival, the *Quarterly Review*, had a similar circulation and both were reprinted as bound volumes. In 1823 the *Westminster Review* was founded by James Mill, Bowring and others, to reflect radical and working-class opinion, and the first article promised that the authors would have 'a vivid and constant consciousness of belonging to a large community', and noticed that 'the prodigiously increased importance of the people is recognized in the speeches of the statesman, the sermons of the divine, the lucubrations of the author, and the criticisms of the reviewer', all of whom were impressed with the rise of a new power to which, blessing or cursing, they owed a certain degree of homage.[3] All these and others, notably the liberal Anglican *Eclectic Review*, the moderate *Monthly Review* and the *New Monthly Magazine*, the Tory *Blackwood's* and *Frazer's* magazines, and, from 1828, Rentoul's Radical *Spectator*, commented on colonial government. What they said had to be taken into account by the ministry.

Years later, after he had become under-secretary at the Colonial Office, James Stephen told Macvey Napier of the *Edinburgh Review* that he deliberately refused to expose himself to the influence of public opinion as expressed in the journals. 'I make it a rule never to read a newspaper', he wrote, 'except for matters of fact, in order to keep my own mind from the contagion of the foul passions to which these people minister, and to which some of them prostitute abilities of the highest order.'[4] This was a luxury which lesser minds could not afford. Embattled colonial governors and his political superiors

---

[1] Mitchell, op. cit., p. 54–5.   [2] *W.R.* V (1826) 263.
[3] *W.R.* I (1824) 2.   [4] q. in Knaplund, *James Stephen*, p. 16.

in the twenties certainly were very sensitive to adverse publicity.
Particularly after 1819, the British Press paid regular if not copious
attention to the overseas Empire and was 'far more enthusiastic than
is generally recognized'.[1] The *Morning Chronicle*, whose recurrent
'exposures' became *causes célèbres* in Australian politics from Governors Macquarie to Bourke, regretted that the British public 'hated to
be troubled' with imperial affairs and that the Press could not do
more to forward the views of colonists. Other journals deplored the
'indifference' shown towards colonies, except when scandal broke, or
complained that 'all in Parliament and most outside, knew as little
about British colonial government as of the administration of the
Khan of Tartary'. The colonies ought not to be 'uniformly ranked in
the lowest scale of minor affairs'.[2]

In fact the Press, together with the many books published during
the period, went far to rescue the Empire from that position, and a
great deal of information and opinion became available on exploration, commerce, emigration, transportation, and other imperial
concerns. Most of the ideas which attracted so much attention in
the thirties had been freely discussed in literary circles for many
years.

The *Edinburgh Review*, always interested in political economy,
laissez-faire, and the expansion of England, followed colonial developments urbanely if somewhat sceptically. Until 1827 the articles on
Australian affairs were usually written by Sydney Smith himself. He
reviewed the works of Collins, Bennet, Wentworth, Bigge, and others;
recounted in detail the various achievements of the colony; recommended the emigration of free labour and respectable capital; and
urged the government towards the implementation of liberal ideals
whenever this seemed possible. But he was puzzled by the moral and
religious problems faced by the colonists, amused at Macquarie's
grand schemes and passion for ornamental architecture, predictably
critical of 'Treasury jobbing' of appointments, and intrigued by the
tempestuous personal politics of the remote British settlements.[3] As
early as 1803 he wrote that there was a risk that transportation would

---

[1] H. F. G. Tucker, 'The Press and the Colonies, 1802–1833' (Bristol Univ.
M.A. thesis 1936), p. 2. This excellent work has provided the source of many of
the references to the contemporary Press in this chapter.

[2] *Morning Chronicle* 19/8/1824; *The Times* 18/9/1832; *Westminster Review*
VIII (1827) 26; *Monthly Review*, n.s. XV (1830) 129.

[3] *The Works of Sydney Smith* (2nd ed. London, 1840), i, 36 ff. (*E.R.* II (1803));
i, 321 ff. (*E.R.* XXXII (1819)); ii, 23 ff. (*E.R.* XXXVIII (1823)).

become 'one of the surest roads to honour and wealth', and in 1826 elicited from Peel an admission of the inefficiency of the penal system. Punishment ought to be disagreeable, and prisons places of 'sorrow and wailing'. His interest in the colony was not merely literary, and his views were heard with respect by Peel, Horton, and Bathurst. He thought that Elizabeth Fry, 'amiable and excellent woman' though she was, placed insufficient emphasis on severity as a deterrent to crime: and his criticism was supported by the Navy Office, who protested that Mrs. Fry was 'totally unqualified' to give an opinion upon such important matters as convict transportation and shipboard conditions. From the colony Archdeacon Scott complained of the interference of 'persons perpetually writing to the Colonial Department and dictating what should be done'.[1]

In this case, as in so many others, the Colonial Office sought to keep an open mind, withstand pressure and introduce an improving measure. Horton had consulted Mrs. Fry and forwarded her confident suggestions and strictures on current administrative practice to the relevant authorities. But here it was hard to make any radical change where advice was divided.[2]

Whereas, earlier, 'listless and procrastinating statesmen' had been stigmatized, perhaps legitimately, for misgoverning the Empire on 'principles vague in their conception, and oppressive in their operation',[3] this was no longer the whole story. Now the central government's shortcomings, though often still the result of carelessness or inattention, were more frequently due to a real anxiety to take the right decisions and to elaborate a more efficient and rational system, just when the men concerned could count neither on the requisite political power or material resources to conduct experiments, nor on any certainty that whatever initiative they took would be acceptable in theory or effective in practice.

To the various opponents of the ministry colonial administration seemed to provide endless examples of aristocratic government at its extravagant and corrupt worst. It was believed that colonies were

---

[1] *E.R.* II (1803), p. 36; Smith–Peel, 13 Mar. 1826, and Peel–Smith, 24 Mar. 1826, in *Sir Robert Peel*, ed. C. S. Parker (London, 1891), i, 400–2; *E.R.* XXXV (1821), p. 286 ff.; XXXVI (1882), p. 354 ff.; E. G. Jones, op. cit., p. 354; A. G. L. Shaw, *Convicts and the Colonies*, Ch. 6; *The Letters of Sydney Smith*, ed. N. C. Smith (Oxford, 1953), i, 316, 391, 425, 484; C.O. 201/165/18, Navy Board–Horton, 7 Mar. 1825; C.O. 201/168/262, Scott-Horton, 5 Dec. 1825.

[2] C.O. 201/146/468, E. Fry–Horton, 8 Aug. 1823; *H.R.A.* I/xi/114, Bathurst–Brisbane, 30 Aug. 1823.

[3] *E.R.* IX (1807), p. 337.

made to suffer because of the unreformed state of a Parliament in which they had no direct voice. They were not so much territorial additions to the mother country as extensions of the ministry, where 'borough patronage' and 'the family system' was maintained.[1] There was no dearth of complaint. 'There never was tolerated a worse colonial minister than that unrespected Lord', wrote *The Times* when Bathurst retired from office. He 'knew nothing of the colonies, and wished to know little more'; and the whole 'vulgar and unsympathizing ministry' was an affliction to the Empire, maintained the *Morning Chronicle*. Military government was essentially rotten. The whole record of the Colonial Office, it was said, was a sorry history of jobbery and the squandering of land and other favours. Reasonable colonial requests for reform and representation were summarily denied. The Stephen family was an expensive incubus.[2]

The ministerialist *Quarterly*, on the other hand, to which Horton, Barrow, Croker and Barron Field contributed, reliably expressed the more enthusiastic Tory view. Wartime doubts that Britain 'with one hundred arms' would not prove to have 'a sufficiency of strength and spirit and blood at the heart' to maintain realm and colonies intact, were replaced in hindsight by assurances that it was only by the possession of ships, colonies and commerce that Britain had been enabled to resist Napoleon. Free-trade theories 'hatched in the brains of Scotch metaphysicians' ought to be rejected if they led to the neglect of the imperial outworks by which the citadel was strengthened, or the atrophy of colonial links through which the British language, laws, and religion circulated to the remotest part of the earth. It ought to be England's aim that the sun never set on her dominions. She should 'plant her standard on every unoccupied spot . . . of the habitable globe'.[3] To the *Quarterly*, Bathurst would remain 'one of the most humane and amiable men of his time, . . . one of the most prudent statesmen reared in the school of Mr. Pitt'.[4]

A country and its colonies constituted a political partnership for the insurance of one another.[5] Infant colonies, like infant children,

---

[1] Tucker, op. cit., p. 43 ff; *W.R.* VIII (1827), p. 4 ff.

[2] *The Times* 20/4/1827; *M.C.* 29/1/1823; *M.C.* 6/9/1827; *The Times* 31/12/1827; *The Times* 8/7/1822; *E.R.* XLVII (1828), p. 95 ff.; *The Times* 11/8/1825, 11/9/1828; *M.C.* 14/3/1828; *Spectator* IV (1831), p. 236; *Blackwoods Mag.* XXVII (1830), p. 245.

[3] *Q.R.* VI (1811), p. 496; XXXIII (1826), p. 410 ff.; XXXIX (1829), p. 340.

[4] *Q.R.* LXVII (1840), p. 463.   [5] *Q.R.* XXXII (1825), p. 579.

must be expensive before they become profitable. They ought to be able to consider themselves as constituent parts of one great Empire, inhabited by children sprung from one common parent; not, as the 'new economists' would have, an unnatural parent, ready to strangle them to avoid the expense of bringing them up.[1] This vision was not far removed from that of Wentworth's *Australian* which asserted that the time was ripe for a liberalization of political and economic policy. 'It is the happiness and welfare of the colonies, their improvement and prosperity, that ought to be considered by the ministers of the parent state, not how they shall contribute to ministerial influence.'[2] Certainly even the *Westminster Review* could agree by 1829 that 'the discouragement of colonization is certainly not the feeling of the great majority of the people of England'.[3]

The *Quarterly* was convinced that the period was witnessing, 'to a degree of which no former age can furnish an example', a powerful impetus on the part of restless and dissatisfied mankind to improve his condition, and that this 'spirit of universal inquisition' demanded the deep, dispassionate attention of all who governed human affairs or thought about them. Its progress ought not to and could not be stopped. Rather it was wiser and safer to confine it within reasonable limits and 'direct it to the attainment of practicable objects'. The Empire was not just an inexhaustible source of wealth and power. It afforded the opportunity and imposed the duty of meliorating the condition of humanity. It was therefore gratifying and no surprise that the claims of the Australian colonists should rise in proportion to their increasing numbers and prosperity. Wentworth's 'dictatorial and menacing tone' could not disguise his considerable ingenuity and the inevitability of an Australian exercise in 'the fashionable occupation of constitution-mongering'.[4]

The Australian colonies had outstripped their origins. They were now viewed more favourably than hitherto, rapidly advancing to 'immense importance', 'something new and amusing'. Material progress, however, as in Canada, seemed surely more urgent than 'new modelling the constitution'. What had already been achieved would force Parliament to modify the hitherto autocratic pro-consular government of the Antipodes. But, though the *Quarterly* noted that some of the colonists foolishly fancied themselves old and strong

[1] *Q.R.* XXXIII (1826), p. 410–13.   [2] 15/10/1824.
[3] *Q.R.* XXXIX (1829), p. 340; *W.R.* XI (1829), p. 50.
[4] *Q.R.* XXIV (1820), p. 195 ff.; 56 ff.; XXIII (1820), p. 400 ff.

enough to 'shake off the easy yoke of paternal authority and . . . set up a Government of their own', there was no clear agreement about what could or should be done. A Colonial Assembly might be the 'patriot's toast of Botany Bay', but the government ought to have learnt from experience of assemblies in the old colonies never to think of adopting them in the new. Wentworth's radical plea for assembly gained the approval only of the *Monthly* and *Eclectic Reviews*, and by 1827 the *Monthly* was prepared to be satisfied if the new and active colonial newspapers were permitted to print the proceedings of Council.[1]

When Joseph Hume, arguing that 'every British interest ought to be represented in that House', recommended direct colonial representation in the Imperial Parliament, he was supported by Sir George Murray who was concerned lest the Reform Bill deprive the empire of the virtual representation they had enjoyed and the 'warm interest' which he had, while in office, noticed certain members take in colonial affairs. Hume was indignant that there should be laughter at the thought of an Australian member, and declared that there were more British subjects in that country than in twenty of the boroughs they proposed should retain members. The Wakefieldian *Spectator* approved; but the *Morning Chronicle*, which claimed that in 1831 a total of 104 members, three-quarters of them returned by rotten boroughs, had more than adequately presented colonial interests to the House, did not.[2] Twenty years later, Disraeli again raised the question of colonial representation at Westminster. But Stanley, who claimed to have given the matter much thought, dissuaded him. Colonial representatives, he thought, would introduce an undesirably democratic element into the House.[3]

Liberal comment, again, dogmatically sympathetic to *laissez-faire*, was divided about the effects of central legislation and the desirability of 'government with a purpose' in the Empire. Colonies should pay their own way and the mother country interfere with them as little as possible. But slave colonies could not be trusted without strict supervision, and it did not seem enlightened to refuse special preference to Australian wool when the granting of this would foster

---

[1] *Q.R.* XXIII (1820), p. 400; XXXI (1824), p. 52 ff.; XXII (1825), p. 311 ff.; *M.C.* 6/8/24; *M.R.* XCVI (1821), p. 68–9; VI n.s. (1827), p. 124; *Ec. R.* n.s. XIV (1820), p. 137.

[2] *P.D.* 3rd Series vi/110 ff., 16 Aug. 1831; *Spectator* V (1832), p. 122; IV (1831), pp. 187, 236; *M.C.* 17/8/1831.

[3] R. Blake, *Disraeli* (London, 1966), pp. 293–4.

the 'absorbing ambition' of the settlers and bring about a 'considerable annual reduction' in 'our tailor's bills'.[1]

Both as part of the nation's penal system and as increasingly prosperous settlements, the Australian colonies and their administration attracted a great deal of public notice from 1818. This attention was impossible to evade. Horton for one welcomed and fostered it. But frequently the task of administrators was greatly complicated by the pressures to which it gave birth. In the course of discussions on the issue of emigration, for example, with which Horton became identified, no real consensus appeared.[2] It was agreed that the processes of demobilization, industrialization and over-population, especially in Ireland, had been accompanied by unemployment, crime, the crowding of cities, and the near collapse of organized systems of poor relief. As the decade advanced, interest in emigration as a partial cure for some of these ills grew. Despite some appreciative judgements, however, that his efforts would be valued 'at a period when his bigoted political adversaries . . . are buried in oblivion', or that the Report of his 1826 Committee showed a 'bold and uncompromising spirit' and marked a 'decided era in the progress of the present ministry' towards true political wisdom and courage, Horton's attempts to give colonization a regular political form and his earnest advocacy of assisted schemes earned him little but suspicion or opprobrium.[3]

The Tory Press, following his opponent Sadler, argued that emigration was an expensive and inadequate remedy. The best would be lost to the country. Cultivation of waste land at home, abolition of sinecures, and the expansion of fisheries were more practical. *The Times* agreed that it was preferable to 'feed the hungry at home'.[4] Radicals and others were doubtful about large-scale emigration and saw no point in diverting emigrants from the United States to the colonies. Plans to raise money by mortgaging the poor rates were criticized, as were the lesser experiments of the administration. It was said that there was little likelihood that loans made to pauper emigrants, especially the large sums needed for a journey to the Antipodes,

---

[1] *E.R.* XXXVIII (1823), p. 485 ff.; XLII (1825), p. 361 ff.; *M.R.* CIII (1824), p. 297; *W.R.* VIII (1827), p. 29; XIII (1830), p. 49; *M.R.* XIII n.s. (1830), p. 268.
[2] Tucker, op. cit., Chs. VIII, IX; Jones, op. cit., Ch. IX ff.
[3] *N.M.M.* XXVI (1829), p. 54; *Q.R.* LXIII (1830), p. 269; *W.R.* VI (1826), pp. 371–2.
[4] *B.M.* XV (1824), p. 35 ff.; XXI (1827). p. 586; *The Times* 19/10/1827, 27/11/1827.

would ever be repaid. Large-scale emigration thence was impossible. Voluntary schemes were well enough, but the public should be protected from enthusiasts.[1]

Even after the Whigs came in and the cause of emigration had become more fashionable, due in no inconsiderable part to that zeal of Horton which had proved so fatal to his own advancement, there was no firm agreement from which vigorous and concerted government action might have sprung. The abortive Bill of February 1831 'drawn up by Mr. Stephen, approved by Senior the friend of Lord Lansdowne', and introduced by Howick, was condemned by the Wakefieldians, now hewing to their own ideas, as Hortonian.[2]

'Orator' Hunt, presenting a Petition from the National Union of the Working-Class of the Metropolis, characterized the Colonial Secretary's 'compulsory emigration scheme' as an 'unjust, wicked, and unconstitutional' transportation;[3] and on 14 March 1832 Alderman Wood introduced Cobbett's bitter petition. Horton, Cobbett felt, had believed in 'transporting' people from their homes like pigs or poultry. Joseph Hume was forced to come to Howick's defence, saying that no compulsory emigration was intended. Lord Goderich intended to offer only information and encouragement.[4]

Whereas Horton had been inclined always towards consultation, Howick tended to act even when an issue was not altogether clear. The *Westminster Review* noted in 1826 that most useful measures introduced by departments were often strenuously opposed in the House. Howick, though he did not escape criticism, was able to profit by the ground-work of his predecessors. He was assiduous, wrote the *Spectator*, 'unremittingly occupied with the business of his office, and most desirous to pursue the best course in whatever may come under his official notice, without much regard either to party politics, or to those more important questions, which, though they agitate the public mind, bear but slightly and indirectly on the subject of colonial administration'. When his land-sale regulations were issued, the little attention they received was at first favourable. 'It was

---

[1] *W.R.* VI (1826), p. 242 ff.; *E.R.* LXV (1826), p. 68; LXVII (1828), pp. 215–6; *Q.R.* XXXVI (1828), p. 547; *M.R.* VI (1827), pp. 119–21, n.s. X (1829), pp. 396–7; *Ec. R.* 28/8/1827; *W.R.* VI (1826), pp. 371–2; *M.R.* C (1823), p. 253.

[2] *Spectator*, 16/4/1831; cf. also 19/2/1831, 26/2/1831; *M.C.* 18/2/1831, 23/2/1831; Howick–Horton, 22 Apr. 1831, q. in Jones, op. cit., p. 323.

[3] P.D. 3rd S. V/927, 8 Aug. 1831.

[4] P.D. 3rd S. XI/ 14 Mar. 1832; *Rural Rides*, ii, 81; *Political Register*, 3/3/1827; 9/4/1831; *E.R.* XCIII (1828), p. 204 ff.

doubtful whether the new system had been the subject of conversation between any two persons in England, not immediately connected with the respective colonies', commented the *Morning Chronicle*, which nevertheless approved of his new system and hoped that the Regulations would be made permanent by Parliament and extended to other parts of the Empire.[1] When the inevitable reaction came, and Dixon, stating New South Wales to be 'the safety-valve of Great Britain', protested against Howick's innovation, he was supported by Henry Bulwer and had letters from the Macarthurs in his hand. But Howick felt confident enough to reject his demand for a Select Committee on Australian lands. Committees were useful enough, said Howick, where information was to be collected, or where facts were to be inquired into which were doubtful. Here all the facts were before the House and he opposed a committee to inquire merely whether government policy was wise or not.[2]

Basic difference of opinion existed too about the part the government had played in the formation of development companies and their employment as semi-official instruments of policy, especially in the field of emigration. The Australian and Van Diemen's Land Companies, privately financed, were suspected as a 'job'. The experience of the Swan River colony and the alleged favouritism of Thomas Peel caused a great outcry. The propaganda-conscious 'systematic' colonizers did not hesitate to call it the 'greatest blunder committed by a colonizing state since the discovery of America'. But their own ideas were quite as controversial as those of Horton or Torrens, from which they were partly derived. Gouger, anxious to try Wakefield's plans out in practice, in Australia rather than in Canada, confided to Horton, with whom he hoped to make common cause, that he had done all that was possible to press his views with Sir George Murray and R. W. Hay at the Colonial Office. 'The Administration *alone* has the power to give effect to the principles in question', he wrote, 'without any assistance from public opinion, to enlist which, in favour of the plan, might occupy much time.' The *Spectator* never forgave Hay, a 'Tory hack of the Castlereagh School', for sinking their 'ideal' South Australian Scheme.[3] When Howick expressed scepticism about the

---

[1] *W.R.* VI (1826), p. 266; *Spectator*, 12/2/1831, 5/2/1831, 19/2/1831; *The Times*, 21/2/1831; *M.C.* 20/1/1831, 3/2/1831, 18/2/1831.

[2] P.D. 3rd S. X/669 ff., 22 Feb. 1832; XIII/509 ff., 7 June 1832.

[3] *B.M.* XX (1826), p. 474; *The Times* 16/4/1824; *Spectator*, 5/2/1831; *M.C.*, 1/6/1829, 18/11/1833, 31/7/1829; *Q.R.* XLIII (1830), p. 270 ff.; Gouger–Horton, 3 Feb. 1830, q. in Jones, op. cit., p. 285 ff.; *Spectator*, 5/1/1833, 9/11/1833, 29/10/1831.

whole genus of colonial companies and the disillusionment of his department at the realization that the Australian Company would ultimately obtain its huge grants at the bargain price of 1s. 8d. per acre, Joseph Hume defended even that 'Macarthur' venture, and maintained that its grants had been, not profuse, but useful and economical.[1]

Long before the advent of the Wakefieldians, however, public attention had been directed, through a spate of parliamentary reports, handbooks, journals, memoirs, and the transactions of various emigration and missionary societies, to the merits and demerits of the several colonies as fields for settlement and enterprise. Australia, 'so high with regard to its physical advantages, capabilities and prospects', and yet so disappointing 'intellectually and morally', seemed to offer very fine prospects to a certain type of settler.[2] The very distance from old Europe and its wars seemed an advantage. It was reported that the natural beauty of the country was great. The natives were not formidable, nor were the animals ferocious. The sky was clear and climate more temperate than Canada with equitable seasons and a spring and autumn like the English summer. Save for 'debauchery and drunkenness', disease was almost unknown. The country was so open that clearing provided little problem; yet there was ample timber and the land was fertile, and easy to cultivate. Stock of all kinds could be pastured on the excellent grass. Hops, barley, cotton, and tobacco flourished. Coal, iron, and other minerals gave hope for future industries. The expense of the voyage, government regulations, and pioneering conditions had to be taken into account. Unskilled pauper labourers could not compete with the convicts, but poor settlers who were skilled, or ready to become domestic servants to respectable families, and artificers such as bricklayers, carpenters, and tailors might do very well. Settlers who possessed capital and could command labour and who had the necessary agricultural or pastoral experience would almost certainly succeed. With £500, a man could obtain a land grant of 500 acres, paying fees amounting in 1825 to only £2. 19s. 7d., as compared with £125 in Canada.[3] The coastal location of land made communications relatively easy, and the existence of the penal establishments guaranteed a cheap supply of labour and a sure market for colonial produce.

On the other hand, Australia was held to be 'beyond the natural

[1] P.D. 3rd S. XIII/511, 7 June 1832.
[2] W.R. III (1825), p. 448 ff.   [3] W.R. III (1825), p. 463.

sphere of European connection, isolated from the mother country by a journey of about eighteen weeks', and the economic advantages of convict labour had to be balanced against the social and moral dangers of life 'among the most murderous, monstrous, debased, burglarious, brutified, larcenous, felonious and pickpocketous set of scoundrels that ever trod the earth'.[1] Even this aspect was controversial. The colony was not established, wrote the *Edinburgh Review* 'to gratify the indolence of Pharisees, but to heal the contrite spirit of repentant sinners';[2] and free settlement would diminish prejudice against the colony, giving a stimulus to the rehabilitation of degraded men. 'From a moral point of view, this place is a complete Hell', said *The Times*.[3] The exploration of the coastline aroused considerable interest. The extension of settlement, the special prospects of Van Diemen's Land, and later that 'more select and moral society' at Swan River gave great grounds for hope.[4]

The *Quarterly* reviewer turned with pleasure from the 'swamps and prairies' of British North America, to the 'fertile and beautiful island' of Van Diemen, 'a land flowing with milk and honey for the farmer and the small landholder, who, from the exaction of high war rents, the depression of agricultural produce, improvident speculation, or any other cause, may incline to emigrate from the land of their fathers'. All who could command a little capital might look hopefully to that part of the globe; though the reviewer was rightly sceptical of the accounts given by a member of Freycinet's expedition of Sydney's 'magnificent hotels, majestic mansions, houses of extraordinary taste and elegance, fountains ornamented with sculptures worthy of the chisel of our best artists, spacious and airy apartments, rich furniture, horses, carriages, and one horse chaises of the greatest elegance, and immense storehouses'. Everywhere these great and flourishing colonies gave signs of exciting progress. Transportation had been a boon, and should be continued; and aided emigration should be developed. Eventually the colonies would set up for themselves. Only Wentworth's *Australian*, 'a vehicle for such opinions, and so expressed, that, for the peace of the country, it will probably soon

---

[1] *B.M.* XXII (1827), p. 603.   [2] *E.R.* XXXVIII (1823), p. 91.
[3] 10/8/1830; *M.C.* 18/2/1831, 23/2/1831.
[4] *Q.R.* XXXIX (1829), p. 315 ff.; *The Times* 17/7/1823; and in general: *B.M.* XXII (1827), p. 603; *Q.R.* XXIII (1820), p. 73 ff., XXVII (1822), p. 99 ff., XXXVII (1828), p. 3 ff., XXXVIII (1828), p. 240, XXXIX (1829), p. 315 ff.; *W.R.* III (1825), p. 452 ff., VIII (1827), p. 241 ff.; *E.R.* XLV (1826), p. 65 ff., XLVII (1828), p. 215 ff.; *M.R.* XLI (1820), p. 58, n.s. VI (1827), p. 119; X (1829), p. 369 ff.

be found expedient to suppress it', spoiled the scene.[1] Meanwhile, monies should be cheerfully voted annually without direct return in the shape of revenue, by the Treasury of the mother country. Soon these colonies would be themselves 'the means of carrying commerce and civilisation into the numerous and populous islands of the Australasian seas'. Already they had conferred wealth and happiness on thousands of families, and had been 'the means of rescuing from vice and misery many tens of thousands, who would otherwise have been thrown back upon society to repeat their former crimes'.[2] It was the colonial department's honour as well as its responsibility to play a civilizing role in this new 'swing to the East'.

*   *   *   *   *

Suggestions, criticisms, sanguine applications for colonial appointments, and enthusiastic plans for colonization flowed in to the industrious Goulburn and his successors. Old soldiers, families of convicts, poor curates, country gentlemen, merchants and labourers seeking new opportunities, Scots and Irish—all demanded and most received at least a routine reading and the courteous 'usual answer'. When the Colonial Office, echoing the Governor's suggestions, was reported to be encouraging the voluntary emigration to New South Wales of persons of 'enterprise and integrity', this initiative was welcomed as a means by which the redeemed colony might become a fit residence for civilized man, and an assistance, instead of a burden, to the homeland.[3]

Many thought that the Australian colonies would provide a loyal and British alternative to the United States. 'How desirable it would be', wrote a correspondent to Lord Bathurst, 'to direct the tide of emigration . . . to our own settlements, instead of letting America reap all the advantage of our labour, intelligence, knowledge, and Industry . . . particularly . . . when so fine a portion of the globe, so capable and willing of its increase, remains almost literally unpeopled.'[4]

'We would rather emigrate to one of His Majesty's Colonies than

[1] *Q.R.* XXVII (1822), p. 99 ff.; XXVIII (1823), p. 346; XXIV (1820), p. 257; XXXII (1825), p. 314.
[2] *Q.R.* XXXIII (1826), p. 410 ff.
[3] e.g. *G.M.* Feb. 1819, *H.R.A.* I/ix/797, Macquarie–Bathurst, 16 May 1818.
[4] C.O. 201/95/385, G. Foulerton–Bathurst, 13 Jan. 1819; also e.g. /30, W. Allen–Bathurst, 11 Dec. 1819.

to any other country that is not under our happy constitution', wrote a group of would-be emigrants from Leicester. 'I cannot bear to go to any country that is hostile to England', wrote another.[1]

Indefatigable supporters of Pacific expansion, the vigorous and progressive exploitation of Australasian potential, and the removal of outmoded restrictions on shipping, commerce, and the movement of people, were not, and could not be entirely ignored, even where necessity, prudence, or the lack of imagination of hard-pressed under-secretaries prevented them from recognizing in some of these submissions the foreshadowing of many future developments.

Colonial officials and correspondents insistently provided ideas and information and strove to forward their views. The lawyers particularly, calling into question most of the presuppositions of colonial government, came to take on the role of political and constitutional as well as legal critics, and it is hard to overemphasize their influence. Ex-Justice Bent wrote often and called at Downing Street to urge reforms. Naval governors, he wrote, had ruled the settlements as they would have done a man-of-war, and military men a regiment. Distance from home had precluded 'public opinion and feelings from being heard', but now at last considerable changes must take place, and 'difference of opinion' even among officials, could no longer be looked upon as a crime.[2]

By 1826 Francis Forbes, who conducted a classic correspondence with the Colonial Office, considered that a 'peaceful revolution' had taken place. To this the appointment of a Supreme Court, Legislative and Executive Councils, the spreading of government over a larger area, and 'frequent points of contact with the best informed of the inhabitants', had contributed. But above all he commended the 'fairness and openness with which the affairs of the colony are now conducted'. Free discussion of the acts of government and public men had given the people an interest and knowledge, and impetus, which it would have been hardy to foretell in the Colony for the next generation'.[3]

Politics had, in fact, come to Australia; an embryonic politics of interest, faction, and bitter intensity—but real politics just the same. The Colonial Office inevitably found itself a participant, in the absence of a truly adequate local forum of debate. Despite attempts made by

---

[1] C.O. 201/101/26, 30 Jan. 1820; /546, W. Savage–Bathurst, 10 Apr. 1820.
[2] C.O. 201/93/38, Bent–Bathurst, 30 May 1818; /92, 3 Aug. 1818.
[3] C.O. 201/178/497, Forbes–Horton, 26 May 1826.

successive Secretaries of State to direct all colonial business through the Governor, and to rely upon their officials on the spot, it proved impossible to dam the homeward flow of documents which expanded in complexity and variety as the needs of the colonies became more sophisticated and colonial issues more controversial and subtle. Settlers took with them the attitudes, opinions and loyalties of Britain, where the Imperial authorities came increasingly under the scrutiny of retrenchers, evangelicals, political economists, and many more besides. Well-established colonists had by now formed ambitious projects in which government intervention or encouragement was expected to play a part. Emancipated convicts, the colonial-born, lawyers, merchants, pastoralists and farmers all had claims to make. Legal documents, the accounts of personal feuds, vengeful or frustrated tirades against administrators, long treatises on colonial conditions, and the constant cry for land, free rations, stock, appointments, convict labour, and other favours, assailed the Colonial Office.[1]

The business connected with the Bigge Commission, the preparation for the Acts of 1823 and 1828, the separation of Van Diemen's Land from New South Wales, the re-modelling of the legal arrangements, and the establishment of Executive Councils and civil departments were all important developments in constructive government aimed at providing an improved framework for the future of a free society. Yet none of these had the effect of reducing the administrative burden of the British authorities. Often, disguised as colonial brawls or personal clashes, issues of real moment were raised, and the department eventually and unwillingly found itself forced to pick its wary way through thickets of confusion and contradiction, scrutinised at every step.

Constant and urgent appeal could have been alarming if colonial correspondents, from the Governor down, had not always insisted, amid passionate requests for official succour, on the extraordinary 'tranquillity' of the colonies. Even the *Australian*, critical of an excited article in the *Morning Chronicle* of 28 September 1825, assured its London readers that, though the time must surely come when New South Wales would sever its connection with England and become an independent State, this process would not come about by revolution.[2] The Office learnt to be sceptical of alarmist representa-

---

[1] e.g. C.O. 201/95/149, Bland–Bathurst, 14 July 1819; /260, Campbell–Bathurst, 1 Mar. 1819; C.O. 201/93/384, Marsden–Bathurst, 20 May 1818.

[2] 28/6/1826.

tions. It had to be careful in its reaction even to the most innocuous-sounding proposals. When John Macarthur's son, Major Edward Macarthur, began a long campaign to set up a colonial militia along the lines of that which had been set up in 'Canada, the West Indies, and the United Kingom', Horton had to keep in mind that one of Macarthur's chief objects was to 'inculcate respect for superiors, observance of the various gradations in society, and that loyal attachment to the Crown . . . now endangered by a democratic spirit sedulously encouraged, preferring the republican institutions of America'.[1]

As a rule, where colonial interests were at one, or where it could be shown that public opinion was strongly felt, the Colonial Office was prompt to act. Bathurst, indeed, withdrew a private official letter which Horton had drawn up for Sir Thomas Brisbane, on the grounds that it 'establishes the principle that if a public servant be unpopular, he must be degraded, altho' any charge brought against him should be disproved'. This was going too far. If it were established, 'in such a rascally community as that of New South Wales we should have no peace hereafter'.[2] But colonists were not slow to grasp the importance of publicity. Young John Macarthur, forwarding as agent the 'exclusives' petition, reported to Horton that the 'respectable inhabitants' had sent £1,500 to England for starting a newspaper, and subscribed £800 p.a. to secure an English Editor of 'loyal and constitutional' principles. The opinions of the 'emancipist' or 'the Republican party' were not those of the moral and respectable part of the community, who were forming a Bank of their own, and most anxious to disclaim their violent and absurd demands.[3]

Much of the criticism which infuriated Macquarie, who wrote with disgust of those 'writing Home false and Malignant representations'; of Brisbane, 'the first Governor who laid himself quietly on the shelf', and of Darling, was unfair and inspired by political opponents.[4] Brisbane particularly was enraged by the offensive 'purely personal' matters which were reported in the Morning Chronicle. He resented accusations that he was lazy, and had shown prejudice against the Church of Scotland and its minister, Dr. Lang, who had returned to Britain to seek support. Above all he denied that he had become subservient to his Colonial Secretary, Frederick Goulburn, whose sarcastic

---

[1] e.g. M.L. A/2913, E. Macarthur–Horton, 4 July 1825.
[2] A/73, Bathurst–Horton, 7 Jan. 1825.
[3] C.O. 201/179/218, John Macarthur Jr.–Horton, 11 July 1826.
[4] H.R.A. I/ix/495, Macquarie–Bathurst, Private and Confidential, 1 Dec.1817; M.C. 21/8/1824; The Times 28/5/1830.

manner and monopolization of the details of administration had soon embarrassed the Governor and led to his falling out with the Macarthurs on the subject of the land grants they had been promised and eventually to the recall of both officials.[1] He suspected the ex-Judge of the Supreme Court, Barron Field, who was rumoured to be writing against him, and refuted the charges at length. Field, who had established himself as a prominent member of the 'exclusive' faction, denied his authorship of the articles which appeared in the *Morning Chronicle* of 19 and 21 August 1824; but he wrote to his friend Marsden that he was reviewing the Bigge Reports and the new edition of Wentworth's book for the *Quarterly*. 'It must be temperate, as that is a ministerial publication.'[2]

Francis Forbes remained convinced that the opposition Press at home, used by 'an ultra-toryism which lies beneath the overt radicalism' was 'far more formidable to us than our own—because what is untruly said here, or unfairly argued or colored, we can always correct at the moment, and bear down by the force of truth—but what is published in the English papers remains uncontradicted until the poison is widespread, and the wound incapable of cure'. The Colonial Office, he insisted, would have to steel itself against those rich and powerful monopolists of land, convicts, and government influence, long experienced in misrepresentation, distortion, and virulent anonymous attacks who menaced governors and others with their influence at home.[3]

Forbes rightly considered that a turning-point had been reached in the government of the colony when Bathurst had decided to have the long and complex Douglass case investigated *in the colony*, thus bringing the 'whole System' to light and threatening to annihilate it. On the surface a complex and tedious colonial scandal, this affair had gradually 'involved within its vortex the Government, its friends, its foes, and many who were neutral'.

* * * * *

[1] *H.R.A.* I/xi/253, Brisbane–Bathurst, 1 May 1824; /327, Brisbane–Bathurst, 23 July 1824; /555, Brisbane–Horton, 24 Mar. 1825; /429, Bathurst–Brisbane, 28 Dec. 1824; /605, Brisbane–Bathurst, 21 May 1825; M.L. A/2899, John Macarthur–father, 22 Aug. 19 Oct. 1823.

[2] *H.R.A.* I/xi/519, Brisbane–Bathurst, 9 Feb. 1825; /550, Brisbane–Bathurst, 24 Mar. 1825; /606, Brisbane–Bathurst, 23 May 1825; /199, Brisbane–Bathurst, 21 Jan. 1824; M.L. A/254 (Piper Papers), Field–Piper, 3 Mar. 1821; *H.R.A.* I/xii/186, Bathurst–Brisbane, 23 Feb. 1826, enc. Field–Bathurst, 12 Feb. 1826; M.L. A/1992 (Marsden Papers), Field–Marsden, 21 Nov. 1824.

[3] C.O. 201/178/495, Forbes–Horton, 10 Sept. 1826.

Henry Grattan Douglass had arrived as a settler in the colony in 1821, recommended by Bathurst. He was appointed magistrate and given charge of the hospital at Parramatta. A confidant of Sir Thomas Brisbane, he was accused by Surgeon James Hall of seducing an assigned convict servant-maid. The Parramatta 'exclusives', whose dominance he had challenged, investigated his conduct at a meeting which he refused to attend. The Governor removed Marsden, Hannibal Macarthur, John Blaxland and J. and G. T. Palmer from the magistracy, even though they were supported by the two judges and other magistrates, when they refused to associate with Douglass on the Bench. Bathurst approved of this, but the next year the dispute was carried further when Douglass was connected with the prosecution of Marsden, who had allowed one of his assigned convicts to become self-employed. This, though common enough, was against existing regulations.[1] Marsden, though a 'perfect stranger', wrote direct to Peel, in an attempt to enlist the support of the Home Office. Peel, however, forwarded the correspondence to Bathurst so that he might learn the relation 'in which two persons of some importance in the Colony stand to each other'. The Secretary of State, expressing 'regret and surprise' that Brisbane should have sanctioned such an intervention to be made to the Home Secretary without Colonial Office knowledge, commanded that Douglass be removed from the magistracy. Brisbane denied that he had approved of Marsden's letter, which he vaguely understood to be a routine plea to the Home Secretary for the convict's life. In the meantime he had nominated Douglass as Commissioner of the new Court of Requests, and, wishing him to have jurisdiction superior to the magistrates, had determined to send him home on an official mission. He ought to be consulted on all matters 'connected with the welfare of the colony'.[2]

When Douglass arrived in England, he was able to defend himself against Marsden's accusations; and Bathurst, who resented the chaplain's 'passing the Colonial Office by attempting to lodge clandestinely in the Home Department a charge against his adversary, under the pretense of interceding for a runaway convict' made the important decision to appoint the Governor, and the newly appointed Chief

---

[1] *H.R.A.* I/xi/960, note 226; /x/744, Brisbane–Bathurst, 6 Sept. 1822; /xi/73, Bathurst–Brisbane, 1 Apr. 1823; /717, Brisbane, Forbes, and Scott–Bathurst, 10 Aug. 1825.

[2] *H.R.A.* I/xi/307, Bathurst–Brisbane, 18 July 1824, enc. Hobhouse–Horton, 29 June 1824, sub-enc. Marsden–Peel, 28 Jan. 1824; /541, Brisbane–Bathurst, 7 Mar. 1825; /230, Brisbane–Bathurst, 21 Feb. 1824.

Justice and Archdeacon (Forbes and Scott) to judge and report on this affair.[1]

The attack on Douglass, however, continued and expanded. Marsden complained to the Bishop of London. Surgeon Hall protested to the Admiralty. Accusations of drunkenness, immorality, flogging of convicts to extort confessions, and the institution of a 'spy' system at Parramatta were made against Douglass.[2] Protests and explanations went to and fro. Brisbane agreed to restore the dismissed magistrates gradually. On the eve of his departure, he wrote that though the colony was peaceful and prospering, he could not bring himself to restore the partisan Hannibal Macarthur and Blaxland to the commission of the peace, much less Sam Marsden. He admitted that Douglass had, probably with an eye to prevent vagrancy, and under outdated regulations of 1810–11, attempted to establish a control on freedom of movement in Parramatta, one of the breaches of civil liberty complained of by the *Morning Chronicle*. Even if his friend had not voluntarily retired, the Governor would not have returned him to the bench 'because I think it is improper to allow any man to fill the Judgment Seat who is opposed in hostility (whether right or wrong) with any considerable portion of the Community'.[3]

Douglass emerged from official inquiries with favourable testimony from a number of witnesses, particularly from Frederick Goulburn, though many years later Henry Goulburn was still trying to recover a £3,500 investment which his brother had entrusted to the doctor.[4] But Archdeacon Scott allied himself with the 'faction' now, according to the Governor, determined to see how far they could count on their influence in England. He was prepared to resign rather than countenance the admission of a 'torturer' into the Council as Clerk.[5] Hannibal Macarthur used his position as foreman of the experimental Parramatta Grand Jury to present further evidence against Douglass,

[1] *H.R.A.* I/xi/351, Bathurst–Brisbane, 2 Sept. 1824, enc. Douglass–Horton, 21 Aug. 1824; C.O. 324/75/3 Minutes of Ld Bathurst, N.S.W. 1824–6.

[2] *H.R.A.* I/xi/388, Bathurst–Brisbane, 30 Oct. 1824; /619, Brisbane–Bathurst, 2 June 1825; /422, Bathurst–Brisbane, 3 Jan. 1825; /557, Brisbane–Bathurst, 5 Apr. 1825; /606, Brisbane–Bathurst, 23 May 1825; C.O. 201/144/5, Barrow–Wilmot, 26 Apr. 1823; etc.

[3] *H.R.A.* I/x/367, Bathurst–Brisbane, 21 Sept. 1824; /557, Brisbane–Bathurst, 5 Apr. 1825; /902, Brisbane–Bathurst, 18 Nov. 1825; /612, Brisbane–Bathurst, 23 May 1825; /903, Brisbane–Bathurst, 18 Nov. 1825.

[4] *H.R.A.* I/xi/717, Brisbane, Forbes, and Scott–Bathurst, 10 Aug. 1825; /782, 11 Aug. 1825; Goulburn Papers, II, 9.

[5] *H.R.A.* I/xi/850, Brisbane–Bathurst, 28 Sept. 1825.

'to attract notice at home' and to get publicity in the colony. The Council examined the records of the various Courts of Magistrates, and found that the practice of passing indefinite and irregular sentences had been pursued by both Marsden and Hannibal Macarthur, before Douglass had come to the Colony. Brisbane and Forbes were rightly convinced that the publicity which this finding was sure to gain in England would discredit the opposition, but 'to put an end to all discussions and recriminations' they had the Council pass a law to stay proceedings against magistrates who had engaged in that practice. This Bill of Indemnity was opposed by Saxe Bannister, the eccentric Attorney-General, by this time under the influence of Hannibal Macarthur and an 'instrument of annoyance to the Government', and by the *Australian*, the 'organ of Marsden and his friends', whose Editor, Dr. Wardell, had been retained by Macarthur.[1]

Forbes was sure that his official participation in this affair had brought upon him the lasting odium of the 'Parramatta party'.[2] He warned Horton that the 'assailants', beaten in the colony, would change the seat of war to England, where their 'coalition of evil', pulled together by their temporary set-back, and 'calculating upon the effect of misstatement and the force of influence at home', would besiege Downing Street with 'files of statements and vollies of oaths'. Douglass the man was perhaps arrogant, but 'his cause became the cause of every publick servant and his sacrifice would have shaken the stability of every independent man in the public departments'. Only the opinion of the Secretary of State, simply expressed, would be all-powerful in the colony. The Colonial Office must defend its servants and resist the 'compact, wealthy and influential body' now acting in union against them. 'Your decrees', he stressed, 'are those of the oracle, the more distant, and obscure, the more decisive and unquestioned.'[3]

Bathurst in this case had correctly judged that such disputes could only be satisfactorily unravelled at the source. But the home government found itself here, as elsewhere, obliged to act, even if only to

---

[1] *H.R.A.* I/xi/850, Brisbane–Bathurst, 28 Sept. 1825; /894, Brisbane–Bathurst, 25 Oct. 1825; /950, Forbes–Horton, 30 Oct. 1825; /881 Brisbane–Bathurst, 11 Oct. 1825; IV/i/676, Forbes–Horton, 15 Dec. 1826.

[2] *H.R.A.* IV/i/740, Forbes–Horton, 20 Sept. 1827.

[3] *H.R.A.* I/xi/950, Forbes–Horton, 30 Oct. 1825; M.L. A/1976, C. Macarthur–King, 22 Aug. 1826 on the effect of the Douglass case in reconciling Marsden, H. Macarthur and Jno. Macarthur Sr.

maintain the effectiveness of local administration and to adjust the working of institutions which were as yet little more than experimental. Where the interests of colonial groups were actively engaged, the initiative rarely belonged to the Colonial Office, but its intervention necessarily played a key role. James Stephen made painstaking reports. Horton could hardly have been more zealous. Bathurst could often correct the clerks on the finer points of colonial squabbles, and even before General Darling had sailed confessed wearily that he thought 'the new Governor will prove a troublesome Gentleman'. Hay never ceased from exhorting troubled officials to beware of dissensions and avoid all taint of party spirit. 'You may repel with perfect confidence', he wrote to Darling, 'any change which may be brought against this Department of attaching more weight than is due to information which may be derived from any other than official quarters.'[1] But distance meant delay, and a certain lack of clarity of definition in the decision-making machinery in London led to confusion and misunderstandings. Despite real attempts to devolve authority in a way more suited to the advancement of the colonies, concrete and practical actions had ultimately to be taken by the Colonial Office, and increasing attention paid to accurate assessments of the motives and activities of individuals and administrators.[2]

The most offensive report made in England against a Governor was that which alleged Brisbane's condonation of widespread prostitution among the women convicts who had been sent as volunteers to a penal farm at Emu Plains when the Parramatta Factory had become overcrowded. Damaging evidence against both Governor and Colonial Secretary was made available to the home authorities who were already concerned about this aspect of the convict system. The chief informants were Surgeon Hall and Sir John Jamison, who owned property near by, and whom Brisbane later regretted to have recommended as a worthy nominee for the new Legislative Council.[3] The Governor appointed a commission of inquiry composed of the Lieutenant-Governor, the Solicitor-General (John Stephen), and Rev. W. Cowper. The report stated that the charge was a 'cool, deliberate

[1] M.L. A/73, p. 4. Bathurst–Horton, 2 Jan. 1825; C.O. 324/85/54, Hay–Darling, 17 July 1826; /56 Hay–Darling, 19 July 1826.

[2] e.g. H.R.A. I/xi/253, Brisbane–Bathurst, 24 June 1824; /466, Bathurst–Darling, 4 Aug. 1826; IV/i/556, Stephen–Horton, 2 Sept. 1824.

[3] H.R.A. I/xi/79, Brisbane–Bathurst, 28 Apr. 1823; /595, Brisbane–Bathurst, 21 May 1825; /418, Bathurst–Brisbane, 21 Nov. 1824; /406, Brisbane–Bathurst, 1 Nov. 1824, later withdrawn—/903, Brisbane–Bathurst, 18 Nov. 1825.

and most outrageous misstatement of facts'.[1] The *Australian* contrasted the Governor's humane encouragement of the women concerned, most of whom married happily, with the official callousness shown at home in the failure to redress the numerical imbalance of the sexes in the colony and with the 'mischievous meddling' of the 'Saints' which had led to the establishment of segregated penitentiaries in England and institutions such as the Parramatta Factory.[2]

Bathurst put Brisbane on his guard, for whatever he wrote officially was 'liable to be called for by Parliament'; but he assured him that he could write privately, and that his honour, like that of every Governor, was safe in the Secretary of State's keeping. Brisbane, however, thought that the Colonial Office had given too much credence to the *Morning Chronicle*'s 'tissue of lies', and was shocked by his letter of recall. He wrote to his patron Wellington and to his friends, begging them not to be misled by hearsay. Like Lachlan Macquarie before him, he felt that the home authorities had let him down badly. The language of their dispatches had been 'harsh, unbecoming, and unjust'. On his return to England, he would demand a full statement of all the foul accusations made against him.[3]

Stephen's report on the Inquiry led Bathurst, satisfied that there had been a conspiracy against the local officials, to command that Hall never be employed again in the convict service, and that Jamison be barred from holding any civil office.[4] Jamison pressed his case and submitted a collection of evidence which must rank among the most lurid ever received by a Department of State.[5] But Hay rejected the attempts of such a 'notorious malcontent' to prove that, even if great immoralities had taken place, either the Governor or the Colonial Secretary had approved of them; and Huskisson refused to modify the censure passed on Jamison.[6]

No one was really satisfied by this kind of government. Frederick Goulburn suspected that the Emu Plains affair had brought about

[1] *H.R.A.* I/xi/812, Brisbane–Bathurst, 10 Sept. 1825.   [2] 7, 21 Apr. 1825.

[3] M.L. f.m. 4/1627, Brisbane–Craufurd, 13 May 1825; Brisbane–Wellington, 20 May 1825; *H.R.A.* I/xi/495, Macquarie–Bathurst, 1 Dec. 1817; f.m. 4, Brisbane–Bruce, 31 July 1825; *H.R.A.* I/xi/814, Brisbane–Bathurst, 10 Sept. 1825.

[4] C.O. 201/175/389, Stephen–Hay, 9 Sept. 1826; *H.R.A.* I/xii/561, Bathurst–Darling, 10 Sept. 1826.

[5] *H.R.A.* I/xiii/297, Darling–Bathurst, 12 May 1827 (enclosures at C.O. 201/182/313 ff.); C.O. 201/188/317, Jamison–Bathurst, 10 May 1827.

[6] C.O. 201/182/337, minute; *H.R.A.* I/xiii/615, Huskisson–Darling, 10 Nov. 1827.

his recall, and wrote from his brother's official residence at Phoenix Park to demand the names of his detractors. He declined profferred new appointments, protesting that military men serving their country as colonial administrators were everywhere betrayed by conspiracies organized in England, and, long after Horton's retirement, was complaining of the habit of encouraging private communications from individuals.[1]

Brisbane was outraged by the letter of recall which had 'equated' him with his colonial secretary, and resolved to confront his enemies boldly. After a stormy interview with Bathurst he had to be placated by Sir Herbert Taylor at the Horse Guards, whom Hay thanked for composing in some degree the Governor's 'ruffled plumes'.[2] He insisted that the Navy Office curtail the political activities of surgeons.[3] He had a series of talks with Stephen and was disappointed with him, remaining convinced that misrepresentation and the Macarthur influence had been at work.[4]

Brisbane intended to conduct a rearguard action to defend his colonial allies, to present memorials, and to further 'liberal' interests when the next New South Wales Bill was discussed. But he judged that he had already given the colony an 'inestimable privilege' in its free Press. Not only would his removal of censorship vindicate his personal reputation as a ruler unafraid that public attention should be directed to his policies, but it would prove a permanent boon. Whenever 'there was deformity in the Constitution, or where Public Abuses existed, the Press would discover them'. He was sure no successor would be bold enough to renew government control over information, for his actions, in introducing a free press and trial by jury, were 'merely ministerial', giving effect to what he believed to be the 'wise policy of H.M. Ministers, to assimilate the Government of this Colony, as nearly as circumstances will admit, to that of the parent State'. Replying to the 'popular address' of 21 October 1825 which urged him to support demands for trial by jury, an assembly

[1] C.O. 201/178/632, Bathurst–Goulburn, 26 July 1826; /634, Goulburn–Bathurst, 27 July 1826; /636, Goulburn–Bathurst, 16 Aug. 1826; 201/197/486, Goulburn–Huskisson, 9 Jan. 1828; /491, 14 Apr. 1828; /503, Goulburn–Murray, 29 Oct. 1828; /507, Goulburn–Murray, 28 Nov. 1828; C.O. 324/86/16, Hay–Henry Goulburn, Private, 2 Feb. 1828.

[2] f.m. 4/1627, Brisbane–Craufurd, 13 May 1825; C.O. 324/85/52, Hay–Taylor, 6 July 1826.

[3] H.R.A. I/xi/844, Brisbane–Bathurst, 13 Sept. 1825; C.O. 201/177/52, Sir Byam Martin–Hay, 6 June 1826; /73, Martin–Hay, 5 July 1826.

[4] F.M. 4/1627, Brisbane–Forbes, 26 Feb. 1827.

of at least a hundred members, and taxation only with representation—and which pointed out that the population now exceeded the entire white population of the West Indies—the Governor showed himself more than sympathetic. He stressed that, though all might agree on the desirability of the extension to Australia of those 'venerated institutions . . . the growth of time, wisdom, and experience under which our beloved Country has attained a height of Civilisation, prosperity and virtue, unexampled in the history of the Human Race', there were grave differences of opinion about the fitness of the colony to receive them in their fullness. The Home Government would not 'retard the communication of any civil right, which it may be convinced the State of the Country prepares it to enjoy', but it was forced to guide its actions by the representations it received; and where contradictory views prevailed, little could be expected. He himself thought that the state of society was such that popular institutions could be further introduced, and he promised to present this opinion at Downing Street.[1] But he had also received an address from the 'landed proprietors' of the colony, dissociating themselves from the 'popular' addresses, attacking 'the continued and systematic dissemination by means of a licentious Press, of doctrines tending to inflame the worst passions of the lower orders, to excite a spirit of animosity towards the upper classes, and contempt for all legitimate authority', and asking Bathurst for a 'truly' independent press, respectable emigrants, education, representation, and other favours, the granting of which would disarm the dangerous forces of a radical faction.[2]

Brisbane, in short, had to recognize that, in addition to the 'vile intrigue, cabal, and malevolence' which he had earlier noted as a blemish on all social life in the colonies,[3] there had arisen in practice groupings which were based less on grounds of personal than of political and economic compatibility. The Governor and his officials were not insulated from this dialogue, and, where local counsels were divided, it became increasingly important for interested parties to bring their influence to bear upon the home authorities, with whom the discretionary power lay.

*　*　*　*　*

[1] F.M. 4/1627, Brisbane–Craufurd, 13 May 1825; ibid. Drafts of replies to addresses of Sydney and Parramatta inhabitants; *H.R.A.* IV/i/627 ff.
[2] C.O. 201/178/102 ff.
[3] P.M.G. 1/1/, Brisbane–Craufurd, 13 Feb. 1823, 14, 17 Sept. 1822.

Brisbane's decision to 'try the experiment of the full latitude of the freedom of the Press', when in 1824 Wentworth and Wardell began to publish the *Australian* without asking his permission, had very far-reaching results.[1] The Colonial Office set great store by obtaining complete files of all colonial newspapers: and asked for copies for Home Office use.[2] Government notices, proclamations, new regulations, and important changes in policy had hitherto been published in the *Gazette*. Macquarie's Colonial Secretary, Campbell, listed the superintendence of the *Gazette* among his chief duties.[3] Official sanction, however, far from precluding controversy, had only tended to exacerbate it, as, for instance, when Campbell became involved in bitter law-suits with Marsden.[4] Eventually, the editor of the *Gazette*, Robert Howe, successfully applied to have the official censorship removed.[5]

At first everything seemed to go well. Forbes was relieved that the *Australian*, 'the *Morning Chronicle* of New South Wales', was soon involved in a squabble with its contemporary, and noted that 'an opposition paper is considered by many here as an unwholesome exotic'. He begged, if the Colonial Office agreed with these critics, that they would act strongly in England, for 'we are not equal to it here'.[6] In fact, Colonel Arthur in Van Diemen's Land had sought guidance, and Brisbane's action caused alarm at Downing St. when the batch of newspapers arrived. James Stephen drafted a dispatch which the new Governor, General Darling, was to take out with him. The 'most cursory examination' of the free newspapers showed that the privilege granted by Brisbane would be 'highly dangerous in a Society of so peculiar a character'. Brisbane had exceeded the limits of prudence and had been more generous than the English laws allowed even at home. There was no reason why similar, or more severe, libel

---

[1] *H.R.A.* I/xi/470, Brisbane–Bathurst, 12 Jan, 1825. C. M. H. Clark, *A History of Australia* (Cambridge, 1968) Vol. II, Chs, 3 and 4.

[2] e.g. C.O. 324/146/63, Horton–Herries, 15 Dec. 1826; *H.R.A.* I/xii/228, Hay–Darling, 20 Apr. 1826; *H.R.A.* III/v/285, Hay–Arthur, 20 June 1826; /588, Arthur–Hay, 12 Mar. 1827; /453, Arthur–Hay, 1 Dec. 1826; /368, Arthur–Bathurst, 7 Oct. 1826; I/xii/63, Bathurst–Darling, 22 Aug. 1825; /257, Darling–Bathurst, 2 May 1826; xiii/840, T.C. Harrington–Hall, 23 Jan. 1827.

[3] *H.R.A.* I/xi/83, Bathurst–Brisbane, 30 May 1823; /348, Bathurst–Brisbane, 17 Aug. 1824; M.L. A/1559/3, Brisbane–Wemyss, 5 Sept. 1825; C.O. 201/120/236 ff.; Bigge Appendix: evidence of J. T. Campbell.

[4] *H.R.A.* IV/i/936 Note 171; I/x/139, Macquarie–Bathurst, 31 Mar. 1819; /313, Bathurst–Macquarie, 14 July 1820; /442, Macquarie–Bathurst, 20 Mar. 1821.

[5] *H.R.A.* I/xi/470, Brisbane–Bathurst, 12 Jan. 1825.

[6] *H.R.A.* IV/i/591, Forbes–Horton, 25 Mar. 1825.

laws, stamp taxes, and the introduction of bonds should not be enacted by the Legislative Council of the colony. A resumable one-year licence, forfeit for blasphemous or seditious libel, and a stamp tax, the produce of which should be sufficient to defray the charges of printing public Acts, Proclamations, and Orders, ought to be introduced at the earliest opportunity.[1] It was fatal advice.

Darling, welcomed by Forbes as a businesslike gentleman, 'easy of approach, attentive to the counsels that are offered, and firm in the execution of his measures', was clearly apprehensive.[2] He told his predecessor that he wished, rather than hoped, to 'promote peace and good fellowship',[3] and he tried to keep an open mind about the addresses which greeted his arrival.[4]

He had, while acting as Governor at the Mauritius, received a letter from Brisbane who told him that it was the settlers and gentlemen, the magistrates and the judges who caused most trouble. Though he later came to think that government officials could be the most troublesome of all, Darling began with a certain sympathy with the ascendant emancipist faction. He was very anxious to ensure that he did not fall victim to the Macarthur group, to whose influence, it was widely alleged, the Colonial Office was particularly susceptible.[5] Hay assured him that no unofficial source would be noticed, that his difficult position was fully understood, and urged him to avoid the 'contagion' of party. Dissension among the colonists about fundamentals rendered them 'totally' unfit for the boons sought by various addresses.[6] The initiative was not coming, therefore, from Downing Street.

Darling wrote to Hay as soon as he realized that party strife would not subside. Archdeacon Scott, very upset by attacks on his new dignity and resistance to the authority he sought to exercise, was, thought the Governor, expecting too much support in his battles—as

[1] *H.R.A.* IV/i/718, Forbes–Horton, 27 May 1827; I/xii/16, Bathurst–Darling, 12 July 1825; IV/i/613, Stephen–Hay, 16 July 1825.

[2] *A*/1819, Forbes–Horton, 26 May 1826.

[3] f.m. 4/1637, Darling–Brisbane, 4 Feb. 1826.

[4] *H.R.A.* I/xii/144, Darling–Bathurst, 1 Feb. 1826. These addresses sought legislatures on the pattern of the British North American and West Indian colonies, deplored the neglect of native-born colonists, and insisted on some powers of nomination to the governing Council.

[5] *H.R.A.* I/xiii/587, Darling–Hay, Secret and Confidential, 1 Nov. 1827; /xii/81, Darling–Hay, Secret and Confidential, 10 Dec. 1825.

[6] C.O. 324/85/54, Hay–Darling, Private and Confidential, 17 July 1826; /56, 19 July 1826.

was John Macarthur, now a member of the Legislative Council and claiming that the *Gazette* was systematically insulting him. Already lack of support from sensible advisers was making itself felt, for the Attorney-General, Saxe Bannister, was no match for Wentworth or Wardell, and had as a precaution opposed freedom of the Press in the first place. He was in favour of suppressing party publications, resented Darling's toleration of the *Australian* and its editors, and sought to be treated more like a minister of state than a subordinate official.[1] The Governor was sure that the Attorney-General was odd, and, as his patron Tooke had hinted in his letters of recommendation, not to be trusted in practical affairs. The Colonial Office must put him firmly in his place.[2]

Darling was ready to be agreeably surprised at the reasonable attitude of the *Australian*, and proud that it had said his government was based on the goodwill of the colonists. He blamed Scott's and Bannister's unpopularity on their friendship with the 'exclusive' party.[3] Though he denied any understanding with Wardell, he considered that the *Australian* could not now be called an 'opposition' paper. Nor could the new, independent, but so far friendly *Monitor* of E. S. Hall. He was conscious of Bathurst's letter of 12 July 1825 about curbing the Press, but he was anxious to avoid a struggle, now that all seemed harmonious. Colonel Arthur had already run into strife. A tax on newspapers would certainly mean the end of their support of the Government.[4]

Hay wrote discursively that he was glad to hear of the improvement in the tone of the *Australian*, but he was sceptical that the 'halcyon' days would last. There were no other settlements where the dangers of a licentious Press could have more serious results than in New South Wales and Van Diemen's Land. Such prints should be restrained and publications with 'the opposite tendency' encouraged. He hoped the *Monitor* would continue as an ally, and assured Darling that he had nothing to fear from the machinations of the Macarthurs. Lord Bathurst was ready to agree to a diminution in the tax to be

---

[1] *H.R.A.* I/xii/210, Darling–Hay, Secret and Confidential, 6 Mar. 1826; /253, Darling–Hay, Secret and Confidential, 1 May, 1826; /437, Darling–Bathurst, 24 July 1826; *Australian* 26 Jan., 16 Feb. 1826.

[2] *H.R.A.* I/xii/437, Darling–Bathurst, 24 July 1826; /445, Darling–Hay, Private and Confidential, 25 July 1826,

[3] *H.R.A.* I/xii/522, Darling–Hay, Private and Confidential, 2 Sept. 1826; *Australian*, 26 Aug. 1826.

[4] *H.R.A.* I/xii/326, Darling–Hay, Private and Confidential, 24 May 1826.

imposed on newspapers, but not to its abandonment. The primary object was to secure tranquillity, not to raise revenue.[1]

The *Monitor*, aspiring to emulate the success of Cobbett, soon embarked on a radical career of criticism of government measures. The Governor, still favourable to the *Australian*, was ready to sanction the prosecution of Hall, the editor of the *Monitor*, an 'ill-disposed, if not a dangerous man' who aimed at arousing the passions of the 'lower classes of the community', especially the Irish. He also determined to refuse Hall's request for permission to purchase more land. Hay, though he deplored the abuse of free expression, vaguely discouraged the Governor from prosecuting. By the time his letter arrived in the colony, the issue of the freedom of the Press had taken a new turning and Darling found himself in very deep waters indeed. He knew that Bannister was incompetent to carry out libel prosecutions successfully; but the Chief Justice, Forbes, refused to certify the restrictive enactment which was proposed after he had brought Bathurst's original letter of 12 July 1825 under the consideration of the Executive Council (in October 1826). Forbes, convinced that a licensing Act was illegal, and that the tide was flowing against laws such as the Six Acts to which Bathurst had referred, told the Governor that, though it would doubtless be 'more *agreeable* to H.M. Government to have the proposed law passed in the Colony, than to have its provisions discussed in Parliament', it was impossible to confine discussion to New South Wales. Parliament alone could effectively come to his rescue. Both Governor and Chief Justice realized the necessity of evading the difficulties presented by any attempt to effect adequate restraints by local action; and Forbes had in mind the expected new Bill which would soon be introduced to deal with the Australian colonies. If Darling was vigorous against the Press, the Bill would be enveloped in acrimonious debate, and 'learned and talented Opposition M.P.s' would so take up the colonial complaints that all authority and influence exercised by the local government would be destroyed. It would be wiser for the Governor to take no action until it was too late for querulous petitions to be sent to Parliament. The Colonial Office must rescue the local government from certain odium by including the contemplated restrictions in the new Act.[2]

[1] C.O. 324/85/77, Hay–Darling, Private, 31 Oct. 1826.

[2] *H.R.A.* I/xii/529, Darling–Bathurst, 4 Sept. 1826; /579, Darling–Hay, 12 Sept. 1826; C.O. 324/85/89, Hay–Darling, 26 Dec. 1826; H.R.A. I/xii/667, Darling–Bathurst, 1 Nov. 1826; /725, Darling–Hay, 4 Dec. 1826, enc. Minute of Ex. Co., 6 Oct. 1826, and Forbes–Darling, 1 Dec. 1826.

The colonial newspapers, however, took up the case of the soldiers Sudds and Thompson, in which serious allegations were made against the governor himself. Darling, fearful of the ill-effects of adverse publicity and now under the attack of the *Australian*'s formidable editor, wrote home hastily to deny reports of his inhumanity and to assure himself of Colonial Office support in what he knew must become a public and a parliamentary scandal, and was already being used as a unifying issue for 'partisan objects' connected with the new Bill.[1] He was satisfied that Wentworth was a demagogue intent on manipulating the emancipist 'opposition', and suspected that Hall, the Methodist Walker, and Father Therry—dangerous because of their close contacts with the convicts—had made common cause. Forbes agreed with him that the agitation over the soldiers' punishment and the subsequent death of Sudds was a 'political juggle'. But he insisted that 'whatever is to be done respecting the Press must be done at Home.'[2]

When the Governor tried to introduce again legislation in accordance with Bathurst's dispatch, Forbes, though not willing to accept the responsibility of pronouncing openly that the Secretary of State's instructions were contrary to law, still refused to co-operate, especially in the plan to issue licences to publishers which would be resumable at the Governor's pleasure. Darling appealed to the troubled state of the colony as an overriding consideration, and pointed out that Chief Justice Pedder in Van Diemen's Land had been more helpful to Colonel Arthur. But Forbes, stressing all along the need for action by the Colonial Office, told the Governor that he should have more active recourse to libel prosecutions if indeed the safety of the colony was seriously threatened, which he doubted. He, who had drafted the 1823 Act, was now the judicial defender of its provisions which the government had guaranteed would protect the rights of British subjects in the colony. Nothing less than parliamentary initiative could legalize an Act of Council so inconsistent with England's laws as that which was proposed. To give the Governor such wide discretionary powers would amount to a monopoly; and the Executive Council would be acting as judges in their own cause if they examined press criticisms of government measures.

---

[1] *H.R.A.* I/xii/716, Darling–Bathurst, 4 Dec. 1826; /730, Darling–Hay, Private, 4 Dec. 1826; /741, Darling–Bathurst, 12 Dec. 1826; /749, Darling–Bathurst, 15 Dec. 1826; /761, Darling–Horton, Secret and Confidential, 15 Dec. 1826.

[2] *H.R.A.* I/xii/765, Darling–Hay, 16 Dec. 1826.

Public outcry at this would inevitably result in appeal not to the home authorities, as hoped, but to the Press and popular opinion in England. It was no time for a local ordinance to oppose the 'declared opinion of the people, and possibly at variance with the sentiments of Parliament' just when a petition was on its way home from the colony thanking Parliament for the advantages of a free Press.[1]

Forbes insisted on the independence of the Chief Justice from the executive, and saw his role as that of a colonial House of Lords. With the awaited Act in mind, he put forward sweeping plans for the devolution of power. New South Wales was as much a civil as a convict colony, and the Governor's powers over finance, taxation, land, trade, and other matters should be less autocratically delineated. A consultative cabinet council, like that of India, should be set up. New South Wales could be governed only in New South Wales. The Governor, seduced by a lust for power, was seeking to overthrow the independence and impartiality of the judiciary and to interfere with the processes of law, and 'make things quiet by suppressing the voice of public opinion'; while the opponents of Darling's régime saw their only hope in the Governor's removal. Although he was himself pressing for home action in the most delicate question of Press freedom, and his own letters were aimed at bringing the Colonial Office around to his point of view, Forbes criticized Darling for being too ready to rely on the authority of the Secretary of State and for sending lengthy dispatches home to be 'stamped with the approval of the home government', thus relieving himself of all responsibility or blame. The Governor should no more be able to evade these, he thought, than the law officers should continue to refer difficult cases home for judgment—a habit deprecated by both the Colonial and the Home Offices. In any case Darling was inexperienced in government, and, attempting too much unpopular reorganization in the absence of fit lieutenants, was too reliant on his family and connections.[2]

Forbes told Horton that he understood that the original Colonial Office intention was a particular response to Arthur's representations rather than a deliberate Colonial Office policy. Darling, having

---

[1] *H.R.A.* I/xii/277, Darling–Bathurst, 8 May 1827, enc. Forbes–Darling, 12, 16 Apr. 1827, and Darling–Forbes, 14 Apr. 1827; III/v/586 Arthur–Hay, 12 Mar. 1827; IV/i/679, Forbes–Horton, 6 Feb. 1827; I/xiii/289, Darling–Bathurst, 11 May 1827.

[2] *H.R.A.* IV/i/679, Forbes–Horton, 6 Feb. 1827; /688, 6 Mar. 1827; /700, 7 Mar. 1827; /703, 22 Mar. 1827.

neglected the normal means of restraining a libellous Press, had sought to force the hand of his Chief Justice when he himself had at length come under attack. Forbes refused to become a party to such misguided pique, to approve of a measure which he was sure would be shown unconstitutional when laid before Parliament, and even to discuss 'political' affairs with the Governor. He agreed with the liberal arguments recently made by the Bombay judges, and refused to certificate the stamp duty as soon as he decided that, though ostensibly for revenue purposes, it would be so excessive as to be clearly punitive and aimed at silencing all opposition journals. If there had been a real danger of violence in the colony, he would have been ready to suspend the Press altogether. But, he warned the Colonial Office, though he was now left in the unpleasant position of having to choose either conflict with the Governor or unpopularity with the people, he would never be 'party to the scheme of reducing the Press to a sensible, adulatory creature of the local government'. A little more temper and deliberation in the colony might, he thought, have prevented much trouble. He might have added, as James Stephen did, that a little co-operation on his own part might have comforted the Governor. As it was, he disclaimed radical sympathies with editors or convicts and regretted the licentiousness of the Press and the 'deep-rooted animosities' it brought to light. He was convinced that the Governor's circle and the 'faction' were now embarked on a narrow and vindictive policy.[1]

Darling, in the absence of Forbes and Bannister, who had resigned, attempted to bring into force Bills based on those which Arthur had had prepared by his law officers and certified by Pedder. But general opposition, and Forbes' action, drove him to suspend the licencing proposals.[2] Incessantly worried and bereft of legal comfort, and desperate for Colonial Office advice and support, Darling continued to come under attack from the radical colonial Press through 1827. He was, he felt, obliged to answer the ceaseless allegations of the *Monitor* and the *Australian*, lest their trenchant and widespread criticisms of his every action find their way into the English papers. The plot to excite popular feeling and to disturb the

[1] *H.R.A.* IV/i/718, Forbes–Horton, 27 May 1827.
[2] *H.R.A.* I/xii/227, Bathurst–Darling, 7 Apr. 1826; /232, Bathurst–Darling, 23 Apr. 1826; /294, Bathurst–Darling, 20 May 1826; /644, Darling–Hay, Private, 10 Oct. 1826; I/xiii/277, Darling–Bathurst, 8 May 1827, and note 70, p. 856; Darling's bills 2 and 3/8 Geo. IV of 25 Apr. 1827, passed 3 May 1827, published *Gazette*, 4 May 1827; 3rd suspended, 31 May 1827.

convict classes was serious, and it could not be expected that he or Colonel Arthur would tamely suffer the abuse lavished on them. Archdeacon Scott's resignation was being hailed as a victory for popular agitation. His magistrates could not be expected to prove trustworthy, nor his new and treasured Boards to continue efficiently if vituperation was the reward of every public servant. Whereas in the Cape and in India only discontent and grumbling could result when the Press was checked, in the Australian colonies a revolution was just possible. The home government must therefore do what was necessary and give him sympathetic legal and political help. Both Judge Stephen and Forbes, though full of noble protestations of judicial independence, were so unco-operative as to snub him when he sought information. He was sure Stephen had given confidential and highly inflammable information to the Press, or to Doctor Douglass, Wardell's friend and the Judge's private physician, which was as bad. Every rumour found its way to the papers, to be distorted and used against him.[1]

If Forbes was right, then the Chief Justice had indeed all powers of legislation, even in financial matters. He had undermined all the Governor's efforts to restrain the Press: and the proposed stamp-duties had had to be rescinded. Undoubtedly Brisbane had allowed the lawyers too much latitude.[2]

The well-attended public meeting of 26 January 1827 which voted for a petition, read by Wentworth, and seconded by Hall, seeking taxation by representation, the establishment of a legislative assembly, and the extension of civil rights, marked a new stage in colonial maturity. A new Bill was known to be in contemplation, and the claims were pitched high. The Australian colonies, it was said, with a

[1] e.g. *Monitor*, 16 Mar. 1827; *H.R.A.* I/xiii/178, Darling–Hay, 23 Mar. 1827; /189, Darling–Horton, 26 Mar. 1827; /79, Darling–Horton, Most Private and Confidential, 6 Feb. 1827; /206, Darling–Hay, 27 Mar. 1827; /259, Darling–Bathurst, 18 Apr. 1827; /318, Darling–Bathurst, 24 May 1827; /589, Darling–Hay, Private and Confidential, 2 Nov. 1827; /650, Darling–Jas. Stephen, Private, 16 Dec. 1827; /374, Darling–Bathurst, 29 May 1827 on Forbes' conversations with Wardell about the proposed Stamp duties.

[2] *H.R.A.* I/xiii/380, Darling–Bathurst, 30 May 1827; /386, Darling–Hay, Private, 30 May 1827; /391, Darling–Bathurst, 1 June 1827, enc. Forbes–Darling, 31 May 1827. MacLeay had claimed that the measure aimed to bring in £500 which would start an official *Gazette*; but, at 4*d.* per issue, the tax ought to have brought in £3,000 (the *Gazette*'s weekly circulation was 2,000, the *Australian*'s 1,200 and the *Monitor*'s 500, bringing a total of 182,000 per annum). The tax, therefore, envisaged a significant decrease in circulation, and seemed to have this decrease as its motive.

population of 55,000, were now paying taxes little short of those paid
fifty years before by the British colonies in North America, where
there had been 3,000,000. Darling would have none of this. There
were, he wrote, *no* direct taxes; most of the revenue came from spirits
and tobacco and the *ad valorem* 5 per cent on foreign goods. He
scouted the suggestion that it was possible to obtain a hundred suitable members for an assembly. Of the existing eighty-three magistrates, twenty were officials and ten military or naval officers. The
Press, 'formidable everywhere', was extremely dangerous in New
South Wales, where it excited convicts, inflamed emancipists, and
offered disappointed settlers opportunities for unfair attacks on a
hard-working and conscientious government. The home authorities
must strengthen his hand. 'The evil of this place is the passion, which
exists, that New South Wales should be the counterpart of England.'
He was impatient of the truculence with which immature colonial
aspirations were urged. Yet if he recruited champions, Lawrence
Halloran's preferred *Gleaner*, for example, he knew he would become
more deeply entangled in an intensified debate.[1]

The Governor, forced to resist unreasonable demands and the
excessive iconoclasm of Wentworth, Hall, and the rest, appeared to be
and in practice was, closer than was comfortable to the 'exclusives',
though he had noted how Archdeacon Scott's impetuous reaction to
opposition and identification with that faction had led to disillusionment and frustration.[2] He knew that the country was not ready for
its precious freedoms, but was by no means sure how to secure
Colonial Office backing. 'The military and the prisoners are seen
constantly reading the Newspapers', he wrote. Forbes was nothing
but a common liberal, an admirer of America, who did not wear a
wig or gown in court. 'America is the Grand Beacon, which Mr.
Wentworth and the opposition papers have in view.' It was more than
ever necessary to repulse 'republicans' and render the government
'purely Aristocratick'.[3]

Darling had enough evidence to suspect that many of his oppo-

[1] *H.R.A.* I/xiii/50, Darling–Bathurst, 31 Jan. 1827; /96, Darling–Hay, Secret
and Confidential, 9 Feb. 1827.
[2] e.g. A/2899 (Macarthur Papers), Jno. Macarthur–son, 16 May 1827; *H.R.A.*
III/v/156, Arthur–Bathurst, 21 Apr. 1826, enc. Scott–Arthur, 13 Feb. 1826;
H.R.A. I/xiii/190, Darling–Horton, Private and Confidential, 26 May 1827;
I/xiv/234, Darling–Huskisson, 21 June 1828; /318, Darling–Bathurst, 24 May
1827.
[3] C.O. 323/149/189, Darling–Horton, 6 Feb. 1827; /260, Darling–Hay, Private
and Confidential, 20 Apr. 1827.

nents had venal motives, or were disgruntled at their failure to obtain undeserved favours or official positions. Forbes had stretched a point by obtaining land from Sir Thomas Brisbane in his mother's name. The popular sheriff MacKaness had imagined that his appointment entitled him to all the traditional functions and perquisites of the sheriff of an English county. Dr. Douglass maintained social contacts with Wardell and Wentworth. The Secretary of State should censure them, he thought, for their mistaken illusions and for daring to give 'marked countenance' to proceedings critical of existing institutions and constituted authorities.[1]

The Colonial Office was, to a degree, willing to help. Archdeacon Scott was told to keep aloof from parties, and to send his communications through the Governor. Stephen was called on to make endless reports about the conduct of alleged offenders. Doctor Douglass' name in the *Gazette*, as seconder of a motion of thanks to MacKaness for presiding at the meeting mentioned above, was enough to earn him a rebuke for conduct highly improper in a man occupying the confidential post of Clerk of the Council. Darling was satisfied to pass on official censures, but his temper went altogether beyond bounds when Douglass and MacKaness took part in a Turf club meeting at the end of 1827, at which offensive resolutions were passed and his own honour insulted when the band pointedly played 'Over the Hills and far away' immediately after his health was proposed.[2] It was a pleasure that the attempts to rally popular feeling on the occasion of the 40th anniversary of the foundation day misfired; and it was a relief to be rid of Douglass, that 'busy, meddling, intriguing, mischievous fellow', friend of Wentworth who had publicly called government measures 'diabolical and damnable' and of Wardell, who named the Governor 'a Tyrant, a Monster, and a scoundrel'.[3]

Worried about the Sudds affair, and the influence at home of Captain Robison, the relation of the Stephen family involved in that case, he sent off his brother-in-law, Colonel Dumaresq, to argue his

[1] *H.R.A.* I/xiii/98, Darling–Hay, Secret and Confidential, 9 Feb. 1827; /251, Darling–Hay, Secret and Confidential, 15 Apr. 1827; /447, Goderich–Darling, 16 July 1827; /640, MacKaness–Darling, 13 Dec. 1827.

[2] C.O. 201/179/40, Scott–Horton, 13 Jan. 1826; /434, Horton–Scott, Minute; C.O. 202/15/13, Hay–Scott, 5 Aug. 1826; C.O. 201/204/282, Stephen–Twiss, 18 Apr. 1829; *H.R.A.* I/xiii/443, Goderich–Darling, 12 July 1827; /647 Darling–Goderich, 15 Dec. 1827; /638, 642, Darling–Goderich, 14 Dec. 1827.

[3] *H.R.A.* I/xiii/784, Darling–Hay, 15 Feb. 1828; /706, Darling–Goderich, 15 Jan. 1828; /712, Darling–Hay, Private, 15 Jan. 1828; I/xiv/356, Murray–Darling, 30 Aug. 1828.

case. Though Forbes would not rise to MacLeay's bait and co-operate in crushing the confident opposition, Darling persisted in his campaign against his calumniators. Litigation gave Wentworth and Wardell opportunities for passing damaging remarks about the administration in open court, which were in turn gleefully reported in the Press. The infuriated Governor could only continue to implore the Colonial Office for understanding and assistance.[1]

In his crusade against privilege and bureaucracy, Hall, who had originally been recommended to Macquarie by Peel as a man trusted by Wilberforce, and whose father claimed to have been a loyal writer for the Government cause at home, got deeper into hot water. He described himself as a 'perpetual commission of Enquiry', whose annual efforts cost the authorities a £2. 12s. 0d. subscription to the *Monitor*, where Bigge's had cost more than £10,000; and he asked if Huskisson had not praised the role of a free Press as a check on autocratic administration and favouritism in high places. When libel suits began to stick, his sojourns in prison gave him opportunities to keep up a regular and voluminous correspondence on the subject of official malignancy. Here again, Darling was sure, a venal motive existed; and he suspected that a little patronage, which he scorned to give, would buy off this adamant paladin of the native-born and the rights of transplanted Englishmen.[2] The Colonial Office, nevertheless, felt obliged to deal with Hall as they dealt with all correspondents. His charges were referred to the Governor for report and comment. Thus the gadfly had its effect.[3]

Darling, though grateful for the support of the *Gazette*, was not enthusiastic about encouraging the Howes with the titles and emoluments of an official government printer, and inclined, as did Arthur more practically, towards the setting up of an official government journal. The home authorities frowned on this, and deplored the

[1] C.O. 323/149/260, Darling–Hay, Private and Confidential, 20 Apr. 1827; *H.R.A.* I/xiv/617, Darling–Murray, 27 Jan. 1829; /618, Darling–Murray, Private, 29 Jan. 1829; I/xiii/869, Note 125; /547, Darling–Goderich, 10 Oct. 1827; /429, Darling–Hay, 5 July 1827; /477, Darling–Hay, 1 Aug. 1827; /692, Darling–Hay, 10 Jan. 1828; I/xv/654, Darling–Murray, 7 Aug. 1830; I/xvi/286, Goderich–Darling, 24 June 1831.

[2] M.L. (Hall Papers) Ah. 14, Peel–Macquarie, 20 Dec. 1810; C.O. 201/95/523, E. S. Hall (Sr.)–Bathurst, 3 Mar. 1819; 201/93/232, Hall–A. Young, 1 May 1818; *H.R.A.* I/xiv/578, Darling–Murray, 2 Jan. 1829, enc. Hall–MacLeay, 3 Nov. 1828 and Hall–Murray, 26 Nov. 1828; 201/207/89, Hall–Murray, 16 Mar. 1829; /101 Hall–Murray, 2 May 1829; *H.R.A.* I/xv/626, Darling–Murray, 27 July 1830.

[3] e.g. *H.R.A.* I/xv/243, Murray–Darling, 6 Nov. 1829; /441, Murray–Darling, 23 Apr. 1830; /843, Darling–Murray, 21 Dec. 1830, etc.

'partisan' use of the *Gazette* by the Government, an accusation rejected by the Governor.[1]

It was, of course, useful to have the assistance of the *Gazette* when Darling thought it had become essential to remove Doctor Douglass from his sensitive post as Clerk of the Council. Where, in Brisbane's time, the Howes' paper had supported that Governor's protégé, they now proved their loyalty to officialdom by turning on him as a dangerous, Canningite liberal. The Governor was determined to place his own trustworthy friends in positions which demanded the confidence of government; but the Colonial Office was aware of his penchant for selecting members of his family and entourage, and moved to send out men 'unconnected with any party', among whom was Edward Deas Thompson, destined to play a very important role in future developments during the thirties. Douglass' own complex career, and his eventual return to England on half-pay, caused the Office much embarrassment. There seemed to be no end to the necessity of examining his official and private life. Stephen was convinced that the Governor's treatment of Douglass was yet another proof of his harshness, intolerance, and lack of dignity when it came to appeasing political foes.[2]

*   *   *   *   *

It was becoming apparent to the Governor that he could not force the hand of the home authorities. He could, however, insist that correct procedures be carried out: and the Colonial Office could usually

---

[1] *H.R.A.* I/xii/548, Darling–Bathurst, 8 Sept. 1826; I/xiv/33, Darling–Huskisson, 23 Mar. 1828; /36, Darling–Stanley, 22 Mar. 1828; /341, Darling–Hay, 18 Aug. 1828; /446, Murray–Darling, 11 Nov. 1828; I/xvi/11, Goderich–Darling, 6 Jan. 1831; C.O. 201/218/441, Hay–Darling, 25 Aug. 1830; *H.R.A.* I/xvi/304, Darling–Goderich, 20 July 1831. Also C. Sec. (N.S.W.) 4/1752, 4 Mar., 6 Apr. 1822 for a typical claim of the Howes to be 'on the alert, night and day, to serve the interests of the government'; and ibid. 4/1790, 9 Feb. 1826, Minute of Darling, lukewarm to the *Gazette*, whose heading 'By Authority' he finds misleading.

[2] *H.R.A.* I/xi/958, Note 212; I/xii/10, Bathurst–Darling, 4 July 1825; /96, Darling–Bathurst, 2 Mar. 1826; /160, Darling–Hay, Secret and Confidential, 4 Feb. 1826; /512, Bathurst–Darling, 31 Aug. 1826; I/xiii/16, Darling–Bathurst, 11 Jan. 1827; /521, Darling–Goderich, 25 Sept. 1827; /588, Darling–Hay, Private and Confidential, 2 Nov. 1827; I/xiv/190, Huskisson–Darling, 17 May 1828—sending Deas Thompson. Also I/xiii/443, Goderich–Darling, 12 July 1827; /647, Darling–Goderich, 15 Dec. 1827; /653, Darling–Hay, 17 Dec. 1827; /706, Darling–Goderich, 15 Jan. 1828; I/xiv/364, Murray–Darling, 30 Aug. 1828; /229, Darling–Huskisson, 19 June, 1828; C.O. 201/195/485, Stephen's Report, 4 Mar. 1828; 324/86/67, Hay–Dumaresq, 4 Oct. 1828.

be relied on to support him in this. It was an old custom for mal-
contents to attempt to send their submissions direct to the Secretary
of State; but in nearly every case Downing St. referred matters back
to the Governor as the proper channel of communication. John
Stephen, Jr., for example, was severely reprimanded for sending his
letters in such a way that Darling could have no knowledge of their
contents, and, when he returned to England to defend his cause,
protested bitterly when the Colonial Office insisted on remitting his
evidence to New South Wales for comment. He commented wryly
that it was customary for the local officials to refer matters home,
while at home the rule was to refer matters to the colony. Wentworth,
no devotee of official courtesy, caused Darling great anxiety by sending his threatened motion of impeachment to England by unofficial
means. In fact, Doctor Douglass was the courier, and the Governor
could be sure that, even if the motion was unsuccessful, he was in for a
painful period of criticism by the English Press and Opposition M.P.s.[1]

Successive Secretaries of State, in turn, grew accustomed to public
criticism of the administration of the Australian colonies. General
Murray was applauded for his liberal attitude and his promise, for
example, to issue an Order in Council aimed at extending trial by
jury; but he came under running fire, not only from those who had
heard bad reports about Swan River, but from O'Connell, Hume, and
Hunt, who urged attacks against Darling, defended freedom of publication, and sought a review of Hall's case. Jephson was shocked at
the coarseness of vituperation and harshness of expression used by
the colonial journals towards those placed in authority, but the
radicals persisted in raising awkward questions and were well primed
with colonial petitions and correspondents' grievances. When Howick rose to answer Bulwer's speech on behalf of the colonists in 1832
he stressed that, with Governor Bourke, a new era had dawned, and
that anything objectionable would be most severely handled. The
Press would be free 'to the fullest extent'.[2]

[1] *H.R.A.* I/xiii/389, Darling–Bathurst, 31 May 1827; /581, Huskisson–
Darling, 31 Oct. 1827; /770, Huskisson–Darling, 11 Feb. 1828; I/xv/678, Murray–
Darling, 12 Aug. 1830; and on Wentworth, I/xiv/690, Darling–Murray, 24 Mar.
1829; /714, Darling–Murray, 20 Apr. 1829; /793, Darling–Murray, 28 May 1829,
enc. Wentworth–Murray, 1 Mar. 1829; I/xiii/789, Darling–Hay, 16 Feb. 1828;
I/xiv/196, Darling–Stanley, Private, 24 May 1829; I/xv/70, Darling–Twiss, 7 July
1829.

[2] P.D. n.s. XXI/914 ff., 1 May 1829; Goderich, P.D. 3rd S. I/1345 ff., 20 Dec.
1830; Jephson, P. D. n.s. XXIII/856 ff., 25 Mar. 1830; Hume, O'Connell, & Co.

* * * * *

Darling's experience was in many ways paralleled by Arthur's in the southern colony. Colonel Sorell had early warned the Lieutenant-Governor of the potential dynamite contained in a factious Press at a time when runaway convicts seemed likely to set up a bushranger's republic. He had sought and obtained Bathurst's advice to curb the Press, with which he soon became embroiled. Lathrop Murray and Gellibrand, Andrew Bent and Fenn Kemp were *his* Hall and Wentworth. Chief Justice Pedder and Alfred Stephen provided him with more comforting advice than Darling's lawyers, but Arthur came to realize the disadvantages of the obvious necessity of keeping in step with New South Wales. He opposed Brisbane's open invitation to the colonial Press, attempted to impose a stamp and licence system with Pedder's help, and was everywhere frustrated by the Sydney developments. He knew that an attack on the liberty of the Press was dangerous for the popularity of his administration, but became stoically convinced that his plans for the colony, based surely on his instructions as commander-in-chief of a penal colony, necessitated an authoritative exercise of government power and hence made a collision course inevitable with those who did not share his vision.[1] He too was worried about his detractors' influence in England, and like Darling, who saw his position as increasingly 'perilous', wrote to refute the charges of the 'igneous spirits' with which he had to deal in the colony and to demand clear and well-defined instructions from home.[2]

As Van Diemen's Land received, together with an increasing number of convicts, a growing accession of respectable and wealthy settlers who resented the suggestion that the colony be viewed as a receptacle for the worst or most troublesome prisoners and who were

---

P.D. n.s. XXIV/288 ff., 11 June 1830; /436 ff., 17 June 1830; 3rd Series X/32 ff.; XII/1089 ff., 28 June 1832; P.D. n.s. XXIV/1110 ff., 8 July 1830; Howick, 3rd Series XII/1108, 28 June 1832; cf. also C.O. 201/215/339, Hume–Howick, 26 Nov. 1830; /345, Hume–Howick, 23 Dec. 1830.

[1] *H.R.A.* III/iv/877, note 89; /366, Arthur–Horton, 14 Sept. 1825; /237, Arthur–Horton, 10 Feb. 1825; III/v/48, Arthur–Horton, Private, 16 Jan. 1826; /130, Bathurst–Arthur, 2 Apr. 1826; /49, Arthur–Bathurst, 17 Jan. 1826; /495, Arthur–Hay, 27 Jan. 1827; /586, Arthur–Hay, Private, 12 Mar. 1827; /665, Arthur–Hay, 23 Mar. 1827, enc. Pedder–Arthur, 10 Mar. 1827; /490, Arthur–Bathurst, 27 Jan. 1827; III/vi/247, Arthur–Bathurst, 24 Sept. 1827; /242, Arthur–Hay, 23 Sept. 1827.

[2] C.O. 280/20/362, Arthur–Twiss, 2 June 1829; 280/28/393, Arthur–Twiss, 2 Apr. 1831; /129, Arthur–Hay, Private, 2 Jan. 1831; *H.R.A.* I/xv/850, Darling–Murray, 22 Dec. 1830.

less than enthusiastic about Arthur's plans for a model penal system, the Lieutenant-Governor found that he also had to cope with a more articulate public opinion. He dealt cavalierly with public meetings and deputations, judged that all demands for legislative assembly were ridiculously premature, and was alarmed when a draft of the abortive 1827 Bill seemed to make provision for this and other liberal measures. His Colonial Secretary, John Burnett, kept up a regular correspondence of near-alarmist tone with Hay, and so accustomed did the colonists become to his personifying authority that they believed the Ripon regulations were simply another example of Arthur's autocratic approach to his power of deciding how affairs should be arranged.[1]

In the affairs of the Press, as in so many other matters, Hay's private correspondence with officials was a dubious blessing. The Governors found themselves often carrying on a phantom 'unofficial' correspondence as well as that contained in the dispatches: and the results could be unfortunate. Undoubtedly they rejoiced at being able to unload their confidences on the under-secretary, but as a channel of decision-making this type of dialogue was ineffective and led to misunderstandings. Hay, during the latter years of the period only intermittently responsible for the Australian colonies, gained from such letters a wealth of additional information; and occasionally, when he settled down to answer a batch of them, was able to pass on important background reports. Thus he explained to Darling that 'great objections' had arisen to including in the proposed new Bill for New South Wales clauses restraining the Press. In fact, the Bill would not get through the House if it did so. But he was less helpful when he offered for promulgation the draft of an Order in Council similar to that which had been framed to meet the problem at the Cape: and his agreement that the colonists' demands for assembly were 'absurd in the extreme' could only mislead the Governor into narrower paths. Hay realized that Forbes, who wrote regularly, was an excellent source of information and of gossip, but their relations were never

---

[1] *H.R.A.* III/vi/351, Arthur–Goderich, 27 Nov. 1827; III/v/653, Arthur–Bathurst, 23 Mar. 1827; C.O. 280/17/75 ff., and /111 ff. Arthur–Huskisson, 5 July 1828; C.O. 280/19/5, Arthur–Murray, 2 Jan. 1829; /22, Arthur–Hay, Private and Confidential, 26 Jan. 1829; on Burnett, e.g., C.O. 323/147/472 ff., Burnett–Hay, Private and Confidential, 18 Mar. 1827; C.O. 280/23/20, Burnett–Hay, Secret and Confidential, 20 Jan. 1829; Ripon Regs., C.O. 280/33/136, Arthur–Howick, 14 Jan. 1832, cf. also E. Morris Miller, *Pressmen and Governors, Australian Editors and Writers in Early Tasmania* (Sydney, 1952); C.O. 280/38/324, G. Robertson (of the *Colonist*—'the Tasmanian Cobbett')—Goderich, 30 July 1832.

as friendly as those which had existed between Forbes and Horton. He realized that the lawyer or the Governor must go, and he deplored Brisbane's 'unfortunate' liberality in removing censorship of the Press in the first place. He satisfied himself with somewhat vague exhortations to both men to show more public spirit and friendly feelings. Gradually he seems to have made up his mind that Darling had, indeed, acted too severely. At no stage did his advice have the force and intelligence needed to break down the antagonisms which bedevilled colonial relations.[1]

Despite continual efforts, therefore, the Governors were not able to derive much protection or comfort from Downing Street. When Murray sent out the 1828 Bill, he described how account had been taken of many opinions. To have the 'benefit of the reaction of public opinion' laws must normally be inserted in the colonial newspapers eight days before their proposed enactment. The powers of the Chief Justice to block legislation were curtailed. The home government had decided, again despite repeated representations, not to restrict that privilege of free publication 'so conducive to the welfare of society', but to leave the onus of decision, an 'arduous duty', on the local legislature, which must neither give way to panic measures nor shrink from unpopularity if the safety or property of the colony required repression. Murray admitted, apologetically but bluntly, that there was no hope for a general mandate from home. Forbes had been right. Licencing newspapers was, it had proved, illegal; but mention was further made of a possible stamp-tax introduced strictly for purposes of revenue, and of a bond which might discourage sensational journalism. A month later, in August 1828, Murray sent a dispatch which aimed to deal compendiously with all the bitter controversies in New South Wales. The actions of all protagonists were impartially appraised. Darling's habit of issuing proclamations about matters of personal taste and behaviour was censured. As in no other country, his authority ought to 'depend upon its possessing the respect of the Colonists'. Harmony was essential for the public service and sensitive feelings should not stand in the way of public duty. There would certainly be 'unfortunate results' if any further report should reach England of disputes between the Governor and the judges. It

[1] e.g. C.O. 324/85/122, Hay–Darling, Private, 19 July 1827; /86/58, Hay–Darling, 3 Sept. 1828; /154, Hay–Darling, Private, 25 Aug. 1830; C.O. 201/182/224, Minute by Hay 17 Nov. 1827; C.O. 201/181/423, Hay–Darling, 23 Mar. 1827 re Brisbane; Forbes; e.g. *H.R.A.* IV/i/731, Forbes–Horton, 20 Sept. 1827; C.O. 201/188/195, Forbes–Horton, 14 June 1827.

was also decided that Forbes would withdraw from the Executive Council, which Darling should consult more, and his relatives less. After an initial reaction of pain and disappointment, the Governor accepted the inevitable. He did not control Downing St. or have sole access to the councils of the imperial government. Instead, he devoted himself to strengthening the libel law. Even here he was to be frustrated as his law was disallowed. Although the editors of the *Australian* and the *Monitor* spent long periods in gaol, Darling felt he had been beaten. He placed the blame squarely on the Colonial Office and his enemies when he was recalled at the end of his six year term on account of 'misunderstandings and dissensions'. In his apologia he judged that Hall's attacks on him, directed at those 'Home Readers' for whom colonial journalists delighted to write, had ruined him. 'His triumph is complete.'[1]

* * * * *

Some of the most illuminating insights, as well as much of the material from which the Colonial Office part in the continual dialogue was fashioned, came from James Stephen. He was conscious of the unpleasant responsibilities which Darling, Forbes, Arthur and others had been forced to bear, and the evidence left him in little doubt that the Press was a potential danger. But the formal decisions, as he insisted to Hay, were not his to take. He was fully prepared to draft severe warnings for his recalcitrant relations, one of whom eventually floated the rumour that Stephen was himself to be sent out to New South Wales to conduct a new Commission of Inquiry: and he insisted against Darling's heated and resentful charges of his anonymous opposition that he had been at all times very careful not to interfere where they were concerned. When he was preparing the 1828 Bill, he showed sympathy with Darling's wish that 'Parliament should take upon itself the odium which it can so much better afford

---

[1] *H.R.A.* I/xiv/260, Murray–Darling, 31 July 1828; /275, Murray–Darling, 31 July 1828; C.O. 408/5/72, Murray–Arthur, 31 July 1828; /356, Murray–Darling, 30 Aug. 1828; /714, Darling–Murray, 21 Apr. 1829; 792, Darling–Murray, 25 May 1829; on libel etc., *H.R.A.* I/xv/345, Darling–Murray, 23 Jan. 1830; /339 Darling–Twiss, 20 Jan. 1830; /355, Darling–Murray, 4 Feb. 1830; C.O. 201/218/441, Hay–Darling, 25 Aug. 1830; *H.R.A.* I/xvi/11. Goderich–Darling, 6 Jan. 1831; /304, Darling–Goderich, 20 July 1830—disallowance of his 11 Geo IV, c.1. Cf. also C.O. 324/86/154, Hay–Darling, Private, 25 Aug. 1830; 201/229/404, Darling–Goderich, 21 June 1832; 202/25/234, Goderich–Darling, Private and Confidential, 15 Mar. 1831; A. H. King, 'Aspects of British Colonial Policy 1825–1837, etc.' (Oxford Univ. D.Phil. thesis 1959), p. 216 ff. Richard Bourke never once had to invoke his still considerable powers to curb the colonial Press.

to bear', and noted that new libel laws were urgently called for. In his report on the accumulated vexed questions concerning New South Wales, which formed the base of Murray's dispatch of August 1828, Stephen was utterly fair in giving credit to Forbes who, though his pride was at fault in refusing the Governor his confidential advice, had merited praise for standing firm against the 'common error (for such to speak plain it was) of the Secretary of State, the Governor, and the Executive Council'.

When Darling sent his new libel laws, Stephen was very uncomfortable. He had ceased to believe that the colony was in a state of imminent crisis, which might have justified emergency measures. He therefore rejoiced to see them disallowed; and he protested vigorously against Darling's abuse of his assignment powers by withdrawing convict labour from the service of his political opponents, the men of the *Australian* and the *Monitor*. He came eventually to think the Governor far too narrow and apprehensive, and he told Hay that he suspected the best solution of the interminable struggles would be, under a new Governor, to offer the situation of Attorney-General to Dr. Wardell, 'just one of those men who are fitted for such rough work as you have to do in New South Wales'. Wentworth would have been even better, had he not offended against Darling past all forgiveness. In his dealings with the Australian colonies he learnt to have constant 'recourse to compromise and anomalies', for in them settlement had been made, so contrary 'to all sound principles, that . . . affairs cannot be administered with reference to the ordinary and established maxims of good government'.[1]

The administration of the Australian colonies in the 1820s took place, therefore, not only against a background of increased comment, but in a context of quite intense ill-feeling, rooted as much in

[1] C.O. 201/186/403, Stephen–Hay, 19 July 1827; *H.R.A.* I/xiii/516, Huskisson–Darling, 21 Sept. 1827; /581, Huskisson–Darling, 31 Oct. 1827; /770, Huskisson–Darling, 11 Feb. 1828; on Darling's accusations, etc.; I/xiv/650, Darling–Stephen, Private, 16 Dec. 1827; I/xvi/304, Darling–Goderich, 20 July 1831, /314, Darling–Goderich, 26 July 1831; C.O. 201/220/224, Stephen–Hay, 14 Jan. 1832; on Cner. of Inquiry rumour by Jno. Stephen Jr., e.g. C.O. 280/24/380, Arthur–Murray, 14 Apr. 1830; *H.R.A.* I/xv/282, Murray–Darling, 14 Dec. 1829; /712, Darling–Murray, 18 Aug. 1830; on 1828, C.O. 201/195/336 ff., esp. at /363 ff.; /398, Stephen–Murray, 15 Aug. 1828; on libel law, C.O. 201/211/77, Stephen–Hay, Minute, 29 Nov. 1830; C.O. 201/212/27, Stephen–Short, 29 Jan. 1831; on Darling, C.O. 201/214/190, Stephen–Hay, 5 Oct. 1830; *H.R.A.* I/xv/418, Darling–Murray, 12 Apr. 1830; /810, Murray–Darling, 8 Nov. 1830; I/xvi/289, Darling–Goderich, 27 June 1831; on Wardell, C.O. 201/219/44, Stephen–Hay, Memo 1831; on anomalies, C.O. 323/47/225, Stephen–Murray, 14 July 1830.

human nature as in the old military system and the makeshift principles of the emerging free government. 'The wonder is', wrote
Frederick Goulburn to Sir Thomas Brisbane, 'not that two persons
should differ upon some points, but that any two should have agreed
upon any.'[1] Not all was sown in despair. Roger Therry accounted the
time correctly as one of high hopes, with 'more materials for a
pleasant society than almost at any subsequent period'.[2] Even Governor Arthur was ready to concede that a person in his station could
profit from opposition. 'There are weaknesses in every character', he
told Goderich, 'and if we have not enemies to watch over and expose
them, they would soon gain an injurious ascendancy.'[3]

[1] f.m. 4/1627, Goulburn–Brisbane, 21 Nov. 1825.
[2] *Reminiscences* (London 1863), p. 54.
[3] C.O. 280/33/249, Arthur–Goderich, 21 Jan. 1832.

V

ASPECTS OF A GOVERNMENT ECONOMY

IN 1819, William Wentworth described the main sources from which the Australian colonies derived 'the means of procuring those articles of foreign growth and manufacture which are indispensable to civilized life' as 'the money expended by the government for the supply of the convicts, and the pay and subsistence of the civil and military establishments'.[1] Government expenditure was, he thought, the determining factor in encouraging or stifling colonial development.[2] By 1831 this contention could not have been so positively maintained. By that time many new features, both of long-term and of more immediate significance, had come to affect the course of economic growth. Some of these were rooted in local circumstance. Others had their origin in the consistent contemporary search for orthodox solutions to economic dilemmas, even in imperial concerns. Even if Australia had not been founded for commercial reasons and remained during the period chiefly as a penal 'safety-valve', at least in official eyes, neither public policy nor private interest could by 1831 rest content with colonial stagnation.

Social and economic change in Britain inevitably had important repercussions in the Australian colonies. Intermittent but widespread violence accompanied the demobilization of the armies after the war and the movements of people and disturbance of habits which followed mechanization. Irish and Scottish tenants were cleared off their lands. Industrial towns grew and created new tensions. Increasing attention was paid to the detection and punishment of crime. The annual numbers of convicts transported mounted significantly. From 1811 to 1815 the average intake grew from 700 to 1,000 each year. After 1816 the average annual number rose to 2,600. After 1825 it was for ten years an average 4,900.[3] A static image of Australia as a transplanted English county devoted chiefly to subsistence farming by reformed emancipated peasants under benign military supervision

---

[1] W. Wentworth, *A Statistical, Historical and Political Description of New South Wales*, etc. (London, 1819), p. 111.
[2] op. cit., p. 178.   [3] A. G. L. Shaw, *Convicts and the Colonies*, p. 147 ff.

could never have survived this influx, if indeed it had ever been consistently entertained by anyone. Certainly it was not real to those who had experienced the quality of a convict society or been excited by the pastoral prospects upon which Bigge had commented so favourably. The nature and spread of settlement on the mainland and in Van Diemen's Land, the discovery of the path over the Blue Mountains, and the arrival of free settlers, some of them clearly men of 'capital and respectability', added fresh dimensions to the task of government. The earlier routine workings of transportation had created regular government *agenda*, to which private aspirations had to be subordinated. Now, although official control over society was so dominant that it would long remain a natural assumption that land, supplies, and convict labour would be made available under government auspices, unlimited commitment to expansion could not be taken for granted. Nor would detailed government direction of the minutiae of trade and agriculture be as acceptable in the 1820s as it had been in the emergencies of the foundation years.[1]

Strong local command, in view of the governor's responsibility for the convicts, was predictable and necessary in economic matters as in all else. Macquarie kept strict control over the routes across the mountains, for he knew that the convicts believed it was possible, having surmounted these obstacles, to walk to China. Yet he had experienced the unpleasant consequences of unauthorized experiments in taxation. His methods proved unacceptable both to the colonists whose commercial expectations had now become enlarged and to a home government quietly engaged in dismantling the Navigation Acts and desirous of fostering *sponte acta* at the periphery. Even in an 'official' colony such as New South Wales, *laissez-faire* and private enterprise seemed to offer opportunities for making retrenchments and for setting up more rational fiscal patterns and a less costly administrative *modus vivendi*.

There was no shortage of ambitious and imaginative ideas. Governor Arthur was sure that Van Diemen's Land would become an Alexandria between India and South America.[2] Edward Eagar made a career out of singing the praises of New South Wales.[3]

---

[1] C. J. King, *The First 50 Years of Agriculture in New South Wales* (Sydney, 1950), p. 530 ff., and Arts, 12, 13, and 14.

[2] *H.R.A.* III/v/667, Arthur–Hay, 23 Mar. 1827.

[3] *Letters to the Rt. Hon. Robert Peel, M.P., on the advantages of N.S.W.* etc. (London, 1824), p. 41 ff.; N. D. McLachlan, 'Edward Eagar 1787–1866; a colonial spokesman in Sydney and London', *H.S.A.N.Z.*, X (1963), p. 431 ff.

Surgeon Cunningham marvelled that the 'seeds of a mighty Empire' had been sown, whose progress towards riches and power even now exceeded in rapidity 'any founded on the American continent'.[1] But the Great South Land tended to be a true Pandora's Box.

The years 1819-25 saw a pastoral boom comparable with that of the thirties, and the elements of a stable and permanent free 'plantation' colony, with convicts providing a guaranteed labour force, began to emerge. The early experiments in sheep-breeding were now producing results in long and fine wools suitable for the new English mechanized methods. Crowding, drought, and a plague of caterpillars forced the opening up of areas beyond the coastal plains, and it was possible to argue that pastoral expansion had presented the colonies at once with a dynamic staple and a full programme for the foreseeable future.[2] Throughout the whole period, of course, the Commissariat's need for grain and meat continued to be a major factor and efforts were made to discover other outlets for colonial products, some of them rather exotic. Brisbane thought that Australian and New Zealand flax and tobacco would displace Russian flax and U.S. tobacco in English markets, and thus 'give activity to our ships, energy to our exuberant population, and fill the Exchequer, instead of exhausting our coffers'.[3] When James Stirling pressed for the occupation of Western Australia, he mentioned coal and iron as incentives to the governor.[4] It was recognized that the economic style of the colonies would compel public authority to play a positive role and exercise a manifest influence, even in fields where there were express plans for eventual government disengagement. The pastoral sector, soon to have a fabulous expansion, was no exception.[5]

---

[1] *Two Years in New South Wales* (London, 1827), ii, Letter 22.

[2] cf., e.g. J. W. McCarty, 'The Staple Approach to Australian Economic History', *Business Archives and History*, iv (1964), p. 1 ff.; but cf. G. Blainey, ibid. 'Technology in Australian History', p. 117 ff., on the role of mining; G. C. Abbott, 'Staple Theory and Australian Economic Growth 1788–1820', *B.A. and H.* v (1965), p. 142 ff.; J. P. Fogarty, 'The Staple Approach and the Role of the Government in Australian Economic Development', *B.A. and H.* vi. (1966), p. 35 ff. on the place of wheat.

[3] P.M.G. 1/1, Brisbane–Craufurd, 18 May 1822.

[4] *H.R.A.* I/xii/777, Stirling–Darling, 14 Dec. 1826.

[5] J. Ker, 'The Wool Industry in New South Wales, 1803-30', *B.A. and H.* ii (1962), p. 18 ff.; E. A. Beever, 'The Origin of the Wool Industry in New South Wales', *B.A. and H.* v (1965), p. 91 ff.

*   *   *   *   *

It had become normal and fashionable in the 1820s for practical statesmen as well as theorists to take an interest in the orthodox maxims of political economy, air their opinions in clubs, and seek to embody them in reformed 'systems'. Colonial government, taking into its ambit all the great questions of classical inquiry, was no exception.[1] Sydney Smith, reviewing the record of Lachlan Macquarie's alleged extravagance in New South Wales, protested that 'an examination on the principles of Adam Smith, and a license from Mr. Ricardo seem to be almost a necessary preliminary for the appointment of Governors'.[2] Even Lord Bathurst, no doctrinaire economist, had given deliberate impetus to an empirical and thoughtful reappraisal of the whole Government economy of the Australian colonies when he gave the Bigge Commission the broadest possible scope.

No irrefutable dogma held the field. Even the classical political economists did not oppose the exercise by the state of a positive function wherever this seemed necessary or useful for the purposes of economic or social improvement.[3] In the Australian colonies, whose economic life was still after thirty years very much directed by the imperial government, a dynamic tension between theoretic doubt and positive determination to forge more rational systems created the need for fresh analysis of colonial goals and led to a wide variety of practical experiments.

Bentham, often invoked as at least the unconscious parent of many reforms, had based his criticisms of Empire in general and of New South Wales in particular, on political, social, and penal as well as on economic grounds. Yet his views fluctuated and his influence with Tory ministers was by no means direct. As a very old man he was stirred by the foundation of the Swan River settlement, and wrote actively in ap-

---

[1] C. Badham, *The Life of J. D. Hume* (London, 1859), Ch. VI; A. Bain, *James Mill* (London, 1882), p. 198 ff.; L. Stephen, *The English Utilitarians* (London, 1900), Vol. II, Ch. v ff.; D. Winch, *Classical Political Economy and Colonies* (London, 1965), p. 2; E. R. Kittrell, 'The Development of the Theory of Colonization in English Classical Political Economy', *Southern Economic Journal*, xxxi (1965).

[2] *Works*, i, 335.

[3] L. Robbins, *The Theory of Economic Policy in English Classical Political Economy* (London, 1961), pp. 170–190; E. R. Kittrell, ' "Laissez Faire" in English Classical Economics', *Journal of the History of Ideas*, xxvii (1966), p. 610 ff.; F. H. Knight, 'Theory of Economic Policy and the History of Doctrine', *Ethics*, Chicago, lxiii (1952), p. 276 ff.; R. N. Ghosh, 'The Colonization Controversy; R. J. Wilmot–Horton and the Classical Economists', *Economica*, n.s. xxxi (1964), p. 385 ff.

proval of Wakefield's new model for colonization in South Australia.[1]

Bentham, James Mill and others who spoke or wrote on colonial affairs, or corresponded with the Colonial Office and other government departments, were often concerned less with the colonies for their own sakes than with the effect which imperial mismanagement might produce at home. But Britain's expansion abroad had its own fascination, and the complex process of colonization grew to become an object of increasing interest to the acknowledged experts. John Stuart Mill, later an effective contributor to imperial theory, had as a small child read Collins' *Account of New South Wales*. His father wrote the article 'Colonies' for the supplement to the *Encyclopaedia Britannica*. Grey Bennet, gadfly to Macquarie, was coached by Francis Place. Anthony Fenn Kemp, the Wentworth of Van Diemen's Land, kept up a correspondence with Brougham. John Dunmore Lang, the Scottish chaplain of New South Wales, whose early efforts in the colony were directed to economical reform of the administration and the emigration of free labour, was a consultant of Chalmers, whose books on political economy dealt seriously with the question of pauper migration. At the end of the decade, Gibbon Wakefield's powerful *Letter from Sydney* was first and foremost an essay in political economy. Alexis de Tocqueville expressly excepted the Australian colonies when, writing of his experience of democracy in America in 1831, he noted the economic factors which had contributed to the emergence of that remarkable 'freedom of the middle and lower orders of which the history of the world had as yet furnished no complete example'.[2]

---

[1] J. Viner, 'Bentham and J. S. Mill: The Utilitarian Background', in *The Long View and the Short* (Glencoe, 1958), p. 308; ed. G. Greenwood, *Australia: A Social and Political History* (Sydney, 1955), p. 99; J. C. Beaglehole, 'The Royal Instructions to Colonial Governors 1783–1854', (London Univ. Ph.D. thesis, 1929), p. 5 and esp. Ch. IX, pp. 683–699; E. Halévy, *The Growth of Philosophic Radicalism* (London, 1928), pp. 115–16; R. C. Mills, *The Colonization of Australia* (London, 1915), pp. 152–3; D. Pike, *Paradise of Dissent* (Melbourne, 1957), Chs. III and IV; L. Robbins, *Robert Torrens and the Evolution of Classical Economics* (London, 1958), pp. 166–7; Winch, op. cit., pp. 128–9, 150. On Bentham's influence with Robert Peel, cf. J. A. Gulland, 'Criminal Law Reforms 1822–27', (London Univ. M.A. thesis, 1930), pp. 10 ff., 226 ff.; N. Gash, *Mr Secretary Peel* (London, 1961), pp. 312, 331–4; L. Radzinowicz, *A History of English Criminal Law and its Administration from 1750*, i, Ch. XVIII; B.M. Add. MSS. 40400 (Peel Papers), f. 134, Bentham–Peel, 28 Mar. 1830. But cf. J. Hart, 'Nineteenth-Century Social Reform: A Tory Interpretation of History', *Past and Present*, 31 (1965), p. 39 ff.

[2] R. H. Murray, *Studies in the English Social and Political Thinkers of the Nineteenth Century* (Cambridge, 1929), i, 378; G. Wallas, *The Life of Francis*

Throughout the period the basic orthodoxy of *laissez-faire* influenced colonial as well as British views. In the Australian colonies so much had always been done and was expected to be done by the government, that even imperial officials become convinced that the full effects of *laissez-faire* would cripple colonial development and, at least in the short term, have illiberal effects in practice. Colonists, though with few exceptions unprepared to defend their vital interests in an academically original or sophisticated way, showed lively partisan concern for the economic mechanism which they knew was so dependent upon the action of governments at many levels. They naturally insisted on protection for delicate colonial growths and fully appreciated that the imperial government was in a uniquely powerful position to foster or destroy their hopes. Incessant demands for direct assistance and indirect patronage were made, and a constructive official response was confidently expected. The workings of the transportation system had from the beginning woven in Australia a tapestry of government design. Now, when colonial advance had opened up new possibilities, revised conceptions seemed to be called for lest dull continuance of outmoded paternal schemes itself produce an expensive acceleration of official growth. Sometimes the government was drawn into new fields of activity through the sheer absence of other competent or credible agencies. Often, to the alarm of those at home determined to reduce even existing commitments, the inexorable spread of settlement brought about a costly reduplication of necessary services. Even to set up, stabilize, or regulate what was intended eventually to become autonomous brought about greater government participation, restriction, or intervention. Neither colonial officials nor the Colonial Office were unenthusiastic about their imperial mission. Yet, as the systematic colonizers were later to discover, it was a baffling task to balance development, expenditure, and aspiration to the mutual benefit of mother country and colony.[1]

It is dangerous to overstress the part played by speculative thought in shaping lives and institutions; but when James Mill advised

---

Place 1771–1854 (London, 1898), p. 178; *H.R.A.* III/ii/350, Macquarie–Sorell, 24 Sept. 1818; J. D. Lang, *Accounts of Steps taken in England*, etc. (Sydney, 1831); A. de Tocqueville, *Democracy in America* (ed. N.Y. 1961), i, 30–32.

[1] C. D. W. Goodwin, *Economic Enquiry in Australia* (Duke, 1966), esp. Ch. 9, 'The State and Economic Growth'; Kittrell, art. cit., p. 615; N. D. McLachlan, 'The Role of Government in New South Wales 1788–1855' (London Univ. Ph.D. thesis, 1957), esp. Section II, 'Government activity'.

Edward Strachey in 1819 to send out some of Bentham's works to Elphinstone, then engaged in the work of improving Indian administration, it was found that William Erskine had already attended to this a year earlier. In New South Wales Macquarie, long harried by the Treasury's repeated 'positive commands' to make every possible retrenchment in the colonies' 'most enormous' expenses, was succeeded by Sir Thomas Brisbane, who desired above all to institute systematic and economical reform.[1] His Colonial Secretary, Frederick Goulburn, was an ardent reader of 'Adam Smith, Ricardo, and other writers of Political Economy'.[2]

Brisbane was delighted with his appointment and enthusiastically outlined his plans to friends at home. In a time of economic recovery and relative political liberalism, when 'Prosperity' Robinson was bringing down cheerfully optimistic budgets and Wilmot Horton set on a course of restless colonial experimentation, the new governor might well have hoped for much. Bathurst, however, was afraid he would fall into Macquarie's 'great Error', and begged well-wishers to remind him that the colony, for all its growing interest and claims, was still a place of punishment and reform. The imperial penal aim was paramount.[3]

Brisbane soon decided that Australia was the finest field in the world for the 'application of Political Economy to the purposes of Life', and determined to extend to 'these remote Regions', still largely unexplored, the beneficial influence of economic science. He regretted that he had not arrived in time to collaborate with Bigge in preparing the formal and detailed recommendations from which so much was expected. Macquarie's 'system' he entirely condemned, and was horrified to learn, for example, that large quantities of grain were regularly imported. Resolving to call forth 'the energies of the place' in accordance with the principles of the immortal Adam Smith, he

---

[1] T. S. Ashton, *The Industrial Revolution* (Oxford, 1948), p. 22; Sir T. E. Colebrooke, *The Life of the Hon. Mountstuart Elphinstone* (London, 1884), ii, 111 f.; K. Ballhatchet, *Social Policy and Social Change in Western India 1817–1830* (Oxford, 1957), and E. T. Stokes, *The English Utilitarians and India* (Oxford, 1959), provide detailed studies of Indian administrative achievements; Mitchell Library mf. A/1626–7 *Letters of Sir Thomas Brisbane* and *P.M.G.* 1/1 for full exposition of his principles.

[2] S. J. Butlin, *The Foundations of the Australian Monetary System, 1788–1851* (Melbourne, 1953), p. 146.

[3] W. D. Jones, *Prosperity Robinson* (London, 1967), esp. Ch. 4 'Economics with a heart'; B. M. Add. MSS. (Bathurst Papers) Loan 57/14/1732, Wellington–Bathurst, 19 Oct. 1823; 57/64/13, Bathurst–Sir George Murray, 11 Nov. 1822.

hoped to repay all the past expenses of the mother country. The net-work of 'plundering John Bull' which he blamed his predecessor for tolerating, especially in the key Engineer's Department, must be forever stamped out. In two years costs would be considerably re-duced if only he could prevail against military incapacity and the dishonesty and inefficiency of his officials. Australia had advantages of climate 'superior to the most favored Nations', an extent of territory, and a command of manual labour 'beyond any other State'. It was monstrous that the government had hitherto supported the people, rather than the people the government. It was surely not Utopian to plan for local effort to supply the needs of the whole population and to provide a large surplus. This surplus would be to the present advantage of convict labourer, overseer, settler and Crown alike, and would give the colony a sure and permanent base for future growth. There were no limits to his vision. Australia's 'incalculable' capabilities, if exploited, could render Great Britain independent of all foreign nations. There was 'boundless scope for the Philanthropist, the political Economist, and the Philosopher'.[1]

Throughout his short administration Brisbane clung to the satis-faction that he studied every new measure in principle before putting it into effect. The wider view he sought became blurred as practical detail obscured his treasured image. Macquarie's groundwork had been sounder and more thorough than the critics were willing to grant.[2] The equilibrium of the Old Viceroy's plans for development had been disturbed less by his age, exhaustion, faults of temperament, or lack of imagination, than by the impact of a number of new factors, most of which were quite beyond his control. The arrival of the Bigge Commission had in fact left his system of personal rule without its reference point. Brisbane, for all his sanguine hopes, was destined for an equal disillusionment.

Brisbane earnestly turned his mind toward the problem of blend-ing into one peaceful and prosperous development the 'amendment of convicts and a system of productive labour'. He discovered, as did James Stirling in a different context at Swan River, how far apart dreams could drift from reality. Brisbane's insight, actually inherited in part from Macquarie, but which his biographer insists came to him instantaneously while he was 'listening to the gospel preached by the

[1] *P.M.G.* 1/1, Brisbane–Craufurd, 14 Feb. 1822, 18 May 1822, 9 Mar. 1822; *M.L.* mf. A/1627, Brisbane–Bruce, 28 Mar. 1822.
[2] *P.M.G.* 1/1, Brisbane–Craufurd, July 1822, and July 1823.

excellent chaplain', seemed to him a comprehensive blue-print.[1] It was a scheme 'for the profitable and pleasurable employment of the convicts', whereby a task force of clearing-gangs, composed of about twenty men each, would provide the means of creating civilization and public services for a maturing community. He placed additional confidence in an adaptation of Macquarie's assignment system, and ruled that land should be granted only to those settlers prepared to keep a convict labourer, free of all expense to government, for every hundred acres of their grant. Thus convict labour would be applied to convict support, the costs of administration met, and English capital attracted by the knowledge that no shortage of labour would be allowed to curtail the prospects of pastoral and agricultural projects.[2] It was a typical colonial paradox that, just when Brisbane was ready to provide a regular supply of labour to private ventures, Horton, himself an ardent theorizer, was taking practical steps to segregate convicts in distant penal establishments in accordance with Bigge's suggestions.[3]

Brisbane's administration saw many changes and experiments, some of which turned out badly. For the governor, disillusionment soon began. The challenge of office, which he had coveted since 1815, turned to ashes. His subordinates 'unhinged' his new and necessary reforms with their petty rivalries, selfish pursuit of landed property and government contracts, and inability to understand his more universal intentions. His genial remarks were misunderstood and distorted, and he felt obliged to withdraw from those unofficial contacts with colonists which might otherwise have led to fruitful collaboration. Fortunately in astronomy he found a science of a less dismal kind to fall back on.[4] The obstructive alliances of offended factions, the Douglass affair, the attacks of the *Morning Chronicle*, and the feeling that the Treasury and Colonial Office distrusted his judgement and hampered the workings of his arrangements, completed his disgust. It was no consolation, as Horton too discovered, that progress, however hopeful, brought with it insoluble political dilemmas. The

[1] Ed. Rev. N. Tasker, *Reminiscences of Sir T. M. Brisbane* (Edinburgh, 1860), p. 47.
[2] *P.M.G.* 1/1, Brisbane–Craufurd, 18 May 1822, 14 Sept. 1822, 8 Apr. 1823, 1 May 1823; *H.R.A.* I/x/723, Brisbane–Earl of Buchan, 30 Aug. 1822.
[3] *H.R.A.* I/x/791, Bathurst–Brisbane, 9 Sept. 1822; C.O. 201/155/500, Minute by Horton, 7 July 1824.
[4] *P.M.G.* 1/1, Brisbane–Craufurd, 21 June 1823, 29 July 1823, 22 November 1823.

governor could not make 'the Departments pull cordially together'. In the course of introducing system, regularity, and rational demarcation into the scattered establishments, the key office of Colonial Secretary had become 'much too overgrown'. Frederick Goulburn's activity and talent had to be weighed against his sarcasm and irritability. He resented the influence which enabled the Macarthurs to overrule local authority in obtaining handsome land-grants; and his attempts to evade and delay the implementation of these orders brought down upon his governor sharp rebukes from Downing St. Brisbane grew sure that transient military officials could never bring about the basic reorganization which sound principles demanded. Few soldiers were capable or willing to study the science of Political Economy. His critics, mistaking his liberal intentions and 'deepest reflection' for lack of attention and laziness, complained to the Colonial Office of his ineffectiveness. Only a new, permanent, and civilian system offered hope, he told the Secretary of State.[1]

* * * * *

The Colonial Office, continually subject to the criticism of retrenchers, could not evade the ultimate responsibility of forming, if not an economic policy, at least a set of coherent goals. Reliance had perforce to be placed on the successive governors, not only for that supply of regular information upon which piecemeal decisions could be based, but for the execution of wider imperial projects concerning trade, investment, labour, land and currency. The governors, in turn, though eager for the most part to exercise local initiative, were only too aware of the tensions imposed by the process of economic change and of the need to have authoritative support in their dialogue with the Treasury or their own subordinates. Private and corporate influence could be brought to bear at all levels, but it was to the Secretary of State that most clients eventually had recourse. Goulburn's *Blue Books* began to show, year by year, the profile of a freer economy, whose progress, fluctuations and imbalances had to be taken into account. Bigge's liberating reports were accepted, private enterprise and capital encouraged, and the official horizon clearly lifted beyond that of merely penal or emancipist economy. Optimism was frequently exaggerated, but it was not altogether out of place.

[1] M.L. mf. A/1627, Brisbane–Bruce, 26 July 1823, 31 Dec. 1823, 30 Jan. 1824; Brisbane–Bathurst, 28 July 1824; *P.M.G.* 1/1, Brisbane–Craufurd, 13 May 1825.

Brisbane's successor, Darling, soon to garner a dour reputation for unimaginative thoroughness, was no economic doctrinaire. Yet he was as impressed with his 'infant Empire' as Governor Arthur had been with Van Diemen's Land. New South Wales, he wrote, was taking 'gigantic strides' to wealth 'which is power'.[1] Certainly both Darling and Arthur grasped the fact that local economic prosperity could give them relief from a host of private and official supervisors.

Though the central government was generally reluctant to take grand imperial initiatives, it rarely interposed deliberate obstacles to private enterprise. Horton, later condemned as a meddler by the systematic colonizers, actively fostered schemes which had their origins in many sources, and showed great readiness to encourage experiments in more fields than that of emigration.[2] Notable were the Australian Agricultural Company and the Van Diemen's Land Company, which had their counterparts in other regions of the Empire.[3] The object was of course to employ British capital profitably as well as constructively. The Companies would not have been launched but for the interest of intelligent and lively men such as John Smith who, avoiding disaster in the banking collapse of 1825, went about, according to Marianne Thornton, like a 'beneficent genius in a fairy tale' not only promising impossibilities, but 'always performing them'.[4] Yet the accusations that the Agricultural Company was a Macarthur job were not altogether groundless, for the venture had their strong backing. In London young John shared fully the contemporary interest in economic doctrine. He attended McCulloch's lectures, along with James Mill, Hume, Hobhouse, Huskisson, Robinson, and those 'young Tories' whom the master rejoiced to see. Indeed he introduced Horton to McCulloch and discussed with them 'the impolicy of the monopoly or mercantile system, as noticed by Adam Smith'. His interest had its practical side, for he also dined

---

[1] M.L. mf. A/1627, Darling–Brisbane, 4 Feb. 1826.
[2] D. Pike, op. cit., p. 37; D. K. Fieldhouse, *The Colonial Empires* (London, 1966), pp. 251–4.
[3] S. H. Roberts, *History of Australian Land Settlement 1788–1920* (Melbourne 1924), pp. 50–70; N. Macdonald, *Canada 1763–1841* (London, 1939), p. 270 ff., and Ch. VIII.
[4] B. E. Fitzpatrick, *British Imperialism and Australia 1783–1833* (London 1939), p. 18; and Chs. 6 and 7; J. A. S. Leighton–Boyce, *Smith the Bankers 1658–1958* (London, 1958), pp. 135–6; Marianne Thornton–Hannah More, 12 Dec. 1825, in ed. T. S. Ashton and R. S. Sayers, *Papers in English Monetary History* (Oxford, 1953), p. 104.

with Horton and Spring Rice, and later 'seated on one of the large sofas' at the University Club talked till 2.15 in the morning about New South Wales and its prospects, the recall of Sir Thomas Brisbane, and Peel's plans to send out henceforth only 'men capable of labour'.[1] In the colony the family formed the backbone of the colonial committee and their strategy was carefully planned.[2]

Horton's reception of the Company plans was friendly, and the Colonial Office was ready to grant special advantages, as its proposals seemed 'so exactly to correspond' with the recommendations of Commissioner Bigge.[3] But there were critics. The *Australian*[4] from the beginning characterized the company as a monopolistic Leviathan which threatened the balanced progress of the colony. Forbes told Horton after the company had been active for a year that its local representatives had, without introducing much capital, disturbed the economic equilibrium of the colony by manipulating stock prices. Its privileges had discouraged emigration. He distrusted the motives of the Macarthurs and contrasted the reality with the expectations that had been entertained of the company's outlay bringing about improvements in stock-breeding, the general reduction of prices, and the swelling of a 'good wholesome population' by the introduction of 'people of skill'.[5] In 1831, when the company had shaken off the control of its colonial committee and was emerging from the near-ruin to which it had come under its unfortunate first agent, Robert Dawson, E. S. Hall described the whole project as a brilliant victory for the Macarthurs. They had in effect created a set of buyers in London for their sheep, cattle and horses.[6] By then John Smith was complaining to the Secretary of State that the Company had in seven years expended more than £230,000 with scant return.[7] But not all was disillusionment. Much painful effort had gone into the venture. Even the Macarthurs were glad enough to be relieved of their responsibility, and rejoiced at the prospective change in fortunes which followed the

---

[1] Macvey Napier, *Correspondence* (London, 1879), p. 39; M.L. (Macarthur Papers) A/2911, Jno. Macarthur–Elizabeth, 25 Apr. 1825.

[2] M. H. Ellis, *John Macarthur* (Sydney, 1955), pp. 492–4, 510–11; M.L. A/4314, Minute book of Australian Agricultural Co. 1824–29; A/4315, Correspondence of Colonial Committee.

[3] *H.R.A.* I/xi/305, Bathurst–Brisbane, 13 July 1824, transmitting 5 Geo. IV lxxxvi.

[4] 3 Mar. 1825.

[5] C.O. 201/178/495, Forbes–Horton, 10 Sept. 1826.

[6] C.O. 201/223/453, Hall–Goderich, 21 Sept. 1831.

[7] C.O. 201/222/512, Smith–Goderich, 6 June 1831.

passing of the long drought and the appointment of Sir Edward Parry.[1]

If in young John Macarthur the Company had a persuasive advocate, in Wilmot Horton such enterprises found a receptive mind. In principle the government would remain faithful to its general attitude of accommodation, but time and experience brought many practical lessons. Some radically affected official attitudes. Others were ill-learnt or remained only half-remembered. In 1824 Horton took considerable care to set the companies off to a good start. Their ambitious prospectuses were examined in detail. The directors were invited to interviews with Lord Bathurst, who cannily pared down their estimates. Parliamentary legislation was necessary, and elaborate charters had to be drawn up. Important questions were at stake, concerning not only commercial and pastoral development, but also colonial order and government. The companies sought very wide terms of reference and hoped to take leading parts in the process of colonization. The conditions of their land-grants and convict assignments and duties had to be determined. Rivalries between them had to be ironed out, and the privileges they sought carefully scrutinized.[2]

The Van Diemen's Land Company lost no time in asserting its claims, purchasing stock in Europe, and seeking what advantages it could. Its competent spokesman, Edward Curr, wrote strongly but intelligently of its expectations. Besides the all important wool, it hoped to partake in such activities as mining, whaling and sealing, distilling and brewing, lending money on mortgage, advancing money to the colonial legislature, and contracting for public works.[3] Curr knew the chaotic conditions of colonial survey and argued firmly for conditions affecting land and valuations to be fixed at home in England. He seems to have confused Horton, who tried to remedy his own inexperience of colonial conditions and geography by consulting

[1] Ellis, op. cit., pp. 510–11, 516–21; M.L. A/4316 Correspondence with Robert Dawson;—for his version cf. *Statement*, etc., and *The Present State of Australia* (London, 1830); Roberts, op. cit., p. 53 ff.; J. Gregson, *The Australian Agricultural Company 1824–1875* (Sydney 1907), pp. 27–54; A. Parry, *Parry of the Arctic* (London, 1963), pp. 136–75.

[2] C.O. 280/2/5, J. Smith & Co., Plans for establishing a Company; /11, J. Macarthur–Horton, Private, 23 Apr. 1824; /18, Smith–Bathurst, 30 Apr. 1824; /34, Smith–Bathurst, 30 Apr. 1824; /34, Smith–Bathurst, 22 May 1824; /52, Smith–Bathurst, 12 July 1824; /339, Stephen's draft of Charter, 27 July 1824; /130 Draft of a Bill, etc.

[3] C.O. 202/13/102, Horton–Curr, 25 Mar. 1825; /121, Bathurst–V.D.L. Co., 15 Apr. 1825; C.O. 280/1/6, Pearse–Bathurst, 22 May 1824; /22, Pearse–Horton, 11 Feb. 1825; /49, Curr–Bathurst, 22 Mar. 1825; /80, Curr–Horton, 30 June 1825; and his book *An Account of the Colony of Van Diemen's Land* (London, 1824).

ex-Governor Sorell. Sorell, with certain misgivings about the company's becoming too mighty, was enthusiastic about the opportunity it seemed to offer for colonial development.[1]

John Smith defended his monopolistic demands on the grounds that such a small colony could not stand the sudden introduction of extensive competition. John Macarthur, vexed at the rival company's more fortunate arrangements for obtaining fresh stock, stressed the desire of 'several of our directors, who are also Directors of the East India Company' to work coal mines in New South Wales, 'under a belief that they may facilitate Steam Navigation throughout the Eastern Seas' by loading empty convict ships with Australian coal for India.[2] Mining concessions were granted, but not before jurisdictional problems forced the Colonial Office to consult the Treasury and even the Duchy of Lancaster.[3]

There were voices of caution. Huskisson at the Board of Trade approved the granting of mining rights to the Agricultural Company, but thought permission should be refused for 'their engaging in the Fisheries, or in brewing, or in distilling'.[4] He did not object to the Van Diemen's Land Company's project of providing *bona fide* loans, as long as credit was not used as a springboard to obtain 'something like a partnership' in other enterprises.[5] James Stephen thought that the V.D.L. Company had driven an 'extravagantly good' bargain with the government in its obtaining handsome commutations of quit rent in place of maintaining convicts, and he urged the use of every precaution to preclude speculation in the formation and practice of the companies.[6]

Once the first steps had been taken, the Colonial Office found that the path of colonization by company was a very thorny one. Continual protests were made about the shortage and quality of convict labour available. Bathurst and Stephen had continually to resist demands for monopolies, e.g. of coal mining. In general they tried to

[1] C.O. 280/1/90, Curr–Bathurst, 1 Sept. 1825; /142, Sorell–Horton, 29 Jan., 1825; /172, Sorell–Bathurst, 25 Apr. 1825; /176, Sorell–Barnard, Private, 4 Aug. 1825.

[2] C.O. 280/2/46, Smith–Bathurst, 12 July 1824; /54, Smith–Horton, 31 Mar. 1825; /70, Macarthur–Horton, Private, 9 Apr. 1825.

[3] C.O. 280/2/100, Hay–Smith, 7 July 1825; /324, Horton–Harrison, Private, 23 May 1825; C.O. 324/145/119, Horton–Bexley, 19 Apr. 1825.

[4] C.O. 280/2/318, Huskisson–Horton, 24 Apr. 1825.

[5] C.O. 280/1/118, Huskisson–Horton, 29 Apr. 1825.

[6] C.O. 280/1/134, Stephen–Horton, Minute, 8 July 1825; /124, Stephen–Horton, 9 Mar. 1825.

delegate decisions on particular matters to the colonial governors.[1] But predictably the colonial and British representatives of the companies claimed special consideration and sought to maintain their interest with government. They never hesitated to approach the Secretary of State, especially when projects ran into difficulties.[2]

The governors for their part accepted the advent of the companies and their patronage from the Colonial Office with cautious optimism at best. They knew that the introduction of capital could only benefit the colonies, but they realized the danger of a local *imperium in imperio* which could exert powerful pressure at home. They were grateful when clear central decisions made it unnecessary for them to antagonize either the companies or their critics, but this too rarely proved possible. The progress of the ventures inevitably led to a host of new problems as well as keen disputes, usually concerning the site of company land-grants.[3] Arthur thought the Colonial Office had been misled into giving far too handsome terms to the V.D.L. Company by way of set-off for the maintenance of convicts, and he correctly foresaw great trouble over the first misguided choice of land in the rugged north-west of the island. Yet he felt a certain responsibility for the welfare of the company in this and other matters. The Colonial Office, too, was ready to reach a compromise wherever possible.[4]

By 1827, as Hay admitted in reply to Arthur's representations, the Colonial Office had every reason to be wary of company plans. James Stephen emphatically agreed.[5] In spite of good intentions, relations seemed destined to be frayed. Even Sir Edward Parry's friendship

[1] C.O. 202/18/2, Hay–Smith, 8 June 1826; /13/134, Horton–Brickwood, 4 Apr. 1825—on coal *H.R.A.* I/xii/237, Bathurst–Darling, 29 Apr. 1826; C.O. 324/85/61, Hay–Macarthur, 25 July 1826 and C.O. minute on C.O. 201/187/462, Nov. 1827.

[2] C.O. 280/14/275, Pearse-Huskisson, 16 Nov. 1827; /283, long précis by Short on the V.D.L. Co.; /358, Arthur–Hay, Private, 9 Oct. 1826; *H.R.A.* I/xiv/541, Darling–Murray, 27 Dec. 1828; C.O. 201/205/353, Brickwood–Murray, 10 June 1829.

[3] *H.R.A.* I/xi/305, Bathurst–Brisbane, 13 July 1824; /563, Bathurst–Brisbane, 17 Apr. 1825, enc. Charter of A. Ag. Co. and recommendation of Robert Dawson; /591, Bathurst–Brisbane, 18 May 1825, on land, survey etc.; *H.R.A.* III/v/25, Arthur–Bathurst, 2 Jan. 1826.

[4] *H.R.A.* III/v/25, Arthur–Bathurst, 2 Jan. 1826; /132, Arthur–Bathurst, 4 Apr. 1826; /394, Arthur–Bathurst, 14 Nov. 1826; /398, Arthur–Bathurst, 15 Nov. 1826; /473, Bathurst–Arthur, 7 Jan. 1827; C.O. 323/157/169, Arthur–Hay, 26 Jan. 1829; *H.R.A.* III/vi/14, Bathurst–Arthur, 18 Apr. 1827; /251, Huskisson–Arthur, 13 Oct. 1827.

[5] C.O. 323/146/353, Arthur–Hay, 9 Oct. 1826; *H.R.A.* III/v/616, Hay–Arthur, 21 Mar. 1827; C.O. 280/14/105, Stephen–Hay, 19 Mar. 1827.

with Governor Darling did not prevent a bitter tone invading the course of negotiations concerning such matters as survey, arrangements for education, police and clergy, and the reorganization of the company's holdings which Howick saw could be combined with their taking up some of the former Church and School lands.[1] It had by this time become apparent that a new wave of corporate enterprise was projected. Swan River and other schemes had cast grave doubts on the ability of the Colonial Office to deal with such business effectively. Stephen told Hay bluntly that 'the whole system of colonization by companies is founded on a mistaken principle'. It combined two baneful characteristics, absenteeism and the alienation of land not intended for immediate occupancy. He thought that time had shown that too much government encouragement of companies was against the best interest of the colonies and their settlers. It is hard to believe that this concern for the welfare of both did not play a large part in making him and Hay wary of any grandiose colonizing plan, even if the proposals claimed to have a base in some completely new principle of 'systematic' colonization.[2]

*   *   *   *   *

Colonists, capitalists, and governors showed themselves fully aware of the commercial importance of both public aid and official expenditure. This held for the maritime industries which were so important in the lives of the colonies, but which tended to develop a momentum of their own.[3] It was also true of wool, from which by 1831 so much had confidently come to be anticipated. Even here, capital and encouragement was not enough, and Arthur made out a powerful case for the speedy provision at public expense of an adequate labour force. Dr. Turnbull, a member of his Political Economy Committee, succinctly expressed a common view when he wrote: 'The colony is poor, because it cannot export, and it cannot export, . . . because it cannot produce cheaply, and it cannot produce cheaply because labour is dear, because it is scarce; therefore a supply of efficient

---

[1] C.O. 201/214/425, Smith–Murray, 23 Mar. 1830; *H.R.A.* I/xv/50, Murray–Darling, 2 July 1829; /429, Murray–Darling, 21 Apr. 1830; /581, Darling–Murray, 13 July 1830, enc. Parry–MacLeay, 13 Apr. 1830; /714, Murray–Darling, 20 Aug. 1830; Roberts, op. cit., pp. 54–8; J. F. Campbell, 'The First Decade of the Australian Agricultural Company, 1824–1830', R.A.H.S. IX (1923), 113 ff.

[2] C.O. 201/214/177, Stephen–Hay, 10 Apr. 1830.

[3] G. Greenwood, *Early American-Australian Relations* (Melbourne, 1944), pp. 79 ff., 144 ff.

labour will enrich the colony and make it prosperous.'[1] Government support had to be generous, and at all levels.

In fact the home authorities had long responded to colonial pressures. In 1819, for example, even Vansittart had recommended plans for viticulture in New South Wales, and the Treasury was ready to admit samples of Blaxland's colonial wines into England on the same favourable terms given to Cape wines.[2] Blaxland restlessly sought a colonial staple and his incessant correspondence with the Colonial Office, Treasury, and Board of Trade was always carefully examined.[3] He won special concessions for his preparation of wines for export.[4] His application for a reduction in the duty paid on rape seed from £39. 10s. to £1 per ton was successful, but his request for a monopoly of tobacco production was turned down.[5] The prospects of tobacco looked attractive and became a great talking point. The Macarthurs' London representatives, Donaldson and Wilkinson, Co., sought to convince the Colonial Office that Australia could take the place of the United States if the right steps were taken.[6] But the Board of Trade would not accept the bait and, pointing out that revenue questions were involved, referred the Colonial Office to the Treasury, who in their turn proved unwilling to make exceptions for the Australian colonies, even when Governor Darling forwarded a strong and persuasive memorial from the colonists.[7]

There were many other attempts during the 1820s to set up colonial trading and commercial concerns. The fortunes of such enterprises as Robert Campbell and Company and the Scottish Australian Company of Leith were directly influenced by government decisions, even if not under official patronage: and all found it necessary to cultivate the interest of both the colonial and the central administration.[8]

[1] C.O. 280/29/168, Arthur–Goderich, 9 July 1831.

[2] C.O. 201/97/117, Vansittart–Bathurst, Private, 23 Feb. 1819; 201/110/163, Harrison–Horton, 10 Dec. 1822.   [3] e.g. C.O. 201/187/233 ff.; 197/110 ff., 1828.

[4] C.O. 201/195/246, Lack–Twiss, 2 July 1828; 202/23/30, Twiss-Blaxland.

[5] C.O. 201/195/244, Lack–Leveson Gower, 28 Feb. 1828; /250, Lack–Twiss, 30 Aug. 1828; C.O. 202/23/40, Twiss–Blaxland, 3 Sept. 1828; 201/206/45, Blaxland–Twiss, 14 Jan. 1829.

[6] C.O. 201/197/235, Donaldson & Co.–Leveson Gower, 6 May 1828; /269, Nov. 1828, Memorial.

[7] C.O. 201/204/168, Lack–Twiss, 4 Apr. 1829; /250/266, Dawson–Twiss, 22 May 1829; H.R.A. I/xv/340, Darling–Murray, 23 Jan. 1830; C.O. 202/26/1, Hay–Stewart, 21 June 1830; /8 Hay–Stewart, 7 July 1830; H.R.A. I/xv/661, Murray–Darling, 8 Aug. 1830, enc. Stewart–Hay, 27 July 1830.

[8] M. Steven, *Merchant Campbell 1796–1846: A Study of Colonial Trade* (Melbourne, 1965), p. 246 ff.; D. S. Macmillan, *Scotland and Australia 1788–1850* (Oxford, 1967), pp. 159–60, 117 and Chs. IV–VI.

Colonial ventures had to stand or fall by their own resources and by the imagination and determination they brought to bear against natural and human obstacles. But government policy could encourage or discourage development at many levels. If tariffs remained in the last analysis an imperial responsibility, adjustments and concessions were readily made, largely in response to the growth of local administration and colonial pressure.[1]

Commissioner Bigge was keen to encourage colonial commerce and the development of profitable exports. His report on trade contained the evidence of people engaged in a wide variety of enterprises, and he examined a good range of questions such as duties, port regulations, and the economic effects of the transportation system and limitations arising from the colonies' being situated within the limits of the East India Company's charter.[2] In the implementation of his recommendations the Colonial Office necessarily played a key long-term role. Horton was eager to follow Bigge's advice and reacted favourably to colonial suggestions, but he could not always fire other departments or officials with his enthusiasm. Thus, though duties on wool and other colonial products were relaxed or conditions otherwise relaxed, the Board of Trade refused to eliminate wool duties altogether.[3]

The Board of Trade was perhaps closer than most other departments to having a definite economic policy by 1830, but it was at this time concerned more with its advisory and consultative functions than with executive action. Its energies were expended in difficult negotiations with the French, Dutch and United States and it was either baffled or uninterested in the infant commerce of the Australian colonies, whose position as convict colonies in the Eastern hemisphere in any case created puzzling anomalies. In James Stephen they shared a common counsel with the Colonial Office, and the Secretary of State was a member of the Board.[4] Piecemeal decisions were of course given, about governors' economic recommendations,

[1] J. A. La Nauze, 'Australian Tariffs and Imperial Control', *The Economic Record*, XXIV (1948), pp. 1–17, 218–35.

[2] e.g. C.O. 201/128, 129, 132 Evidence.

[3] *H.R.A.* I/x/782, Brisbane–Bathurst, 7 Sept. 1822, enc. Memorial from Landholders and Proprietors, etc.; I/x/793, Bathurst–Brisbane, 9 Sept. 1822; I/xi/60, Bathurst–Brisbane 24 Mar. 1823; C.O. 201/153/133, Lack–Horton, 3 Apr. 1824; J. Ker, art. cit., pp. 18–36.

[4] L. M. Brown, 'The Policy of the Board of Trade in Relation to British Tariffs and Foreign Trade, 1830–1842' (London Univ. Ph.D. thesis, 1955), pp. 21, 31, 438; Young, op. cit., pp. 196–200.

for instance, and friendly advice given, as in 1827 when Hay was advised that a proposed seal for Van Diemen's Land portraying convicts landing might be considered tactless by the colonists.[1]

The Board of Trade could be helpful. In 1822 it forwarded reports from the consul at Rio and showed how ships returning from Australia with cargoes of wheat and coal could avoid paying foreign dues.[2] But it was also cautious. When Australian merchants raised the question of the payment of duty on tea and the granting of bounty on linen imported at the colony, the Board pointed out that, though the colonies were within the limits of the East India Company charter, they could not be considered as in the East Indies. They could not or would not make exceptions in their favour, or award them some special status between Europe, America and India.[3]

The contacts between the Government of India and the Australian colonies were largely routine, to the disappointment of some imperial visionaries. The great imperial link which appealed to so many who corresponded with the Colonial Office did not emerge, but individual and corporate ventures were launched with varying success. Such was the activity of the East India Trade Committee of 1823–4 which was instrumental in the colonization experiments in Northern Australia.[4] When the Colonial Office took action to remove the disabilities which the colonists resented, especially that restricting colonial shipping to vessels over 350 tons, no objection was raised.[5]

The Board of Trade clearly had no intention of supplanting the Colonial Office. In 1826 the government was approached by French merchants about their Eastern trade and the effect of commercial treaties then in negotiation.[6] Huskisson told Horton that he had always understood the Eastern colonies were the responsibility of the colonial department. 'At the Board of Trade we know very little of their concerns.'[7] There was at this time at the Board of Trade great

[1] C.O. 323/149/496, Lack–Hay, 5 June 1827.

[2] C.O. 201/144/36, Lack–Horton, 23 Oct. 1823.

[3] C.O. 201/144/40, Lack–Horton, 28 Nov. 1823; 202/11/76, Horton–Lack, 12 Aug. 1823; /144, Horton–Whiston and Hewitt, 2 Dec. 1823.

[4] e.g. C.O. 201/144/371, Larpent, etc.–Horton, 16 Dec. 1823.

[5] H.R.A. I/x/18, Macquarie–Bathurst, 1 Mar. 1819, enc. Memorial of Merchants, 19 Nov. 1818; C.O. 201/97/266, T. Courtenay–Bathurst, 22 June 1819; J. M. Ward, British Policy in the South Pacific 1786–1893 (Sydney, 1948), p. 28 ff.

[6] C.O. 201/179/24, Hervell–Bathurst, 20 May 1826; /175/205, Lack–Hay, 26 July 1826, enc. Stephen–Lack, 22 July 1826.

[7] C.O. 325/6/67, Horton-Huskisson, 1 Aug. 1826; /70, Huskisson–Horton, 2 Aug. 1826.

impatience with the whole subject of its responsibilities concerning the *minutiae* of colonial arrangements, James Stephen could be relied upon for advice about particular cases. The troublesome trade of New Zealand and Australian questions were best left to the Secretary of State.[1] Efforts were made to clarify the legal position, but a policy of *quieta non movere* won the day. Hay was willing to concede that the uncertainty and confusion caused great inconvenience, but discussions were interrupted by Huskisson's illness. Neither Bathurst nor Hay wanted to foster an accession of foreign shipping around the Australian coast. Clearly more was at stake than conditions of trade.[2] Even at the end of the decade when foreign contacts with Australia were expanding, the Board of Trade would not, at least in answer to individual inquiries from entrepreneurs such as the insistent Peter Dillon, commit itself to official interpretations of what it still maintained was a vexed and difficult point.[3] By this time, the Board's statistical department under G. R. Porter was anxious to obtain detailed colonial statistics. With a certain poetic justice Hay maintained that the Colonial Office Blue Books contained all that could possibly be wanted.[4]

*   *   *   *   *

The decade saw important changes, beginnings and experiments in the field of banking and finance. An enlightened mercantilism was perhaps the best and most welcome policy for colonial expansion. But many functions which in a more mature society would have been carried out by established bankers and private entrepreneurs were in New South Wales performed by the government. Goods sold to the Crown were in effect an export to Britain. The Commissariat acted in its multifarious workings as far more than an organization concerned only to ensure supplies for convicts and soldiers in extended penal settlements.[5] Barter and dealings carried out in kind long

[1] C.O. 201/175/203, Lack–Hay, 6 June 1826; /204/170, Lack–Twiss, 23 Apr. 1829; Young, op. cit., pp. 196–200.

[2] C.O. 324/93/35, Hay–Grant, 15 Sept. 1826; /33, Hay–Stephen, 15 Sept. 1826; /35, Hay–Huskisson, 27 Sept. 1826; 324/85/73, Hay–Huskisson, Private, 1 Oct. 1826; /100, Hay–Grant, 14 Mar. 1827; 201/187/393, H. Donnison–Hay, 21 June 1827; /185/389, Stephen–Hay, 27 June 1827.

[3] C.O. 201/215/192, 5 Apr. 1830; 202/24/193, Hay–Lack, 3 May 1830; 201/214/82, Lack–Hay, 11 June 1830; 202/26/2, Hay–Dillon, 22 June 1830.

[4] C.O. 323/214/67, Auckland–Hay, 23 June 1832; /81, Lack–Howick 27 Aug. 1832; /82, Minute by Hay.

[5] K. Dallas, 'Transportation and Colonial Income', *H.S.A.N.Z.* III (1949), pp. 297, 305; R. M. Hartwell, *The Economic Development of Van Diemen's Land 1820–1850* (Melbourne, 1954), esp. Ch. 12; A. G. L. Shaw, op. cit., p. 260 ff.

remained central in colonial life, but progress naturally demanded more satisfactory and sophisticated means of exchange. The governors had of necessity become involved in continual attempts to control, develop and stabilize the primitive but complex financial system in process of evolution. There had been various suggestions for a more formal participation by government in banking. Very early after his arrival Macquarie, impressed by what Lord Caledon had told him of his banking arrangements at the Cape, and alarmed by the widespread use in New South Wales of unreliable private promissory notes, tried to set up a government Bank.[1] He was sharply told that the British government had 'many objections'. But the idea persisted and the Governor returned to his plan in 1816, when he obtained the backing of Judge-Advocate Wylde. The result of his actions, more positive than permissive, was the establishment of the Bank of New South Wales.[2]

Despite certain qualms about his powers to grant a charter which assured the shareholders of limited liability, Macquarie thought this development of 'more real benefit' to the colony than any other public measure. He recommended that, if things went well with the bank, the government 'should either become a party in it, or that it should at least make it the depository and Medium of all Government Monies and payments'.[3] The home government were ready to send out shipments of specie when necessary, and approved where they did not inspire the gradual emergence of a rational monetary system. They appreciated the difficulties which had led Macquarie to improvise methods for creating a more adequate and reliable local currency, such as the circulation of the 'holey-dollars' and restrictions on dollar exports.[4] It was recognized that the role of government expenditure was pre-eminent, at least until regular and staple exports could be developed. John Macarthur complained that 'our chief, indeed almost our only import is bills upon the Treasury'.[5] George Johnston

[1] E. H. D. Arndt, *Banking and Currency Development in South Africa 1652–1927* (Cape Town, 1928), Pt. I, Chs. 2 and 3; Pt. 2, Ch. 1; Bigge Appendix, C.O. 201/125/70 ff. Evidence of Wylde.

[2] Butlin, op. cit., pp. 76 ff., 108 ff.; *H.R.A.* I/vii/242, Macquarie–Castlereagh, 12 Mar. 1810; /264, Macquarie–Castlereagh, 30 Apr. 1810; /343, Macquarie–Liverpool, 27 Oct. 1810; /365, Liverpool–Macquarie, 26 July 1811; I/ix/215, Macquarie–Bathurst, 29 Mar. 1817; IV/i/234, Wylde–Goulburn, 31 Mar. 1817; I/x/347, Macquarie–Bathurst, 1 Sept. 1820, enc. Wylde–Bathurst, 3 Mar. 1817.

[3] *H.R.A.* I/ix/215, Macquarie–Bathurst, 29 Mar. 1817.

[4] *H.R.A.* I/ix/74, Macquarie–Bathurst, 22 Mar. 1819, enc. Port Regulations, 6 Feb. 1819.

[5] Macarthur–Davidson, 3 Sept. 1818, *Early Records*, p. 247.

told Wentworth that the whole value of colonial property in an 'immense gaol' could be jeopardized by the 'scratch of a pen' in Downing Street. But Bathurst, advised by the Crown lawyers that the governor had exceeded his powers, rejected the objectionable suggestion that a public bank was needed. Indeed, Macquarie's denial that the Bank 'was in any manner guaranteed by government' was somewhat doubtful, and Commissioner Bigge found it necessary to stress the invalidity of the charter. Brisbane was warned against renewing it, but found it inconvenient to discourage what had now become an important colonial institution.[1]

The incomplete experiment of the 'Dollar System' which began in 1822 was an ambitious if confused attempt to set up a uniform local circulation. The high conventional valuation of the dollar at 5s. made the coins a profitable import. It was planned to replace sterling in the colony with Spanish dollars, which Brisbane compared rhapsodically to 'the air we breathe'. He hoped that the change-over would be as easy and acceptable in practice as it was logical and beneficial in theory. But the Commissariat would accept dollars only at their estimated bullion value of 4s. 2d., and many colonists thought the experiment with 'a foreign coin of doubtful and fluctuating value' a misguided effort to reduce colonial expenses by depreciation all round. The Bank, now pursuing dangerously adventurous policies, complained that new doctrines were unjustly elevating 'an unauthorized and illegal circulating medium'. 'The money transactions of an infant Colony', write the Directors, 'can bear no comparison with those of the greatest and most Commercial Nation in the Universe'.[2]

It proved in any case difficult to establish a stable valuation for the dollar, even for use in government transactions. Brisbane told Bathurst that he had long delayed fixing the rate of the Spanish Dollar with reference to English Sterling because of decisions which he had heard were about to be made at home about imperial monetary systems.[3] In 1824 a Board of Commissariat officers appointed by Brisbane recommended a rate of 4s. 4d. which was the same as that ordered

[1] M.L. (Wentworth Papers), Johnston–Wentworth, 1 Mar. 1819; *H.R.A.* I/ix/840, Bathurst–Macquarie, 29 Oct. 1818; I/x/347, Macquarie–Bathurst, 1 Sept. 1820; I/xi/100, Bathurst–Brisbane, 31 July 1823; I/xi/586, Brisbane–Bathurst, 14 May 1825; Bigge, 3rd Report, 67.

[2] Butlin, op. cit., ch. 6; C.O.202/11/32, Horton–Harrison, 31 Mar. 1823; *Sydney Gazette*, 30 Aug. 1822; *H.R.A.* I/x/729, Brisbane–Bathurst, 2 Sept. 1822, enc. Memorials of Colonists and Bank of N.S.W.; I/xi/73, Bathurst–Brisbane, 31 Mar. 1823.

[3] *H.R.A.* I/xi/518, Brisbane–Bathurst, 9 Feb. 1825.

by the Treasury when a sterling exchange standard was imposed.[1] Early in 1825 the Treasury decided to introduce into the Empire 'a fixed and uniform medium of exchange for all transactions connected with the public service, in the place of the various fluctuating and anomalous currencies which had been created under the pressure of temporary emergency, or with views of local and peculiar expediency'. British silver and copper coin was to be circulated, convertible on demand into British gold coin through the medium of Commissariat Bills.[2] Bathurst told Brisbane that the government's object was to establish an 'unobjectionable and unvarying medium for the payment of the troops', and a 'uniform Currency in the whole of His Majesty's Foreign Possessions, founded upon and having reference to the currency of the United Kingdom'.[3] It was the wreck of Brisbane's dollar experiment.

Bathurst had himself been consulted on the subject, for the Treasury was concerned about Brisbane's monetary policy. There was even talk of introducing paper money, but Hill convinced Horton that the colonies should first become familiar with the use of British silver. Herries felt that the scheme would need Parliamentary legislation 'for it would in fact be raising a Ways and Means by the creation of Debt', and would necessitate tiresome precautions against forgers. Yet Governor Darling was forced to revive the idea when he assessed the crisis caused by the shortage of coin.[4]

Supplies of coin were to be shipped to the various colonies, to be exchangeable for bills on the Treasury at a fixed rate of £103 of coin for a bill of £100. Where foreign coins such as the Spanish Dollar would still be allowed a restricted use for government purposes, fixed rates were set down. An Order in Council laid down the rate at 4s. 4d. Schedules of rates and duties payable to the Crown were to be drawn up, and accounts to be kept, in sterling terms.[5] Though these decisions had to some extent been anticipated, the process of retreat from Brisbane's attempted experiment proved long and complex, with different nuances in each colony. Imperial action had overruled an

[1] *H.R.A.* I/xi/668–9, enc. in /648, Brisbane–Horton, 16 June, 1825; Butlin, op. cit., pp. 150–64.

[2] Treasury Minute, 11 Feb. 1825; R. Chalmers, *A History of Currency in the British Colonies* (London, 1893), pp. 23 ff., 242 ff., 414 ff.

[3] *H.R.A.* I/xi/635, Bathurst–Brisbane, 5 June 1825.

[4] C.O. 323/202/31, Harrison–Horton, 12 Feb. 1825, enc. Treasury Minute, 11 Feb. 1825; /79 Hill–Horton, Private, 25 Apr. 1825; *H.R.A.* I/xii/450, Darling–Hay, Private, 26 July 1826.

[5] 23 Mar. 1825. enc. in I/xi/635, Bathurst–Brisbane, 5 June 1825.

interesting local initiative.[1] Bathurst, who had been bombarded with colonial complaints, showed a somewhat cynical sympathy with the governor's plight. But he noted that Brisbane should have remembered that men always protest when their 'main, and almost exclusive object, the acquirement of wealth' was affected. 'I confess', he wrote, 'I feel so doubtful of understanding the Questions of Currency that I am not prepared to cast blame on those who may err on the subject, unless there are any reasons for suspecting corrupt Motives.' In general governors should not tamper with such subjects without instructions from home. 'But it is a very common error', he added, 'and whenever the governors undertake it they are pretty sure of being in the wrong.'[2] Governor Darling was in 1828 still trying to be 'rid' of dollars, and in Van Diemen's Land the process took much longer.[3]

In New South Wales there were unexpected results. Only those who held British coin, which was in short supply among the general public, could demand bills on the Treasury from the Commissariat. Merchants were forced, lacking bills, to pay for their purchases in dollars, which were shipped from the colony to an embarrassing extent. In May 1826 two ships alone exported over $100,000.[4] A financial crisis ensued. The Bank of New South Wales, which had in January 1826 been able to declare a dividend of over 50 per cent per annum, was forced in May to seek a loan of £20,000 in specie from the government. There were now several banking establishments in the colonies. The Bank of Van Diemen's Land, in whose foundation Sorell claimed to have taken the initiative, opened in 1824.[5] Early in 1826 a second bank, the Bank of Australia, was formed in New South Wales by the 'pure Merinos'.[6] A third, the Sydney Commercial Bank, was proposed, but its planners soon entered into close connection with the original bank.

Darling, though he had been reluctant to give the Bank further patronage, in accordance with what he believed to be Colonial Office policy, was, nevertheless, persuaded to save the day by providing

[1] *H.R.A.* I/xi/690, Bathurst–Brisbane, 23 July 1825.

[2] C.O. 324/85/14, Minutes of Lord Bathurst, 1824–6.

[3] Butlin, op. cit., p. 175 ff.; *H.R.A.* I/xiv/122, Darling–Huskisson, 10 Apr. 1828.

[4] Butlin, op. cit., p. 168.

[5] *H.R.A.* III/iv/138, Sorell–Arthur, 22 May 1824, enc. in Arthur–Bathurst, 9 June 1824. It, too, made the necessary adjustments to be reorganized as a joint-stock company in 1827–8 when the 'charter' of the Bank of New South Wales was abandoned.

[6] *Monitor*, 13 Jan. 1827.

government credit for the required sum rather than a loan. A Committee of his Board for General Purposes was appointed as a Board of Inquiry, consisting of the Colonial Secretary, Auditor, and a Commissariat officer on 11 May 1826. Next day it reported capably on the state of the bank's affairs. The rapid dollar drain and the immediate consequent need for cash was disclosed. But the bank's general practice of providing wide accommodation and its specific dealing with a relatively small number of clients came under scrutiny. On a real money capital of less than $50,000 the Bank had accepted liabilities to the extent of over $565,000. The Board recommended that, if assistance was given, 'it should be made an indispensable condition that the management of the Bank should be conducted with more circumspection than appears to have been lately observed'.[1]

The Bank of Australia agreed to help restore credit, but refused to incur risks. The Executive Council laid down conditions for giving help. The government must approve of three new directors. The bank's discounts must be radically reduced and its capital paid up. The claims of government must be satisfied before a dividend of profits could be declared; and the Bank must take effective means to keep its amounts and make its payments in sterling.[2] Darling hoped that the very promise of government backing would sufficiently restore public confidence and also that the existence of two sound banks would prove beneficial. He asked for more British coin to be sent from home as the only means of replacing dollars with sterling circulation. He had permitted the appointment of Auditor Lithgow as a director of the Bank 'in compliance with the wish of the Public', though he was fully aware of the danger of having public officials on bank boards. He noted that he had earlier refused Lithgow permission to become a director of the Australian Bank.[3] The Governor and Council were clearly influenced in their actions by the fact that the colonial Treasurer and Naval Officer[4] had had considerable funds deposited in the Bank. From the time of Macquarie the Bank had been used as a place of deposit for many government accounts.[5] Darling wrote to

---

[1] *H.R.A.* I/xii/268, Darling–Bathurst, 5 May 1826; /296, Darling–Bathurst, 20 May 1826, enc. /299, Minute, 11 May 1826 and /300 ff. Report of Board, 12 May 1826.

[2] loc. cit. /306, Directors–MacLeay, 16 May 1826; /307, Memo of Ex. Co. 16 May 1826.

[3] loc. cit., p. 297–8.

[4] John Piper, also President of the Bank.

[5] Bigge, 3rd Report, p. 65, 84. Butlin, op. cit., p. 130.

Bathurst about Treasurer Balcombe's transactions with the Bank. He suspected that the Treasurer, who had placed nearly $100,000 in cheques in the Bank on the day of the inquiry, had been engaged in private money transactions which he was now seeking to conceal. The governor proposed not only to inspect the Treasury henceforth at uncertain and irregular intervals, but to forbid Balcombe 'lodging the public money on the Bank, or making use of it, as he appears most improperly to have done, for his private purposes.'[1]

The Treasury was consulted about these events and Hill's long letter to Hay formed the basis of the dispatch sent to Darling.[2] The Bank's illegal charter and the improvidence of its directors were castigated. But, as long as the private status and unlimited liability of its partners were clearly recognized in the colony, there was no objection to its legitimate activities. Darling's moves to save the Bank were approved as judicious and proper; but Lithgow's appointment as director was disallowed. There must never grow an impression 'that the Government are in some way or other participants in the affairs of this Bank, and that they would ultimately protect them, who deal with it, from loss, should the Bank fail'. Lithgow might exercise a supervisory role, however, especially during the existence of the Bank's obligation to the government. More British silver would be sent.[3] The Governor, relieved that his actions had been approved, wrote that Lithgow, whose presence as a director had in any event been intended only as a temporary measure to guard the fate of government funds deposited at the Bank, had now retired.[4] He had already been able to report that the government aid which had saved the Bank had been repaid with interest.[5]

When the Treasurer tried to explain his activities, he was able to argue that he had no specific instructions concerning the keeping of public monies. He claimed that his desire for security adequately explained his large deposits with leading merchants. His own house had no vault and only one sentry guarded his office. The Commissariat Stores recently had suffered heavy losses from theft.[6] Bathurst, how-

---

[1] *H.R.A.* I/xii/321, Darling–Bathurst, 22 May 1826.
[2] C.O. 202/18/92, Hay–Hill, 10 Oct. 1826; 201/176/180, Hill–Hay, 6 Nov. 1826.
[3] *H.R.A.* I/xii/702, Bathurst–Darling, 1 Dec. 1826.
[4] *H.R.A.* I/xiii/519, Darling–Goderich, 24 Sept. 1827.
[5] *H.R.A.* I/xiii/128, Darling–Bathurst, 26 Feb. 1827.
[6] *H.R.A.* I/xii/336, Darling–Bathurst, 27 May 1826, enc. Balcombe–MacLeay, 26 May 1826.

ever, shared Darling's suspicions and in consultation with the Treasury set out more practical regulations for the safeguard of government funds.[1] All revenue collected at Sydney should henceforth be paid over weekly to the Treasurer, and regular transmissions set up from the outstations. There should be available a secure and fireproof vault, with three separate keys, one for the Treasurer, one for the Auditor, and one for the Colonial Secretary, all of whom should be represented at the opening. The Treasurer must keep accounts at each of the Banks, as long as they were in good credit. All revenue, except small amounts for immediate needs, should be paid into the Banks so as to give a 'fair and equal share of business' to each.[2] The Governor must receive monthly a copy of the Treasurer's report to the Auditor on the state of government holdings. Sums in excess of a balance of £10,000 (£5,000 in each bank) were to be deposited, in specie, in the vault, and inspections regularly carried out.[3]

The embarrassment of the Bank, which had been precipitated by the rapid export of dollars, resulting in a general exercise of restriction in the granting of credit, coincided with Darling's attempts to put dollars out of circulation. He sought to encourage the circulation of British money by retaining dollars received in exchange for Treasury Bills and prohibited by a Currency Act colonial notes under £1 in face value. But his efforts were rendered even more strenuous by the necessity of coping with the effects of the transfer of the cost of the colonial civil establishment to colonial revenues. There were also increased imports to be paid for.[4] The chairman of the new Chamber of Commerce, Edward Wollstonecraft, wrote to ask for government action to remedy the crippling shortage of cash, and to present a catalogue of the causes of the crisis. Among others he mentioned Brisbane's economy campaign, with its accompanying 'dollar system' and curtailment of drafts made on the Treasury. It was a melancholy coda to Brisbane's earlier career as a practical theorist. His successor was forced to ease the situation by issuing Treasury Bills to the amount

---

[1] *H.R.A.* I/xii/590, Bathurst–Darling, 29 Sept. 1826; /705, Bathurst–Darling, 1 Dec. 1826; Butlin, op. cit., pp. 526–8.

[2] Both these decisions—to encourage equally respectable banks by the deposit of government funds and to maintain a Treasury vault—led to important developments during the thirties when a revenue boom caused the specie deposit in New South Wales to grow enormously: cf. Butlin, p. 532 ff.

[3] *H.R.A.* I/xiii/579, Darling–Goderich, 24 Sept. 1827.

[4] *H.R.A.* I/xii/506, Darling–Bathurst, 30 Aug. 1826; /450, Darling–Hay, Private, 26 July 1826; /214, Hay–Darling, Private, 9 Mar. 1826; /426, Darling–Bathurst, 23 July 1826.

of $60,000 which was due from the Commissariat to the Colonial Treasury. He directed that the Commissariat should make its payments in British coin, which would be supplemented by the issue of £5 and £10 notes. At home the Treasury was more inclined to blame the crisis on the 'improvident accommodation' of local speculators afforded by the Bank of New South Wales rather than on a shortage of cash or on Brisbane's ill-fated experiments.[1]

The new instructions on revenue and expenditure of 1825–6 were aimed at preventing the Governor incurring debts and forbade the raising of money 'by way of loan, or by the issue of debentures, or paper of any description', without first obtaining sanction from home. Darling thought it wiser to withdraw most of his notes, but the Colonial Office, again in consultation with the Treasury, authorized him to continue a moderate issue until more coin became available. By the time this decision arrived in the colony, Darling had already called in the outstanding notes and destroyed the plates.[2]

Late in 1827 the faction-ridden Bank of New South Wales was encountering strong competition from the Bank of Australia and in process of becoming a joint-stock company after the final repudiation of its 'charter'. By this time the state of the colony had entered into depression in which a severe two-year drought, a fall in wool prices, and the aftermath of the 1825 crisis in England all played a part.[3] In December 1828 the directors applied for a loan of £15,000. The Governor was forced again to assess whether the Bank was really helpful to the colony or just a means by which speculators could work in fictitious capital. He was vulnerable to the charge of favouring the Bank of Australia. He decided, despite contradictory advice and evidence of egregious mismanagement, that the enterprise was worth saving in hard times. The Executive Council agreed, but rigorous conditions were imposed; though Darling was not able to force the directors to wind up their affairs 'in the course of twelve months' as he had intended. He maintained that the two banks were not only still desirable, but, 'considering the encreasing Trade, etc., of the

[1] *H.R.A.* I/xii/506, Darling–Bathurst, 30 Aug. 1826, enc. Wollstonecraft–MacLeay, 15 Aug. 1826; I/xiii/257, Bathurst–Darling, 18 Apr. 1827, enc. Herries–Hay, 10 Apr. 1827.

[2] I/xii/488, Bathurst–Darling, 11 Aug. 1826; I/xiii/130, Darling–Bathurst, 28 Feb. 1827; /725, Huskisson–Darling, 17 Jan. 1828, enc. Lewis–Hay, 15 Dec. 1827; I/xiv/323, Darling–Huskisson, 6 Aug. 1828.

[3] Butlin, op. cit., p. 203 ff.; R. M. Hartwell, 'Australia's First Trade Cycle 1820–1832', *R.A.H.S.*, 42 (1956), pp. 51–67.

Colony, . . . absolutely necessary'. Again his decisions were approved, with appropriate warnings, from home.[1] Next year, in fact, he was ready to re-establish the government deposit in the Bank of New South Wales. This move also was approved, but, though the admonition took some time to bear fruit, it was urged that banks which accepted government deposits must publish returns.[2]

In Van Diemen's Land different economic conditions were more favourable to the expansion of banking. The success of the Bank of Van Diemen's Land, which Arthur thought had exercised too tight a monopoly, encouraged certain officials to form a new bank, the Derwent. Their motives and activities were by no means above suspicion and the governor tried to make them dissociate themselves from the enterprise. Prompted by the Treasury, where complaints had been received about the financial dealings of public servants in the colony, Murray supported Arthur. Public servants should not be directors; financial officers should surrender all shares.[3]

Arthur showed great respect for the Banks and their contribution to colonial life. He was selective in the exercise of his patronage, however, and infuriated John Dunn of the Commercial Bank by repeated refusals to award the Bank the privilege of government deposit.[4] He supported Charles Swanston of the Derwent Bank for membership of the Council. Arthur was himself a shrewd investor and fully appreciated the need for increased capital in the colony to be encouraged. His Act 11 Geo. IV c. 6 of 1830 declared English usury laws to have no application in Tasmania, and the lead thus given was followed in 1834 by the senior colony.[5]

In 1831 the Treasury, concerned about the deposit of Commissariat Funds, asked for detailed information about the 'constitution, regulation, capitals, and resources,' of the colonial Banks; and sought information about the terms which Banks could offer in return for being entrusted with government deposits. Darling replied generally

[1] *H.R.A.* I/xiv/549, Darling–Murray, 29 Dec. 1828; I/xv/731, Darling–Murray, 21 Sept. 1830; /101, Murray–Darling, 9 Aug. 1829.

[2] *H.R.A.* I/xv/731, Darling–Murray, 21 Sept. 1830; I/xvi/228, Goderich–Darling, 30 Mar. 1831; Butlin, op. cit., p. 528.

[3] S. J. Butlin, 'Charles Swanston and the Derwent Bank 1827–40', *H.S.A.N.Z.*, II (1943), p. 161 ff.; C.O. 280/18/293, Arthur–Huskisson, 13 Oct. 1828. The officials were the Colonial Treasurer, Collector of Customs, Sheriff, Solicitor-General, Clerk of the Council, and Master of the Supreme Court; C.O. 408/5/156, Murray–Arthur, 14 June 1829; 280/22/252, Stewart–Twiss, 26 Mar. 1829.

[4] Butlin, *Foundations*, p. 530; C.O. 280/38/69, Dunn–Goderich, 16 Jan. 1832.

[5] C.O. 280/35/212, Arthur–Goderich, 9 Sept. 1832.

that the Banks would offer suitable deposit facilities.[1] The home government, in short, had come to terms with colonial banking developments. Howick urged that the government make full use of the facilities offered.[2]

Throughout the period the government on the spot had had to play a continuously active role, but intervention from home, even if merely to prevent improper practices, had been conclusive. From about 1830, in a significant new phase, more orderly and constructive attention had to be paid to the structure of colonial banking. Public interest in joint-stock banking grew after the 1826 Act, and eventually British capital came to be attracted by the high rates of interest which seemed to be offered in the colonies. The Bank of Australasia, with its royal charter, was the first of these truly imperial ventures designed to make profits for British shareholders under the close supervision of directors in London. Its incorporation raised important issues which required attention from the Board of Trade and the Treasury as well as the Colonial Office. Hay's agreement to a Treasury demand that the control and issue of Bank charters should be on a 'settled and consistent principle' was no more than a recognition of a fact. For there could be no denial that in 1831 the Treasury was ultimately the department 'more peculiarly charged with questions relating to the Finances and Currency of Empire'.[3]

---

[1] *H.R.A.* I/xvi/38, Goderich–Darling, 29 Jan. 1831, enc. Ellice–Howick, 13 Jan. 1831; /310, Darling–Goderich, 26 July 1831.

[2] C.O. 324/140/352, Howick–Stewart, 20 Jan. 1832.

[3] Butlin, op. cit., p. 524; A. S. J. Baster, *The Imperial Banks* (London, 1929), Chs. 2 and 3, esp. pp. 24, 29; Arndt, op. cit., Pt. II, Ch. 3; C.O. 323/213/227, Spring Rice–Hay, 12 Nov. 1831.

VI

TREASURY CONTROL

AT almost every step of the government process, and in the working out of every public or private vision for the future development of the Australian colonies, the British Treasury was of necessity a formidable presence. During the Napoleonic Wars various attempts had been made to reduce the confusion which characterized the nation's financial administration. In the course of a major reorganization in 1805 sub-sections within the department were set up to deal more rationally with its business, and a non-political assistant secretary, George Harrison, was appointed. It was the beginning of the modern higher permanent civil service.[1]

Harrison, the son of a former attorney-general of Jamaica, was an efficient and influential public servant, expert in law and taxation. He was responsible for drawing up Treasury Minutes, now the formal vehicle for the expression of policy; for co-ordinating a web of committees, boards and offices; and for conducting the interdepartmental correspondence in which general financial decisions were given and particular directions concerning special expenditure communicated. This last formed a lifeline of colonial government, for the routine business of the Australian colonies consisted mainly in obtaining regular authorization from the Secretary of State for the payment of bills on the Treasury, drawn by the governors from parliamentary funds for colonial expenses.[2] The Treasury was also the normal channel for the conduct of the affairs of the Commissariat, which had in 1812–13 become a branch of the Army Commissariat and a Treasury sub-department as a result of reforms carried through by Herries and Willoughby Gordon.[3]

Demands for a greater regularity of system and for retrenchment at home and abroad were perennial Treasury themes. The drive towards economical reform and Treasury control embarrassed Goulburn and Bathurst in their attempts to create a more efficient Colonial

[1] D. Gray, *Spencer Perceval* (Manchester, 1965), p. 305 ff.
[2] D. M. Young, op. cit., p. 184 ff.
[3] *H.R.A.* I/ix/ note p. 863.

Office. Untempered, it could have seriously maimed the prospects of the Australian colonies, for only the most unfavourable attention was likely to be attracted by the expenditure of large sums of money by a complicated variety of official bodies on the other side of the world. But the Treasury was itself subject to many pressures and a victim of its own technical shortcomings. The details of colonial finance, by no means a central preoccupation in a country whose own financial system was undergoing gradual reform, were often bewildering and difficult for Treasury auditors already notoriously prone to delay and to cultivate complexity for its own sake. Bathurst resisted all efforts to supplant his department in its direction of imperial affairs, and his political status enabled him to prevail. While the Colonial Office could be relied upon to encourage economies at all levels, it became accustomed to act from more informed and comprehensive motives than those which generally inspired the Treasury.

In 1816, during the post-war retrenchment, Bathurst forwarded to Macquarie a Treasury circular enclosing ancient Minutes of 28 November 1764 and 12 August 1791 on the regulation and reduction of expenditure at foreign stations. He warned the Governor against sanctioning any 'prodigal or incautious expenditure'. A close scrutiny of every branch, civil and military, was to be made and Macquarie was urged to bring the colonial costs 'within some more reasonable limits'. This was to be 'paramount to every consideration of Improvement'. At the same time the Treasury requested David Allan, chief officer of the Colonial Commissariat since 1813, to provide reliable estimates of the likely expense to be incurred by the colony during the next year. Macquarie was ready to co-operate with the retrenchment plan up to a point, but refused to submit a colonial budget to his subordinate.

The Governor resented criticisms based on a false appreciation of his efforts to cope with a growing number of convicts; and the Commissary objected to Macquarie's autocratic approach to expenditure from the Police Fund. The Treasury received from Allan a number of recommendations aimed at reducing costs. Many of his suggestions raised wide questions of policy and ran counter to traditional practices which the governor considered essential to the welfare of the colony and the encouragement of local enterprise. But the Secretary of State commanded a careful report to be made on the Treasury's recommendation that recourse be had to open competition and public tender for the purchase of grain and supplies. The time had come for prices to be regulated rather by the salutary workings of supply and demand than by the arbitrary dictate of the governor. Soon, wrote Bathurst, 'the Internal Commerce of the Colony must be placed in its Natural State and its present Restrictions removed'.

In his reply Macquarie agreed to reduce the issue of rations to new settlers, though he supported the continuation of assistance for ex-convicts during the first months after their release. He had long stood out against the admission of settlers who did not possess sufficient capital to maintain themselves. But he denied that any substantial economies could be made consistent with the 'interior Prosperity and Safety' of the colonies, except, he noted pointedly, in the much inflated Commissariat for which the Treasury itself bore responsibility, and to which he obviously objected as a potential *imperium in imperio*. The colony could not possibly be ready for the freedom of commerce envisaged by the Treasury until at least the end of 1818. A mere desire to bring about regularity of imperial practice and a doctrinaire conformity to the principles of *laissez-faire* must not, he thought, be allowed to override the practical experience which had since 1788 been amassed by the administrators of these 'most peculiar colonies'. Open contracts would bring about the engrossing of grain and a monopoly of the meat market by the wealthier graziers. Allan's notions had been derived from a short stay and his views of the merits of the tender system were more influenced by his being a large owner of cattle than by his zeal for the public service. If the Commissary was sincere then reform and reduction was possible and necessary in his own department where there was a 'vast accumulation of Business and writing'. The adoption of 'a few official Forms' should not be allowed to disguise a history of speculation, fraud, and maladministration. The Governor thus took the attack into the Treasury's camp. Although Bathurst insisted that the Governor adopt a less cavalier attitude towards the obtaining of Treasury sanction for his ambitious programme of public works (even if this was to be financed from the growing colonial funds), Macquarie's views were respected by the Secretary of State.[1]

---

[1] *H.R.A.* I/ix/150, Bathurst–Macquarie, 24 July 1816, enc. Harrison–Goulburn, 6 July 1816, Lushington–Goulburn, 5 Jan. 1816, and Allan–Herries, 25 Sept. 1813; /236, Macquarie–Bathurst, 31 Mar. 1817; /248, Macquarie–Bathurst, 1 Apr. 1817; /830, Bathurst–Macquarie, 24 Aug. 1818; C.O. 201/139/86, Macquarie–Allan, 28 Feb. 1818; /89, Macquarie–Harrison, 4 Mar. 1818; /91, Allan–Harrison, 17 Mar. 1818;—on the authorization of settlers, *H.R.A.* I/ix/52, Macquarie–Bathurst, 18 Mar. 1816; /237, Macquarie–Bathurst, 31 Mar. 1817;

Macquarie was right. Despite continuous if intermittent Treasury bids to eliminate corruption, many Commissariat officers took advantage of their business connections and government office to feather their own nests. Delay, inefficiency, and inter-departmental jealousies allowed them to escape with impunity or at least to escape from inquiry relatively unscathed. One of the most notable imperial achievements of the 1820s was the gradual establishment of an honest and effective colonial audit. In the Australian colonies the record of Commissariat officials was black enough. The system indeed put a premium on fraud. Macquarie and his successors moved towards the institution of a better colonial revenue service, but the process was often a painful one. In 1817 the Governor asked urgently for the appointment of a Collector of Revenue on a 'liberal salary, or with allowance sufficient to prevent his resorting of necessity to fraudulent means'. It was one of the recurrent nightmares of governors that they would be held personally responsible for the financial consequences of a succession of officials whose defaults were little short of spectacular. For ultimate success, the goodwill and co-operation of a considerable number of public bodies was needed, and this often proved difficult to bring about. Default, oversight and misapprehensions were of course no colonial monopoly. Chinnery, the London agent, had for example been discovered to have a deficit of over seventy thousand pounds.[1]

Macquarie's Instructions commanded him to make periodical returns to the Treasury and the Board of Trade as well as to the Colonial Office, but after the reorganization of the Commissariat in 1812 there had seemed little need for this: it was presumed that the local Treasury officials would maintain direct communication with their superiors. The Colonial Office exercised firm, if not unlimited control in the conquered colonies and in New South Wales, but it was naturally the custom for important economic proposals to be laid before the Treasury. With the establishment of the Colonial Audit Office in 1814,[2] the post-war expansion, and the beginnings of parlia-

/797, Macquarie–Bathurst, 16 May 1818; —on public works, e.g., /201, Bathurst–Macquarie, 30 Jan. 1817; /830, Bathurst–Macquarie, 24 Aug. 1818; /708, Macquarie–Bathurst, 12 Dec. 1817.

[1] *H.R.A.* I/ix/213, Macquarie–Bathurst, 22 Mar. 1817; I/xi/58, Brisbane–Lushington, 20 Mar. 1823; /186, Harrison–Brisbane, 13 Dec. 1823; Gray, op. cit., p. 318.

[2] 54 Geo. III. c. 184, extended to N.S.W. and V.D.L. by Treasury Minute, 20 Dec. 1822.

mentary interest in the details of colonial expenditure, it was inevitable that the Treasury's role would be widened.

The first results of 'Treasury initiative' in New South Wales were disreputable and precipitated a colonial crisis. David Allan, forced to return to England under a cloud, had been replaced by Frederick Drennan, who had served in Canada and the West Indies. Drennan claimed to have Treasury authority for his radical programme of Commissariat and financial reorganization. He quoted precedents from his past experience to justify a complete 'reform' of the store-receipt system which had become the kernel of public exchange and finance in the colony. Macquarie, whose experience in this field with Allan had been chastening, was nevertheless without the advice of a public auditor or a controller of accounts. He was anxious not to defy what Drennan assured him was an explicit Treasury instruction. He went so far as to sign general orders drawn up by the Commissary to introduce the new arrangement. Yet he was concerned about the impact of Drennan's centralized, independent and unaudited position on the commerce of the colony, especially when it was insisted that Bills from Van Diemen's Land could only be accepted for payment in Sydney. Quite apart from certain suspicious reports the Governor had received against an official whose declared aim was to eliminate fraud and inefficiency, Macquarie felt that his authority as governor was being gravely undermined. He wrote to the Treasury and to Bathurst to protest. Even if Drennan's methods were genuinely the produce of Treasury reform, a wooden insistence on system and economy without respect to the wider purposes of government was no basis for intelligent administration. In the event it emerged that Drennan's claim to have received Treasury authorization to act independently of the Governor and to assert immediate and direct control over colonial matters was much exaggerated, if not dishonest. He had been told to report on the system with an eye to economy, but not to change the system of his own initiative or to act as though his jurisdiction was not subject to the authority of the Governor. By 1822 a chastened Drennan was returning to England under arrest, with over six thousand pounds unaccounted for. A committee of investigation into the affair undoubtedly led Bigge, who was a member, to turn his attention more closely to the mechanics of colonial finance.[1]

[1] *H.R.A.* I/x/84, Macquarie–Bathurst, 24 Mar. 1819; /100, Macquarie–Treasury, 24 Mar. 1819, enc. Drennan–Macquarie, 5 Feb. 1819, Macquarie–

Bigge heard a great deal of evidence about the conduct of Commissariat affairs, the purchase of supplies, the issue of rations, methods of store-keeping and stock-taking, and the granting of government contracts. The store-receipt system was a typical colonial improvisation which had evolved to satisfy the peculiar requirements of scattered communities for whom the Commissariat was chief provider. The receipts had taken the place of bank notes as a sort of circulating medium. In rejecting the system, both Allan and Drennan claimed to be introducing normal Treasury practice, but the privileged position they allotted to themselves under their substitute scheme clearly offered a suspiciously wide field for personal gain and speculation.[1]

After a period of misunderstanding and confusion, the Treasury issued a circular to all foreign stations on 12 February 1822 commanding that governors should countersign all Commissariat Bills. Brisbane, after a short acquaintance with the history of default and Commissariat practice in New South Wales, protested that to do so would be to involve himself personally in the intricate public expenditure of the colony. This was surely unjust to his own interest, and would not lead to any positive improvement in the protection of the public interest. He pressed the Treasury to send out an honest accountant. Drennan's successor, Wemyss, he found an able official, but the confused and complex state of the public accounts could never be cured unless they were attended to by a permanent professional. Harrison replied that it was not the Treasury's intention to hold governors personally responsible for 'the application of the money raised by the negotiation of Commissariat Bills', but only to ensure that the officers of the department had official sanction in their proceedings. He agreed, however, to the establishment of an accounts branch of the Commissariat in New South Wales, whose chief officer would be responsible for countersigning all Bills.[2] By this time the Colonial Office had finally been moved, on the advice of Bigge and

---

Drennan, 8 Feb. 1819, etc.; /153, Macquarie–Treasury, 12 June 1819; /408, Macquarie–Bathurst, 15 Mar. 1821, enc. Harrison–Drennan, 17 Apr. 1818 and Harrison–Drennan, 28 Jan. 1820; /629, Brisbane–Bathurst, 6 Apr. 1822; C.O. 201/103/83, C.O. Minute of 1821 calling attention of Harrison to report and recommendations of the Committee of Inquiry.

[1] e.g. C.O. 201/128/71, Allan–Bigge, 13 May 1822; 201/139/204, Harrison–Allan, 25 Apr. 1818; 201/139/267, Allan–Herries, 29 Apr. 1815.

[2] *H.R.A.* I/x/802, Lushington–Brisbane, 5 Aug. 1822; I/xi/58, Brisbane–Lushington, 20 Mar. 1823; /186, Harrison–Brisbane, 13 Dec. 1823.

others, to establish a Colonial Treasury, whose tasks would obviously grow as the colonies advanced.

It was hoped that the appointment of William Balcombe would initiate a general reform of the colonies' financial arrangements. Hitherto the system had been very odd. In addition to the Commissary, who was responsible for all drafts on the English Treasury, the financial officers had included the Treasurer of the Police Fund, the Naval Officer, and the Treasurer of the Orphan Fund. The Naval Officer was responsible for the collection of colonial revenues derived from import duties, royalties on timber and coal, wharf taxes, fees on shipping and auction duties. The Treasurer of the Police Fund collected tolls on public roads and bridges, market and fair dues, and fees paid on the slaughtering of cattle. Seven-eighths of the revenue received by the Naval Officer was paid into the Police Fund at the end of every quarter. The purpose of this Fund was to defray the costs of gaols and police and of public works generally, as well as to provide a general fund for rewards, grants in aid of salaries, etc. The orphan fund, composed of the remaining one-eighth—it had been more earlier—had been created specially for the maintenance of the 'Orphan Institution', but by this time contributed also to the purchase of requirements for public works and towards the expenses of certain military officials. Now Horton realized that this structure was outdated, but he was bewildered by its primitive complexity. It is typical of the empiricism of the Colonial Office that Balcombe should set out without instructions. He comforted himself with the thought that he could find guidance in his new post from the practice of Treasurers in other colonies.[1]

* * * * *

The Colonial Office, though not prepared to surrender authority or control over the workings of colonial government, was of course willing to consider constructively whatever the Treasury had to say. For the Australian colonies this routine business included a great number of perennial proposals based on the recommendations and submissions of individual colonial officers or Boards. By a Treasury Minute of 20 December 1822, the examination of the accounts of the Australian colonies was assigned to the Commissioners of colonial audit. During 1823 the Commissioners tried to grapple with the

---

[1] *H.R.A.* I/xi/95, Bathurst–Brisbane, 31 July 1823; /138, Bathurst–Brisbane, 2 Oct. 1823; /282, Brisbane–Bathurst, 8 June 1824; /493, Bathurst–Brisbane, 6 Feb. 1825; note 36, ibid.; C.O. 201/155/58, Balcombe–Horton, 20 Apr. 1824.

documents they collected from the Colonial Office and the Treasury, and from that time they became a leading source for suggestions about the application of general principles to the financial administration of Australia. Early in 1824 they presented a report which outlined the peculiar financial structures which had evolved in the colonies, in so far as they had been able to understand them. They were puzzled and dissatisfied at the accounting system and the haphazard methods of colonial appropriation. It was recognized that the revenue in both New South Wales and Van Diemen's Land was 'rapidly and regularly increasing,' but no concrete proposals were made for a major alteration until further information became available. They asked that all colonial accounts, including those of the agents in Britain, be henceforth regularly and promptly submitted to them; and they admitted surprise and interest in the amount of the sums which seemed to be involved.[1]

In the same year the Colonial Audit asked to deal directly with colonial officials, but was refused. They also judged, upon review of the existing system, that it was unreasonable to expect governors to bear the responsibility for neglect, omissions and defaults over which they had no control. Responsibility for the due accounting of funds throughout the colonies should be transferred therefore from the Governor, whose sanction for expenditure would remain necessary, to 'the officer in whose hands the Funds are lodged and by whom only the monies are received, and paid out'. These recommendations should, they thought, be kept in mind when Instructions were being framed for the projected Department of Audit in New South Wales and appropriate information issued to the Governor, the Treasurer and the local auditor.[2]

Brisbane's position was vindicated, and although the Colonial Office had no intention of surrendering its general control over colonial finance, it welcomed the opportunity of establishing a more rational *modus vivendi* with both Treasury and overseas governors. Brisbane was elated at the appointment of William Lithgow, a most competent official, as Commissary auditor. He lost no time in asking

[1] C.O. 201/104/259, Harrison–Goulburn, 17 Aug. 1821; 201/110/79, Harrison–Wilmot, 24 Jan. 1822; 201/144/296, Herries–Horton, 31 Oct. 1823; 324/143/245, Goulburn–Harrison, 15 Aug. 1821; 323/197/208, Treasury Minute; 201/153/262, Harrison–Horton, 26 May 1824, enc. Report of Col. Audit, 5 Mar. 1824.

[2] C.O. 323/203/366, Brande–Horton, 8 Mar. 1825; 323/203/94, 9 Jan. 1825, enc. Rept. Col. Audit 27 Apr. 1824; /385, Brande–Horton, 6 May 1825; /45, Harrison–Horton, 16 Feb. 1825, enc. Rept. Col. Aud. 17 Dec. 1824.

for Lithgow's duties to be extended to embrace the whole colonial revenue 'in order that he may have the entire financial state of the Colony under his eye.' In 1825 Bathurst, having consulted the Treasury, complied with this request, even though he remained wary of the Colonial Audit as a general rule and refused permission for them to conduct a direct correspondence with the governors. The Secretary of State, caught between ardent fires, had to assert himself against Treasury encroachment on the one hand and the exercise of independent initiative by governors who could now rely on distance and the healthy state of colonial funds to protect them from the more annoying consequences of their growing habit of presenting the home authorities with *faits accomplis*, on the other. When Darling wrote that he had found it necessary because of the expansion of public business to separate the offices of accounts from that of Colonial Auditor, Huskisson replied that the arrangement was approved and that a commissary accountant would be sent to succeed Lithgow who could now devote his energy to the general audit of the colony and the execution of the completely reorganized financial measures which had been decided upon in 1826.[1]

Firm decisions taken on the spot often seemed called for, but even after the appointment of local auditors and colonial treasurers accountable for the expenditure of the colonies, the Secretary of State remained the final court of appeal in economic and financial as in other matters. This could be frustrating for the energetic Colonial Audit Office, which remained concerned about the complexity of the Australian accounts and alarmed over the growing sophistication and expense of colonial establishments far away, about which they had only the most sketchy information and over which they suspected the Treasury was not able to exercise its 'salutary' control. In 1825 Brande wrote to Horton to protest the 'general want of system' and confusion of colonial accounts which led to great irregularities and losses. He proposed bluntly that 'the supervision of all matters of Colonial Revenue and Expenditure' be placed in their entirety under a special office, either of the Treasury or the Colonial Department, which would attend to them in detail, inspect and superintend revenue operations and prepare 'all necessary information for His Majesty's

---

[1] *H.R.A.* I/xi/379, Brisbane–Bathurst, 2 Oct. 1824; /644, Bathurst–Brisbane, 14 June 1825; C.O. 324/145/177, Hay–Harrison, 31 Aug. 1825; *H.R.A.* I/xiii/249, Darling–Bathurst, 12 Apr. 1827; I/xiv/163, Huskisson–Darling, 30 Apr. 1828; —on new Instructions, I/xii/483, Bathurst–Darling. 11 Aug. 1826.

Government or for Parliament'. Bathurst's minute noted acidly that 'the neglect and incompetency of the Treasury and the Colonial Department being thus established, the remedy is perfectly clear and simple. Appoint the writer to the Office here proposed'. He refused to transfer all the correspondence with the colonies concerning expenditure and finance to Brande. But the suggestion was not an unreasonable one, and in 1832 the Treasury acted on Goderich's comments on the final report of the Commissioners of Colonial Enquiry in which he mentioned favourably the possibility of assimilating the Colonial Audit Board to the general Audit Office. They were pleased that years of effort had led to the simplification of the financial transactions of colonial governments and noted that the authority of local officials had been limited and defined in such a way that a final audit was made easier. They agreed that there was now no need for a separate board. The Colonial Audit Board was therefore merged with the Audit Office. Brande was appointed to an office very similar to the one he had outlined seven years earlier.[1]

* * * * *

In the letter which accompanied Darling's Commission and Instructions, an attempt was made to clarify the governor's responsibilities in financial matters. His authority *vis-à-vis* the Colonial Secretary, Alexander MacLeay, a shrewd, experienced and very able old Treasury hand, and the other colonial officials was delineated. Regular reports on the colony's finances were to be made. Money earmarked for specific purposes could be spent only on them. Horton had, after the Bigge Reports, made earnest but confused attempts to divide the costs of colonial government more rationally. Now, in place of vague hopes that strictly colonial costs would soon be met by local revenues and exhortations to reduce colonial establishments and discontinue fees and allowances, there were practical discussions between the Treasury and the Colonial Office. It was decided that a distinction should be clearly made between 'the regular Civil Establishment of the Colony in its character as a British Settlement, and those whose employments originate from its appropriation as a Place of Punishment for persons convicted of offences in this country'. The expenses

[1] C.O. 324/146/267, 31 Dec. 1830, Hay–Stewart; 323/214/11, Treasury Minute, 20 Jan. 1832; 201/153/262, Harrison–Horton, 26 May 1824, enc. Rept. Col. Aud. 5 Mar. 1824; 323/203/362, Brande–Horton, 25 Feb. 1825; Young, op. cit., p. 190 f.

of the latter would henceforth be met from an annual parliamentary appropriation. The fixed expenses of the civil establishment, the necessary remittances to the Colonial Agent, and all essential colonial services would now be defrayed from colonial revenue. Any surplus should be devoted to 'meet the charges incurred by Great Britain on account of the colony'. In both divisions, authorization from home was necessary before the government would approve colonial action.[1]

The Colonial Office was uneasy about the Treasury's insistence that the immediate initiative of governors be limited to matters involving an expenditure of less than two hundred pounds and about other aspects of the Treasury's attempt to 'exercise departmentally a check over the expenditure of particular colonies'. The whole question of imperial finance should be re-examined. Horton felt that estimates drawn up by the governors and presented to Parliament would ensure a more effective and flexible control over colonial expenditure than regulations which often could not or should not be observed. Enraged by Treasury attempts to cut back his own office, Horton demanded from Herries a 'definite understanding respecting the jurisdiction of the Secretary of State and of the Treasury' without which he refused to continue in office. A conference was held between the Chancellor of the Exchequer and Horton, and the accounts of New South Wales were chosen as a test case. The great difficulty was to agree on practical ways and means by which imperial and merely colonial expenses could be separated and an equitable assessment made of each colony's readiness to contribute from its surplus fund towards the costs of the former.[2]

Sweeping new instructions were sent to the Governor, Treasurer and Auditor, which aimed at covering all essential procedures concerning the collection of revenue, government expenditure, stocktaking of supplies, and the inspection and audit of colonial accounts. An accurate and up-to-date, and hopefully definitive schedule of all colonial appointments was to be drawn up and maintained, showing the *ordinary* expenditure of the colonial governments. This was to

---

[1] *H.R.A.* I/xii/18, Bathurst–Darling, 14 July 1825; /44, Hay–Darling, 28 July 1825; /214, Hay–Darling, 9 Mar. 1826, enc. Hay–Harrison, 6 Feb. 1826; I/xi/64, Bathurst–Brisbane, 29 Mar. 1823; C.O. 201/144/296, Herries–Horton, 31 Oct. 1823; 202/16/68, Horton–Herries, 4 Jan. 1826; /92, Hay–Harrison, 6 Feb. 1826; /114, Hay–Hill, 30 Mar. 1826; 201/176/66, Hill–Horton, 30 Mar. 1826; 202/19/131, Hay–Hill, 31 July 1827.

[2] C.O. 325/35/3, Horton, Private 1825–6, Minute of P. Smith on Treasury Control of Finance; /37 and 45, Horton–Herries, 9 Aug. 1826.

state the original authority under which respective appointments had been made, and whether and when the Treasury had authorized them in advance or sanctioned them in retrospect. To this fixed *establishment* the Governor was forbidden to add without the express authority of the Treasury and the Secretary of State unless it was 'indispensably necessary', in which case subsequent permission must be obtained. If the Governors' reasons were thought insufficient, they would be held personally responsible for recovering the unauthorized expenditure. Precise conditions were set down for leave of absence, allowances, and for officials seconded from the military. Another schedule must show the more stable and *fixed* of the '*contingent*' or *extraordinary* expenditure. The Governors were not to add to this list of recurring items of variable cost without sanction from home. Expenditure on *unfixed contingent* charges, such as the construction or repair of public buildings, should never be incurred except in 'very pressing emergency' without prior authorization, unless the whole charge was less than two hundred pounds. Regular checks were to be made and reductions carried out. Full explanations must be made of any variation in government revenue and expenditure. The practice in Van Diemen's Land was to conform as nearly as possible to that of New South Wales. Colonial Auditors were to send all relevant information home, Gazettes and Government Orders as well as accounts. At home the opportunity was taken to transfer the accounts of the 'Parliamentary Agent', who had hitherto been responsible for the payment of the expenses of the civil establishment proper, to Barnard, whose instructions were also revamped. It was expected, optimistically in view of the rather doctrinaire categories of the plan, that the effect of the changes would soon put an end to the 'very irregular and careless manner' which had characterized the transmission and handling of colonial accounts.[1]

Darling went ahead with these arrangements and tried desperately to sort out the intricate transfers which would be necessary to conform colonial practice to what was required. But he had not been able to work an instant miracle. Nor had the colonial revenue proved elastic enough to cover all that the Treasury suspected it ought. In general the Treasury approved of what had been done, but they now launched a campaign to pare the colonial departments down to a

[1] *H.R.A.* 1/xii/483, Bathurst–Darling, 11 Aug. 1826, enc. Instructions of 13 June 1826, Signed by Liverpool, F. J. Robinson, etc.; C.O. 201/176/84, Hill–Hay, 13 June 1826; 202/18/170, Hay–Herries, 20 Feb. 1827.

minimum. The lists of the establishment could not be too carefully revised with regard to due economy. Colonial and commissariat funds should be kept strictly apart, and they scouted Darling's proposal that the Colonial Treasurer should exercise an overall control over the financial structure. All surplus colonial funds should be paid over into the Military Chest in aid of the general expenditure, or be applied in 'some other manner as H.M.G. at home should direct'.[1]

Towards the end of 1827, Darling, under great strain of overwork, complained to Hay that 'the Machinery of this Government is totally inadequate to the performance of its various and important duties'. He had, from 'perfect Anomaly and Confusion, gone far to establish regularity and order'. The business to be done was urgent and increasing. The reforms and changes introduced from home, welcome as they were as a sign of interest and care, demanded 'numerous and comprehensive Reports and Statements' which could only be kept up to date and accurate if more men were employed. He found it quite impossible to comply with Treasury Instructions 'by reporting every Augmentation and trifling increase of salary'. Later, when the government and departments were fixed and consolidated, this could be done. Now it was far more important to obtain useful and fit men to try to keep pace with the administrative changes called for by the colony's rapid advance. Hay, who had often told Darling of his desire to set up a fine colonial service for Australia to supply 'well-trained and efficient public Servants', doubtless understood. But, given the non-representative character of the colonial constitution and the massive financial dependence of the Australian colonies on the British Government whose Treasury was bent on radical reductions, there was no alternative but to keep a tight rein.[2]

In 1827, Darling took the opportunity to strike a bargain by purchasing a brig for colonial use. He made no apologies for not obtaining prior authorization for this expenditure. Without it the new settlement at Westernport would have starved, and the Port Essington project to the far north been indefinitely delayed. Compliance

[1] *H.R.A.* I/xiii/88, Darling–Bathurst, 9 Feb. 1827; /170, Goderich–Darling, 30 July 1827; /685, Darling–Goderich, 8 Jan. 1828; /742, Huskisson–Darling, 30 Jan. 1828; I/xiv/367, Darling–Huskisson, 30 Aug. 1828, enc. Lithgow–Mac-Leay, 26 Aug. 1828; C.O. 201/186/302, Frankland Lewis–Stanley, 27 Nov. 1827, sent to Darling and Arthur in Jan. 1828.

[2] *H.R.A.* I/xiv/585, Darling–Hay, 1 Nov. 1827; C.O. 324/85/49, Hay–Darling, Private, 14 June 1826.

with the rules would have been more expensive than ignoring them. Outstations simply could not be run cheaply, he maintained, and mere adherence to Treasury regulations could bring everything to a standstill. Once again, though the Colonial Office was sympathetic, the Treasury made no concession. In cases of real necessity the Governor must act, but the subsequent report which he was obliged to make would act as a salutary penance which would teach him to anticipate expenditure and deter him from any 'incautious and unauthorized spending'. This attitude was frustrating for the most conscientious of governors, and Darling and Arthur learnt to circumvent it uneasily as colonial revenues grew in such a way as to give them increasing resources which could be applied to satisfy the urgent needs of the colonies they governed. In 1829, after Darling had insisted on civil service readjustments to meet the realities of colonial requirements, a Colonial Office minute noted with alarm: 'It is quite impossible to allow General Darling to persist in the course of increasing salaries at pleasure.' Yet the Office deserves great credit for cushioning the clamour of the Treasury for mindless reductions which could only have retarded colonial development. James Stephen in 1832 wrote an exasperated minute against a Treasury attempt to prevent urgently required legal appointments in Van Diemen's Land: 'It is in the spirit of our times to confound parsimony and economy with each other.' About the same time Horton, who had done so much in his busy way to bring about the advancement of the colonies and was now governor of Ceylon, wrote to his old colleague Hay to complain of the confining effect of economies imposed from home. Hay marvelled that Horton, after all he had witnessed in office, should suppose it possible 'that any expensive Establishment can be kept up in our colonies'. He also noted wryly that it was impossible to have at home 'the advantages of Reform, without the pinching inconveniences to which it must subject a number of individuals in all quarters of the world'.[1]

* * * * *

In the later twenties there was indeed taking place in England a great debate about economic policy and the principles of public finance.[2]

[1] H.R.A. I/xiii/301, Darling–Hay, 14 May 1827; I/xiv/10, Huskisson–Darling, 5 Mar. 1828; C.O. 201/203/109, M. after H.R.A. I/xv/200, Darling–Murray, 9 Oct. 1829; C.O. 280/37/147, Minute by Stephen, 4 Oct. 1832; C.O. 324/87/70, Hay–Horton, 4 Feb. 1833.
[2] cf. e.g. L. M. Brown, 'The Policy of the Board of Trade', thesis cit., esp. Ch. I, 'Parliament and Economic Policy in 1830.'

This debate was far more complex than a mere battle for the principles of *laisser-faire*. All parties could at least agree that more accurate
and detailed information would be necessary about the practical
workings of administration if effective and systematic reforms were to
be carried out. Attention was paid to the way all public accounts were
kept and the reports of the non-party Finance Committee of 1828
gave great impetus to a thoroughgoing review of government expenditure. Among its strong recommendations of Treasury control and
retrenchment all round were admonitions against each department's
seeking to exalt its own importance, wishing to accomplish its respective object 'complete and perfect', and setting the desirable above the
economically possible. Imperial administration was not overlooked,
though the Colonial Office was by now long accustomed to scrutiny
and aware of its need to consider carefully ways and means even when
bent on making the most urgent improvements. Hay, who had high
hopes for such imperial projects as a regular colonial civil service,
lamented to Darling that expense alone was the 'great obstacle' to
this and other desirable reforms. He told the Governor that the
Financial Committee was expected to look narrowly into every item
of colonial expenditure, and warned him that very little could be done
to follow up interesting and worthy suggestions now being received
from the colonies, because of the unreceptive financial climate of the
time. Against all his wishes, he told Arthur, he would be forced to
continue on the haphazard course of appointing individuals without
any set principle, a procedure which he was aware was unsatisfactory
and troublesome to the disappointed colonial governors.[1]

Goulburn, in many ways the architect of the modern Colonial
Office, might have been expected to offer radical solutions, but he
was now Chancellor of the Exchequer in the Wellington Administration (January 1828–November 1830) and his commitment was now
to a Treasury point of view. Hay and Goulburn conducted a correspondence and had conversations about colonial finances in which the
Chancellor, though helpful, was clearly uneasy about the obvious lack
of an over-all system. Hay begged him not to allow the appointment
of a Parliamentary Committee to investigate colonial finance. It
would, he thought, be a measure 'most objectionable in any point of
view' and would tend to retard rather than advance reforms already

[1] P.P. 1828 V; C.O. 324/85/48, Hay–Darling, Private, 14 June 1826; /122,
Hay–Darling, Private, 19 July 1827; 86/12, Hay–Darling, Private, 27 Dec. 1827;
/58, Hay–Darling, 3 Sept. 1828; /55, Hay–Arthur, 14 Aug. 1828.

taking place. He frankly confessed that the method of dealing with colonial requisitions, especially from the convict colonies, was very unsatisfactory. In theory the Secretary of State should have seen and approved all submissions before they were sent to the Treasury.[1] In practice the Colonial Office was often side-stepped and at the Treasury there was apparently little or only intermittent examination and revision of costly details. Greater departmental co-operation was necessary. More important, the whole question of transportation to Australia should be reconsidered from the point of view of expense. Goulburn, busy about many greater affairs of state, took the view that the Treasury should have the management of colonial revenues. He was, however, ready to wait for the returns expected soon from the colonies to the various questionnaires and inquiries that had been sent out, before he made firm decisions; and he was prepared to defend the Colonial Office in the House against the negative attacks of Joseph Hume.[2]

In 1830 a Commission of Colonial inquiry was appointed, intent on reappraisal and reductions. Although Goulburn was included, Sir Willoughby Gordon, another experienced and able administrator-member, thought it rather weak. It was, in any case, rendered inconclusive and incomplete on the death of George IV and the political decline of the Wellington régime. The Commission re-emphasized the necessity of 'strict and efficient' Treasury control over 'every branch and every article of Colonial Expenditure' (to which Goderich noted 'Quite right'), stressed the need for proper audit, and, under the influence of Herries, recommended again the 'encouragement of private enterprise' in the granting of colonial contracts and the renting rather than building of accommodation for government purposes. There was a formal effort made to unravel the system of departmental consultation so that confusion and delay would be lessened. The Treasury would accept responsibility, but the Colonial Office must be consulted at every level.[3]

On the receipt of the Report of the Commissioners, Hay wrote to the Treasury to give them Goderich's first impressions. The Secretary

---

[1] After the Commissioners made formal recommendations on this subject, Goderich insisted that the Secretary of State should examine requisitions before the Treasury gave their sanction; C.O. 324/146/273, Hay–Stewart, 31 Dec. 1830.

[2] C.O. 323/156/61, Goulburn–Hay, 8 Oct. 1828; 201/205/219, Goulburn–Hay n.d. 1829; 324/93/170, Hay–Goulburn, 25 Feb. 1830; 324/211/34, C.O. Minute, 24 June 1829.

[3] Young, op. cit., p. 193 f.; C.O. 323/212/177, 13 Dec. 1830.

of State agreed that the Treasury should exercise control over colonial expenditure and that rules laid down for colonial officials should be strictly obeyed. But he noted that supervision from home and the enforcement of policy from a distance was not easy. He agreed that colonial accounts should be reported accurately and punctually, and was prepared to recommend changes in the style and method of presentation so that a uniform system might be employed throughout the Empire. The measures suggested by the Commission had all been the subject of 'much anxious deliberation and in many cases of positive instruction' from the colonial department, he wrote. The recommendation that adequate salaries everywhere replace housing and living allowances and fees had already been anticipated. Goderich was not quite so willing to support a universal change to a system of open competition for tenders and contracts. This was a question upon which the Colonial Office had received much contradictory advice. In many cases the lack of real capital among colonists would almost certainly lead to monopolistic practice and to increased expense rather than the economy and liberalization hoped for. He was more ready to examine the idea that Colonial Agencies be con-solidated and placed under 'the immediate eye' of the Colonial Office and to follow up other suggestions concerning the tabulation of information about colonial revenue and expenditure, the sharing of the costs of Audit by a wider number of colonies, and a general reorganization of the Colonial Audit.

The Commissioners, though they felt uncomfortable about de-manding severe reductions in the colonial civil service and declared themselves deeply conscious of the inequities, inconvenience and personal hardships that might result from radical and sudden action, were clearly interested primarily in systematic retrenchment. The Colonial Office was more patient and more empirical, ready to take the opportunity of carrying through a number of reasonable reforms and simplifications; but was also at pains to defend its own establish-ment at home, to represent the colonial point of view, and was reluctant to allow doctrinaire reform to erupt into piece-meal or petty economies which would override essential imperial objects. Thus, when, in 1832, the Treasury commented adversely on the position of the new settle-ment in Western Australia, remarking that the colony appeared 'to have been preserved rather with a view to the necessary protection of private adventurers, than from any prospect of national advantage' and insisting that the unexpectedly large expenditure be reduced,

Hay sprang to the defence of the Swan River colony. Though he had earlier been as sanguine as the Treasury in hoping that the colony would not prove an expense to the public, he now defended the settlers. The colony was and would be most useful to India and the other Australian colonies. They would be able in the long run to defray their own expenses and were entitled to the protection of the Mother country.[1]

*   *   *   *   *

From the first the experience of Western Australia showed how chimerical were the aspirations of strict Treasury control. The administrators had been strongly advised that the strictest attention must be paid to costs. The Colonial Office assured the Treasury that there would be very limited financial responsibility for the home government. Even salaries, Murray wrote to Stirling, must be paid in land-grants rather than fixed annual amounts. 'You cannot be too cautious of creating new offices,' he told the Lieutenant-Governor, who was informed by Twiss that he could not himself expect any salary 'in the present reduced state of the public finances.'[2] Yet arrangements were made for Stirling to take out specie and for co-operation to be given, at least in the settlement's early days, from the Commissariat of New South Wales. Stirling and others connected with the venture were naturally keen to ensure the support of the Treasury, especially if emergencies should arise, and to secure firm commitments from the British government. The frail and uncertain beginnings of the colony had convinced Stirling that 'the question as to the undertaking of the Enterprize would be decided in reference to the attendant Expenses', and he was prepared to waive the question

<hr>

[1] C.O. 323/146/267, Hay–Stewart, 31 Dec. 1830; C.O. 323/213/107, Stewart–Hay, 28 Jan. 1831;—on colonial audit C.O. 323/214/113, Stewart–Hay, 31 Jan. 1832;—agents, /136, Stewart–Hay, 10 Feb. 1832; /150, Stewart–Howick, 25 Feb. 1832;—on regular information, etc., /156, C.O. circular, 28 Feb. 1832. (In 1833 Hay, despite years of efforts to produce reliable Blue Books, thought the Colonial statistics only 'an approximate to the truth'; C.O. 324/193/296, Hay–Auckland, 2 Apr. 1833. It would need a G. R. Porter to straighten out colonial statistics);—on W.A., C.O. 323/214/248, Stewart–Hay, 4 Sept. 1832; /252, C.O. Minute, draft of Hay–Stewart, 24 Sept. 1832;—Treasury attack on C.O. establishment, e.g., 324/146/300, Hay–Spring Rice, 22 July 1831.

[2] C.O. 397/1/34, Hay–Dawson, 30 Dec. 1828; 397/2/5, Murray–Stirling; 30 Dec. 1828; /10, Murray–Stirling, 22 Jan. 1829; 397/3/21, Murray–Stirling, 30 May 1830; /23, Twiss–Stirling, 22 June 1830.

of outfit and a regular salary for a time, particularly as he had his
promise of a hundred thousand acres. Yet he sensed that the Colonial
Office would be sympathetic.[1]

By 1830 it was clear that emergencies had arisen, and that the
venture was certainly going to be more costly and more troublesome
than had been hoped. Stirling had been forced to urge that the settlement be declared in every respect a British colony, or else peremptorily
abandoned. Anything in between would be ruinous. He could not
continue without acknowledgement, without an official establishment, and without instructions concerning revenue and finance.
Respectable people of capital had been attracted to the colony; but
all the preliminary confusion about land grants and conditions of
settlement which had so disturbed the Colonial Office in London was
surpassed by the realities of the hardships encountered on the spot.
Gradually the home government, convinced of the need for action
by these and other reports coming from New South Wales and Van
Diemen's Land, became involved beyond all prediction and expectation. Barnard, who had extended his services as Agent to meet the
pressing requests now arising from Swan River, demanded to know
how the bills would be met. The Audit Office complained that they
were receiving a chaos of bills, without vouchers, authorities or
relevant information; and they protested against the Colonial
Secretary Peter Brown's assumption of the title of 'commissioner of
audit'. Hay, anxious to avoid a débâcle, fought the Treasury to
obtain the urgent establishment of reasonable colonial arrangements.
Official neglect to provide the apparatus of government, a proper
system of accounting and financial responsibility must not be allowed
to culminate in a public spectacle of ruin and collapse. He scornfully
rejected an absurd Treasury suggestion that the colonial establishment, if granted, should be formed on the meagre pattern of New
South Wales in 1788. No matter how much they might regret the
original optimism which had led to this contretemps, the under-
secretaries at the Colonial Office were not prepared to see the colonists starve or to stand idly by while the situation deteriorated beyond
repair. They might, and did, exhort Stirling to keep the colony within
reasonable limits, and pare his establishments to an irreducible
minimum, but they held out for a reasonable treatment of his
earnest requests and refused to accept facile suggestions that the

[1] C.O. 18/3/5, Stirling–Hay, 13 Jan. 1829; /7, Stirling–Twiss, 16 Jan. 1829;
/214, Stewart–Hay, 6 Feb. 1829, enc. Minute 23 Jan. 1829.

colony could be redeemed by the sending out of boat-loads of convicts.[1]

The Treasury remained far from helpful. The Audit wrote patronizingly of Stirling's incapacity as a naval officer for keeping accounts, yet when it was agreed to send out an experienced commissariat officer lack of co-ordination between the departments led characteristically to his setting off without explicit instructions. Finally the Colonial Office got round to issuing instructions to the Governor. Predictably he was commanded to consult the home authorities about all revenue arrangements and, though he was at last empowered to set up formally his colonial departments, the strictest economy was enjoined upon him.[2]

The Colonial Office, which had hitherto appeared to expect from the Governor reports as detailed and accurate as those they were accustomed to receive from Darling and Arthur, at last settled on a salary of eight hundred pounds for Stirling. They were unwilling, however, to sanction remuneration for the various boards which he had found it necessary to employ in the redemption of what had in some ways already earned the title of the 'Cinderella' settlement. He was told that 'on no account' would additions be allowed to the slender establishment approved, and he was warned not to allocate money from any colonial funds which might be raised in the colony. He should consult the new Council on revenue matters and take all steps to make the colony pay its own way 'at no distant period' so that it would become, as had been originally intended, independent of the home country for its support. The Colonial Office clearly found his unauthorized additions and habit of helping needy settlers from government funds almost as alarming as the Treasury had done, but they tried to explain as best they could the actions which the

[1] C.O. 18/7/6, Stirling–Murray, 17 Jan. 1830; /104, Stirling–Sec. of State, 18 Oct. 1830; /32, Stirling–Sec. of State, 20 Jan. 1830; /68, Stirling–Twiss, Private, 26 Jan. 1830; 18/3/123, Barnard–Twiss, 7 Dec. 1829; 18/7/222, Dawson–Hay, 11 Aug. 1830; 397/3/27, Hay–Stewart, 5 Aug. 1830; /29, Hay–Stewart, 6 Aug. 1830; /37, Hay–Dawson, 15 Sept. 1830; 18/7/240, Stewart–Hay, 2 Dec. 1830; 397/3/44, Howick–Stewart, 11 Dec. 1830; 18/9/54, Stewart–Howick, 27 Jan. 1831; 397/3/48, Howick–Latour, 14 Jan. 1831.

[2] C.O. 18/9/179, Stewart–Howick, 16 Mar. 1831; /186, Stewart–Howick, 14 May 1831, enc. Audit–Treasury, 5 May 1831; 18/10/40, Stewart–Goderich, 2 Apr. 1832; 18/9/86, Stirling–Hay, Private, 14 May 1831; 397/2/90, Howick–Stirling, 30 Aug. 1831; 397/3/37, Hay–Dawson, 15 Sept. 1830; /110, Hay–Stewart, 19 Sept. 1832; 397/2/46, Stirling's Instructions, 5 Mar. 1831; /64, Goderich–Stirling, 28 Apr. 1831.

Governor had taken to drag the colony back into a state of relative confidence and prosperity.[1]

In mid-1831 Stirling was so impatient with his position, bereft of any coherent financial system, that he threatened to return home in person to seek redress. In some ways the material situation and morale of the colony had improved, but he had had to make a number of civil appointments and he was alarmed by the effect of the new land regulations upon the modifications which he had introduced into land-alienation in Western Australia. In early 1832, just when the Treasury was threatening to dishonour Bills from Swan River on the ground that they felt the Treasury had no control over the public expenditure there, Stirling made up his mind to represent the colony's demands in England. In this resolution he was supported by the new Executive Council and other colonists who took the opportunity of asking for an elective representation in the Legislative Council and various other privileges of a mature British colony. Thus the horrified Colonial Office found the Swan River, with all its hopes and fears, woes, grievances and expectations, flowing through its sighing-rooms. Stirling vigorously argued his case, blaming the home authorities for their neglect, carelessness and inefficiency. He demanded support, more time to work out reasonable colonial arrangements, more financial backing, and more inducements for would-be immigrants. Hay indignantly set out the department's case. He described how the Colonial Office had been dragged half-reluctant into the foundation of the colony, and how everybody had known that economy was of the essence of the new venture. At no time had there been commitment by the home authorities for anything more than a handsome but short-term support. He conceded Stirling's contention that there could be no question of allowing the Government's investment of fifty thousand pounds and the settlers' of over one hundred and fifty thousand pounds to go for nought. But he stressed that the time was not opportune for the home country to be giving open-handed assistance to distant colonies, no matter how hopeful their prospects. It was an embarrassing illustration of the weaknesses and strengths of the Colonial Office. Hay was obviously still interested in backing

---

[1] C.O. 397/2/64, Goderich–Stirling, 28 Apr. 1831; /90, Howick–Stirling, 30 Aug. 1831; 397/3/53, Howick–Stewart, 22 Feb. 1831; /56, Howick–Stewart, 11 Mar. 1831; /144, Howick–Stewart, 20 June 1831; /98 Hay–Spring Rice, 3 Mar. 1832; /121, Hay–Stewart, 12 Jan. 1833; /174, Hay–Stewart, 20 July 1833; 18/9/12, Stirling–Murray, 13 Mar. 1831; /212, Stewart–Howick, 10 Aug. 1831; /235, Stewart–Howick, 27 Aug. 1831.

the colony, but prevented by the Treasury from doing what he thought necessary. He recognized that grave mistakes had been made, but was to a point justified in passing the blame on to the Treasury. Stirling, having failed in his set-piece battles concerning land regulations and help for needy settlers, had really won the war. The home government would not be permitted to wash its hands of the settlement. Despite tension, strain, bad feelings, and accusations of abandonment and lack of understanding, another huge slice of Australia had been added to the Empire. From desperate beginnings a new colony had taken root and refused to be torn up. The consequences had to be admitted.[1]

* * * * *

The Colonial Office expected that the new legislative and executive councils would share with the Governor the increasing business of colonial government and modify his autocratic exercise of power. They had also encouraged the establishment and procedures of the various boards and committees which the governors had found necessary, in the absence of a mature constitution and civil service, to help them understand and administer the colonies. In principle the home authorities were ready to consider sympathetically colonial suggestions whatever their origin, but in practice the Secretary of State frequently opposed the unanimous recommendations of his colonial advisers and officials on grounds of expense.

The granting of the Church and Schools charter, for example, was an elaborate attempt to set up an administrative structure which could deal with urgent current problems of religion and education, and anticipate future demands in an orderly and systematic way. Yet here, as elsewhere, the local officials soon found that an empirical adaptation of the original scheme was necessary. Darling proposed to make money available from the colonial treasury when he found that the ambitious arrangements aimed at in the charter would not have the desired effect. He was sharply reminded that, although nothing could be more important than the 'religious and moral welfare of all

---

[1] C.O. 18/11/38, Treasury Minutes, etc., 17 Feb. 1832; 18/9/92, Stirling–Murray, 13 Mar. 1831; /96, Stirling–Goderich, 17 June 1831; 18/10/5, Stirling–Goderich, 7 Jan. 1832; /42, Stirling–Goderich, 5 Apr. 1832; /56, Stirling–Goderich, 28 June 1832; /93, Stirling–Goderich, 14 July 1832; /218, Stirling–Goderich, 20 Sept. 1832, enc. Ex. Co. Minute, 29 June 1832; /240, Stirling–Hay, Private and unofficial, 20 Dec. 1832; /242, Stirling–Hay, Private, 22 Dec. 1832; 397/2/122, Hay–Stirling, 2 Jan. 1833; /138, Goderich–Stirling, 8 Mar. 1833; /165, Stanley–Stirling, 28 July 1833; 18/12/18, Stirling–Hay, 5 Jan. 1833.

classes' in the colonies, the greatest circumspection was required in thus appropriating the resources of the country. Prior consultation and positive authorization from home must precede any expenditure as large as was envisaged. The Governor must never presume to use 'his discretion' in matters involving such expenditures. 'It is by such acts,' wrote Robinson, 'that we get involved in unforeseen and indefinitely increasing expense.' The Commissioners of Audit, Darling was warned, would consider any breach of this rule a sufficient reason for not passing the charge. The Secretary of State must not be expected to rescue delinquent officials.[1]

The Governor replied that he had no intention of deviating from Treasury instructions in this affair, or of exercising a discretionary power over public money. But he urged strongly that the Treasury's instructions be modified. They must lead to 'great inconvenience and injury to the service, besides entailing additional expense on the Public'. Years might elapse before decisions could be reached concerning contingent expenditure such as urgent but expensive repairs to government buildings. The Governor, 'acting on the spot and on the most prudential motives' could be relied on to take informed and responsible measures, he argued. 'A colony, making rapid strides as this is, and situated 16,000 miles from the Mother Country, can hardly be bound without injuring its advancement by the common rules, which are applicable to colonies under ordinary circumstances.' Huskisson was receptive to this complaint and the Colonial Office uncomfortable lest a strict interpretation or overstressing of the rule which commanded prior reference home should lead to the breakdown of administration and crush all spontaneity in colonial government. The Treasury, however, was unwilling to concede any change, except a grudging permission for unforeseen repairs to be carried out 'if it can be stated that a larger Expense would be necessarily incurred by deferring the Work'. In the case of the Church and Schools corporation they found proof of their suspicions that improvisation would be very expensive. The charter had to be revoked and the best made of a bad deal. The reclamation operations were lengthy, complex, and costly. No similar corporation was set up in Van Diemen's Land.[2]

---

[1] *H.R.A.* I/xii/324, Darling–Bathurst, 24 May 1826, enc. Archdeacon Scott–Darling, 4 May 1826; /607, Bathurst–Darling, 6 Oct. 1826, founded on a minute by the Chancellor of Exchequer at C.O. 201/171/375, 29 Sept. 1826.

[2] *H.R.A.* I/xii/308, Darling–Bathurst, 22 May 1826; /324, Darling–Bathurst, 24 May 1826; /607, Bathurst–Darling, 6 Oct. 1826; /738, Bathurst–Darling, 11

Darling continued to report expansion in the colonial departments and the adoption of new salary scales. He was able to show that his Executive Council fully backed what he had done. The Secretary of State, however, complained that the Governor had, in the three years before 1830, raised *all* the colonial salaries. He was reproved for taking it upon himself 'without sufficient authority' to change the existing arrangements, and his practice of acting first and then seeking permission was thought 'exceedingly objectionable'.[1]

Darling had, by 1830, come into a very awkward position. He had, under the workings of the 1828 Act, submitted the colonial accounts to the Legislative Council. Further, he had had to take steps to ensure by local legislation the continuance of those lucrative duties on spirits and tobacco which had once been entirely within the governor's competence to impose but which now, according to Chief Justice Forbes, needed the consent of Council. He sought more latitude in his financial administration, finding it particularly irksome to have to refer home matters where all costs would be adequately met from the Colonial Treasury.[2] The Colonial Office could only urge him to consult the Council and then refer all proceedings home for approval, with any minutes, or additional information that he could offer.[3] Darling, exasperated, insisted throughout that he was most attentive to economy and was adamant that if he had erred it had been 'in endeavouring too rigidly to carry into effect the orders addressed to me from Home, when satisfied from local circumstances that they could not be acted on here without serious injury to the public Service'. He quoted cases taken from the daily workings of his government, against the practicability of employing the proposed private contract system of making roads when there were so many idle convicts available. He stressed the vast arrears which now occurred in the departments because they were so short-handed.

Dec. 1826; I/xiii/122, Darling–Bathurst, 22 Feb. 1827; /462, Goderich–Darling, 27 July 1827; I/xiv/76, Darling–Huskisson, 30 Mar. 1828; I/xiii/113, Darling–Bathurst, 16 Feb. 1827; C.O. 201/222/298, Stewart–Howick, 30 June 1831; 202/26/191, Howick–Stewart, 16 July 1831; *H.R.A.* I/xiii/668, Huskisson–Darling, 26 Dec. 1827, enc. Planta–Stanley, 27 Nov. 1827; C.O. 202/20/18, Hay–Hill, 8 Nov. 1827.

[1] *H.R.A.* I/xv/409, Murray–Darling, 10 Apr. 1830; /200, Darling–Murray, 9 Oct. 1829.

[2] I/xv/436, Darling–Murray, 22 Apr. 1830, enc. Darling–Judges of N.S.W., 16 Feb. 1830, and reply, 22 Feb. 1830.

[3] I/xv/817, Murray–Darling, 12 Nov. 1830.

There was, he argued, no point in false economies which merely robbed Peter to pay Paul. The home government should trust him to capitalize on the huge expenditure already made. New South Wales was not an old settled colony which could be governed by rote. Between 1825 and 1829 the revenue had increased by 50 per cent (from £67,000 to £95,000); eleven thousand convicts had arrived, and a great number of new establishments and settlements had been founded. He was in a very unpleasant dilemma. On the one hand the settlers demanded more services and amenities, and his officers complained that they had insufficient means to carry out their tasks. On the other he was thought prodigal at home. In fact, he insisted, what he had done had been accomplished by ceaseless labour and great personal sacrifice. His own salary was quite insufficient to meet basic costs, much less to enable him to fulfil his social obligations in a community where the governor needed to give special example and provide leadership.[1]

The Act of 1828 had indeed introduced a new element into the financial structure of the Australian colonies. From 1827 the civil expenses were expected to be met from colonial revenue. This had hitherto been raised largely from duties levied under the governor's authority. Now the council must be consulted. Arthur wrote that this would be a great source of future embarrassment and that it would lead to great difficulties in carrying out instructions from home which should direct the particular expenditure of any part of the colonial revenue. He declared himself ready to act with the Council, but was reluctant to initiate local legislation concerning the levy of duties until he could be sure that thereby he would not be contributing to a significant impairment of the authority of the Secretary of State. He preferred, therefore, to act under a proclamation rather than through a colonial law. The Treasury, who had welcomed and in part inspired the changes by which 'fixed' establishments were set up and a division of costs made between the civil and convict sections—with every prospect that colonial surplus funds should be applied to pay for at least the 'mixed' expenses such as police—were anxious about Arthur's action. They were concerned also that the workings of the 1828 Act would, by devolving authority, weaken their control over the expenditure of colonial revenue. The question was an important one and raised legal difficulties. James Stephen drew up for Hay an exhaustive report on the history of taxation in the Australian colonies.

[1] *H.R.A.* I/xv/742, Darling–Hay, 30 Sept. 1830.

He described how complaints about the arbitrary exercise of power in 1819 had led to the reaffirmation of the 'sound doctrine' that in an occupied country of vacant territory 'the Crown could not exercise, nor delegate to the Governor, any legislative authority, and least of all an authority for imposing and levying taxes'. He noted that the indemnifying Act of 1819 and the continuing Acts which gave temporary powers to the Governor had been acknowledged in the 1828 Act. Henceforth the powers to determine amounts of duties and the manner by which surplus revenue should be expended were vested in the governors in council. Huskisson's aim had been to supersede the autocratic legislative powers of the Governor. Stephen thought that, as the Act applied prospectively, Arthur's proclamation was in order as attached to revenue raised before the promulgation of the new law. But he admitted that there was obscurity in the Act and accepted responsibility for it. He recommended a new Bill which would clarify the situation and place the civil list beyond the reach of the Council's interference. Such an Act might also deal with such other questions as had caused dissension among the colonial lawyers; for example, the problem of masters' rights in their assigned convicts' labour.

Stephen apologized for the necessity of amending an Act drawn up so recently but confessed 'the extreme difficulty of legislating upon a very extensive subject with perfect precision'. He admitted the validity of Arthur's remarks about the changed status of the Legislative Council, but did not share his qualms. The Act, he stated firmly, had deliberately contemplated a development of the powers of the Council and this was no 'reasonable subject for regret'. After all, the Council was appointed by the Crown, on the recommendation of the Governor himself. One half of the members were *ex officio*. The Governor had the original and casting vote, and he prepared laws for adoption. Difficulties might indeed be raised, but financial measures rejected in such circumstances probably deserved to be rejected. This might cause embarrassment but important powers could not be entrusted to anyone without some inconvenience. He also noted that the House of Commons, now determined to examine imperial expenditure in growing detail, would surely be more ready to approve an estimate if it was known to be sanctioned by the local legislature. In any case the Council in Australian colonies was largely composed of officers who needed money and support for their departments and were 'so connected with the Crown as scarcely to be free Agents on such questions'.

He felt that 'the concession made to popular feeling has been more nominal than real'. The Governors had gained in being relieved 'from much obloquy' without any erosion of their former powers. But he stressed that henceforth any proposals to add to, or change, the public establishments financed from local revenue in New South Wales and Van Diemen's Land must be made in the form of recommendations to the Governor-in-Council and not as peremptory instructions to the Governor.

Arthur was told to consult and work through his Council. Stephen's views proved to be justified for a time, and certainly the Australian colonial legislatures did not create as many serious obstacles to their administrations in matters of finance as did those of British North America. But inevitably problems arose, and inevitably the task of the governors became more complicated during the thirties as attacks on the system of appropriation of public monies by a non-representative body mounted and the home authorities unwisely withheld revenues derived from the *droits* of the Crown and the sale of land from colonial control. For the governors there were compensations. Bourke obtained great public acclaim for merely carrying out Colonial Office instructions to give greater publicity to financial statements. Arthur took the opportunity of rejecting a number of men recommended from home for possible colonial employment and making a number of new appointments, saying that in these and other measures he had been following the advice of his Council 'for the good government of the country'. At all events the Treasury were certainly right in thinking that the administrative and legislative changes of 1827–9 had rendered their control over colonial costs and finance more remote, more delicate, and more difficult.[1]

* * * * *

After the Whigs came to power the uneasy dyarchy of Colonial Office and Treasury continued. Much of the groundwork had been

[1] C.O. 280/24/323, Arthur–Twiss, 8 Mar. 1830; /26/92, Stephen–Hay, 30 Aug. 1830; /216, Dawson–Hay, 15 Nov. 1830, enc. Brande–Treasury, 12 Aug. 1830; 408/6/132, Hay–Stewart, 12 Aug. 1830; 408/7/84, Murray–Arthur, 12 Nov. 1830; 280/37/92, Stewart–Hay, 19 Jan. 1832, enc. Col. Audit Report, 15 Dec. 1831, and Audit–Treasury, 16 Feb. 1831; 280/28/383, Arthur–Murray, 2 Apr. 1831; /29/104, Arthur–Goderich, 30 June 1831; A.C.V. Melbourne, op. cit., pp. 99, 119–20, 170, and esp. pp. 177 f. 'Financial Problems'; and e.g. D. G. Creighton, 'Struggle for Financial Control in Lower Canada', *C.H.R.* XII (1931), pp. 120–44.

done and was respected. In 1831, when arrangements were being made for Bourke's instructions to be drawn up, the Treasury reviewed the changes of the past decade. They noted that, when New South Wales was placed under the colonial audit and the new instructions formulated for Governor, Auditor and Treasurer, it had been agreed that the Treasury should be consulted on all matters of colonial finance. Reports were to be made to both departments, and no additions or changes introduced without the sanction of both. Bathurst had then insisted that all correspondence between the Treasury and the colonies was to pass through the Secretary of State. This system was approved and adopted in practice since early 1827, and had been extended to the Cape, Mauritius, Malta and Trinidad. Now they saw that, in the proposed new instructions to the governors, the Secretary of State could 'authorize by his separate order' the raising of money by the colonial government, without any reference to the Treasury. They could not forego 'that effectual control and supervision which they consider to be their undoubted duty on all occasions to exercise on all matters relating to the Revenue in the Colonies, as over every other Branch of the Public Revenue and Expenditure'; and they linked this demand with recent legislation providing that surplus colonial crown revenue should accrue to the Consolidated Fund. Howick, in reply, pointed out that the 1828 New South Wales Act had been framed to give the Council wider powers, and, except for revenues originating from crown rights and property, the Governor-in-Council possessed appropriation powers over all local revenue. Neither the Governor nor the Treasurer could legally authorize the issue of any part of these funds, except with the consent of the Council. Bourke would be instructed to lay before the Legislative Council each year an estimate of accounts. This must be previously approved by the Treasury, through the Secretary of State, and, despite the opposition of the Colonial Audit, given wide publicity in the colony. No particular difficulty was anticipated concerning the fixed and permanent expenses of the civil establishment, but Howick thought it was good that a governor should have to defend his policies and their administration in matters involving contingent appropriation, such as wage-rates, the price of labour and contracts, etc., where the Council could exercise disapproval or impose conditions. How far the Governor was responsible to the Treasury was now a real problem. Howick was anxious lest concessions rightly forced on him by his Council run him into difficulties at home. If a governor had in emergency to amend his approved estimates, he must formally register his protest in council and report the circumstances.[1]

The Treasury agreed to absolve the Australian governors from personal accountability where the Councils compelled them to actions or expenditure which were not in conformity with their instructions from home, but viewed with alarm any prospect that the Councils should be able to evade Treasury control. The governors must act strongly to control the expenditure and keep the home government well informed. They proposed that if necessary the existing laws should be changed so that the local Councils should not be encouraged to usurp altogether the function of financial appropriation. At all times the governors must observe the strictest economy and continue the attempt to devote surplus colonial revenues to help pay the colonies' convict and military expenses.

Howick replied that Bourke would be told of the Treasury's fears. He thought that experience had shown that the Councils were prepared to take upon the colonial revenues a fair proportion of the convict and military expenses, but opposed legislation which must only disturb good relations with rising colonies. Few reductions, indeed, could be hoped for while the colonies were still the instruments of a transportation system, but the progress of the colonial economies would soon allow great burdens of expense to be transferred. Goderich firmly rejected the untimely transfer of these costs merely 'for the sake of a small immediate saving to this country'. Even the revenue from land, which could be expected to be handsome, and on which the Treasury had its eye, should be looked on 'not so much as Income but Capital,' and would best be invested in emigration schemes, especially of females. In this way Britain would gain and a strong and prosperous community be built up. The Secretary of State also came to an arrangement whereby the Treasury would be approached formally only about significant changes in the colonial finances. Otherwise they might safely assume government supervision and approval through the auspices of the Colonial Office and the Audit. The Treasury, surrendering to a subtle change in the status of the Australian colonies, nevertheless continued to insist on receiving regular accounts of colonial revenues, taxation, and all statistics.[2]

---

[1] This would of course raise political issues, over which the Secretary of State would be primarily concerned.

[2] C.O. 323/213/188, Stewart–Howick, 29 June 1831; 324/85/29, Hay–Herries, Private, 25 Feb. 1826; C.O. 202/26/179, Howick–Stewart, 4 July 1831; 201/222/

The changes which took place in the audit system at home in 1831 and 1832 ensured that the Treasury would maintain its demands for regular, detailed, and up-to-date returns from the colonies. Early in 1832 a Circular was sent out insisting on a punctual submission of accounts in order that the Treasury might have 'periodically laid before them a distinct and comprehensive view of the whole expense which is incurred in our colonial establishments'. Despite the inevitable delays which continually held up the compilation and transmission of Blue Books, Brown Books and financial abstracts, much had been done to meet this aim. But whereas the Colonial Office had maintained and even strengthened its influence over the constructive government of the Australian colonies, constitutional and administrative change had made it less and less likely that the Treasury would ever be able entirely to succeed in achieving its avowed end of 'exercising a prompt control over the whole expenditure of the colonial government'.[1]

306, Stewart–Howick, 8 July 1831; 202/26/189, Howick–Stewart, 16 July 1831; /193, Howick–Stewart, 21 July 1831; 323/213/209, Stewart–Howick, 16 Aug. 1831; /222, Stewart–Hay, 17 Oct. 1831; 201/222/324, M. of Brande, 18 Oct. 1831.

[1] *H.R.A.* I/xvi/320, Howick–Bourke, 12 Aug. 1831, enc. Stewart–Howick, 6 Aug. 1831 sub. enc. Audit–Treasury, 27 June 1831; /534, Goderich–Bourke, 28 Feb. 1832, Circular, enc. Stewart–Hay, 17 Oct. 1831; /467, Goderich–Bourke, 24 Nov. 1831, circular—the salary of Colonial Treasury to be suspended if accounts are late; /478, Hay–Bourke, 21 Dec. 1831, enc. Stewart–Hay, 16 Dec. 1831, sub. enc. Audit–Treasury, 5 May, 2 Dec. 1831—on N.S.W. and V.D.L. accounts 1827–30;—on delays, *H.R.A.* I/xiv/649, Darling–Murray, 17 Feb. 1827; /720, Darling–Murray, 23 Apr. 1829; I/xv/556, Hay–Darling, 16 June 1830, enc. Stewart–Twiss, 14 June 1830 and Audit–Treasury, 24 May 1830; /61, Darling–Hay, 1 Feb. 1831.

VII

THE SEARCH FOR EFFECTIVE
COLONIAL ADMINISTRATION

THE years 1818–31 did not see the Treasury achieve a direct controlling influence over the development of colonial finance, but Treasury participation was a *sine qua non* of almost every colonial arrangement. Certain factors strengthened the hand of local administration. Among these were the simple facts of distance and the very intricacy of colonial affairs in process of change. The devolution of authority which resulted from the appointment of legislative and executive councils and the increasing use of colonial boards and departments also had their effect. Neither Darling nor Arthur were frightened to take the initiative. When Darling, for instance, decided to separate the commissariats of New South Wales and Van Diemen's Land, he acted first and only consequently informed the Treasury and Colonial Office. He had the support of the local commissaries in making this sensible move, and the decade saw an increase in the readiness shown by men on the spot to consider events from a colonial point of view. Brisbane's confused but significant efforts to institute civil service departments had affected colonial administration irreversibly. In the place of autocratic rule there sprang up a wide variety of special agencies each with its own style, interest and competence. The Home Government was now confronted with a number of official sources of information. In view of the growing tide of documents in which the financial proceedings of the colonies were communicated there was room for complaint by the Treasury about the complexity of colonial reports but surely not, as Bathurst noted, for Herries' charge that the Treasury was kept 'uninformed, not only of the measures which have from time to time led to occasional and extraordinary expenses in the colonies, but even of the state of their ordinary revenues and the permanent charges upon them'.[1]

[1] *H.R.A.* I/xii/424, Darling–Harrison, 22 July 1826, enc. Gen. Order, 1 July 1826, and Report of Board, 31 Jan. 1826; /458, Darling–Bathurst, 27 July 1826; III/vi/1, Hay–Arthur, 2 Apr. 1827, enc. Herries–Hay, 29 Mar. 1827; C.O. 323/207/126, Herries–Horton, 24 Mar. 1827, and ff.; C.O. 280/4/326, Sorell–Horton, 28 Feb. 1825.

The effect of conflicting advice upon practical administration could be confusing both for the home authorities and for the governors. In 1828 Darling tried to dismiss a commissariat plan to reduce the convict expenditure by initiating a broad programme of open contracts for stores and public works. He could not have been more brusque. Commissary Maddox had offended by sending his recommendations confidentially to the Chief Commissary W. Hill, who had forwarded them to Dawson at the Treasury, who in his turn submitted the documents for Colonial Office comment. Maddox's communication with the Treasury, wrote the Governor, 'was not founded on any correct data, and his deductions were speculative and erroneous'. But in fact the debate about the desirability of advertising for the supply of stores and services for the colonial government by means of open and competitive contract could not be decided by Darling's angry reaction. Issues were raised and attitudes expressed which called into question wide areas of the colonial governments' aims and achievements.[1]

The Treasury had long been uncomfortable about the traditional use in the convict colonies of government activities and finance to control the colonial economy, regulate wages and prices, and encourage supply and production. Commissariat officials, mindful of their duty to cut costs, were inclined to criticize the governors' actions as wasteful. Bigge broadly approved of Macquarie's policy of preventing monopoly, but the Colonial Office looked to Brisbane for a relaxation of government controls in the more developed state of the colony now emerging. Instead, there had followed the peculiar episode of the adoption of a dollar standard, when the settlers claimed that their property had depreciated by over 20 per cent because of the sudden change of commissariat practice. (The commissariat used a standard of 5s. = $1, but private merchants would only offer 4s. 2d. because of a glut of imported specie.) The Secretary of State commented that the settlers would have had less grounds for complaint had the measure been accompanied by an instruction to the Commissary 'to advertise for his supplies of all descriptions and to have accepted the lowest offer'. This was doubtful, as the pattern of Commissariat buying was a very delicate one which had grown up over many years, but it illustrates the Colonial Office's scepticism about the traditional

[1] *H.R.A.* I/xiv/172, Huskisson–Darby, 12 May 1828, enc. Dawson–Hay, 26 Apr. 1828, and Maddox–Hill, 4 Nov. 1827; /696, Darling–Murray, 7 Apr. 1829; 1/xv/152, Murray–Darling, 1 Sept. 1829.

fixed maximum price for the purchase of agricultural produce; and it warned the governor that he should 'as much as circumstances will admit' make use of open tenders and competitive contracts.[1]

What seemed to be at stake was an expensive protected system versus a freer 'market' arrangement which Treasury officials tended to think would prove much cheaper. The Treasury, though it had learnt to consult the Colonial Office about any measures suggested by commissariat officers on the spot which appeared to affect 'the general interests of the Colony', persistently raised the question of government contracts. Just about the same time as Darling was putting Commissary Maddox in his place, the Treasury was insisting that the recommendations of their men in the colonies be taken into consideration when the 1828 Bill should come into operation. Murray sharply reminded the Governor that he could not cavalierly dismiss matters which called for a full and considered report which could be forwarded by him to pacify the Treasury. Darling stuck to his guns.

Maddox's plan, he replied, was speculative and visionary. He pointed to a number of contracts which had ended in disaster and heavy expense. The very convict nature of the colony had effects upon the conditions and price of labour and material which simply made the workings of a normal liberal or market economy impossible.[2]

The Treasury, confusedly grasping that the accounts of their colonial subordinates were telling a tale of large expenditures under abnormal headings, did not relent in its efforts to make the convict colonies act in ways more conformable to the accustomed financial and commercial pattern. Early in 1830 Lord James Stewart pressed Hay and Twiss to urge the Governor to hasten the expansion of the assignment system, so that the convicts would not have to be supported at public expense and would, presumably, appear unmistakably on the credit side of Treasury ledgers. He again recommended that public works be carried out under a contract system.[3]

Hay and his political colleagues found it difficult to come to a clear decision. The whole basis of Australian colonization and its

---

[1] *H.R.A.* I/xi/95, Bathurst–Brisbane, 31 July 1823; I/x/729, Brisbane–Bathurst, 2 Sept. 1822, enc. Petition, 10 May 1822; I/xi/73 Bathurst–Brisbane, 31 Mar. 1823; /571, Brisbane–Bathurst, 14 May 1825.

[2] C.O. 201/176/44, Harrison–Hay, 24 Feb. 1826; /196/264, Hill–Gower, 16 Apr. 1828; *H.R.A.* I/xv/152, Murray–Darling, 1 Sept. 1829; /578, Darling–Murray, 12 July 1830.

[3] *H.R.A.* I/xv/828, Hay–Darling, 14 Dec. 1830, enc. Stewart–Twiss, 11 Feb. 1830.

future development was in question. Advice varied widely. They passed the better suggestions on to the Treasury but would not accept Treasury verdicts without query. Captain Montagu, who had been Arthur's private secretary from 1824 to 1826 and then clerk of the Councils, was available in England for consultation. He agreed with the Treasury. Public works carried out by convict labour were inefficient. Increase in assignment was possible, desirable, and would lead to significant reductions. He held that by 1828 the colonies were costing fully half a million pounds annually and possibly much more. Yet they were now advanced communities where there were private contractors quite capable of coping with government contracts on the spot. Much more recourse should be had to a competitive system. The Treasury, primed by Maddox, pointed out that the proper division of convict and colonial costs from which so much was hoped for, would be quite vitiated if great numbers of convicts were to be kept on in government service and employed in purposes which could only be termed colonial. But Howick refused to be hastened into making recommendations which seemed to be so much against the advice of the governors.[1]

Arthur, asked to give his views, firmly presented the case against the indecision now apparent at home. The very nature of the colonial government of Van Diemen's Land was endangered. Whatever might be said of New South Wales, where there existed a number of impressive buildings, etc. his own colony was relatively immature. Montagu's appreciation was wrong, he thought. Maddox, too, was premature in his views, and over-ambitious. It was, of course, he wrote, desirable to have a firm and intelligible division of accounts between the convict and colonial establishments. But the simpler the accounts could be kept, the cheaper and more efficient it would be both for the home government and the local community. The home authorities should not suppose that a penal colony did not have weighty disadvantages in its innermost structure. The burdens of transportation were heavy enough without the heavy-handed imposition of harsh and bureaucratic exactions. True economy, he maintained, 'will be found, —not in exhausting the limited resources of the colony, but, in improving and calling them more extensively into action by sending out a much larger body of convicts'. This was Arthur's special vision,

---

[1] C.O. 280/27/169, Montagu–Twiss, 5 Jan. 1830; 408/6/95, Hay–Montagu, 19 Feb. 1830; 280/27/173, Montagu–Hay, 8 Mar. 1830; 280/32/94, Stewart–Howick, 3 Jan. 1831; 408/6/187, Howick–Stewart, 27 May 1831.

but it was clear and coherent. It is an illustration of the great variety of opinions expressed about the future of the Australian colonies that Arthur could continue, at a time when humanitarian interest was rising against the brutalities of transportation, and when the liberal aspirations of Hay and others at the Colonial Office were looking favourably to the metamorphosis of convict colonies into free settlements, to suggest seriously that first offenders should be sent to Van Diemen's Land in the interest both of economy and reform. At the end of 1832 he was able to send home a report of a Board which opposed the contract system and supported his plea for more convicts. Arthur was not by any means against assignment. Indeed he spent long hours each day engaged on administering the details of assignment. But he had put a strong case against any dogmatic opinion which asserted that the colony was ready for radical liberalization. Hay, at least partly convinced by Arthur and Darling, wrote to Stewart that the Governor's letters confirmed 'the truth of what has been on more than one occasion stated by this Department . . . that much inconvenience results from officers of the Commissariat making the practice of sending home suggestions connected with colonial matters, without previously communicating upon them with the local government'.[1]

When Goderich communicated the report of the Commissioners of Colonial Enquiry to the new governor of New South Wales, the tone of his dispatch was very different from those which had from time to time so harassed General Darling. The recommendations of the Commission were treated with respect and in great detail, and the opportunity was taken to review the financial arrangements of the colony with a view to reduction. Attention was drawn to proposals aimed at simplifying the revenue-collecting machinery, and the office of Controller of Internal Revenue—established in 1827 by Darling to help relieve the Surveyor in the heavy duty of collecting quit rents on land, etc.—was abolished. Goderich supported a proposed tax on assigned convicts' labour which it was suggested might be employed to raise ways and means to subsidize emigration. The Colonial Office seemed convinced that the tax was justified and unwilling to consider the liabilities of settlers who accepted convict servants. Other matters mentioned concerned the containment of settlement within defensible

[1] C.O. 408/7/88, Hay–Arthur, 14 Dec. 1830; 280/33/368, Arthur–Howick, 18 Feb. 1832; /34/104, Arthur–Howick, 14 Apr. 1832; /36/359, Arthur–Hay, 12 Dec. 1832; 408/8/88, Hay–Stewart, 31 Oct. 1832.

limits, and the conditions of the civil service, where no pettifogging detail was too small for Treasury scrutiny. In addition the Governor was recommended to open again the old question of contracts for stores and public works. But Darling's protests had borne fruit. It was recalled somewhat guiltily that the Governor had argued persuasively for expansion and the insufficiency of existing arrangements just at a time when the home government seemed most insistent on the close examination and radical reduction of colonial costs. Stephen's views on the changed status of the Australian colonies had also had their effect. The Secretary of State seemed more ready to allow the Governor a wider field for his initiatives and encouraged that the new Legislative Council had caused little financial trouble. The way ahead seemed clear for the colonies gradually to take over the charges of the Commissariat and convict establishments as their economies matured. Henceforth many of the animadversions of the British Government would be couched in terms of advice rather than of command. It was, wrote Goderich, 'almost impossible to draw up instructions in this country with any confidence that they will be applicable to the actual situation of the Colony on their arrival'.[1]

* * * * *

Questions concerning stores and rations gave particular trouble. In 1824 drought and scarcity of grain forced Brisbane, at the request of the Commissariat, to import a cargo of rice and flour from Batavia, then within the trading preserve of the East India Company. When the ship *Almorah* returned to Sydney early the next year it was seized by Captain Mitchell of the visiting naval sloop H.M.S. *Slaney*. The Governor discovered that there were on board a large quantity of tea, over 100,000 dollars, and other articles ordered by the Commissariat but unauthorized by him. He was persuaded by Wemyss the Commissary was to give a reluctant sanction for these imports, but when Attorney-General Bannister tried to recover what he now considered Crown property, his boarding-party was fired on. Shortly

---

[1] *H.R.A.* I/xvi/34, Goderich–Darling, 23 Jan. 1831, on tax on convicts; 201/214/369, Stewart–Hay, 2 Dec. 1830 and 202/26/131, Howick–Stewart, 5 Apr. 1831, ditto; c.f. also I/xvi/346, Darling–Goderich, 10 Sept. 1831; *H.R.A.* I/xvi/382, Goderich–Bourke, 29 Sept. 1831; /587, Bourke–Goderich, 2 Apr. 1832; /814, Goderich–Bourke, 12 Dec. 1832; on Collector of Internal Revenue *H.R.A.* I/xiv/25, Darling–Huskisson, 15 Mar. 1828; /516, Murray–Darling, 12 Dec. 1828.

afterwards the *Almorah* departed without clearance.[1] Brisbane felt that he had many causes for complaint, and not least at the Commissary's assuming for himself 'a latitude he was by no means authorised to exercise'. In sending nearly £30,000 to Batavia (in Treasury Bills to be negotiated) the Treasury official had 'never deigned to consult me, or even acquaint me of his intentions', the Governor told Bathurst. He thought Wemyss an honest man, but 'full of weakness, caprice and malevolence', and, like Frederick Goulburn, a source of friction which must be removed if his own authority was to be upheld.[2]

Bathurst had no intention of allowing a governor's authority to be eroded by Treasury officials, even though he had already decided that Brisbane must go. He engaged in a brisk correspondence with his friend Lord Melville at the Admiralty.[3] Quite apart from the fine legal points involved, which it was agreed would require expert advice and litigation, departmental dignity was at stake. Melville regretted the incident, but strongly defended his officers. The warrant of the local Superintendent of Police under which the boarding-party had attempted to recover the property of the crown was 'flagrantly illegal,' he told Hay, his old colleague now under-secretary at the Colonial Office. Bathurst must recognize 'the extreme jealousy with which the Admiralty look at any attempt to limit or control the necessary authority of the King's Naval officers to prevent any person, on any pretence whatever, from coming on board either by stealth or forcibly, unless armed with some superior authority of unquestionable validity, military or civil'. Bathurst, for his part, could be relied on to insist on official etiquette. 'I assure you I only care about it,' he had written to Canning, 'because the observance of it is I think generally the best mode of preventing confusing collisions in Departments.'[4]

The Secretary of State suspected that the Commissary's importation of tea was a 'filch', but the Treasury defended Wemyss' action. 'It is the obvious duty of the Commissary', wrote Harrison to Hay, 'to obtain all supplies, required for the Publice Service, particularly of

[1] *H.R.A.* I/xi/529, Brisbane–Bathurst, 4 Mar. 1825.

[2] *H.R.A.* I/xi/556, Brisbane–Horton, 24 Mar. 1825.

[3] B.M. Add. MSS. Loan 57/16/1970, Hay–Bathurst, 5 Nov. 1825; 1 Nov. 1825.

[4] C.O. 323/146/296, Melville–Hay, 30 Oct. 1825; /300, Melville–Hay, 19 Nov. 1825; *H.R.A.* I/xii/674, Bathurst–Darling, 12 Nov. 1826; C.O. 201/176/185, Hill–Horton, 18 Nov. 1826; *H.R.A.* I/xiv/32, Darling–Huskisson, 20 Mar. 1828; B.M. Add. MSS. Loan 57/14/1710, Bathurst–Canning 29 Sept. 1823.

Articles not the produce of the Colony, from the best Market and upon the most favourable terms.' The Comptrollers of Army Accounts noted that, in this case, as opposed to former ones concerning Treasury officials, the honesty of the local Commissary was not disputed. They maintained that he had proceeded 'with a view to the Public interest, and to reduce the Public expenditure' and that he should be supported even though his importation of dollars had interfered with 'the private advantage of a large class of the most influential persons in the Colony'.[1]

Bathurst finally decided that it was reasonable to allow the Commissariat to import the stores and specie required for the public service, but he insisted that only emergency and the express authority of the Governor could excuse 'interference with the speculations of private commerce'. Private entrepreneurs should be encouraged and not exposed to ruin by the trading activities of the Commissariat. Officials who used their position for private profit were acting against Treasury instructions and must be removed from the service. Darling, already engaged in a thorough examination of the colonial departments, assured the Secretary of State that he would keep the Commissariat in its proper place. The Treasury officials had too long considered themselves 'an independent body not under the immediate control of either the civil or military Authority'. This error could not too soon be checked.[2]

The Governor's requisitions for supplies, based on the real needs of isolated colonial communities, were subject at intervals to the most minute examination by the home authorities. At first efforts were chiefly directed to eliminate waste and to avoid the stock-piling of expensive equipment. Gradually, as Lithgow and other colonial officials provided a more accurate picture of the machinery on which the soldiers, convicts and free settlers depended so much, it was possible to draw up more realistic scales of rations and institute more orderly reforms. Towards the end of 1828 Darling sent home his detailed annual requisition list. It had been prepared by a board 'in concert with the heads of the several Departments', but it had proved difficult to separate adequately the items required for the convict

---

[1] B.M. Add. MSS. Loan 57/57, Bathurst–Hay, 30 Oct. 1825; *H.R.A.* I/xii/130, Bathurst–Darling, 30 Dec. 1825, enc. Harrison–Hay, 9 Dec. 1825, and Drinkwater and Stewart–Harrison, 28 Nov. 1825, alluding to the 'Memorial of Certain Merchants of New South Wales to Sir Thos. Brisbane' of 13 July 1825.

[2] *H.R.A.* I/xii/141, Bathurst–Darling, 5 Jan. 1826; /660, Darling–Bathurst, 27 Oct. 1826.

service from those intended rather for civil or more general colonial purposes. The Colonial Office told him that the Treasury had agreed to send out the tools and stores requested, but had demanded that in future the Governor should give more particulars and render more accurate accounts. Goderich suggested that in future a new system of requisition be employed. Lists of articles required for colonial ends should be forwarded to the Agent, who would submit them to the Secretary of State. These should be distinguished from the lists of requisitions drawn up for the convict establishments, which should be sent to the Colonial Office direct. Darling thought this instruction impracticable. Colonial reality could not be neatly divided into categories in order to please the Treasury, but he promised to report in greater detail, and to observe as scrupulously as possible the heads —Colonial, Military and Convict. He also took the opportunity of complaining that stores were often of low quality and slow to arrive. Barnard, finding his business expanding uncomfortably, did not satisfy either Governor or Treasury. He noted that there were now fourteen colonial departments in New South Wales, all actively contributing to the list of requisitions. When the matter came up for review in 1829 the Colonial Office was pleased at Darling's efforts, but the Treasury had reversed their former opinions and suggested that it would be cheaper and more efficient if stores could be obtained by government departments in England rather than through private contracts and agencies. Once again it had proved almost impossible to co-ordinate neatly the retrenchment aims of the Treasury, a general government desire to encourage free enterprise under supervision, and colonial aspirations. When Darling, for example, asked that a number of iron bedsteads be sent to the colony for his troops, the request went to the Commander-in-Chief, the Colonial Office, the Treasury, the Commissariat, the Ordnance, and finally back to the Treasury and Colonial Office again. Eventually the Governor was given wider discretion. Throughout, the Treasury's object was to ensure that, somewhere along the line, the lists of requisitions were judged by an 'independent' scrutineer.[1]

[1] *H.R.A.* I/x/309, Harrison–Macquarie, 5 July 1820; /404, Macquarie–Bathurst, 7 Feb. 1821; /669, Bathurst–Lushington, 29 Sept. 1821; C.O. 202/11/53, Wilmot–Harrison, 13 June 1823; 201/165/309, Lithgow–Harrison, 30 Aug. 1824; *H.R.A.* I/xii/571, Darling–Bathurst, 11 Sept. 1826; I/xiii/298, Goderich–Darling, 13 May 1827, enc. Herries–Hay 3 Apr. 1827; C.O. 202/19/64, Hay–Herries, 7 May 1827; /95, Hay–Herries, 27 June, 1827; *H.R.A.* I/xiii/696, Darling–Goderich, 12 Jan. 1828 enc. his M. of 15 Aug. 1827; /699, of 11 Jan. 1828; C.O. 201/195/106,

The issue of rations and the storing of requisitions remained long a topic of interest to the Treasury. In Van Diemen's Land the question was complicated by the primitive conditions which existed in some of Arthur's penal settlements, the para-military activity which he conducted in connection with the clearing out of the bush-rangers, and the 'campaign' to collect the aborigines in 1830–1. Treasury concern could only be modified by repeated assurances that checks were maintained, and that the colonial revenues could bear an increasing share of the costs.[1]

* * * * *

One of the most important reforms which affected the colonies during the period after 1818 concerned the collection of customs and excise. Herries and Huskisson, the prime movers, became involved in long and wearisome discussion of principle with Horton, Bathurst, and Stephen at the Colonial Office. The arrangements for colonies possessing legislative assemblies caused great trouble.[2] Herries asked that the new principles of appointment and employment be applied even in those colonies where the officers were appointed by the Secretary of State and had not been placed under the Commissioners of Customs. He promised Horton that in settling the new arrangements the Treasury would take no step without fully consulting the Colonial Office.[3] It so happened that the customs activity, reform of the

---

Barnard–Twiss, 9 Aug. 1828; *H.R.A.* I/xiv/17, Darling–Barnard, 7 Mar. 1828; /18, Darling–Huskisson, 7 Mar. 1828; /601, Murray–Darling, 3 Jan. 1829; C.O. 201/205/251, Stewart–Hay, 6 Mar. 1829; /255, Stewart–Twiss, 30 Apr. 1829; /283 and /318, Dawson–Hay, 16 Nov. 1829; C.O. 201/205/330, Stewart–Twiss, 22 Dec. 1829;—on difficulty of drawing up requisitions, *H.R.A.* I/xv/3, Darling–Murray, 1 June 1829, enc. Rept. Board, 17 May 1829; I/xvi/545, Goderich–Bourke, Circular, 1 Mar. 1832.

[1] e.g. *H.R.A.* I/xvi/398, Darling–Goderich, 3 Oct. 1831; /671, Goderich–Bourke, 3 July 1832; I/xv/413, Murray–Darling, 12 Apr. 1830, enc. Stewart–Twiss, 3 Apr. 1830, and Audit–Treasury, 21 Jan. 1830; /397, Hay–Darling, 7 Apr. 1830; I/xvi/800, Hay–Bourke, 14 Nov. 1832, enc. Treasury–Hay, 13 June 1832; C.O. 280/28/180, Arthur–Hay, 10 Feb. 1831; /32/154, Stewart–Hay, 22 June 1831; /224, Arthur–Murray, 1 Mar. 1831; /240, Arthur–Murray, 1 Mar. 1831; /120, Stewart–Hay, 19 July 1831; /126, Stewart–Hay, 13 Sept. 1831; /28/317, Arthur–Murray, 31 Mar. 1831; /29/106, Arthur–Goderich, 30 June 1831; C.O. 408/6/119, Hay–Stewart, 20 May 1830; /211, Howick–Stewart, 6 Sept. 1831; /22, Twiss–Stewart, 2 Mar. 1829; /159, Howick–Stewart, 10 Jan. 1831; /181, Howick–Stewart, 26 Apr. 1831.

[2] Young, *op. cit.*, p. 209 ff.; C. R. Fay, *Huskisson and His Age* (London, 1951), pp. 113, 285 ff.; C.O. 323/203/137, Horton–Huskisson, Private, 30 Aug. 1825.

[3] C.O. 323/203/108, Herries–Horton, 8 Aug. 1825; /241, Herries–Horton, 4 Dec. 1825.

administration, abolition of fees, and the great consolidation of laws which took place in 1825, coincided with urgent local demands for improvement.[1]

Governor Arthur had successfully applied to have the office of Treasurer separated from that of Naval Officer in Hobart, where the popular Dr. Bromley was discovered to have defaulted by many thousand pounds. Sorell, who had trusted Bromley, told Horton that the two offices had been combined by Macquarie to save money, there being at that time no salary set aside for colonial Treasurers.[2]

Arthur tried to introduce changes into the Naval Officers' department which aimed at bringing its practice into line with English and imperial precedent. These changes were naturally not favoured by some local merchants who had found Bromley's personality attractive and his inefficiency, or worse, convenient. But the Governor obtained the backing of the Colonial Office who were alarmed at the defection and evidence pointing towards large-scale dishonesty, smuggling, thievery, and the corruption of the convict clerks. Hay consulted the Treasury and Bathurst sent Arthur a report (4 July 1826) from the Commissioners of Customs which clarified the Governor's position, backed the local authorities against the complaints of the colonial merchants and generally approved of what Arthur's appointee Hamilton had done to bring his department into 'unison with the practice in British America and in the United Kingdom'.[3]

In 1826 Bathurst sent a circular dispatch to the Australian colonies informing the governors that the colonial collection of customs would henceforth be directly administered under instructions from the Commissioners of Customs in London. Darling took the opportunity to inquire into the highly idiosyncratic administrative methods of Captain Piper, Naval Officer at Sydney. He set up a board which included, along with the official members, two prominent merchants, Richard Jones and Edward Wollstonecraft, the Chairman of the new Chamber of Commerce (who later withdrew because of attacks made in the *Australian*). The report from Sydney gave a full account of the multifarious duties of the Naval Officer, the port regulations, system

[1] *H.R.A.* 1/xiii/545, Darling–Goderich, 8 Oct. 1827.

[2] *H.R.A.* III/v/19, Hay–Arthur, Private, 22 Dec. 1825; III/iv/204, Arthur–Bathurst, 27 Oct. 1824; /298, Bathurst–Arthur, 4 July 1825—appt. of O'Ferrall in place of Arthur's appointee Hamilton; 280/4/394, Sorell–Horton, 6 June 1825.

[3] *H.R.A.* III/v/49, Arthur–Bathurst, 17 Jan. 1826; C.O. 280/8/180, Herries–Hay, 20 May 1826; /9/94, B. Broughton–Bathurst, 13 Nov. 1826; C.O. 408/2/29, Hay–Herries, 3 May 1826; *H.R.A.* III/v/301, Bathurst–Arthur, 10 July 1826.

of fees, etc. Obviously the existing establishment was quite inadequate for the proper collection of revenue or the prevention of smuggling. A regular Custom House with salaried officers was recommended. The board also proposed a full reform of methods of procedure, the registry of vessels engaged in colonial trade, and an efficient system of warehousing. Deacon Hume's work in England to consolidate the customs laws was noted with approval and envy. It was urged that the colonial system should follow as closely as possible that now adopted at home. But a number of special and largely protective duties were proposed.[1]

A very large deficit was discovered in Piper's accounts. The Governor set about to carry through in detail reforms aimed at correcting the 'neglect and inefficiency' which had distinguished a department from which so much revenue was now hoped for. Salaries were substituted for fees and pains taken to select honest men for the minor appointments.[2] Judge Forbes wrote to Horton commending Darling's efforts to follow out Treasury instructions and replace Piper's private empire with a sound, well-staffed office. He was critical of appointments made from home and thought the governors should have a freer hand. Darling and Arthur had discussed the problem of civil service appointments. It was essential that dishonest and ineffective men be removed. Yet the home government was unwilling to surrender its patronage and insisted that each decision, practical step, or appointment made on the spot be checked and approved at home by both C.O. and Treasury.[3]

[1] *H.R.A.* I/xiii/136, Bathurst–Darling, 1 Jan. 1826; III/v/25, Bathurst–Arthur, 1 Jan. 1826; I/xii/653, Darling–Bathurst, 21 Oct. 1826, enc. M. of 12 Oct. 1826; approved in /418 Goderich–Darling, 12 June 1827; C.O. 201/182/121, 2 Apr. 1827.

[2] Arthur's officials later pointed out a discrepancy between their regulations, which had been adapted from imperial practice elsewhere, and the local practice. The regulations envisaged that the salaries would be deducted first from the revenue which would then be subsequently turned over to the Colonial Treasurer. Arthur, however, had commanded them to send all the revenue to the Treasurer in the first place. When they were consulted, the Commissioners of Customs agreed that, although their 1827 arrangements had been in the former sense, in fact the governor of New South Wales had acted in the same way as Arthur. They approved, and stressed that the practice of both colonies always be assimilated as much as possible.

[3] *H.R.A.* I/xiii/245, Darling–Bathurst, 10 Apr. 1827; /246, 247 Darling–Bathurst, 11 Apr. 1827; C.O. 280/24/33, Arthur–Murray, 1 Feb. 1830; 408/6/136, Hay–Stewart, 17 Aug. 1830; 280/26/212, Stewart–Hay, 29 Sept. 1830; 408/7/74, Murray–Arthur, 8 Oct. 1830; C.O. 201/188/103, Forbes–Horton, 15 May 1827; 323/146/243, Arthur–Horton, 23 Apr. 1826; 201/186/308, Frankland Lewis–Hay, 7 Dec. 1827; *H.R.A.* I/xiii/592, Huskisson–Darling, 4 Nov. 1827.

Co-operation between the two departments was often most un-satisfactory in practice. Arthur complained that the methods followed by Bromley's successor as Naval Officer, Rolla O'Ferrall, a young man commended to the Colonial Office by the Duchess of Suther-land, made him 'quake'. The Collector of Duties at Launceston was just as bad. Yet his efforts to encourage honesty and reform were frustrated by his inability to offer reasonable salaries or to count on his nominations to office being confirmed when he did find a capable man. Undoubtedly the Colonial Office had good intentions. Hay urged Lewis at the Customs to make good appointments when the Australian colonies should become the responsibility of the Treasury. Huskisson, in addition to reserving to himself the appointment of the first Comptroller of Customs at Sydney under the new system, tried to take care that Darling's minor appointments be continued. He was also willing to confirm Arthur's nominations if this was compatible with engagements already entered into by the Colonial Office or the Treasury.[1]

Much damage was caused by the absence of a single, impartial, professional source from which nominations to Colonial appoint-ments might flow and by which a vigilant scrutiny might be main-tained of subsequent performance. It was reasonable for men to be appointed from England, particularly in the absence of respectable and large communities in the colonies. But the haphazard patronage which frequently characterized Colonial Office appointments seriously hampered colonial governors, who learnt only gradually to have the confidence to suspend and dismiss men highly recommended from home, and to insist on supporting their own nominees. In 1827 Arthur had to report a serious robbery from the Colonial Treasury, and he suspected worse. He protested that O'Ferrall's slipshod examinations of departing ships had failed to prevent the escape of runaway convicts. Mere routine observance of even the best imperial customs practice was insufficient for the special vigilance required in the ports of a penal settlement. The Colonial Office refused to inter-fere in what was now a responsibility of the Treasury. Hopefully

[1] *H.R.A.* III/vi/291, Arthur–Goderich, 1 Nov. 1827; /314, Arthur–Hay, Separate, 1 Nov. 1827; /245, Arthur–Hay, 23 Sept. 1827; C.O. 202/20/25, Hay–Frankland Lewis, 17 Nov. 1827; C.O. 202/20/32, Hay–Hill, 28 Nov. 1827; /142, Leveson Gower–Hill, 26 May 1828; 324/86/1, Hay–Lewis, 7 Nov. 1827; 202/20/57, Hay–Planta, 22 Jan. 1828; 408/4/135, Gower–Dawson, 26 May 1828; *H.R.A.* I/xiii/246, Darling–Bathurst, 10 Apr. 1827; /592, Huskisson–Darling, 4 Nov. 1827; /652, Darling–Goderich, 17 Dec. 1827.

O'Ferrall had improved and could be confirmed in office. The next year the collector at Launceston was found to be over £3,000 short in his accounts. Van Diemen's Land offered special difficulties and Arthur called urgently for detailed instructions if the new arrangements were to be effective. He complained that, though smuggling was not now so widespread and he had acted to purify the corrupt establishments, he needed more support and guidance from home. The Colonial Office forwarded his dispatches to the Treasury, who at least grasped that a uniformity of practice must exist in both Australian colonies. Early in 1829 decisions were at last made about the size and make-up of the Tasmanian establishment. Cotton, the new Collector at Sydney, was sent to investigate and towards the end of the year Arthur was able to report that, despite delay and confusion, the revenue was being collected and was growing steadily.[1]

Under the new system, the Commissioners of Customs were to be consulted about regulations, procedure, and salaries. Although of course it was not intended that revenue should leave the colonies, accounts were to be examined in England as well as submitted to the Governor. Darling prepared instructions for the Collector and Comptroller. Both the Treasury and the Commissioners of Customs were ready to approve technical reforms suggested from the colony, but were concerned about the colonial board's 'questionable policy' of recommending increases of duties aimed at protecting local enterprise. Huskisson and Stanley agreed. The Secretary of State was sympathetic to all attempts at colonial advancement and ready to encourage local growth, but baulked at the imposition of new protective duties 'as tending to diminish the inter-colonial intercourse, as well as that with the Mother country'.[2]

The Treasury was hesitant to interfere in matters of colonial government as such, but firmly supported 'the imperialism of free trade'. Under no circumstances would they approve of a principle which would lead to the imposition of taxes on the produce of the

[1] *H.R.A.* III/vi/191, Arthur–Bathurst, 23 Sept. 1827; C.O. 280/16/192, Arthur–Hay, Private, 12 Apr. 1828; 408/4/169, Twiss–Stewart, 30 Oct. 1828; 408/6/54, Hay–Stewart, 30 July 1829; 280/19/60, Arthur–Murray, 2 Feb. 1829; /20/21, Arthur–Murray, 3 Apr. 1829; /19/346, Arthur–Murray, 20 Feb. 1829; /22/230, Stewart–Twiss, 3 Jan. 1829; /21/468, Arthur–Twiss, 9 Oct. 1829; /470, Arthur–Commissioners of Customs, enc. Rept. 9, 1829.

[2] C.O. 201/186/308, Frankland Lewis–Hay, 7 Dec. 1827; *H.R.A.* 1/xiii/545, Darling–Goderich, 8 Oct. 1827; instructions enc. at C.O. 201/183/373 ff.; C.O. 201/186/314, Minutes by Huskisson and Stanley on Lewis–Hay, 7 Dec. 1827; 202/20/47, Stanley–Lewis, 26 Dec. 1827

United Kingdom. When the colonial governors, acting under different local pressures, adopted different scales of duties in 1828 neither Treasury nor Colonial Office was slow to notice the division of opinion. Whatever could be said of the scales, and it was argued that the Treasury and Board of Trade did not go out of their way to assist colonial imports to the United Kingdom, it was agreed that a more careful eye should be kept on maintaining uniformity of practice in New South Wales and Van Diemen's Land.[1]

Darling felt strongly the handicap which a shortage of capable officials imposed on all his civil service reforms. He succeeded in bringing out of retirement Macquarie's outstanding colonial secretary J. T. Campbell to take Piper's place as Collector, and moved Captain Rossi, who had been sent from home to organize the new police force, to the position of Controller. When Campbell resigned, Rossi acted as Collector. The governor feared that, despite a notable drive to stamp out smuggling, it continued 'to no inconsiderable extent'. This was not a law-abiding community.[2]

Hand-to-mouth measures dissatisfied the governors who were both determined to lay down the regular and stable framework of a civilized colonial society. Darling welcomed the appointment of both Collector and Controller, the first of whom, Michael Cotton, became a member of the Legislative Council under the 1828 Act. By the time they arrived the Governor was convinced that a more numerous establishment would be needed to keep pace with the great expansion of business brought about by the growth of commerce and trade than the Treasury had foreseen. Among 'purely experimental' measures he had appointed more clerks and storekeepers and his actions were supported by the new arrivals who pushed ahead with a thorough remodelling of the customs service to assimilate it as far as possible to that of Great Britain.[3]

[1] C.O. 201/205/235, Dawson–Twiss, 22 Jan. 1829; 280/19/187, Arthur–Murray, 10 Feb. 1829, enc. Memorial of Merchants 15 Sept. 1828, protesting against the inequality of duties between the high level of V.D.L. and that of N.S.W.; 408/4/165, Twiss–Stewart, 15 Oct. 1828; 280/22/44, Dawson–Twiss, 22 Jan. 1829.

[2] H.R.A. I/xiii/246, Darling–Bathurst, 10 Apr. 1827; /652, Darling–Goderich, 17 Dec. 1827; I/xiv/566, Darling–Murray, 31 Dec. 1828.

[3] H.R.A. I/xiii/246, Darling–Bathurst, 10 Apr. 1827; /652, Darling–Goderich, 17 Dec. 1827; I/xiv/566, Darling–Murray, 31 Dec. 1828; /249, Murray–Darling, 19 July 1828; /623, Murray–Darling, 1 Feb. 1829; /566, Darling–Murray, 31 Dec. 1828; /123, Darling–Huskisson, 10 Apr. 1828; /693, Darling–Murray, 6 Apr. 1829, enc. Langa and Cotton–MacLeay, 26 Mar. 1829; /641, Darling–Murray, 12 Feb. 1829.

The Treasury felt more comfortable now that the Commissioner of Customs had entered into the dialogue and was able to accede more gracefully to requests for the enlargement of the colonial establishment, for better buildings, equipment and conditions of employment, when the Governor's advice was supported by their own appointed officials. In New South Wales, by the time Governor Bourke succeeded Darling, the customs department was well under way to becoming an effective as well as a very productive instrument of local and imperial policy. (The Western Australian customs establishment never came under the imperial system, as duties were collected by the Collector of Colonial Revenue, a local official.) On the whole, customs arrangements satisfied both local and imperial needs until, with the repeal of the Navigation Acts and the movement towards self-government in the 1840s, it became inevitable that the colonies would exercise clear autonomy over customs affairs.[1]

In Van Diemen's Land, it did indeed seem that O'Ferrall had improved, though the Colonial Secretary, John Burnett, a regular and voluminous correspondent of Hay's, spoke of his 'total incompetence' and Arthur continued to try to drop him. Even Bromley's case seemed more excusable when his convict clerk, Bartholomew Broughton, was said to have left over £8,000 in his will. But in 1832 it emerged that O'Ferrall had, since 1828, been involved in an extraordinarily bold series of frauds, in collusion with other officials, chiefly the Colonial Treasurer Thomas. Both principals had been members of the Legislative Council. Both had taken part in considerable land and commercial speculation. They had avoided detection by the simple expedient of rushing large sums of money back and forth between their offices during the process of audit. A sudden simultaneous check disclosed major defaults. The discovery followed the decision to place all surplus colonial funds in the banks, now deemed respectable, though O'Ferrall had, contrary to Arthur's policy, been a large shareholder in the Commercial Bank. The Governor wrote bitterly that O'Ferrall, who had arrived penniless and in debt, was now rich. O'Ferrall added insult to injury by accusing the businesslike and

---

[1] C.O. 201/214/336, Stewart–Twiss, 24 June 1830; /353, Stewart–Hay, 23 July 1830; 323/213/131, C.O. Returns to Treas. letter of 15 Mar. 1831; /211, Stewart–Hay, 22 Aug. 1831; *H.R.A.* I/xiv/712, Murray–Darling, 19 Apr. 1829; I/xv/567, Murray–Darling, 28 June, enc. Stewart–Twiss, 24 June 1830; I/xvi/358, Darling–Goderich, 19 Sept. 1831; /668, Goderich–Bourke, 18 June 1832; J. A. La Nauze 'The Collection of Customs in Australia: A Note On Administration', *H.S.A.N.Z.* 4 (1949).

competent governor of nepotism, moneylending and abuse of authority. He even blamed his default impudently on the sheer inefficiency of the colonial audit in failing to catch him out earlier. Arthur agreed that the auditor, a commissariat official, had, by his unimaginative following out departmental rules, allowed O'Ferrall to conceal his activities. The cost to the public of this episode, he wrote gloomily, amounted perhaps to over £20,000.[1]

* * * * *

In instituting a thorough cleansing and reorganization of the colonial departments the governors had continually to balance costs against improvement and efficiency. Thus, for example, in the aftermath of the Bigge Report, the intended reform of the Police Department, so important in the life of convict colonies, led in New South Wales to the appointment of a new superintendent, Captain Rossi, an experienced colonial official, and assistants chosen from the ranks of the Metropolitan Police. Brisbane was very happy with Rossi's 'zeal, discretion and activity' and supported a memorial arguing strongly for a salary higher than the £600 from colonial funds which Bathurst had approved. This plea was predictably refused, but a report of Rossi's demanding that the colonial police must have more men, better salaries and improved conditions of service raised wider issues. Darling was convinced and, on the unanimous agreement of the Executive Council, acted accordingly. He judged that the colony could well afford the cost of an efficient police force. Faced with a *fait accompli* the Colonial Office acquiesced, but Goderich sharply reminded Darling that he was forbidden except in cases of extreme necessity to 'incur any expense exceeding £200 or to authorize any augmentation of salary to take place, or any new appointments to be made, until you shall have reported the grounds . . . and until the sanction of the Secretary of State shall have been first obtained'. It was merely one shot in a continuing battle. The governors refused to be as impressed by Treasury protests that no exceptions might be made in favour of the Australian colonies in the general rule of

---

[1] C.O. 280/23/18, Burnett–Hay (Secret and Confidential), 20 Jan. 1829; /47, Bromley–Murray, 26 Aug. 1829; /59, C.O. Minute, 8 Mar. 1830; 408/8/132, Hay–Stewart, 19 Mar. 1833; /118, Goderich–Arthur, 13 Mar. 1833; 280/36/162, Arthur–Goderich, 3 Nov. 1832; /36/252, Arthur–Goderich, 10 Dec. 1832; /346, Arthur–Hay, 11 Dec. 1832; /39/199, Arthur–Goderich. 22 Feb. 1833.

reduction all round as the Secretary of State hoped his repeated warnings would make them.[1]

Neither the Treasury nor the Colonial Office could quite concede that the economic life and social requirements of distant colonies and the home-land might have a subtly distinct rhythm and pace. Undoubtedly the colonies relied on the British link as on a life-line, and developments at home could be relied on to have immediate impact, but the governors could safely have been trusted with more initiative in making provision to meet the special demands of their expanding charges. While it was encouraging to be commended for conscientious efforts to bring about improvements in the public service 'notwithstanding the commercial depression, which has prevailed throughout the world, and from which therefore Van Diemen's Land could not be expected to be exempt', Arthur found it frustrating to have his reasonable requests for salary adjustments to be rejected on the grounds that the salaries of all public servants were undergoing revision at home in a time of retrenchment and that he could expect no different treatment.[2]

Darling had learnt before he left England of plans to reorganize and increase the civil establishment of the colony 'so as to provide more effectually for its growing interests'. He had rightly insisted on a competent financial adviser to attend to the accounts. Lithgow had already made his mark and the Treasury had in his reports and those of the various colonial boards a source of detailed information and recommendation about revenue, expenditure, fees, rations, public works, accounts, salaries and conduct of the public officers. This mass of detail created considerable problems when it came down to making concrete decisions, even when the local Treasury officials threw their weight behind the Governor's policy. In cases where economy seemed to be against advancement it was left to the Colonial Office to pick

[1] *H.R.A.* I/xii/95, Bathurst–Brisbane, 31 July 1823; /322, Bathurst–Brisbane, 23 July 1824; /457, Bathurst–Brisbane, 2 Jan. 1825; A. G. L. Shaw, op. cit., pp. 195–7; *H.R.A.* I/xi/904, Brisbane–Bathurst, 21 Nov. 1825; I/xii/357, Bathurst–Darling, 11 July 1826; I/xi/159, Darling–Hay, 4 Feb. 1826; /679, Darling–Bathurst, 15 Nov. 1826, enc. Rossi–MacLeay, 7 Oct. 1826, and Minute of Ex. Co. 1 Nov. 1826; I/xiii/419, Goderich–Darling, 15 June 1827; I/xiv/188, Huskisson–Darling, 16 May 1828; I/xiii/519, Darling–Goderich, 23 Sept. 1827; I/xvi/547, Goderich–Bourke, Circular 1 Mar. 1832, enc. Stewart–Hay, 23 July 1829; 201/222/334, Stewart–Howick, 10 Aug. 1831; 408/7/220, Goderich–Arthur, 3 Nov. 1831; 408/7/92, Goderich–Arthur, 28 Dec. 1830.

[2] C.O. 408/5/77, Murray–Arthur, 21 Aug. 1828; /87, Murray–Arthur, 2 Oct. 1828; cf. also R. M. Hartwell, 'Australia's First Trade Cycle, 1820–1832', *R.A.H.S.* 42 (1956), p. 51 f.

up the pieces and to try to co-ordinate diverse views. Here the observance of departmental propriety and consultation was vital, and the Colonial Office stood firm on its priority. When the Treasury, for example, sent Bathurst the instructions drawn up for the guidance of the Governor and other revenue officials by the Commissioners of Colonial Audit in 1826 with the help of Lithgow's reports, Hay, among other emendations, took good care to insert a direction that 'all correspondence between the Treasury and the Colonies is to pass through the Secretary of State'. It was also regularly insisted that all colonial correspondence should pass through the Governor. That which did not was liable to be, and most frequently was, referred back to the colony for his perusal and comment.[1]

A constant Treasury complaint was that colonial governors appeared to be expanding their civil service departments without reference home. In 1822 Harrison had demanded to have all particulars of colonial appointments before he would sanction the payment of salaries. Darling, encouraged by the optimism of his early communications with Horton and Hay, and confirmed by his initial experience of running the government machine of New South Wales, found it essential to make or support a great variety of new appointments. It was necessary to obtain the services of good men who would stay on as settlers after they had finished their period of office. Salary scales must be raised to attract better and more trustworthy clerks. Convict clerks simply should not be employed in revenue business or on confidential matters. To his requests that the Colonial Treasurer's office be enlarged the Colonial Office was sympathetic, but by 1826, when Horton's own establishment in Downing St. was under attack, it was natural that Darling's action to expand the office of his Colonial Secretary should be resisted.[2]

Hay and Horton, forced to enter into discussions with the Treasury

---

[1] C.O. 201/163/18, Darling–Bathurst, 4 Jan. 1825; /32, Darling–Bathurst, 2 Mar. 1825; 201/165/309, Lithgow–Harrison, 30 Aug. 1824; /305, Treasury Minute, 18 Aug. 1825, founded on Lithgow's reports; /346, Lithgow–Harrison, 30 Dec. 1824; /176/44, Harrison–Hay, 24 Feb. 1826, enc. Brisbane–Harrison, 16 Apr. 1825; B.M. Add. MSS. Loan, 57/58, Bathurst–Hay, 2 Nov. 1826; C.O. 201/176/38, Hill–Hay, 21 Feb. 1826; 324/84/29, Hay–Herries, Private, 25 Feb. 1826; 201/176/90, Hill–Hay, 13 June 1826.

[2] C.O. 201/110/79, Harrison–Horton, 24 Jan. 1822; H.R.A. I/xii/366, Darling–Bathurst, 20 July 1826; /368, Darling–Bathurst, 20 July, enc. rec. of Board including Lithgow and MacLeay re convict clerks, and enc. MacLeay–Darling, 28 June 1826; /371, Darling–Bathurst, 20 July 1826; /712, Bathurst–Darling, 3 Dec. 1826; /691, Darling–Bathurst, 16 Nov. 1826; I/xiii.420, Goderich–Darling, 16 June 1827.

about the expenses of their own department, did not forget the regulations, conditions, equipment, passage allowances, etc. of civil servants proceeding from England. They were keen, as part of a practical reform of colonial administration, to have a regular and efficient system of appointment, salaries and conditions. In 1825 when Herries had arranged that Alexander MacLeay, Colonial Secretary Designate of New South Wales and ex-Secretary of the Transport Board, should receive £2,800 per annum, Horton pointed out that the Treasury were here acting inconsistently with agreed and accepted principles. MacLeay had had a handsome pension. Now his proposed salary, if considered merely as salary, was too much, especially as it would be met from locally raised funds. He protested that the Treasury should themselves observe their own principle that 'Pensions should be dormant whenever the pensioner should accept new office'.[1]

No detail of the colonial establishments was too small to escape scrutiny. Darling's colonial boards busily produced reports, and their recommendations found their way into departmental practice as the complicated apparatus of administration for a freer society was constructed. At home a continual barrage of criticism exasperated and discouraged the governors.[2]

Even the work of drawing up registers showing details of colonial appointments and the authorities under which they had been made and keeping them up-to-date for the Audit at home was not an easy task. The changes which followed the reforms of 1826–7 had not simplified the duties of either Colonial Secretary or Colonial Auditor. Darling had also been called on to send home, in anticipation of the Public Accounts probes into colonial finance, answers to a number of questions which required more detail and attention than the normal Blue Book. He had found the process of dividing expenses and accounts between convict and colonial heads very complex and difficult. It could not be disguised that expenditure had risen in the previous three years. But there was a corresponding increase in revenue

[1] C.O. 324/146/53, Hay–Hill, 20 Sept. 1826; 63, Horton–Herries, 15 Dec. 1826; 323/203/259, Hill–Horton, 20 Dec. 1825; 201/165/236, Horton–Hay, Minute of 1825.

[2] H.R.A. I/xiii/76, Darling–Hay, 6 Feb. 1827; /242, Darling–Bathurst, 8 Apr. 1827; /568, Darling–Hay, 30 Oct. 1827; I/xiv/24, Darling–Huskisson, 13 Mar. 1828; /80, Huskisson–Darling, 31 Mar. 1828; /624, Darling–Murray, 1 Feb. 1829, I/xvi/300, Darling–Goderich, 16 July, 1831; C.O. 201/229/404, Darling–Goderich, 21 June 1832.

and he thought it unjust that the urgent requirements of expanding colonies should be shelved or rejected because of the passion now being felt at home for retrenchment. In New South Wales everything had to be done. Eventually all the expensive setting up of departments and bringing about of other improvements would lead to real savings. It was absurd, e.g. to cancel the salt rations from England on grounds of economy, if the home government really wanted new settlements at Melville Island, Fort Wellington, Western Port and King George's Sound; for only salt rations were suitable, and the locally cured meat was dear and unsatisfactory.[1]

The Governor insisted that his enlargement of the Colonial Secretary's staff was necessary to keep up with the vast growth of official business. No matter how helpful various boards proved or how much the Superintendent of Convicts could accept responsibility for convict affairs and assignment, the Colonial Secretary was the great engine of administration. His office must inevitably bear the brunt of colonial correspondence. Murray reluctantly capitulated.[2]

The Colonial Auditor, pressed to render a more prompt account of the colonial finances, was able to point out that his work had been hampered by a lack of competent men on his staff. The changes of 1826–7 were bad enough, completely disturbing the continuity of all ledgers, etc. Now he was expected, with inexperienced and underpaid clerks, to provide ever more detailed and accurate reports and statistics. The Governor forwarded Lithgow's request for an increased establishment and supported his demand that salaries be raised so as to attract more efficient and trustworthy men. Characteristically he had already acted in the interests of order and efficiency. The Colonial Office, anxious to obtain reliable information from the colony, approved what had been done. The increase in salaries should be offset, however, by the clerks' working for longer office hours. Thus the new passion for statistics and method had its effects. The production of the Blue Book for the year of transition 1827 had placed great strain on the Colonial Secretary, and MacLeay was uncomfortable at being held responsible for delays over which he had not the slightest real control. The Governor tried to hasten the returns by transferring the duty of preparing the Blue Book to the Auditor. But on receiving

[1] C.O. 201/186/276, Hill–Hay, 24 Aug. 1827; *H.R.A.* I/xiv/11, Darling–Huskisson, 5 Mar. 1828; I/xiii/426, Goderich–Darling, Circular, 1 July 1827; /786, Darling–Goderich, 16 Feb. 1828.

[2] *H.R.A.* I/xiii/564, Darling–Goderich, 27 Oct. 1827; I/xiv/217, Murray–Darling, 31 May 1828.

the Colonial Office Circular of 6 June 1828 he cancelled this sensible arrangement and the irksome duty reverted once more to MacLeay. In London the Treasury made little account of the difficulties which change, improvisation and overwork created on the spot.[1]

The Colonial Office, bombarded by the Treasury and Colonial Audit with inquiries about colonial finance, could reply that the restless activities of the previous two years would soon bear fruit in an orderly and intelligible system. From official and private correspondence a stronger case could have been made. Dumaresq, for example, had given Horton a clear and impressive picture of the revised working of bureaucracy in New South Wales, of the endless difficulties which arose in the administration of a colony where the Governor had to report home each petty item of expenditure and the Colonial Secretary dealt with over 9,000 letters a year. But Horton, with his flair for change, improvement, and liberalization, had moved on. At least one of his successors had to be convinced that the accounts of the Australian colonies did not make utter nonsense. There was, runs an under-secretary's minute, 'quite extraordinary' confusion in the first efforts of Darling and Arthur to tabulate convict and colonial costs separately; and he expressed doubts about the very existence of an audit section in the colonies. More important, he thought that the statistics, such as they were, did not conceal that the mother country was paying for a great number of purely colonial expenses. Henry Short, more conversant with the ebb and flow of colonial correspondence, assured him that the Governors' efforts had brought about great improvements and that they had done nothing which was unreasonable or out of line with their instructions. Even the most impatient Treasury officials, (and few of them seemed able to tolerate the existence of apparently redundant clerks in the colonies for a moment), could hardly press for the bold transfer of the 'mixed' costs, for example those of the inflated police establishment needed because of the existence of convicts in the community, to colonial funds which were still so slender.[2]

---

[1] *H.R.A.* I/xiv/252, Darling–Huskisson, 28 July 1828, enc. Lithgow–MacLeay, 28 May 1828; /277, Darling–Huskisson, 31 July, enc. Lithgow–MacLeay, 9 July 1828; /701, Murray–Darling, 12 Apr. 1829; /222, Murray–Darling, 6 June 1828, Circular (Finance) No. 3; I/xv/68, Darling–Murray, 7 July 1829; enc. MacLeay–Darling, 7 July 1829; /1, Murray–Darling, 1 June 1829, enc. Stewart–Twiss, 19 May 1829.

[2] C.O. 201/205/261, Stewart–Twiss, 19 May 1829, enc. report of Col. Audit, 6 May; 202/23/177, Twiss–Stewart, 10 Mar. 1829; 201/191/41, Minutes of 30 Mar.

Darling told the Secretary of State that it was quite impossible to fix the establishments of some colonial departments in the way ordered by the Treasury. The advancement of the colony could not be permanently frozen; nor did he have control over the numbers of convicts which the Home Office thought fit to transport. He could report regular improvements in the colonial revenue, which doubled in his time in the colony without the additions of new duties or taxes. But it was odious and burdensome to have to explain each petty adjustment in every minor clerical department of his government and he demanded that his non-compliance should not stand against the final audit of Public Accounts at home. The Treasury conceded, against the scrupulous views of the Colonial Auditor of Van Diemen's Land, that no special report was required at home about changes in the names of persons holding colonial appointments or the filling up of vacancies in offices already approved, but they reaffirmed that their object was 'to prevent the creation of any new office, with a new salary, or any new distribution of the salaries already approved of' except with Treasury sanction.[1]

The governors reacted strongly to any suggestion that the Australian colonies were merely the passive recipients of vast and increasing sums from the home country. They had good reason to resent the attacks of Joseph Hume and others, but could not avoid continual criticism. When the Whigs came to office, Hume wrote to Howick complaining of the 'shameless extravagance' of the governors of New South Wales and Van Diemen's Land. They had created, he maintained, useless appointments for creatures of their own family and favourites, and fixed upon salary scales disproportionate to the state of the colonies. 'The governors do as they please and having three purses to draw from they take care to do so freely, whilst no kind of control whatever exists over them.' He proposed that their own salaries be reduced, the heavy charge on Britain decreased, and the colonists freed to make their own arrangements. It was a firm,

---

1829; after Darling–Goderich, 8 Jan. 1828 (in *H.R.A.* I/xiii/685 ff.); 201/197/281, Dumaresq–Horton, Private, 10 Jan. 1828; *H.R.A.* I/xv/90, Murray–Darling, 1 Aug. 1830; /863, Goderich–Darling, 25 Dec. 1830; /403, Hay–Darling, 7 Apr. 1830, enc. Stewart–Hay, 1 Apr. 1830.

[1] *H.R.A.* I/xiv/649, Darling–Murray, 17 Feb. 1829; C.O. 201/229/404, Darling–Goderich, 21 June 1832; *H.R.A.* I/xvi/300, Darling–Goderich, 16 July 1831; C.O. 280/22/360, Stewart–Twiss, 5 Dec. 1829.

coherent, and entirely unrealistic viewpoint; and one long familiar to the Colonial Office.[1]

In 1824 William Sorell, consulted about the costs of governing Van Diemen's Land, made some intelligent criticism of those who would 'force . . . the colonies upon their own immature resources by the rigorous application of a principle of sparing the Mother Country'. He said that since 1817 when he took over the administration of the small community in Hobart his aim had been so to foster the colonial revenues that the colony 'should as far as possible defray the charges incurred for its improvement, and internal security'. He had taken it for granted, though he had had no explicit instructions, that the home government 'expected a reduction in the demand upon the Mother Country'. But permanent, if gradual, savings could only be made if the colonists had official encouragement; and he questioned the wisdom of Horton's proposed commercial 'liberalisation' as too doctrinaire. 'Total and sudden' departures from the traditional protective system, for example—whether ordered from home or from Sydney—could have a restricting rather than a liberating effect. He had no doubt that an abandonment of price-fixing in favour of a tender system would discourage many local growers and set back much of what had been accomplished to bring about prosperity and self-reliance. His experience taught him that a governor needed strong powers and more discretion to judge what was necessary for the balanced advance of the colony. He supported Arthur's insistence that the two Australian colonies should be now parted and an opportunity given for the decentralized development of a new and independently equipped community. In many ways he was right; and the separate advance of Van Diemen's Land, calling for the duplicating of departments and administration at every level in the Antipodes, was the test case to prove the ability and will of the imperial authorities to provide constructive government or to rest satisfied with colonial stagnation or worse.[2]

In Van Diemen's Land, George Arthur undoubtedly emerged as an articulate and persistent advocate of constructive government. New South Wales had, by the mid-twenties, fifty years of survival upon which to build a free society. Van Diemen's Land was relatively

[1] *H.R.A.* I/xv/850, Darling–Murray, 22 Dec. 1830; C.O. 201/215/339, Hume–Howick, 26 Nov. 1830.

[2] C.O. 201/152/54, Sorell–Horton, 24 Aug. 1824, enc. Sorell–Arthur, 22 May 1824; 280/4/316, Sorell–Horton, 26 Jan. 1825; /326, Sorell–Horton, 28 Feb. 1825; 280/4/354, Sorell–Horton, 26 Apr. 1825.

embryonic and its future uncertain. The achievements of the decade can hardly be overrated, for many of them were against the grain.

Arthur was informed of the financial arrangements contained in Darling's instructions and later of the rules drawn up for revenue officials. He too set up boards and committees to help him report on ways and means, revised the system of colonial audit, and in every way emphasized the rights and special needs of Van Diemen's Land. He found it almost impossible to decide about the costs of the 'mixed' departments, noting that 'every transaction of the colony is so interwoven with its convict character that the measures of the government are everywhere bottomed upon it'. A system of transportation, to be efficient rather than merely harsh or severe could not be entirely inexpensive to the home country. He welcomed free settlement, but, though 'very reluctant to interfere with the measures of speculating men in any way' and unwilling to 'impede the unrestricted exercise of capital' he could see no alternative to special measures if costs were ever to be covered by the government. Those measures must in the nature of the colonial economy be protective.[1]

It was agreed that care would have to be taken that financial arrangements in both colonies were kept in harmony. For a time the accounts of Van Diemen's Land were sent to Sydney, but as the case for local government was pressed and separate establishments grew up, both Colonial Office and Treasury came to acknowledge the active participation of Governor Arthur in the administrative dialogue. From 1827 he acted to carry out the project of dividing financial responsibility between the Commissariat, which would attend to convict matters, and the colonial Treasury. He objected, however, to any move which would tend to reduce his immediate control over those workings of the transportation system, such as the assignment of convicts and conditions on the penal settlements, upon which his administration placed such emphasis. He argued persuasively also against the Treasury's premature recommendation that stores be purchased locally. The extravagant demands of the colonial merchants would be ruinous, he thought, and it would be far better to continue a system whereby the Commissariat would be responsible,

---

[1] *H.R.A.* III/v/195, Bathurst–Arthur, 23 Apr. 1826; /393, Arthur–Bathurst, 14 Nov. 1826; III/vi/113, Goderich–Arthur, 31 July 1827; /415, Arthur–Goderich, 31 Dec. 1827, enc. Ex. Co. M. 29 Dec. 1827; /57, Arthur–Bathurst, 22 May 1827, enc. Ex. Co. M. 26 Dec. 1826; /230, Arthur–Bathurst, 23 Sept. 1827, enc. G.G.O., 3 Sept. 1827; /108, Goderich–Arthur, 12 July 1827; /396, Arthur–Goderich, 22 Dec. 1827.

under his supervision, for the purchase and general storage of all government needs. His painstaking submissions almost always forced consent.[1]

Arthur also carried out a full reappraisal and reorganization of the colonial departments. He had efficiency and economy always in mind, of course, and made every effort to provide the home authorities with the prompt, regular and hopeful reports they so continually asked to have. But, though he described his object as making sure that 'nothing unreasonable' was charged against the Mother Country, he had become the apologist *par excellence* of the convict system, and in his special vision transportation and the advancement of Van Diemen's Land were inextricably linked. His demands for increase in the local establishment were therefore more often clothed in language which defended his régime of penal reform, and pleaded for the instruments which might make it more effective, than were those which came from the older colony. Yet he too was coping with the influx of free capital and the development of settlement and society which could not take place without an expansion and reform of the financial and administrative activities of the government. His special boards and committees were just as necessary as had been Darling's to help and advise in matters concerning land, public works and the more general workings of a freer community. His task was not made easier by the 'effect of the great depression in England, which operates exceedingly upon this colony'; nor by the continual course of change upon which the home government embarked in its attempt to settle financial and revenue arrangements in a permanent way. He could report progressive increases in colonial revenues, even during times of economic stress; but he insisted that a short-term view must not be taken. If convicts were a great boon to a struggling community, their presence also imposed great burdens. Things might be vastly better if the home government, instead of sending 'idiots, madmen, cripples . . . boys, ignorant clerks, and weakling idle pickpockets', would transport robust mechanics, farming men, or labourers. Then the case for colonial contributions to the cost of transportation would be more clearly justified. In the meantime, the colonial revenues could and

---

[1] *H.R.A.* III/vi/113 Goderich–Arthur, 31 July 1827; C.O. 408/4/54, Hay–Hill, 2 Aug. 1827; 408/3/157, Huskisson–Arthur, 30 Jan. 1828; 408/4/122, Leveson Gower–Hill, 7 May 1828; /134, Gower–Dawson, 24 May 1828; 280/16/93, Arthur–Hay, 26 Feb. 1828; 280/19/52, Arthur–Murray, 2 Feb. 1829; 280/21/520, Arthur–Twiss, 1 Dec. 1829; 280/26/172, Stewart–Twiss, 8 May 1830; 280/28/338, Arthur–Murray, 2 Apr. 1831; 280/37/114, Stewart–Howick, 31 Jan. 1832.

should be built up 'with prudent arrangement, by relaxing a little when the settlers are pressed, and stimulating their speculations, both Agricultural and Commercial, by fair and reasonable arrangements'. In this way Van Diemen's Land might soon be expected to defray entirely its own colonial expenditure and help very substantially in meeting convict costs. It was 'quite impossible that one single day can elapse without some urgent demand for some unauthorized expenditure'. Colonial demands were incessant and pressing. The £200 rule, for example, was unrealistic. He could, he hoped, be relied upon to conduct colonial affairs with the most precise attention to economy of detail, but he must be allowed more latitude from home. As it was, the home country was obtaining great benefit from its convict colonies and should not carp at the appointment of officers, such as worthy judges, who were needed because of the increase of convicts, especially when their salaries would be met from monies raised locally.[1]

The compilation and transmission of accounts from Van Diemen's Land from 1818 caused particular complaint in England. The auditors could not grasp what had happened. In 1830 they were still puzzled about the accounts of 1820–5 as well as about the more recent ones. There was confusion about the formal transmission of reports and accounts and it appears that the Colonial Office sometimes failed or forgot to forward them to the Treasury. In the colony Arthur welcomed open publication of the colonial estimates and assured his superiors that the local audit was working hard to keep the audit up to date under very difficult colonial conditions. Apart from the problems of pioneering, he noted, there was perhaps 'a kind of incubus upon all Accountants that seems to render it next to impossible to get the accounts through their hands'. In 1830, when he sent back the returns for the previous year, he outlined what had been accomplished to expand the colonial departments and to establish reasonable conditions of employment in order to attract reliable men into government service. When Goderich wrote in the routine way to ask

[1] C.O. 280/19/215, Arthur–Murray, 10 Feb. 1829; /306, Arthur–Murray, 17 Feb. 1829; /346, Arthur–Murray, 20 Feb. 1829; 408/5/183, Murray–Arthur, 5 Nov. 1829; 280/20/14, Arthur–Murray, 3 Apr. 1829; 280/25/158, Arthur–Murray, 17 Aug. 1830;—land Boards, etc.: 280/16/509, Arthur–Huskisson, 5 May 1828; /526, Arthur–Huskisson, 2 June 1828; 408/4/91, Murray–Arthur, 2 Dec. 1828; 2nd Judge: 280/21/302, Arthur–Murray, 10 Sept. 1829; /22/206, Stewart–Hay, 30 June 1830; 408/6/13, Hay–Stewart, 24 July 1830; 280/26/216, Dawson–Hay, 15 Nov. 1830.

for fuller explanations, the Governor reacted strenuously. His Executive Council, 'unanimous and unqualified', had rightly refused to reduce salaries. The proposed alternative of sending out clerks from England on very small salaries was injudicious. They would lose no time in bettering their conditions by taking employment at the new banking and commercial enterprises. The home authorities must reconcile themselves to a new stage of colonial growth.[1]

Arthur's autocratic government and the minute attention he gave to detail led to an abnormal amount of office work. The Colonial Office had hoped that, with the establishment of a full Colonial Secretary's department, the post of private secretary would become redundant. But the Governor insisted that he needed a private secretary with a full clerical staff which could be trusted, particularly as he was not convinced of the capacity of John Burnett, the conscientious but hypochondriac Colonial Secretary whose voluminous confidential correspondence with Hay angered Arthur. He pointed out that, in the place of Sorell's largely verbal administration, he had started efficient government departments from the beginning. Force of habit had led everyone in the colony 'to imagine that nothing can be done without a direct application to the Lieutenant-Governor'. There was, besides, all the laborious business connected with the councils, local boards, the churches, etc. to be conducted, as well as insistent home requests for information and reports to be satisfied. Unlike Burnett and other colonial correspondents, he was responsible for the execution and administration of policies and the Colonial Office could rely more confidently in his practical 'prudence and discretion' as well as in his intentions and motives.[2]

Arthur became so convinced of the virtues of transportation, both as an economic system of penal reform for the home country, and as a mechanism for the advancement of his colony, that he tended to eye

---

[1] C.O. 280/28/103, Arthur–Murray, 6 Mar. 1830; /26/216, Dawson–Hay, 15 Nov. 1830, enc. Audit–Treasury, 12 Aug. 1830; /32/198, Brande–Howick, 18 May 1831; /25/3, Arthur–Murray, 1 June 1830; 408/7/92, Goderich–Arthur, 28 Dec. 1830; 280/29/121, Arthur–Goderich, 5 July 1831, enc. Minutes of Ex. Co. 4 July 1831.

[2] C.O. 280/28/31, Arthur–Murray, 2 Jan. 1831; 408/7/31, Murray–Arthur, 5 Apr. 1830; 408/3/164, Huskisson–Arthur, 17 Apr. 1828; 280/23/18, Burnett–Hay, Secret and Confidential, 20 Jan. 1829; /38/10, Burnett–Hay, Private, 10 Jan. 1832; /30/19, Arthur–Goderich, 8 Sept. 1831; /36/202, enc. *Hobart Town Gazette*, 10 Mar. 1832, with estimates, etc.; /36/25, Arthur–Goderich, 10 Oct. 1832; 280/17/453, Arthur–Hay, 25 Nov. 1828; /403, Arthur–Murray, 5 Nov. 1828; /19/30, Arthur–Hay, Private, 26 Jan. 1829.

suspiciously any changes which seemed likely to disturb the autocratic equilibrium he aimed at. His principles were, debatably, narrow; and he did not altogether convince the Colonial Office, whose devotion to transportation was far more empirical than dogmatic. But he held clear and consistent views. When the question of free emigration became immediate, Arthur wrote that the colony could welcome large-scale assisted emigration; but he insisted that 'whatever aid this colony gives, sending its limited capital out of the territory must be, by all means, steadily and systematically avoided'. He directed the attention of the Colonial Office to positive measures aimed at encouraging the growth of stable and reliable exports rather than to concentrate on increased taxation or the remission home of the proceeds of land-sales. In the last analysis the local governors proved admirable servants of both colonial and imperial interests. By standing firm for local progress against imperial exploitation they went far to temper the zeal of Treasury retrenchers and Whig systematizers which might otherwise have confined colonial development considerably if not indeed precipitated serious crises.[1]

---

[1] C.O. 408/7/135, Goderich–Arthur, 29 Jan. 1831; 280/34/338, Arthur–Goderich, 31 July 1832; 280/29/168, Arthur–Goderich, 9 July 1831; 408/7/242, Goderich–Arthur, 27 Jan. 1832; 280/34/175, Arthur–Goderich, 28 June 1832; 408/7/220, Goderich–Arthur, separate, 3 Nov. 1831; and e.g. *H.R.A.* I/xiv/332, Darling–Huskisson, 12 Aug. 1828; I/xiii/767 Huskisson–Darling, 10 Feb. 1828.

VIII

LAND SETTLEMENT

DURING the years between 1818 and 1831 no field of administration raised more puzzling problems than those which seemed to be created by the vast empty continent itself. Time had proved that the convict colonies could thrive as well as survive: but success brought its own ironies. Lachlan Macquarie's controversial emancipist policy appeared to be based on a determination to enable ex-convicts to aspire to the level of expectation and achievement which John Macarthur and others had already attained. His opponents, official and private, raised economic as well as social objections. The ownership and use of land necessarily became a central theme of government.[1]

Commissioner Bigge, in his attempts to discover the most effective way to employ colonial resources, was not bigoted against small holdings as such, but he seized on the importance of wool, which required for its production large acreage. Many already looked forward, with William Broughton, to the day when wool would become the 'staple commodity' of the colony, forming 'the most prominent feature in its commerce'; and with Sam Marsden urged the government to 'take the sheep into its special consideration—as they will be the source of unknown national wealth'. John Macarthur, whose devotion to wool was unshakeable, appealed to the salutary effect of pastoral solitude on the criminal mind. He argued that, if convicts were to be reformed as well as to be put to the best and most economical use, great powers would have to be entrusted to 'intelligent and Honourable Men', subject of course to the 'inspection and control of a vigilant government'. All agreed that the convicts would be better employed clearing and burning rather than constructing ambitious public works.[2]

In addition, Bigge's liberalizing social recommendations seemed

[1] S. H. Roberts, *History of Australian Land Settlement 1788–1920* (Melbourne, 1924), p. 19.
[2] Bigge Report, pp. 161–3; C.O. 201/118/362 ff., Bigge Appendix, evidence of John Macarthur, W. Howe, W. Cox, S. Marsden, John Jamison, G. and J. Blaxland, W. Broughton, W. Lawson, Rev. R. Cartwright, *et. al.*

to require the encouragement of 'respectable' settlers and pastoralists rather than emancipist farmers. His questioning of the overworked colonial surveyors shows his concern for the orderly spread of settlement as well as the position and use of Crown reserves. He received much conflicting advice about the connected question of convict labour and its profitable employment, whether under private assignment, in clearing gangs, or in public works.[1] In principle, it was agreed that land and other advantages should be offered to free settlers, but in practice there were many pitfalls. John Oxley, among detailed proposals for the reorganization of the Lands Department, presented a revised scale of grants, to be always proportionate to the amount of capital available to colonists for the purpose of improvements; and he argued for the supplementary sale of land for revenue purposes.[2] Macquarie, remitting returns of land grants which he had neglected to send home since 1812, supported his views, as did Bigge in his official report. The governor urged, however, that stricter investigation be made of the assets of settlers, whose capital he suspected was largely 'fictitious'.[3]

Sir Thomas Brisbane's Instructions contained outmoded clauses about land grants and the traditional admonitions concerning the regular submission of returns and maintenance of Crown reserves.[4] But the new governor soon wrote to complain of Macquarie's prodigality in leaving his successor to confirm grants for upwards of 340,000 acres. To redeem the situation, Brisbane announced that he would insert in each grant an express stipulation that a convict must be supported for each one hundred acres granted.[5]

In London Horton, primed with advice from Bigge, but at first unable to consult the ex-governor, was keen to formulate a policy which would not only cover Macquarie's unconfirmed grants but have a more general application. He was persuaded that Brisbane had been misled and proceeded to outline what he hoped would be a new and systematic land policy. He did not believe that settlers would accept Brisbane's terms, as they seemed to presume that all land was

---

[1] e.g. C.O. 201/118, Evidence of Cox, Jamison, the Blaxlands, and Cartwright.
[2] C.O. 201/123/379, ff. Evidence of Oxley and Meehan; 201/150/66, Oxley–Macquarie 29 Jan. 1821.
[3] H.R.A. I/x/408, Goulburn–Macquarie, 15 Mar. 1821; I/x/559, Macquarie–Goulburn, 24 Nov. 1821; /568, Macquarie–Bathurst, 28 Nov. 1821; Bigge, 3rd Report, pp. 48–50.
[4] H.R.A. I/x/596, 5 Feb. 1821.
[5] H.R.A. I/x/630, Brisbane–Bathurst, 10 Apr. 1822.

the same in quality. He preferred to think, with Bigge, that the encouragement of settlers was more important than the imposition of a rigid 'tax'. As colonists prospered, they would take more convicts off government hands. The commissioner had recommended, on Oxley's advice, that land near grants be put up for sale—estimating values at ten shillings per acre for good land, and five shillings for that which was less good. Horton now supported a quit-rent, at three levels depending on the quality and the circumstances of the location, at a rate of 1½ per cent of an 'estimated' value of 10s., 7s. 6d., and 5s., payable after five years and perpetual, but redeemable at twenty years' purchase. Whatever had happened in the past these quit-rents must be collected in earnest. Settlers must improve their land, or it would be resumed after five years. Special cases could be referred to the Secretary of State. In five years' time terms would be revised and the whole question ripe for reconsideration. Brisbane must not forget the penal aspects of transportation in his schemes. In accordance with the Commissioner's Report special penal settlements would be set up to cope with the worst criminals, but the governor must be prepared for a diminution of numbers. The feelings and needs of the settlers must be sought out and reported so that the government might encourage 'an Emigration of free labour proportioned to the precise nature of the case'.[1]

Brisbane, perhaps justifiably confused by the mixture of delay and indecision which seemed to characterize most Colonial Office initiatives in questions concerning land policy,[2] accepted that he had a wider discretion than was actually intended. He imposed a uniform quit-rent but ignored the suggestion that land be divided into three classes; and wrote that the settlers, despite some initial hesitation, were ready to accept his original terms. For his part, he could be trusted to lose no opportunity of assisting in every way in the growth of fine wool, 'the staple of the colony', the productive employment of convict labour, through the use of clearing-gangs, and in a thorough reform of the system of land alienation.[3]

The Colonial Office did not appreciate this brusque modification of their plan, nor Brisbane's neglect to carry out instructions con-

[1] *H.R.A.* I/xi/83, Bathurst–Brisbane, 30 May 1823; /86, Bathurst–Brisbane, 30 May 1823; /87, Bathurst–Brisbane, 31 May 1823; C.O. 201/142/348, Bigge–Horton, 10 Feb. 1823.

[2] *H.R.A.* I/xi/553, Brisbane–Bathurst, 24 Mar. 1825.

[3] *H.R.A.* I/xi/323, Brisbane–Bathurst, 23 July 1824; /179, Brisbane–Bathurst, 29 Nov. 1823.

cerning the Macarthurs' hard-won land grants.[1] Horton had become uncertain whether to allocate a convict to a settler on a pastoral property was to grant him a favour or to impose a burden on him. Hobbes Scott, consulted in Bigge's absence, argued firmly that grazing and the production of fine wool for export offered the best economic prospects and provided an ideal employment for convicts; and he thought the sale of land would yield very large returns.[2]

Some principle of sale appealed to Horton. He had Bathurst's agreement with his view that, once a proper valuation was put on land, the conditions of alienation should be rigorously applied, but he was now prepared to go further. *Bona fide* settlers would be assisted and revenue raised if gratuitous grants were everywhere abandoned in favour of enforceable quit-rents. He wrote angrily to Frederick Goulburn about Brisbane's *de facto* rejection of his original ideas. Questions were liable to be asked in Parliament. It was not right for a long and considered Colonial Office dispatch insisting on the classification of land to result in a brief colonial proclamation based on a contrary principle.[3]

Horton was further incensed when he learnt in discussion with Scott, Stephen, and Douglass, who represented the Governor's views in Downing St. in 1824, that Brisbane rarely bothered to examine settlers' claims to capital. He thus seemed to be tolerating an alarming speculative element in the transportation system.[4] Douglass tried to explain that Brisbane's plan was not intended to supplant Horton's. He argued that the two systems were not incompatible. Flexibility was needed if the convict system was to be constructively re-styled. Rigid valuations of land could only be nominal and were impossible to maintain. Brisbane was merely improving on some of Macquarie's more worthy visions. The best proof of a settler's effective intention to work colonial land lay in his actual residence and maintenance of convicts rather than in possession of a dubious 'real capital'. He showed his bias, however, in arguing that agricultural proprietors were of more value to the colony, would provide more employment, and be of less political embarrassment to the government than those

---

[1] *H.R.A.* I/xi/92, Bathurst–Brisbane, 31 July 1823; /349, Bathurst–Brisbane, 17 Aug. 1824; /698, Brisbane–Bathurst, 4 Aug. 1825.

[2] C.O. 201/157/194, Scott–Horton, 19 June 1824; /204, Scott–Horton, 29 July 1824; /267 ff., Observations by Scott 1824.

[3] C.O. 201/155/499, Horton–F. Goulburn, Private, 7 July 1824; /509, Horton–Bathurst, Minute.

[4] C.O. 202/12/155, Horton–Douglass, 25 Sept. 1824.

who invested their capital in extensive 'grazing establishments'.[1] Horton refused to be convinced and the two men engaged in a furious interchange of opinions about the nature of rent and the contribution of labour to a growing economy.[2]

Horton passionately argued the virtues of a free market. Every received opinion, he maintained, demonstrated 'that the most inexpedient course, which any government can pursue is, that which forces and fetters the direction of Industry instead of leaving it to the discretion of individuals influenced by a due sense of their own interests.' Capitalists should not be forced to engage in tillage for export or to reside on their holdings. Grazing held out great hopes, whereas tobacco, hemp and flax seemed to him to be doubtful quantities. He scouted the idea, often enough suggested by champions of the Antipodes, that New South Wales should use cheap convict labour to outbid the United States, Holland, and Canada, in the English market. Indeed, he wrote, 'the opinion has long been exploded both in theory and practice, that it is the interest of England to bolster up the exports from her colonies by bounties', or to allow them to 'come into that market at a far lower duty than foreign Articles'. He was ready, however, to 'encourage the colonies' to develop exports which could compete fairly, especially in cases such as hemp, used for naval stores, where considerations of defence or strategy were involved.[3] His theoretical objections were backed by practical arguments brought forward by William Sorell. The ex-governor had already expressed fears about the cumulative effect of measures aimed at throwing the colonies upon their own still slender resources.[4] Now he condemned Douglass' strenuous defence of Brisbane's assignment terms of one convict to each hundred acres granted as an 'overstrained application of a principle good in the abstract'. The plan took insufficient account of the diversity of available land and the pursuits already open to settlers. By placing undue emphasis on an 'extended scale of tillage' it might injure the reputation of those colonies for sheep 'that had been the mainspring of recent emigration'.[5]

Meanwhile Brisbane, claiming to be following up Bigge's sugges-

---

[1] C.O. 201/155/402, Douglass–Horton, 12 Oct. 1824.

[2] C.O. 201/155/414, Douglass–Horton, 26 Oct. 1824; 202/13/11, Horton–Douglass, 5 Nov. 1824; 201/166/476, Douglass–Horton, 1 Jan. 1825.

[3] C.O. 201/13/20, Horton–Douglass, 16 Nov. 1824.

[4] C.O. 201/152/44, Sorell–Horton, 24 Aug. 1824, enc. Sorell–Arthur, 22 May 1824.

[5] C.O. 201/152/94, Sorell–Horton, 19 Nov. 1824.

tions, wrote seeking approval of new rules and regulations for the sale of at least 100,000 acres. This land was to go at a general fixed rate of 5s. per acre, with a limit of 4,000 acres for individuals and 5,000 for families, on a deposit of 10 per cent and at six monthly payments. In deference to the Colonial Office the best land would sell at 7s. 6d. and 10s.[1]

This cut across Colonial Office discussions about the introduction of systematic changes in colonial land administration. A draft letter of 3 November 1824 reproached Brisbane for his errors and neglect. It was essential to establish that every colonist either possessed or commanded capital. Land must be surveyed and valued before sale. The average price fixed by the Surveyor General should be made public and termed the 'upset' price. A limit of 10,000 acres would normally be imposed. The object was 'to encourage the real settlement of Capitalists proposing to embark their fortunes in Agriculture', and to discourage land-jobbing. There must be a uniform, simple and efficient system. In addition to sale, the principle of quit-rent would continue, but the practice must be reformed. A credit of sixteen pounds per *annum* would be recognized for each convict maintained. Quit-rents on grants, payable after seven years, were fixed at 5 per cent of the estimated values, redeemable within twenty-five years at twenty years purchase.

This introduced in effect a principle of purchase by quit-rent.[2] The Governor-in-Council was to be allowed to make only small changes in these 'plain and permanent rules' which were aimed at terminating the existing confusion.[3]

There followed a delay while arrangements were being made for the management of the Church and Schools Estates. The actual dispatch of 1 January 1825 proved to be one of those grand official blueprints which refused to measure up to reality. It was forwarded to Canada as a guide to official thought.[4] To round out the circle, the new Colonial Secretary of New South Wales, MacLeay, was instructed in methods of land administration current in Canada.[5]

---

[1] *H.R.A.* I/xi/330, Brisbane–Bathurst, 24 July 1824.

[2] R. G. Riddell, 'A Study in the land policy of the Colonial Office 1763–1853,' *C.H.R.* XVIII (1937), pp. 390–2.

[3] *H.R.A.* I/xi/925 ff.

[4] G. C. Patterson, *Land Settlement in Upper Canada 1783–1840* (Toronto, 1921), Ch. VI, pp. 144–5; P. Burroughs, *Britain and Australia 1831–1855* (Oxford, 1967), pp. 46–7; *H.R.A.* I/xi/434, Bathurst–Brisbane, 1 Jan. 1825.

[5] *H.R.A.* IV/i/591, Stephen–Horton, 27 Mar. 1825.

Commissioners were to be appointed to survey the colony, which was to be divided into counties, hundreds, and parishes of twenty-five square miles. All land was to be valued and the progress of the survey regularly reported. Special arrangements were made concerning crown reserves, roads, and towns. The new Church and Schools Charter would take care of land intended for religious and educational purposes. Emigrants to the colonies would be accurately informed of what they could expect.

Brisbane set up a land commission, but predictable objections were made to his allowance of five hundred pounds a year to each member.[1] The incorrigible Governor claimed that the new regulations closely resembled those already in operation. Certainly Oxley reported hopeful signs of colonial interest in the sale of land.[2]

*　　*　　*　　*　　*

Before Governor Darling sailed for the colony, his instructions on the subject of land were revised in the light of Australian and Canadian experience: and he was allowed to appoint a Land Board to assist him.[3]

There was soon a great deal to report, little of it plain or simple. Darling found that little progress had been made in survey and valuation. He asked that settlers be allowed to receive land before survey where necessary and advised that set-offs for the maintenance of convicts be discontinued. To bridle the sprawl of settlement in unlocated lands and curb the issue of temporary permits to graze or 'tickets of occupation', he laid down more realistic 'limits of location' than those hitherto recognized. But pastoral expansion and restless experimentation had left a complicated structure of land administration which seemed to defy all efforts at control. Already in 1826 Oxley reported that nearly two million acres in the colony had been appropriated under a variety of arrangements with the government. Survey was hopelessly in arrear. Even the Land Board's insistence on the employment of a full-time collector of land revenue seemed to offer slender chance of success.[4] Darling promised

[1] *H.R.A.* I/xi/680, Brisbane–Bathurst, 30 June 1825; I/xii/153, Bathurst–Darling, 3 Feb. 1826; /651, Darling–Bathurst, 19 Oct. 1826.

[2] *H.R.A.* I/xi/691, Brisbane–Bathurst, 31 July 1825, enc. Oxley–Ovens, 23 May 1825.

[3] C.O. 201/164/305, C.O. Minute of 1825; I/xii/113, 120, 124, in /107 ff. Darling's Instructions 17 July 1825; I/xii/18, Bathurst–Darling, 14 July 1825; /266, Darling–Bathurst, 5 May 1826.

[4] *H.R.A.* I/xii/374, Darling–Bathurst, 22 July 1826, enc. Minutes of Executive Council, Oxley's Report, and Proceedings of Land Board.

that every precaution would be taken not to squander the natural assets of the colony, but the institution of a fair and efficient system seemed to be doomed. Sales proved as difficult and delicate to administer as rents and leases.[1]

It is no bad fault in an administrator to listen to advice, but Hay and Horton were perhaps too ready to fuss over the conflicting opinions of interested parties. John Macarthur forwarded letters from James Atkinson, then in England obtaining stock for the colony, who recommended leniency and flexibility towards colonists in land matters.[2] High quit-rents or an exclusive principle of sale could have discouraged that free migration of settlers with capital which seemed to offer the Australian colonies a new start. Horton had already received many proposals for Antipodean development in the course of his conduct of the Emigration Committee, and the Colonial Office received still more. James Dixon, for example, a later influence on Wakefield, suggested that ships bringing tea to England for the East India Company could export ten thousand migrants, especially labourers and females, to Australia at relatively little expense.[3]

There was pressure not only from private correspondents, but from officials such as Forbes who never hesitated to criticize the silly misapprehensions of government about convict maintenance or the collection of quit-rents.[4] Saxe Bannister, another prolific and imaginative writer of manifestoes, was a protégé of William Tooke, whose lasting and confident interest in the colonies formed a link between the era of 'colonisation by company' and Wakefield. By 1825 Tooke was ready to combine the words 'systematic' and 'colonisation' in his praise of the Australian Agricultural Company, of which he was a proprietor.[5]

Horton's plan of 1825 and its subsequent modifications attracted free settlement and encouraged the growth and development of substantial holdings, as was generally intended, though smaller proprietors were not totally forgotten. But detailed regulations had a

---

[1] *H.R.A.* I/xii/502, Bathurst–Darling, 26 Aug. 1826; I/xiii/128, Darling–Bathurst, 24 Feb. 1827; I/xii/536, Darling–Bathurst, 5 Sept. 1826.

[2] C.O. 201/178/12, Atkinson–Bathurst, 17 July 1826; /17, Atkinson–Bathurst, 11 Aug. 1826; cf. also Atkinson's book *An Account of the State of Agriculture and Grazing in New South Wales* (London, 1826).

[3] C.O. 201/178/405, Dixon–Bathurst, 24 Feb. 1826.

[4] e.g. *H.R.A.* IV/i/431, Forbes–Horton, 6 Mar. 1823; /688, Forbes–Horton, 6 Mar. 1827; /703, Forbes–Horton, 22 Mar. 1827.

[5] Pike op. cit., p. 57; C.O. 201/178/302, Tooke–Bannister, 15 July 1825; /187/89, Bannister–Bathurst, 9 Sept. 1826.

way of soon becoming dead letters, with quit-rents and bad titles causing particular trouble.[1]

Just as the efforts of Macquarie, Goulburn and Bathurst to prevent 'by every legal means' the arrival in the colony of settlers without capital had run into difficulties, so the later attempts to allocate land grants in proportion to settlers' capital proved unenforceable.[2] When Brisbane proposed the sale of land, he included among his reasons the 'considerable deceptions' practised by applicants for land and, despite intermittent attempts at home and in the colony to follow up settlers' references, he wrote to an indignant Horton that 'great frauds' were taking place.[3]

Some of the accusations of favouritism made against the colonial governors may have been justified, for the apportionment or withholding of land grants and the allocation or withdrawal of convict servants could obviously be employed to political ends or as patronage. But the decade saw several quite elaborate government settlement schemes. The discharge of the armies after the war had created expensive pension problems and left great numbers of active men on half-pay. By 1822 five million pounds per annum was being paid in half-pay and pensions.[4] Here the Empire could be an asset. It was reasonable to hope that some at least would be able to make a new life in the colonies. The Veteran Companies sent to New South Wales, however, turned out very badly.[5] But from 1826 Hay was at work reviving plans which seemed to hold out much more hopeful prospects. Officers were encouraged to commute their half-pay in exchange for grants of land and other special concessions. The co-operation of the colonial governments and the military and naval authorities, all

[1] *H.R.A.* I/xv/17, Darling–Murray, 23 June 1829; /716, Murray–Darling, 21 Aug. 1830; Roberts, op. cit., pp. 35–9; Burroughs, op. cit., pp. 42–4, 124; R.M. Hartwell, *Economic Development of V.D.L.*, pp. 38–41; D. N. Jeans 'Crown Land Sales and the Accommodation of the Small Settler in New South Wales 1825–42' *H.S.A.N.Z.*, XII (1966), pp. 207–12.

[2] *H.R.A.* I/ix/792, Macquarie–Bathurst, 16 May 1818; C.O. 201/107/563, Minute on Pinsent–Bathurst, 25 June 1821; C.O. 201/112/245, Minute of 5 Dec. 1822.

[3] *H.R.A.* I/xi/302, Brisbane–Horton, Private, 1 July 1824; /552, Brisbane–Horton, 24 Mar.; Roberts, op. cit., pp. 94–6.

[4] H. Martineau, *The History of England during the Thirty Years Peace 1816–46* (London, 1849), p. 325.

[5] *H.R.A.* I/xii/430, Darling–Bathurst, 23 July 1826; /480, Hay–Darling, 8 Aug. 1826, enc. Taylor–Hay, 31 July 1826; I/xiii/86, Darling–Hay, 8 Feb. 1827; /448, Hay–Darling, 17 July 1827, enc. Taylor–Hay, 2 July 1827; /590, Darling–Hay, Private, 3 Nov. 1827; I/xiv/612, Darling–Fitzroy Somerset, 20 Jan. 1829.

eager for humane retrenchment, was enthusiastic.[1] In time the system was extended, and adaptations were introduced as colonial land regulations changed.[2] When Darling suggested that officers of the East India Company receive similar concessions on retirement the Colonial Office sent him the rather crabby answer that the Indian administration had given when Hay had asked them if they wished to partake in the original scheme. Their officers were not presumed to be capable of starting a new life once they had completed their service, they wrote; and fit men should not be given temptation to quit.[3]

In 1831 the Colonial Office made the 'strongest possible objection' to a War Office request that a retiring officer, who had been already nine years in Van Diemen's Land, should receive land instead of half-pay. Grants to officers were not made merely as a commutation, it was pointed out, but 'as an inducement to emigrate to a class of persons who make valuable settlers, and who benefit the colony by the capital they carry out with them'. There was no intention of charging the Colonial revenues with the purchase of an annuity due by the mother country.[4] This kind of response went far to substantiate the Colonial Office's claim to have the interests of the colony at heart.[5] But land for colonial officials and other civil servants proved a more thorny question. In 1817, Macquarie suggested, as a measure of retrenchment, that land grants to civil officers be discontinued. Such indulgences could no longer be excused by necessity, and their cessation would curb the various abuses which stemmed from a confusion of the roles of public servant and landed proprietor.[6]

---

[1] C.O. 324/85/22, Hay–Barrow, 12 Jan. 1826; /22, Hay–Sir Herbert Taylor, 13 Jan. 1826; /24–5, Hay–Taylor, 21 Jan. 1826; C.O. 323/146/317, Taylor–Hay, Private, 15 Jan. 1826; General Order, 8 June 1826; *H.R.A.* I/xii/593, Bathurst–Darling, 1 Oct. 1826, enc. G.O., 8 June 1826; Riddell, op. cit., pp. 143–51.

[2] C.O. 324/85/106, Hay–Taylor, 7 Apr. 1827; /109, Hay–Taylor, 12 Apr. 1827; /111, Hay–Taylor, 14 Apr. 1827; /115, Hay–Taylor, 1 June 1827; 201/185/147, Taylor–Hay, 19 Apr. 1827; /155, General Order, 16 May 1827; /160, Taylor–Hay, 3 June 1827; /171, Taylor–Hay, 25 July 1827; /208, General Order, 24 Aug. 1827; General Order, 11 Aug. 1827; Admiralty Circular, 11 Aug. 1827; *H.R.A.* I/xiii/485, Goderich–Darling, 3 Aug. 1827, enc. G.O., 16 May 1827; /595, Huskisson–Darling, 5 Nov. 1827, enc. G.O. 24 Aug. 1827; I/xv/805, Murray–Darling, Circular, 1 Nov. 1830, enc. Sullivan–Twiss, 10 Sept. 1830.

[3] *H.R.A.* I/xiv/191, Darling–Huskisson, 17 May 1828; I/xiv/494, Murray–Darling, 27 Nov. 1828, enc. Hay–Courtenay, 15 June 1826 and Courtenay–Hay, 4 Sept. 1826, sub. enc. J. Dart–Courtenay, 17 Aug. 1826.

[4] C.O. 201/237/84, M. on Sulivan–Hay, 27 Sept. 1831.

[5] C.O. 408/7/242, Goderich–Arthur, 27 Jan. 1832.

[6] *H.R.A.* I/ix/392, Macquarie–Bathurst, Private and Confidential, 13 May 1817.

Liberal land grants and other concessions formerly afforded had also been very costly. Bathurst agreed, and Goulburn gladly informed the Treasury of the welcome reduction. Fulminations against land jobbing among colonial officials became a consistent theme of the decade.[1]

When Brisbane introduced land sales, Bathurst reluctantly withdrew the prohibition concerning civil officers, but insisted that if they took up land, they should employ resident agents on their properties.[2] Darling thought that land grants, as incentives or rewards to public servants given after a suitable time in office would attract better men, render them loyal supporters of his government, give them a stake in the colony, and serve instead of pensions.[3] He supported an elaborate hierarchical scheme which would apply even to the ranks of minor officials. It would, he thought, mean a considerable saving in the costs of the civil establishment.[4]

The governor found no difficulty in granting attractive holdings to the leading civil servants of his administration,[5] but criticism of his actions made a wary Colonial Office decide that applications for land by public servants should be referred home.[6] Darling bitterly resented the implications behind the withdrawal of his power to grant land to his officials and defended his record in detail.[7] In time the tighter policy had to be relaxed in the interests of efficiency, to allow for the building of town residences and offices.[8] Even these relaxations were grudgingly accorded to the soldiers, though of course the Colonial Office had no objection to military officers receiving land grants on retirement.[9]

Naval and military officers attracted by the Australian colonies

[1] C.O. 324/140/145, Goulburn–Harrison, 24 July 1818; *H.R.A.* I/ix/823, Bathurst–Macquarie, 24 July 1818;/830, Bathurst–Macquarie, 24 Aug. 1818.

[2] *H.R.A.* I/xi/638, Bathurst–Brisbane, 5 June 1825.

[3] *H.R.A.* I/xiii/76, Darling–Hay, 6 Feb. 1827.

[4] *H.R.A.* I/xiii/568, Darling–Hay, 30 Oct. 1827.

[5] I/xiv/41, Darling–Huskisson, 26 Mar. 1828; G. Nesta Griffiths, *Some Houses and People of New South Wales* (Sydney, 1949).

[6] *H.R.A.* I/xiv/237, Murray–Darling, 22 June 1828.

[7] *H.R.A.* I/xiv/475, Darling–Murray, 24 Nov. 1828.

[8] *H.R.A.* I/xv/154, Murray–Darling, 4 Sept. 1829; /241, Murray–Darling, 3 Nov. 1829; I/xv/278, Murray–Darling, 11 Dec. 1829; /387, Murray–Darling, 6 Apr. 1830; /404, Hay–Darling, Private, 7 Apr. 1830; /752, Darling–Hay, 1 Oct. 1830; /592, Murray–Darling, 21 July 1830; /737, Darling–Murray, 23 Sept. 1830; I/xvi/118, Goderich–Darling, 25 Mar. 1831.

[9] *H.R.A.* I/xiv/644, Darling–Murray, 13 Feb. 1829; I/xv/91, Darling–Murray, 1 Aug. 1829; /239, Murray–Darling, 1 Nov. 1829; C.O. 324/86/136, Hay–Taylor, 30 Mar. 1830.

naturally sought to take advantage of their interest with the colonial government by obtaining land grants from the governor. Darling, writing to curtail the 'great abuse' of speculation in land, was inclined to insist strongly on residence as a qualification for grants. But Hay maintained the view that proper agencies were sufficient guarantee, provided of course that care was taken that 'the Grantees are Capitalists of the highest respectability.'[1] The governor persisted in his misgivings, even opposing the *sale* of land to absentee proprietors, but could not quite convince the Colonial Office of his views, though they nevertheless gave qualified approval of his measures.[2]

The Colonial Office was open, no less than the governors, to charges of favouritism by reason of its liberal recommendations of individuals and groups. When T. C. Harington, who had sold his assets in India and moved to Australia, applied for an increase in his holdings, he promised to use his capital of £6,500 to 'create and uphold an opulent gentry', which was, he thought, the aim of the home government. Lord Bathurst favoured the application and ordered him a very liberal grant for his flocks of fine wool sheep, adding: 'I should prefer a Capitalist of £5 or £10,000 receiving as many acres than one of £500 receiving 500.'[3] Potter Macqueen confidently sought and obtained concessions for capitalist investment.[4]

In 1826 Darling told Hay that he welcomed 'Agriculturalists and Mechanics' as well as 'persons possessing available capital'. He complained of the 'Class of "Shop Keepers"' who seemed to imagine they had some right to land. A 'batch of four . . . from Cheapside; vouching for each others' property, and evidently not . . . knowing a potato from a turnip' roused his particular ire.[5] But the Colonial Office, while it approved of his caution, reminded him that even merchants, businessmen and tradesmen could be very rich and ready to spend their money on improving land; and instructed him that it was neither 'just nor politic' to discriminate against such men merely because of their class.[6] In 1829 the governor, disclaiming any bias

[1] *H.R.A.* I/xii/61, Hay–Darling, 23 Sept. 1825; /70, Hay–Darling, 13 Oct. 1825; /799, Darling–Hay, 25 Dec. 1826; I/xiii/434, Hay–Darling, 6 July 1827.

[2] *H.R.A.* I/xiii/531, Darling–Goderich, 1 Oct. 1827; /306, Darling–Hay, 15 May 1827; /597, Hay–Darling, 6 Nov. 1827; I/xiv/215, Murray–Darling, 31 May 1828.

[3] *H.R.A.* I/xi/231, Brisbane–Bathurst, 23 Feb. 1824; C.O. 201/146/599, Minute on Harington–Bathurst, 30 Dec. 1823.

[4] C.O. 201/147/23, Macqueen–Bathurst, 21 July 1823; *H.R.A.* I/xv/294, Darling–Murray, 19 Dec. 1829; /661, Murray–Darling, 24 July 1830.

[5] *H.R.A.* I/xii/766, Darling–Hay, 16 Dec. 1826.

[6] *H.R.A.* I/xiv/215, Murray–Darling, 31 May 1828.

against tradespeople, unless they deceived the government, wrote that 'such people should defer becoming landed proprietors until they have done making shoes and selling stockings'. The Colonial Office agreed that settlers should have real capital before taking up land grants, and referred somewhat inaccurately to the 'invariable' principle of apportioning grants to the amount of available capital.[1] Favours concerning the allocation of land were as eagerly sought after as the assignment of efficient convict labour, and both caused trouble for the governors.[2] Darling considered that the Colonial Office was too gullible in accepting the plans of such speculators as Blaxland at face value. In practice, whatever they might suspect or hear from colonial critics, the Colonial Office had as always to entrust judgements to be made on the spot by the governors.[3]

* * * * *

In Van Diemen's Land separate arrangements had been made for survey and the Lieutenant-Governor empowered to allocate grants on his own initiative, subject to registration and confirmation at Sydney.[4] Governor Arthur was predictably active but canny in land matters, as in most other fields of administration. He chafed under the rule of New South Wales and he too obtained the assistance of a local Land Board. He complained of the prevalence of land jobbing which was 'notorious in both Colonies', and of the delays and shortcomings which arose from his Survey Department being unable to keep up with its work. He also resented any neglect of the special needs of the colony, or any failure to consult his views. He was particularly exercised about the control of land titles and the enforcement of conditions concerning the assignment of convicts and carrying out of improvements.[5]

Arthur disapproved of the 1825 regulations and delayed action

[1] *H.R.A.* I/xiv/618, Darling–Twiss, 28 Jan. 1829; /677, Darling–Twiss, 17 Mar. 1829; I/xv/308, Twiss–Darling, 28 Dec. 1829; /250, Murray–Darling, 16 Nov.1829.

[2] C.O. 201/229/404, Darling–Goderich, 21 June 1832.

[3] On assignments: *H.R.A.* I/xv/346, Murray–Darling, 30 Jan. 1830; /662, Darling–Murray, 9 Aug. 1830; /391, Murray–Darling, 6 Apr. 1830. Also cf. *H.R.A.* I/xv/192, Murray–Darling, 8 Oct. 1829, Circular; /202, Murray–Darling, 10 Oct. 1829; /864, Goderich–Darling, 27 Dec. 1830; I/xvi/298, Darling–Goderich, 14 July 1831; /490, Goderich–Bourke, 28 Dec. 1831.

[4] *H.R.A.* I/xi/109, Bathurst–Brisbane, 28 Aug. 1823; III/iii/66, Sorell–Macquarie, 5 Dec. 1820; I/x/233, Bathurst–Macquarie, 24 July 1820; III/3/39, Goulburn–Sorell, 24 July 1820.

[5] *H.R.A.* III/v/49, Arthur–Bathurst, 17 Jan. 1826; /120, Arthur–Bathurst, 8 Mar. 1826; /136, Bathurst–Arthur, 7 Apr. 1826; /230, Bathurst–Arthur, 14 May

on them. He therefore rejoiced when Hay forwarded the modifications of April 1827 discontinuing the set-offs previously allowed for the maintenance of convicts and allowing allocation without survey. Like Darling, he found it impossible to get reliable information about the means and intentions of would-be settlers, and suggested that the full estimated value of the land should be spent on its cultivation. 'Cultivation', he stressed, should be understood in its pastoral setting and 'improvements' could mean draining and fencing as well as building.[1]

* * * * *

The Colonial Office was more disposed under the influence of Robert Hay to favour conditional grants, which might be controlled, rather than purchase, which could not. Darling's representations were generally accepted. Alienation could go ahead, if necessary without survey and prior valuation, but great efforts must be made by all concerned to improve the colonial survey. Set-offs for maintaining convicts were unnecessary now that it was clear that colonists were competing for the available men.[2] The Governor's detailed assignments were largely approved, but indecision continued. Patronage and efficiency had both to be served. At first it was decided that a collector of land revenues would be sent out from England.[3] Then Darling was instructed to select one of the Assistant Surveyors to do the work.[4] In six months over £16,000 was collected and Darling had appointed his aide-de-camp de la Condamine to the job, thinking it improper to employ a surveyor's clerk in such a responsible post.[5] Huskisson insisted that a surveyor would be more suitable than a soldier, but the Governor still objected and the Colonial Office finally capitulated, agreeing that the office had been underestimated. W. Macpherson was sent out, at a salary of £500, and under security.[6]

1826; /479, Arthur–Bathurst, 7 Jan. 1827; Roberts, op. cit., pp. 42–5; Hartwell, op. cit., pp. 36–40, 58; ed. A. McKay, *Journals of the Land Commissioners for Van Diemen's Land 1826–28* (Hobart, 1962).

[1] C.O. 280/16/346, Arthur–Huskisson, 18 Apr. 1828.

[2] C.O. 324/85/91, Hay–Horton, 10 Jan. 1827; *H.R.A.* I/xiii/219, Bathurst–Darling, Private, 2 Apr. 1827.

[3] *H.R.A.* I/xiii/219, Bathurst–Darling, 2 Apr. 1827.

[4] *H.R.A.* I/xiii/232, Bathurst–Darling, 4 Apr. 1827; /232, Hay–Darling, 4 Apr. 1827.

[5] *H.R.A.* I/xiii/585, Darling–Goderich, 1 Nov. 1827; /616, Darling–Hay, 10 Nov. 1827; /240, Darling–Bathurst, 7 Apr. 1827.

[6] *H.R.A.* I/xiii/613, Huskisson–Darling, 9 Nov. 1827; C.O. Minute at 201/192/119 ff., on I/xiv/25, Darling–Huskisson, 15 Mar. 1828; I/xiv/516, Murray–Darling, 12 Dec. 1828.

Meanwhile Darling had suspended sale altogether because of delays in the colonial survey.[1] The effect of Brisbane's ambitious schemes for land sales and clearing gangs combined with depression, drought, and the plain desire of some proprietors to evade their obligations, to try even the perseverance and ingenuity of his network of boards and committees.[2]

Perhaps the Colonial Office would have profited by the services of a 'Colonial Crown Land and Emigration Board' which Huskisson had already taken preliminary steps to form about this time in London. But Goderich and Wellington had insisted that no expense be incurred and the project fell through. Huskisson himself, though ready to set up a Land Office and sympathetic with the search for colonial export staples, was a firm believer in local initiative and could never bring himself to share Horton's passion for emigration as a panacea for English and Irish ills.[3]

By 1828 Darling was sure that the former Colonial Office insistence on a division of land according to its quality was 'utterly impracticable'. It would be more sensible to draw up new regulations for settlers instead. A general average value should be fixed and quit-rents rigidly collected. When dispatches mentioned 'cultivation' and 'improvements' it was, he thought, improbable that their writers had fully grasped the realities of pastoral life.[4] Early in 1829 the governor reported that almost three million acres had been alienated, and he had again redefined the 'limits of location'.[5] The question of colonial land was attracting much public attention. Colonel Dumaresq agreed with those who held that high land prices would discourage emigration fatally. He had interviews with Murray as Darling's 'representative'

[1] *H.R.A.* I/xiii/254, Darling–Bathurst, 17 Apr. 1827, enc. General Order, 10 Nov. 1826; /614, Huskisson–Darling, 9 Nov. 1827.

[2] *H.R.A.* I/xiii/236, Darling–Huskisson, 5 Apr. 1827; /602, Huskisson–Darling, 7 Nov. 1827; I/xiv/206, Darling–Huskisson, 28 May 1828, enc. Memorial of Landholders, etc.; /345, Darling–Huskisson, 27 Aug. 1828; /605, Murray–Darling, 6 Jan. 1829.

[3] C.O. 323/209/135, Moody and Cockburn–Murray, 13 June 1828; /132/407, Torrens–Murray, 26 June 1828; P.P. 1836 XI (512), q. 1177, p. 640–Torrens; B.M. Add. MSS. 38757 (Huskisson Papers), f. 216, Cockburn–Huskisson, 9 Feb. 1829; f. 228, Huskisson–Cockburn, 25 Feb. 1829; Huskisson–Horton, 23 June 1828, q. in E. G. Jones, *Horton*, pp. 274–5; Torrens–Horton, 28 Feb. 1828, q. in Burroughs, op. cit., p. 227.

[4] *H.R.A.* I/xiv/284, Darling–Huskisson, 2 Aug. 1828; /311, Darling–Huskisson, Private, 2 Aug. 1828; /375, Darling–Hay, 1 Sept. 1828; /383, Darling–Huskisson, 4 Sept. 1828.

[5] *H.R.A.* I/xiv/671, Darling–Murray, 1 Mar. 1829; T. M. Perry, *Australia's First Frontier* (Melbourne, 1963), p. 43 ff.

and impressed Hay with plans of his own concerning the need to encourage a southern spread of settlement.[1] From Major Mitchell, Oxley's successor as Surveyor General of New South Wales, the Colonial Office had long reaped a whirlwind of paper. Mitchell had from the beginning stood on his dignity, campaigned against the Land Commission, and given himself a free hand to experiment.[2] He too had interesting suggestions for Hay about smallholdings and the progress of agriculture. He favoured the production of sugar to the north of the colony, as well as a southern development. But he bitterly resented Darling's 'interference' in the works of survey.[3] Indeed Mitchell's temperament, and his inability to work with the Land Board, the Colonial Secretary, or the Governor, go far to explain how land administration became deadlocked. Mitchell could not be ignored. His demands embarrassed Hay, who had done his best to supply the needs of colonial survey in consultation with, among others, Thomas Telford.[4] Meanwhile, Darling had had to defend himself against accusations of arbitrariness and partiality. It was eventually decided to wind up the colonial land commission which had been set up in 1825.[5]

Constant demands for easier terms and concessions came in to both the central and colonial governments. It was very easy for inexperienced Wakefieldians to propose a 'great revolution of colonial policy' and to insist on a two pounds per acre valuation for land-sale. But Twiss and Hay knew that there were other practical opinions, based on real contact with the conditions of colonial grazing and agriculture rather than on vague enthusiasm and devotion to a 'sufficient price'.[6] Dumaresq, for instance, told the Secretary of State, as an interested party, that three shillings and four pence per

---

[1] C.O. 201/206/277, Dumaresq–Murray, 10 Apr. 1829; /215/172, Dumaresq–Murray, 2 June 1829; 323/155/119, Dumaresq–Hay, 2 May 1828; /162/56, Dumaresq–Hay, Private, 26 May 1830; 324/86/160, Hay–Dumaresq, Private, 18 Oct. 1830.

[2] C.O. 201/198/75, Mitchell–Hay, Private, 30 Sept. 1828; /110, Mitchell–Hay, 15 Dec. 1828; /207/258, Mitchell–Hay, 7 Sept. 1829.

[3] C.O. 323/162/210, Minutes of Hay, 1830; /212, Mitchell–Hay, 24 May 1830; 324/86/155, Hay–Mitchell, 25 Aug. 1830; /161, Hay–Mitchell, 22 Oct. 1830; H.R.A. I/xvi/119, Darling–Murray, 28 May 1831; /219, Darling–Hay, 28 May 1831.

[4] C.O. 202/24/180, Hay–Mitchell, 5 Apr. 1830; /210, Hay–Mitchell, Private, 31 May 1830.

[5] H.R.A. I/xiv/356, Murray–Darling, 30 Aug. 1828; /716, Darling–Murray, 22 Apr. 1829; I/xv/466, Murray–Darling, 6 May 1830.

[6] C.O. 201/206/468, Gouger–Hay, 25 July 1829, pamphlet on Colonization and Minutes of Undersecretaries.

acre was far too high a price for pastoral land.[1] James Macarthur gave very persuasive colonial advice against the existing system.[2]

The Colonial Office was clearly uneasy again about the whole question of land grants as an incentive to settlers; and the débâcle at Swan River caused a failure in nerve. Hay did not possess the political influence to initiate a major reform even if his distaste of doctrine had not rendered him temperamentally incapable of doing so. He had to be thoroughly convinced from his own experience or his correspondence that the time was ripe before he would support changes that his instinct rejected. He could only promise that some systematic re-examination would soon take place.[3] When Stirling recommended that a policy of simple sale after the American model be established in Western Australia once original engagements had been met, Murray replied that all arrangements must now be considered as makeshift, for the subject of land was 'shortly to be completely revised'.[4] Once a revision finally took place through the energies of Howick, who was horrified at what he learnt of Australian land administration, the uniform principle of sale found its way into Stirling's belated instructions. This rude and sudden departure from Colonial Office flexibility upset both Governor and settlers.[5]

Howick was sure his new arrangements would sweep away the debris of the past. He hoped that his solution of the land question would have wide-reaching social and economic effects, such as the growth of free labour migration, to the benefit of both imperial and colonial interests. Goderich's dispatches announcing the new measures bluntly acknowledged the substantial failure of previous expedients.[6] The Ripon Regulations indeed proved a watershed in imperial land policy. But they did not imply a complete break with the past. Still less did they herald a Wakefieldian triumph, though the doctrines of systematic colonization had received much airing in 1830–1. Howick's

[1] C.O. 201/206/315, Dumaresq–Murray, Private, 21 Oct. 1829.

[2] C.O. 201/207/208, Macarthur–Twiss, 10 Jan. 1829.

[3] C.O. 202/24/210, Hay–Mitchell, Private, 31 May 1830; /26/45, Hay–Dumaresq, 10 Oct. 1830.

[4] C.O. 18/7/32, Stirling–Murray, 20 Jan. 1830; 397/2/24, Murray–Stirling, 20 July 1830.

[5] C.O. 397/2/46, Stirling's Instructions, 5 Mar. 1831; /64, Goderich–Stirling, 28 Apr. 1831; 18/10/5, Stirling–Goderich, 7 Jan. 1832; /232, Memorial of Settlers; M. Harris, 'British Migration to Western Australia 1829–1880' (London Univ. Ph.D. thesis 1934), pp. 165 ff., 170 ff.

[6] e.g. H.R.A. I/xvi/19, Goderich–Darling, 9 Jan. 1831; /34, Goderich–Darling, 23 Jan. 1831; Burroughs, op. cit., pp. 38–9.

vigorous executive action, however, put paid to the era of leisurely experimentation which the Tories had encouraged or allowed and which could now safely be condemned as neglect or 'torpor'. The die was cast in favour of simple sale, in which after all the Colonial Office had long shown a fluctuating interest.[1]

Hay remained sceptical of Whig fervour. What was good in Howick's plan, he thought, was not really novel. What was not supported by the colonists would be found unworkable in practice.[2] He hoped at least that the new regulations would mean some relief for colonists still struggling to cope with ancient quit-rents.[3] In time he learnt to use the jargon of 'concentration' and 'sufficient price', when writing to Major Mitchell, who thought the new system would work better than the old.[4] The administrative dialogue would not, however, stay mute for Howick or for anybody else; and gloomy reaction in the colonies showed that the search for definitive solutions had by no means ended. Sale seemed to many to be merely quit-rents writ large.[5]

There was never any shortage of colonial advice, which was usually forceful as well as plentiful. Busby, who told Darling bravely in 1829 that the 'patriarchal period' had ended in Australia and that land should now be allocated without reference to station in society, respectability of connections, or capital, drew on his experience as collector of internal revenue to make some shrewd observations to Howick about his new regulations. The Colonial Office had, he thought, been misled by parallels between Canada and Australia and had underestimated the radical differences between grazing and agriculture.[6] E. S. Hall of the *Monitor*, always ready to complain of Darling's alleged 'family compact', added to his attacks on the Land

---

[1] Riddell, art. cit., pp. 399 ff., and 'A Study in Imperial Land Policy 1783–1848' (Oxford Univ. B.Litt. thesis 1934), Chs. III and VI, esp. pp. 163 ff.; Burroughs, op. cit., Ch. II is a detailed study of the genesis of the Ripon Regulations; J. Philipp, 'Wakefieldian Influence and New South Wales 1830–1832', *H.S.A.N.Z.*, IX (1960), pp. 173–8; Pike, *Paradise of Dissent*, pp. 52–60, and 'Wilmot Horton and the National Colonization Society', *H.S.A.N.Z.*, VII (1956), pp. 205–10; Roberts, op. cit., pp. 33–9.

[2] C.O. 324/93/224, Hay–Howick, 3 Jan. 1831.

[3] C.O. 324/87/10, Hay–Dumaresq, Private, 17 Jan. 1831.

[4] C.O. 324/87/38, Hay–Mitchell, 9 Jan. 1832; C.O. 201/230/190, Mitchell–Hay, 22 Sept. 1832.

[5] R. C. Mills, *Colonisation of Australia 1829–42*, pp. 194 ff.; *Sydney Gazette*, 1 Oct. 1831; and esp. the volumes at C.O. 201/220 and ff., e.g. /463 Memorial of landholders, etc. enc. in Darling–Goderich, 28 Sept. 1831.

[6] C.O. 201/223/120, Busby–Darling, 1 Aug. 1829; /157, Busby–Howick, 21 Aug. 1831.

Board more constructive recommendations concerning the rights of the native born.[1] Young John Stephen did not hesitate to characterize those who had advised the introduction of sale as a set of incompetents who would frighten away migrants and drive pastoralists out into the bush.[2] But George Frankland, surveyor in Van Diemen's Land, and one of Hay's livelier geographical experts, wrote in July 1831 that his head was full of pauper emigration, free labour, convict labour, 'exchangeable commodities—Ricardo, Adam Smith, and Gouger with all their train'. The arrival of the new regulations in the colony had come like 'a sudden discharge of grape-shot from a masked battery . . . upon a body of marauders who are plundering the baggage in the rear'.[3]

In Van Diemen's Land the Ripon Regulations had a mixed reception. Economic conditions were different from those which maintained in New South Wales, and Arthur's convict system as a socially and economically profitable venture coloured his reaction to the principle of sales and emigration. He thought the Colonial Office's new approach to emigration and land showed insufficient awareness of the requirements and realities of a pastoral economy. He promulgated the regulations but obviously treated them as just another attempt by the Colonial Office to systematize at a distance. Everything must, however, be discussed *ad nauseam* by his enthusiastic committees.[4] If his support was lukewarm at best, he did not nevertheless escape criticism, despite his previous generous grants and strong support of substantial outstanding claims.[5] The young Alfred Stephen made himself useful by bringing up to date his lengthy reports on the legal and historical complications which had characterized land administration in the island. Unfortunately he discovered that all land titles seemed to be in doubt.[6] In both colonies difficult

---

[1] C.O. 201/207/68, Hall–MacLcay, 3 Nov. 1828; *H.R.A.* I/xiv/578, Darling–Murray, 2 Jan. 1829, enc. Hall–Murray, 17 Nov. 1828; C.O. 201/207/101, Hall–Murray, 2 May 1829; *H.R.A.* I/xv/153, Darling–Murray, 6 July 1829; /244, Murray–Darling, 6 Nov. 1829; C.O. 201/223/447, Hall–Goderich, 15 Aug. 1831.

[2] C.O. 201/224/470, Stephen–Goderich, 20 July 1831.

[3] C.O. 323/165/566, Frankland–Hay, 10 July 1831; C.O. 324/87/36, Hay–Frankland, Private, 9 Jan. 1832.

[4] Hartwell, op. cit., p. 58 ff., Burroughs, op. cit., pp. 90–7; C.O. 280/29/168, Arthur–Goderich, 9 July 1831, esp. pp. 182 ff., and enc. Appendices.

[5] C.O. 280/30/224, Arthur–Goderich, 27 Oct. 1831; 280/33/136, Arthur–Howick, 14 Jan. 1832.

[6] C.O. 280/33/204, Arthur–Howick, 17 Jan. 1832; /396, Arthur–Goderich, 18 Feb. 1832, enc. Stephen–Arthur, 25 May 1830, 27 May 1830, 14 June 1830, 1 Sept. 1830, 19 Jan. 1832.

questions remained to be determined concerning the collection of overdue quit-rent.[1]

Critics tended to chastise the administration of land before 1831 for chaos and neglect. The chaos certainly existed. Wakefield's claim that he had collected a rag-bag of two hundred different methods of disposing of colonial waste lands may have been exaggerated, but it was not without some truth.[2] Perhaps the most telling evidence of the need to cut back a choking jungle-growth came in the painfully detailed reports of the Collector of Internal Revenue in New South Wales. Macpherson's intention was to put forward ideas of his own, and later to save his job. He described with a clinical eye the complex and unsatisfactory results of successive government measures to cope with the insatiable hunger of colonists for land.[3] The principle of sale, he thought, would eventually prove beneficial to the colonies, particularly if they did not inhibit a suitably assisted immigration. But it is clear that the new regulations would at least in the short term add complication to complication; for his remarkable accounts showed that there had grown up in the colony a crazy structure of no less than twenty different methods of appropriating Crown land. Such results were surely the consequence of well-intentioned but misguided piecemeal activity rather than of ordinary neglect. It was probably more from disgust and disillusionment than from laziness that Hay should wash his hands of Macpherson's correspondence.[4]

[1] *H.R.A.* I/xvi/341, Darling–Goderich, 1 Sept. 1831; /833, Goderich–Bourke, 26 Dec. 1832; C.O. 280/36/280, Arthur–Goderich, 11 Dec. 1832.

[2] P.P. 1836 XI (512), Colonial Waste Lands, p. 550 ff., q. 503.

[3] C.O. 201/221/149, Macpherson–Murray, 19 Feb. 1831, enc. his colonial correspondence, e.g. /161, Macpherson–MacLeay, 15 Jan. 1831; /171, Macpherson–MacLeay, 14 Apr. 1830.

[4] C.O. 201/230/146, Macpherson–Goderich, 7 Nov. 1832, enc. Macpherson–MacLeay, 19 Jan. 1832; /167, Macpherson–Goderich, 23 Nov, 1832.

IX

SUB-IMPERIALISM IN AUSTRALIA

THE expansion of British settlement in Australia was rapid but complex. If historical hindsight has awarded almost unrelieved black marks to the regulation and administration of land in the Australian colonies before 1831, the same cannot be said of wider questions concerning the spread of settlement and the occupation of the continent. The desire to segregate and classify convicts or the need for places of secondary punishment led to the establishment of many outstations.[1] The service of the penal system came first, but there were usually commercial or strategic reasons to provide additional motives for settlement as the reports of the explorers became available.[2] Macquarie's proposals to set up a new convict station north of Sydney were backed by schemes for the cultivation of sugar, tobacco and coffee. The Governor, though he later had doubts, favoured a combination of private capital and government assistance. Bigge visited Port Macquarie and heard evidence of what had been done to encourage colonial sugar.[3] The Commissioner was in favour of employing convicts on sheep runs, but he also advised that segregated settlements be established.[4] He called for the separate administration of Van Diemen's Land, which had by this time developed its own outstations.[5]

There were already detailed blue-prints for the administration of convict settlements and they were to be called upon and modified often in the 1820s, with a consequent elaboration of the colonial administrative structure.[6] The Colonial Office accepted in principle

[1] C. M. H. Clark, *History of Australia* (Melbourne, 1962), i, 236 f.; A. G. L. Shaw, *Convicts and the Colonies*, p. 184 f.

[2] Clark, p. 296 f.

[3] *H.R.A.* I/x/257, Macquarie–Bathurst, 24 Feb. 1820; /364, Macquarie–Bathurst, 1 Sept. 1820; C.O. 201/118/382 ff. esp. evidence of W. Cox; C.O. 201 /142/16, Bigge–Bathurst, 20 Nov. 1819.

[4] At Moreton Bay, Port Curtis, on Pt. Bowen, *3rd Report*, pp. 161–3.

[5] *H.R.A.* I/x/381, Macquarie–Bathurst, 7 Feb. 1821; /527, Macquarie–Bathurst, 18 July 1821 (Macquarie Harbour); Bigge, *Judicial Report*, p. 46.

[6] e.g. C.O. 201/119/264 ff. Bigge Appendix—Instructions to Commandants, etc., Newcastle records, etc. (Newcastle was founded in part to segregate the troublesome Irish from the rest of the convicts); /120/246 ff. Evidence of Morrisett;

the idea of segregating convicts being punished, so that they might be encouraged to earn those 'comforts and advantages that seem to be inseparably connected with the Progress of Colonisation', and Brisbane was instructed to have Oxley examine the north for likely settlement areas.[1] He reported that Moreton Bay and Port Curtis were satisfactory for the purpose, that a major new river had been discovered, and that he would go ahead to establish a station at Moreton Bay.[2] The Colonial Office, however, was not enthusiastic about locking up such good country as a place of secondary punishment and suggested the re-occupation of Norfolk Island.[3] Brisbane considered that the convicts, if carefully classified, could play a pioneering role. The very worst could be assigned to Norfolk Island; the merely bad could open up Moreton Bay. At Port Macquarie, he reported, the work of the convicts was already acting as 'the best means of paving the way for the introduction of free population'.[4] After his inspection in 1827, Darling was not so hopeful of Moreton Bay; but he agreed that Port Macquarie should now be opened to free settlers.[5]

Meanwhile the internal expansion of the colonies had opened up new areas, some of them with quite different styles of life.[6] But while the convicts, explorers and sheep played the leading parts in opening up the coast and hinterland of Eastern Australia, credit for the take-over of the rest of the continent must be shared between the Colonial Office, the Admiralty, and the French.

In 1817 Lachlan Macquarie told Henry Goulburn that neither the French nor any other European nation should be allowed to form 'any settlement in any part of this continent' and the end of the war allowed voyages of survey and exploration to recommence in earnest.[7]

H.R.A. I/x/479, Macquarie–Bathurst, 21 March 1821, enc. Instructions for Commandant at Port Macquarie.

[1] *H.R.A.* I/x/791, Bathurst–Brisbane, 9 Sept. 1822.

[2] *H.R.A.* I/xi/215, Brisbane–Bathurst, 3 Feb. 1824, enc. Oxley–Goulburn, 10 Jan. 1824.

[3] *H.R.A.* I/xi/321, Bathurst–Brisbane, 22 July 1824.

[4] *H.R.A.* I/xi/409, Brisbane–Bathurst, 3 Nov. 1824; /553, Brisbane–Bathurst, 24 Mar. 1825; /603, Brisbane–Bathurst, 21 May 1825; I/xii/170, Bathurst–Darling, 19 Feb. 1826.

[5] *H.R.A.* I/xiii/523, Darling–Goderich, 26 Sept. 1827.

[6] T. M. Perry, op. cit., Chs. 5–8; Louise T. Daley *Men and a River*: *Richmond River District* (Melbourne, 1966), Chs. 1–2; R. B. Walker, *Old New England*: *Northern Tablelands of N.S.W. 1818–1900* (Sydney, 1966), Chs. 1–4.

[7] *H.R.A.* I/ix/488, Macquarie–Goulburn, 24 Sept. 1817; /207, Bathurst–Macquarie, 8 Feb. 1817.

Phillip Parker King had kept a wary eye on Freycinet's activities in the course of his survey.[1] It was in writing about King's voyages that Macquarie first introduced the term 'Australia' into official correspondence.[2] King's reports, the foundation of Singapore, war experience, and the growth of private trade in areas once the preserves of the Dutch or English East India Companies, created a practical interest in northern Australia.[3]

Horton sought and respected King's advice on such matters as the lifting of limitations on colonial commerce and the re-occupation of Norfolk Island.[4] William Barnes, a naval adventurer who had served in the East, successfully puffed ambitious prospects of a prosperous entrepôt trade in the area. The Colonial Office forwarded his ideas to the Board of Trade, at that time attempting to revise the rules governing Anglo-Dutch commercial rivalry; and gave a favourable hearing to the representations of private merchants and shipowners belonging to the East India Trade Committee who had been impressed by Barnes.[5]

Early in 1824 Horton, primed by John Barrow's enthusiastic appraisal of King's reports, was ready to act.[6] Barrow's forward interest was very influential and could normally be presumed. Indeed it was one of Lord Bathurst's standing jokes. 'Barrow is a great Authority', he wrote to Hay in 1826, 'but it has been often said that if *coveting* islands and now settlements is a breach of the tenth commandment he is the greatest violator of the Decalogue in the Kingdom.'[7] Now Barrow acclaimed the birth of a potential new Singapore and supported the effective claiming of the whole of Australia.

The merchants interviewed Bathurst; Barnes plotted his own advantage; and Horton welcomed every initiative with whatever

---

[1] C.O. 201/95/609, King–Goulburn, 9 Nov. 1819.

[2] *H.R.A.* I/ix/747, Macquarie–Goulburn, 21 Dec. 1817.

[3] C.O. 201/91/23, Barrow–Goulburn, 8 Dec. 1818, enc. King–Croker, 10 June 1818; D. Howard, 'English Activities on the North Coast of Australia in the first half of the 19th century' (London Univ. M.A. thesis, 1924), pp. 14–21, 30–42, 50 ff. and esp. Ch. IV, 76 ff.

[4] C.O. 201/146/644, King–Horton, 25 June 1823; /646, King–Horton, 26 June 1823.

[5] C.O. 201/146/178, Barns [*sic*]–Bathurst, 23 July 1823; *H.R.A.* III/v/737, Horton–Lack, 9 Oct. 1823, enc. Barns–Horton, 15 Sept. 1823; /741, Begbie–Horton, 13 Dec. 1823; /747, Larpent–Horton, 16 Dec. 1823; /750, Barns–Bathurst, 21 Jan. 1824; /750, Larpent–Bathurst, 21 Jan. 1824.

[6] *H.R.A.* III/v/751, Barrow–Horton, Private, 22 Jan. 1824.

[7] C.O. 324/75/266, Miscellaneous Minutes, 1824–6.

assistance he could give.[1] A dispatch was sent to Sir Thomas Brisbane outlining the commercial and military motives behind the decision to go ahead with the venture; and the necessary steps were taken to assure the possession of North and North-Western Australia up to the western edge of Bathurst Island. The Governor was told that the settlement would 'give security to the East India Company's and the Indian Private Trade to China by the Eastern Route'. Captain Bremer must be afforded every assistance at Sydney, and would-be settlers should be encouraged. If a foreign power should prove to be already in possession, however, then they should not be disturbed.[2] Bremer at first selected Port Essington and on 20 September took over the 'north coast of New Holland'. But lack of water drove him to move the settlement to Melville Island a week later.[3] In November he wrote hopefully of what had been done;[4] and towards the end of the year sailed away leaving the uninspired soldier, Captain Barlow, in charge of the pathetic establishment.[5] Barrow happily urged the Colonial Office to follow up the scheme but the Treasury would not turn a blind eye.[6] But Melville Island was unhealthy, out of the track of ships passing through Torres Straits; and the expected Malay fishing fleet, whose trepang fields were further East, failed to appear. Communications became almost impossible. Efforts to encourage settlers ran into predictable difficulties. There followed a dreary and in part tragic chronicle. In February 1826 Major Campbell succeeded Barlow and in six months more optimistic news was reported from the post.[7]

In London there was disappointment, at the first information of failure, and the Colonial Office agreed to a retrial of the district to the eastward which Bremer had abandoned.[8] James Stirling was sent in the *Success* to carry out the new plans.[9] It was his presence on the

[1] *H.R.A.* III/v/753, Begbie–Horton, 29 Jan. 1824; /757, Barns–Bathurst, 7 Feb. 1824; /763, Horton–Barns, 6 Apr. 1824.

[2] *H.R.A.* I/xi/227, Bathurst–Brisbane, 17 Feb. 1824; III/v/758, Bathurst–Admiralty, 17 Feb. 1824; I/xi/338, Brisbane–Bathurst, 12 Aug. 1824.

[3] *H.R.A.* I/xiii/858, Note 78.

[4] C.O. 201/155/165, Bremer–Bathurst, 12 Nov. 1824.

[5] *H.R.A.* III/vi/645, Barlow–Ovens, 19 May 1825 and ff.; Howard, op. cit., pp. 96 ff.

[6] III/v/793, Barrow–Horton, 30 Apr. 1825; /796, Herries–Horton, 12 Oct. 1825.

[7] *H.R.A.* III/vi/658, Campbell–MacLeay, 10 Oct. 1826; /677, 20 Dec. 1826; /687, 7 June 1827; /695, 8 June 1827; /721, 20 June 1828.

[8] *H.R.A.* I/xii/224, Bathurst–Darling, 7 Apr. 1826, enc. Hay–Barrow, 6 Apr. 1826 and Begbie–Hay, 18 Mar. 1826.

[9] *H.R.A.* III/v/798, Barrow–Hay, 26 May 1826.

coast rather than official absence of mind which gave the great impetus to the westward course of Empire. For on his arrival he strongly recommended Swan River as the most eligible place for settlement. Darling had reservations, but saw some advantages in such a project; for he thought it could improve communications with the penal settlement planned for King George's Sound to the far south-west of the continent. In any case Swan River occupied, he thought, too strategic a position to be allowed to fall into the hands of the French. Encouraged by Campbell's more sanguine recent reports from Melville Island, he was inclined to allow that settlement more time to prove itself.[1]

Stirling spent some fateful months exploring Western Australia while he waited for the season suitable for sailing north; and in May 1827 proceeded on his ordered expedition.[2] He soon reported that he had planted another small settlement, at Raffles Bay, after rejecting Croker's Island.[3] But naval zeal and the occasional visits of warships could not save the doomed northern stations.[4] Neither the first military commandant at Raffles Bay nor his more imaginative successor Collet Barker had much good news to send. The settlements seemed under a curse, and dogged by sickness, difficult lines of communication, and attacks by the natives. The Malay trepang fishers did not show their faces the first year and when at last they did arrive in 1828 it was too late, for the authorities had been having second thoughts and decisions had been taken to abandon the settlements. Patience might have brought about a different result, for Campbell at least thought that success was in sight.[5] But patience could not be presumed.

By 1827 Darling had grown concerned at the formidable difficulties and expense which the regular service of the outstations created; and listed the details of the settlements under his care: Newcastle, Port Macquarie, Moreton Bay, 'Port Essington', Melville Island, King George's Sound, Western Port, the Illawarra district, and Norfolk Island. He was still in favour of any steps necessary to exclude the

[1] *H.R.A.* I/xii/773, Darling–Bathurst, 18 Dec. 1826, enc. Stirling–Darling, 8 Dec., 14 Dec. 1826.

[2] *H.R.A.* I/xiii/315, Darling–Bathurst, 2 May 1827.

[3] *H.R.A.* III/v/808, Stirling–Darling, 20 June 1827; /811, Barrow–Stanley, 9 Jan. 1828, enc. Stirling's Reports.

[4] *H.R.A.* I/xiii/762, Huskisson–Darling, 8 Feb. 1828, enc. Barrow–Hay, 31 Jan. 1828.

[5] *Journal of the Royal Geographical Society 1834* (4); cf. also, Howard, op. cit., p. 105 ff.

French, whose interest in King George's Sound and Western Port he thought suspicious. But he had qualms about proposals which would lead to yet another colony in the far west coming under his admini-stration.[1] Nor was he alone in his criticisms. The *Australian*, engaged on one of its anti-imperial campaigns and demanding that New South Wales must withstand 'England's parsimony, England's neglect and inattention', had grumbled in 1826 that the Colonial Office was 'scattering British subjects along the coast of New Holland like so many bats in a forsaken dwelling'.[2] Forbes warned Horton against the settling of Swan River from Sydney. 'This colony is yet too young for distant dependencies', he wrote. Such a venture would draw off capital, increase the costs of administration, and divide the attention and means of government. The northern Australian settlements had been 'absolutely useless', ending 'like all creative systems of commerce' in ultimate disillusionment. He thought the south offered more interesting prospects. More attention should be devoted to solving the riddle of the rivers and finding an inland sea if it existed.[3]

At the end of 1827 Darling was willing to support the expediency of a settlement at Swan River, but convinced that the dismal estab-lishment at Melville Island should be transferred to Raffles Bay as a measure of consolidation.[4] Barrow agreed but now had his eyes firmly on Western Australia. He felt that both Western Port and King George's Sound should be retained as well as Raffles Bay. 'I think we may consider ourselves to be in unmolested possession of the Great Continent of New South Wales', he told Hay.[5]

Early in 1828 the Governor advised that the settlements in Northern Australia had by no means fulfilled their promise. Barnes had been, he thought, 'an unprincipled adventurer, totally unworthy of notice'.[6] Consultations were again held between the Colonial Office and the Admiralty. Croker told Twiss that he had always been doubtful of the whole affair and thought the settlements had been undertaken 'inadvertently'. Perhaps he underestimated or forgot what was being done by the left hand of those statesmen in disguise,

---

[1] *H.R.A.* I/xiii/301, Darling–Hay, 14 May 1827; cf. also I/xiv/11, Darling–Huskisson, 5 Mar, 1828.

[2] *Australian* 8 Nov., 11 Nov. 1826.

[3] C.O. 201/188/108, Forbes–Horton, Private, 15 May 1827.

[4] *H.R.A.* I/xiii/549, Darling–Goderich, 13 Oct. 1827.

[5] C.O. 201/195/40, Barrow–Hay, 23 May 1828; *H.R.A.* I/xiv/214, Murray–Darling, 31 May 1828.

[6] *H.R.A.* I/xiii/793, Darling–Huskisson, 25 Feb. 1828.

Robert Hay and John Barrow. At all events Sir George Murray decided on withdrawal.[1]

The discovery in 1824 of a 'new and valuable country of great extent' to the south by Hume and Hovell did not have immediate results, despite Hume's application for a land grant; for Brisbane was understandably reluctant to stretch his already strained line of command beyond breaking point.[2] Hay was very interested in these discoveries, however, as in all others. He was eager to establish settlements or convict outposts linking New South Wales and Van Diemen's Land. Western Port and Port Phillip again came up for discussion.[3] In particular Hay thought it important to forestall the French whom he knew to be considering the question of transportation.[4] By 1826 Hay, thoroughly alarmed by the sailing of D'Urville's expedition, saw an opportunity to combine penal and strategic purposes by planting a convict settlement on the west coast of the continent. Bathurst instructed Darling to throw open Port Macquarie to settlement, replacing it with Moreton Bay as a first place of secondary punishment. Shark's Bay in the west could be next in severity.[5] Shortly afterwards, King George's Sound was substituted for Shark's Bay.[6]

Darling entered into the spirit, though he had his doubts about all distant outposts.[7] He asked for his commission to be extended to take in the whole continent and suggested that the maps be changed to show that British occupancy was real. He gave secret instructions to Lockyer and Wright, Commandants-elect at King George's Sound and Western Port, concerning their possible encounter with the French. Lockyer should avoid 'any expression of doubt of the whole of New Holland being considered within this government'. Wright, at Western Port, could be firmer; for the Governor's instructions had extended his jurisdiction from the 135th to the 129th meridian of east longitude, and Western Port lay well within both these determina-

---

[1] C.O. 201/195/46, Croker–Twiss, Private, 31 July 1828; *H.R.A.* I/xiv/462, Murray–Darling, 15 Nov. 1828.

[2] *H.R.A.* I/xi/552, Brisbane–Horton, 24 Mar. 1825; I/xii/655, Hay–Darling, 22 Oct. 1826; enc. Hume–Bathurst, 20 Apr. 1826; H. G. Turner, *A History of the Colony of Victoria* (London, 1904), i. 49.

[3] *H.R.A.* I/xii/192, Bathurst–Darling, 1 Mar. 1826.

[4] *Bathurst Papers*, p. 595, Memo. of Secret Intelligence from Paris, 30 Nov. 1825.

[5] *H.R.A.* I/xii/193, Bathurst–Darling, 1 Mar. 1826; /194, Bathurst–Darling, Private, 1 Mar. 1826.

[6] *H.R.A.* I/xii/218, Bathurst–Darling, 11 Mar. 1826.

[7] *H.R.A.* I/xii/639, Darling–Bathurst, 10 Oct. 1826.

tions. Indeed it had been tried as a convict settlement twenty years before.[1] Wright, therefore, must warn any French he met away from what would be an 'unjustifiable intrusion on His Britannic Majesty's Possessions'.[2]

The Governor was not really convinced that the French interest in Australia was anything but purely scientific. He was glad of the ostentatious presence of British warships at Sydney, however, when D'Urville arrived, and thought the French had their eyes on New Zealand.[3]

The settlement at Western Port was a half-hearted affair and proved abortive, despite distinct efforts by Hovell and Captain Wetherall of the *Fly* to rehabilitate the reputation of the area in general.[4] Darling was unenthusiastic and when he advised that the experiment be discontinued in April 1827, Goderich allowed him to exercise his discretion, which he did.[5] Too late to save this particular station, the Colonial Office had second thoughts. It seemed to Hay more reasonable to concentrate on the development of the south-eastern corner of the continent, especially if, as Horton hoped, the East India Company could take over responsibility for the settlement of Western Australia. If Western Port itself was unsuitable for settlement, the hinterland was reported to be excellent; and Huskisson rightly surmised that time would shortly see a renewed interest in the area both from New South Wales in the north and Van Diemen's Land in the south.[6]

Darling was not hopeful about King George's Sound from the beginning, and he thought both Shark's Bay, which had been mentioned as a likely spot for a penal settlement, and King George's Sound too distant and desolate to attract the French anyway.[7] Once established, the settlement promptly caused the expected anxiety.[8] The Governor came to the conclusion that King George's Sound

[1] *H.R.A.* III/v/889, Note 167.

[2] *H.R.A.* I/xii/699 ff. Darling–Bathurst, 24 Nov. 1826.

[3] *H.R.A.* I/xii/729, Darling–Hay, 4 Dec. 1826.

[4] *H.R.A.* III/v/827, MacLeay–Wright, 4 Nov. 1826; /830, Wetherall–Barrow, 7 Nov. 1826; /831, Wetherall–Darling, 27 Dec. 1826; /835, Wetherall–Darling, 24 Jan. 1827; /850, Wright–MacLeay, 26 Jan. 1827; /854, Hovell–Darling, 27 Mar. 1827.

[5] *H.R.A.* I/xiii/73, Darling–Bathurst, 4 Feb. 1827; /239, Darling/Bathurst, 6 Apr. 1827; /450, Goderich– Darling, 19 July 1827; /667, Darling–Goderich, 24 Dec. 1827.

[6] *H.R.A.* I/xiii/734, Huskisson–Darling, 20 Jan, 1828; Minute at 201/182/19 ff.

[7] *H.R.A.* I/xii/639, Darling–Bathurst, 10 Oct. 1826.

[8] *H.R.A.* III/vi/453, MacLeay–Lockyer, 4 Nov. 1826; I/xii/773, Darling–Bathurst, 18 Dec. 1826; III/vi/460, Lockyer–MacLeay, 22 Jan. 1827; /501, Lockyer–MacLeay, 18 Apr. 1827; /506, Wakefield–MacLeay, 21 May 1827.

should be retained for strategic purposes, or in case the French really were interested; but considered that the government would have to re-examine its whole policy of establishing penal outstations. The question of the western half of the continent should not be just allowed to drift. If Swan River were to be settled, then King George's Sound should certainly be kept. It would probably be a sound decision to settle Swan River, but this should be done from England or India. Experience had taught him that lack of resources made settlement of the far west impossible from Sydney.[1] At the same time as he took advantage of Goderich's permission to withdraw from Western Port he wrote of his impatience with King George's Sound. Communications were 'tedious', difficult and uncertain, and it was, he wrote, 'a barren Waste.' Only the Secretary of State could decide about its future which was 'entirely a matter of policy'.[2]

At last the hunt was up. Stirling's preliminary bias in favour of Western Australia had been strengthened by the expedition he had made early in 1827. Darling admired Stirling's ability. He was the very man to be governor of a new colony in the west. The captain's application for the job went off with Darling's cordial endorsement. A colony in Western Australia would soon form commercial and strategic connections with the Indian Empire, they imagined.[3]

For the Colonial Office, the moment of truth had come. Once the French scare was over, it recoiled from the results of its own work. Commitments would have to be re-assessed. Hay told Darling that there was no need to take formal possession of New Holland, which was probably too barren for the French to want it.[4] Yet he had certain reservations, for it appeared that the French really had been favourably impressed by the British transportation system. When a French committee of inquiry sought detailed information, the Colonial Office was not prepared to offer more than a copy or two of the Bigge Report.[5]

At the Admiralty Barrow was furious when he heard that Stirling

[1] *H.R.A.* I/xiii/272, Darling–Bathurst, 3 May 1827; /301, Darling–Hay, 14 May 1827; /264, Darling–Bathurst, 21 Apr. 1827.

[2] *H.R.A.* I/xiii/667, Darling–Goderich, 24 Dec. 1827.

[3] *H.R.A.* I/xii/773, Darling–Bathurst, 18 Dec. 1826, enc. Stirling–Darling, 14 Dec. 1826; I/xiii/264, Darling–Bathurst, 21 Apr. 1827, enc. Stirling–Darling, 18 Apr. 1827; /306, Darling–Hay, 15 May 1827, enc. Stirling–Bathurst, 15 May 1827; III/vi/551 ff. reports of Stirling and Fraser.

[4] C.O. 202/17/44, Hay–Darling, Private, 8 Mar. 1827.

[5] E. de Blosseville, *Historie des Colonies Pénales de L'Angleterre Dans L'Australie* (Paris, 1831); C.O. Minute at 201/188/240, Grenville–Horton, 17 June 1827.

had sailed off on a 'Quixotic' expedition 'in direct contradiction to his orders, and in utter ignorance of what he has proposed'. He regretted that Darling had been deceived about D'Urville; and expected to hear that the *Success* had been wrecked on the notorious western coast.[1] When the reports came in, he wrote soberly to Horton that he was impressed by the reports of Swan River which Stirling and Fraser had made. But he thought Stirling's 'anticipations of a commercial intercourse with India, with the Malays, etc.' quite fallacious. The West Coast was dangerous to shipping, and had been long avoided rather than sought out by Indiamen. Swan River would be a new colony almost as much separated from New South Wales as from England. If the Colonial Office wanted to keep a convict establishment at King George's Sound, then it would be right to establish another colony at Swan River. The land between was reported to be good. But all the machinery of an independent colony would be needed to govern the new settlement. On the whole he thought it would be better to develop the eastern side of the continent. Only the political motive of forestalling the French or the Americans should induce Britain to colonize South-Western Australia. Little would be lost even if the area fell into foreign hands. Western Port, however, lying between the two existing colonies, should not be abandoned. As for the settlements to the north, he expected nothing. Only Sir Stamford Raffles had been able to learn the secret of dealing with the Malays.[2]

Stirling's request to be appointed governor of Swan River was, therefore, not well received. The Colonial Office curtly minuted 'no intention of settlement'.[3] Neither Huskisson nor Horton allowed themselves to succumb to the enticements he offered them in his reports. Both men had weighty political problems on their mind. Horton told Hay that he thought a colony in Western Australia would be inexpedient and expensive, unless the East India Company could be interested. In January 1828 Huskisson sent Darling a dispatch which rejected any prospect of a separate colony in Western Australia without support from India.[4] This support he thought unlikely.

[1] C.O. 323/149/135, Barrow–Hay, Private, 13 June 1827; 324/85/118, Hay–Darling, 13 June 1827.
[2] C.O. 202/20/2, Horton–Barrow, 13 Oct. 1827; 201/185/23, Barrow–Horton, Private, 15 Oct. 1827.
[3] 201/189/193, Stirling–Bathurst, 15 May 1827.
[4] C.O. 201/195/10, Barrow–Stanley, 9 Jan. 1828; Minute at C.O. 201/179/206, Horton–Hay, 24 Dec. 1827, on Darling–Bathurst, 21 Apr. 1827 (*H.R.A.* I/xiii/

Despite the benevolent energies of India merchants such as Prinsep, and doubtless Mangles, Stirling's father-in-law, the Company declined to become formally involved.[1] But in 1828 political upheavals had brought to the Colonial Office in Murray and Twiss two friends of James Stirling, who had returned to England determined to carry through his ambitions.[2] Barrow, too, declared a change of heart after discussions with Stirling and reconsideration of his reports. Taking care to disclaim responsibility for the mistakes made in settling Northern Australia, he declared himself ready to support a colony at Swan River.[3] Major Moody joined forces with Stirling in offering suggestions for a cheap occupation of Swan River along the lines of the Australian Agricultural Company.[4]

To Barrow's readiness to give prompt naval support, Hay now added a trump card. On 19 August he wrote to his friend Stuart de Rothesay, then ambassador at Paris, asking for information about French colonial aspirations.[5] A few days later the ambassador sent a dispatch which was very successful in spurring on the doubters. Stuart de Rothesay enclosed a copy of *Le Moniteur Universel* for 22 August 1828 in which proposals for a French Penal settlement, perhaps in New Holland, were discussed. He also reported that a Committee of the *Ministère de Marine* had examined the possibility of French transportation to Australia. Perhaps they had after all read their copies of the Bigge Report. Stuart had warned the authorities that, 'the extension of the British Establishments in that country having already embraced every part of the coast', unpleasantness might arise if they had serious intentions about New Holland; which, however, he doubted.[6]

By October, Hay thought that the abandonment of all the settlements on the northern coast was likely to make a new colony more acceptable at Swan River; and Barrow wrote that the only obstacle

---

264); C.O. 201/182/19, M. of Jan. 1828; I/xiii/739, Huskisson–Darling, 28 Jan. 1828; /741, Huskisson–Darling, 30 Jan. 1828.

[1] C.O. 323/155/201, Prinsep–Hay, 24 Jan. 1828; 324/86/112, Hay–Prinsep, 30 July 1829; 18/1/124, George Bankes–Hay, 1 Aug. 1828.

[2] *H.R.A.* III/vi/585, Stirling–Hay, 30 July 1828.

[3] C.O. 18/1/75, Barrow–Twiss, 2 Aug. 1828.

[4] C.O. 323/155/187, Moody–Hay, 6 Aug. 1828; *H.R.A.* III/vi/586, Stirling and Moody–Hay, 21 Aug. 1828; Mills, op. cit., pp. 53–4.

[5] C.O. 324/93/98, Hay–Stuart de Rothesay, 19 Aug. 1828.

[6] C.O. 201/195/256, J. Backhouse–Twiss, 3 Sept. 1828, enc. Stuart's dispatch, 22 Aug. 1828.

was expense.[1] On 5 November the territorial course was run. Sir George Murray asked the Admiralty to send a ship of war to take formal possession of the Western Coast of Australia. There followed not only swift naval preparations but a tragi-comedy of mismanagement and maladministration as the Colonial Office attempted to cope with the eager appetites of candidates for government patronage at Swan River. Thomas Peel and his companions made their bid in November and their grandiose claims soon ran into misunderstandings. Twiss's absence in Paris, Murray's geniality and Hay's vagueness about detail all played a part.[2] The Colonial Office did not wish to incur expense, but it had no intention of surrendering political authority to private groups. especially inefficient ones.[3] The devolution of authority to colonial officials did little to dissuade British capitalists that the real power lay in London. Colonizers, whether systematic or not, were unwilling to entrust the administration of their schemes to any but the central government.[4]

James Stephen, who had not been consulted, later summed it all up admirably when he said that Twiss fell into 'many errors of form which eventually proved errors of substance'.[5] Yet Stirling sailed in February 1829 with high hopes for his own future and his colony's.[6] Hay wrote optimistically to the Treasury, Foreign Office, and East India Company to tell them of what had been decided. Darling was told that the new colony would be independent of Sydney, but that all possible help was to be given.[7] Complications arose, not only from problems arising from the requirements of the entrepreneurs, but from the fact that this was not to be a convict colony. Difficulties

[1] C.O. 324/86/68, Hay–Barrow, 3 Oct. 1828; C.O. 202/23/75, Murray–Admiralty, 5 Nov. 1828; III/vi/587, Barrow–Twiss, 7 Nov. 1828.

[2] *H.R.A.* III/vi/593, Hay–Peel and Co., 6 Dec. 1828; /608, Twiss–Peel, 21 Jan. 1829; /611, Twiss–Peel, 28 Jan. 1829; C.O. 323/157/295, Peel–Hay, Private and immediate, 21 Jan. 1829.

[3] A. Hasluck, *Thomas Peel of Swan River* (Melbourne, 1965), p. 26 ff.; M. Harris, 'British Migration to Western Australia 1829–1850', pp. 46–51, 124, 163.

[4] e.g. C.O. 201/206/85, Badnall–Murray, 23 May 1829; /91, 25 May 1829; /117, 25 June 1829 and ff. Badnall, a friend of Gouger's, proposed a scheme for the emigration and employment of 100,000 poor European migrants; C.O. 201/206/304, J. C. Denham, etc.–Murray, 12 Oct. 1829, for a scheme of labour emigration.

[5] q. in M. Harris, op. cit., p. 160.

[6] M. Uren, *Land Looking West* (Oxford, 1948), p. 52 ff.; *H.R.A.* III/vi/600, Murray–Stirling, 30 Dec. 1828; /603, Hay–Stirling, 1 Jan. 1829.

[7] C.O. 324/86/84, Hay–Bankes, 8 Jan. 1829; /91, Hay–Planta, 20 Feb. 1829; 18/1/142, C.O.–Dawson, 31 Dec. 1828; 397/1/34, Hay–Dawson, 30 Dec. 1828; *H.R.A.* I/xiv/610, Murray–Darling, 12 Jan. 1829.

encountered on the spot were to become notorious, despite all the efforts of Hay and other supporters of the colony to defend it from destructive criticism.[1]

Despite everything, by 1831 it was possible for a shrewd observer to decide that 'of the final success of the colony there can be no doubt'.[2] Life moved on. Even the terrible example of pioneering in Western Australia could not kill the colonizing spirit. The Hentys, dissatisfied at Swan River, moved on to greater things in Van Diemen's Land and the opposite coast.[3] James Stephen, surprisingly on holiday and bored to be at Cowes away from his official papers, welcomed the chance to give Barrow advice about the reservation of Crown land at Perth and reserves for future public needs.[4] Barrow, who had been anxious to have scientific marvels from New South Wales on display in the beautiful new British Museum, and justifiably expected much of the MacLeays, was fascinated by all questions concerning the internal exploration and coastal survey of the continent.[5] In the years to come he would have much to read.

By 1829 Hay was convinced that earlier reports, including King's, had been far too harsh about Western Australia. He was inclined to round out his conquests with a settlement at Shark's Bay, and again approached Stuart de Rothesay for some French rumours. The ambassador discounted any news which could imply that the French were interested in the Antipodes, and told Hay that his attention would be more profitably employed in countering the United States by settling North-West America and the Falkland Islands.[6] When Hay approached Barrow about potential French claims to Shark's Bay on grounds of discovery, Barrow was sure that good Canningite doctrine and world-wide experience showed that 'priority of discovery must give way to priority of occupancy'.[7] Neither man was in

---

[1] Riddell, op. cit., p. 84 ff.; Harris, op. cit., pp. 220, 293, 300; Mills, op. cit., pp. 55–67; *Morning Chronicle*, 26 Jan. 1830; C.O. 397/1/131, Twiss–Joseph Hume, 20 Apr. 1829.

[2] 5 Mar. 1831, in ed. M. Doyle, *Extracts from the Letters and Journals of G. F. Moore* (London, 1834), p. 50.

[3] M. Bassett, *The Hentys* (Oxford, 1954), p. 2 ff. and e.g. C.O. 18/9/306, Henty–Goderich, 7 Sept. 1831.

[4] C.O. 323/162/297, Stephen–Barrow, 29 July 1830.

[5] C.O. 323/149/125, Barrow–Hay, 12 Mar. 1827; C.O. 201/204/5, Barrow–Hay, 1 Jan. 1829; /26, Barrow–Hay, 19 May 1829.

[6] C.O. 324/86/98, Hay–Stuart, 5 May 1829; 323/157/142, Stuart–Hay, 11 May 1829.

[7] C.O. 324/86/102, Hay–Barrow, 1 July 1829; 323/157/95, Barrow–Hay, 2 July 1829.

a position to wield much political power, but both could take prac-tical measures to satisfy their tastes. Perhaps it was to sublimate their unappeased expansionist appetite that they assisted in the foundation of the Royal Geographical Society. Lord Goderich consented to become the first President and they all read papers about exploits at the Antipodes. Colonial correspondents were prompted to send in detailed reports. The works of the explorers were carefully noted and Hay was offended when reports of Charles Sturt's expeditions were printed in the *Morning Chronicle* before he had received official notice.[1]

In the forward movement of Australian settlement, the Admiralty's East India Station played a leading role. The vessels regularly stationed off the coast were a friendly presence, fought for and valued by colonial governors.[2] Their visits were occasions for local celebra-tion and their participation in setting up outstations, particularly those in Northern and Western Australia, was essential.[3]

Neither Croker nor Barrow allowed considerations of expense alone to prevent the service coming to the aid of colonial expansion, but even the navy was not beyond criticism in times of retrenchment; and the vast emptiness of Australasia made impressive displays of power impossible as well as unnecessary.[4] Questions of defence therefore were largely the concern of the military departments, whose contacts with the Australian colonies were, by the nature of the convict system, close, cordial, but—since the end of the 'Rum Corps' —essentially routine. Soldiers were as much a part of the colonial scene as convicts and indeed their juxtaposition created many problems. The governors were all military men. All pressed for increases or complained at being treated as a staging-point for the service of India. Reductions were resented as settlement spread. A colonial militia was frequently discussed. Macquarie objected that

[1] Howard, op. cit., p. 118 ff.; *Journal of the Royal Geographical Society*, London 1831 ff.; and e.g. C.O. 323/168/105, Barrow–Hay, 12 Apr. 1832; 157/218, Frankland–Hay, 9 Feb. 1829; /223, Frankland–Hay, 16 Aug. 1829; 324/87/36, Hay–Frankland, 9 Jan. 1832; /38, Hay–Mitchell, 9 Jan. 1832; 202/28/94, Hay–MacConochie, 4 Feb. 1832; 323/162/48, Dumaresq–Hay, Private, 5 May 1830.

[2] *H.R.A.* I/x/498, Bathurst–Brisbane, 8 May 1821; enc. letter of Sir Henry Blackwood, 13 Mar. 1821, promising to 'keep a vessel always stationed on the coast of New South Wales'. This resulted from Melville's agreement to a sugges-tion by Bathurst, C.O. 201/104/16, Barrow–Goulburn, 13 Mar. 1821.

[3] Admiralty I/4239, Secretary of State IN-Letters, 1822–4: Melville Island; /4240, 1825: Northern Australia; /4242, 1828: West Australia.

[4] e.g. p.p. 1829 VI (290) Report of Public Accounts Commissioners.

any 'factious Demagogue' could 'light the torch of "Sedition" '. But India and the Treasury usually prevailed over the good offices of the Colonial Office and friendly intentions at the Horse Guards.[1]

Bigge looked into defence matters as into all else; but one at least of his consultants, Major Taylor of the 48th, seems to have thought there was more danger to be feared from fraternization between the Irish soldiers and the convicts than from attacks by the French or the Americans.[2] He did forward to Goulburn a copy of a letter of 1813 which had been intercepted by Captain Bowler, R.N. In this letter the American consul at Rio put forward a suggestion that a surprise attack on Port Jackson might in time of war cause considerable destruction, encourage an uprising of the convicts, and create a general diversion. Bigge seems, however, to have judged correctly that the colonies were too distant and unimportant to attract much hostile attention, though the prevention of escape by convicts on board foreign ships remained a perennial concern.[3]

* * * * *

Much more important were the routine workings of transportation, in which the navy perforce had an integral part to play. By 1818 an impressive administrative and maritime apparatus had been constructed for meeting the requirements of the convict system. After the abolition of the Transport Board in 1817, the direct responsibility for contracts and supervision fell on the Navy Board. Sir Byam Martin, who was the Board's Comptroller until its amalgamation with the general Admiralty Board in the remodelling of 1832, was an efficient and reliable public servant. On the whole the system was effective, skilful and comprehensive, and even, according to the standards of

[1] Difficulties and misbehaviour: *H.R.A.* I/xi/441, Macquarie–Bathurst, 25 July 1817; I/x/343, Macquarie–Bathurst, 31 Aug. 1820; C.O. 201/142/126, Bigge–Goulburn, Private, 17 Aug. 1821; *H.R.A.* I/x/626, Brisbane–Taylor, 4 Mar. 1822; C.O. 201/100/53, Taylor–Goulburn, 6 Nov. 1820;—shortage of troops, militia, and Treasury: *H.R.A.* I/ix/358, Macquarie–Bathurst, 4 Apr. 1817; /837, Bathurst–Macquarie, 29 Sept. 1818; I/x/183, Macquarie–Bathurst, 19 July 1819; C.O. 201/97/26, 3 Mar. 1819, Henry Torrens–Goulburn, and /48, C.O. Minute on Torrens–Goulburn, 1 Dec. 1819; *H.R.A.* I/x/315, Bathurst–Macquarie, 17 July 1820; I/x/609, Brisbane–Taylor, 26 Jan. 1822.

[2] C.O. 201/132/74 ff. Bigge Appendix, 4 Sept. 1820.

[3] C.O. 201/142/132, Bigge–Goulburn, 31 Oct. 1821, enc. extract Sumpter–Poinsett, 18 Nov. 1813.

the time and the nature of the work, humane. This is not to say that considerable moral or medical horrors did not exist.[1]

The private trade of officers of convict ships in spirits and other commodities raised special problems and doubtless renders inaccurate most early colonial statistics. Complaints from colonial merchants caused Goulburn to remonstrate with the Navy Board, who drew up a graduated plan whereby a master would be restricted to ten tons free trading-space, the chief mate three, and so on. Bathurst found this unsatisfactory, and when Bigge also recommended against this lucrative but clandestine commerce, the importation of private merchandise on convict ships was forbidden. By 1825 Brisbane was optimistically reporting that the trade no longer took place.[2]

Regulations concerning food, conditions, and medical care were after 1817 the special responsibility of the Victualling Board. They were carefully drawn up, but difficult to enforce. Adaptations aimed at the separation of juvenile from hardened offenders and various improvements suggested by the Home Office, Bigge, and others were introduced piecemeal. The importance of medical questions and the need for authoritative superintendance by surgeons resulted in the evolution of the 'surgeon system', which seems to have been broadly successful and doubtless goes far to explain the social prominence of doctors in Australian life.[3] One of the many advantages of Admiralty management of the transportation of convicts was that mounting costs were to a certain extent masked. Yet even the tolerant Navy could not remain silent before arrangements which seemed to mean that the expense of female emigration from Cork would find its way under the head of general service expenditure.[4]

Relations between the Admiralty and the Colonial Office were

[1] C. Bateson, *The Convict Ships 1787–1868* (Glasgow, 1959), Ch. 3; A. G. L. Shaw, op. cit., Ch. 5, 'The Voyage', p. 107 ff.; B. Pool, *Navy Board Contracts 1660–1832* (London, 1966), pp. 111 ff., 137–8; C. J. Bartlett, *Great Britain and Sea Power 1815–53* (Oxford, 1963), pp. 9–28, 48.

[2] C.O. 324/142/21, Goulburn–Navy Commissioners, 20 Mar. 1820; C.O. 201/100/267, Navy Board–Goulburn, 17 Apr. 1820; 324/142/138, Goulburn–Commissioners, 27 May 1820; *H.R.A.* I/xi/62, Bathurst–Brisbane, 27 Mar. 1823; I/xi/571, Brisbane–Bathurst, 14 May 1825; Shaw, op. cit., p. 114.

[3] *H.R.A.* I/ix/811, Bathurst–Macquarie, 4 July 1818; /807, Macquarie–Bathurst, 30 May 1818; I/x/142, Goulburn–Macquarie, 9 Apr. 1819; C.O. 201/144/141, Hobhouse–Horton, 9 June 1823, enc. Navy Office–Hobhouse, 29 May 1823; Bigge: at C.O. 201/124 f.; *H.R.A.* I/x/815, note 40; C.O. 201/177/52, Byam Martin–Hay, 6 June 1826; Bateson, op. cit., Ch. IV.

[4] C.O. 201/205/115, Martin–Hay, 18 Nov. 1829; /214/406, Navy Office–Treasury, 23 Dec. 1830; /222/157, Martin– Hay, Costs, 1826–30; C.O. 324/93/185, Hay–Martin, Private, 24 Mar. 1830.

close and friendly, even if there were, as in the case of the *Almorah*, controversial passages. There could be dangers in the wide initiative which had to be entrusted to officers on the spot, and service reports always repaid careful examination. In 1829 the Colonial Office, for example, set a pattern in rejecting a project put forward by Admiral Gage in favour of heavy Indian immigration into the recently abandoned northern areas of Australia.[1]

Most commanders in the area were sanguine about the continuing prosperity and development of the British connection with Australia, and James Stirling was not alone in noticing that Britain's Eastern Empire by the end of the decade did not mean merely India.[2] In 1829 three of the seven vessels belonging to the East India Station were engaged in Australian duties.[3] The dispatches of the various captains and the admiral commanding, Sir Edward Owen, gave the central authorities a lively and direct source of information about colonial development and aspirations. The Admiralty had special concern for the Swan River settlement,[4] coastal surveys,[5] and supplying out-stations from New South Wales.[6] They were interested too in all strategic aspects of the area, and kept a watchful eye on French, Dutch and American activities, literally from China to Peru: hence their interest in Cocos Island[7] and even New Guinea, though there was little but private support for competition with Dutch aspirations there.[8]

But while the Navy was prepared to play a constructive part, there was no great enthusiasm to overtax resources in accepting more than a limited police role in the South Pacific.[9] This reluctance to move

---

[1] C.O. 201/204/12, Croker–Twiss, 21 Apr. 1829, enc. Gage–Croker, 25 Oct. 1828 and Minutes.

[2] Harris, op. cit., p. 312.

[3] Adm. I/194/S.43, Owen–Croker, 2 Sept. 1829.

[4] Adm. I/194/S.57, Owen–Croker, 1 Oct. 1829; /195/S.98, 9 Nov. 1829; /S.112, 4 Jan. 1830; /S.147, 20 Mar. 1830; /S.149, 19 Mar. 1830; /197/S.201, 17 June 1830; /199/S.53, 20 July 1830; /201/S.141, 8 Jan. 1831; /S.164, 9 Mar. 1831; /S.179, 5 Apr. 1831; /203/S.275, Owen–George Elliott, 15 June 1831.

[5] Adm. I/200/S.122, Owen–Croker, 10 Nov. 1830.

[6] Adm. I/198/S.33, 29 Sept. 1830; /201/S.167, 22 Mar. 1831.

[7] Adm. I/195/S.99, 15 Nov. 1829; /S.146, 20 Mar. 1830; /196/S.154, 8 Mar. 1830; /200/S.101, 5 Jan. 1831.

[8] C.O. 201/214/9, Barrow–Twiss, 16 Jan. 1830, enc. Schomberg–Croker, 8 Sept. 1829; /21, Barrow–Hay, I June 1830, enc. Owen–Croker, 30 Nov. 1829, and Laws–Owen, 29 Sept. 1829; and C.O. 201/206/34, J. Andrews–Murray, 9 Oct. 1829.

[9] Adm. I/194/S.67, 29 Sept. 1829; /S.83, 1 Feb. 1830 (Marianas); /197/S.222, 20 July 1830 (Society and Friendly Isles); /204/S.3, Owen–Elliott, 5 Aug. 1831 (New Zealand); C.O. 201/204/35, Barrow–Twiss, 5 Sept. 1829, enc. Laws –Croker 11 Mar. 1829 (Escaped convicts and Society Isles).

formally into the Pacific was shared by the Colonial Office, who had tried unsuccessfully to interest the Foreign Office.[1] New Zealand, however, proved a continual source of administrative concern, especially as it had vaguely become an Australian colony. The whale fisheries, escaped convicts, rumours of lawlessness, missionary claims, the expectation of commercial gain and Sam Marsden finally had their effect.[2]

Macquarie had been interested in New Zealand flax for naval purposes, but against formal settlement. Yet he had allowed some of the missionaries to act as magistrates. Bigge was puzzled by the subject, but there were further advances under Sir Thomas Brisbane, when the Americans seemed to be ready to arm the Maoris and assist runaway convicts.[3] By 1823, serious colonizing proposals were being received by the home government, and these were acclaimed by the *Sydney Gazette*. Lord Bathurst was very cynical of Colonel Nicholl's project to employ 'industrious' Maoris, but Horton predictably tried to make something of every scheme.[4] Nor did Charles de Thierry, an ambitious rather than a systematic colonizer, have much better luck. New Zealand, he was told, was not 'considered as a possession of the Crown'.[5] The Lambton flotation of 1825, whose backers disclaimed all plans of conquest at Bathurst's insistence anyway, proved an expensive failure.[6]

[1] C.O. 324/93/46, Hay–Planta, 8 Dec. 1826; /48, 15 Dec. /57, 24 Jan. 1827; 323/147/347, Planta–Hay, Private, 26 Jan. 1827; On Tahiti, C.O. 201/144/90, Planta–Wilmot, 1 Feb. 1823; /175/231, Planta–Horton, 30 Dec. 1826; Adm. I/4243, Twiss–Barrow, 29 Oct. 1829.

[2] J. M. Ward, *British Policy in the South Pacific 1786–1893* (Sydney, 1948), p. 45 ff.; J. W. Davidson, 'European Penetration of the South Pacific 1779–1842' (Cambridge Univ. Ph.D. thesis 1942). pp. 46 ff., 99 ff., 119 ff., 130, 189 ff.; A. F. Madden, 'The Attitude of the Evangelicals to the Empire and Imperial Problems 1820–1850' (Oxford Univ. D.Phil. thesis 1950), esp. pp. 71, 450 ff.; A. J. Harrop, *England and New Zealand* (London, 1926); E. J. Tapp, *Early New Zealand: a Dependency of New South Wales 1788–1841* (Melbourne, 1958), Chs. 1–4.

[3] *H.R.A.* I/ix/264, Macquarie–Bathurst, 1 Apr. 1817; C.O. 201/91/8, Barrow–Goulburn, 22 June 1818; 202/9/27, Bathurst–Bigge, 24 Apr. 1819; 201/130/186, ff. N.Z. evidence, and Report, etc., at 201/142/486 ff., 27 Feb. 1823; 201/104/23, Barrow–Goulburn, 1821, Information on N.Z. with C.O. Minutes.

[4] C.O. 201/147/181, Nicholls–Bathurst, 16 Sept. 1823; B.M. Add. MSS. 38744 (Huskisson Papers), f. 314 ff. The project had the support of the Enderbys; *Sydney Gazette* 4 Nov. 1824.

[5] C.O. 202/11/146, Horton–de Thierry, 10 Dec. 1823; /155, Horton–de Thierry, 30 Jan. 1824.

[6] C.O. 201/167/229, Littleton–Bathurst, 30 Mar. 1825; /231, Bathurst–Littleton, 29 Mar. 1825; /179/91, Littleton–Horton, 22 Mar. 1826; *H.R.A.* I/xiv/122, Darling–Huskisson. 10 Apr. 1828.

Still the government held back. Then in 1826 Lack at the Board of Trade sent Barrow a strong Memorial of the 'Merchants and Shipowners of the Southern Whale Fishery', signed by most of those engaged also in the Australian trade. This Memorial urged official British intervention in New Zealand on commercial, humanitarian and strategic grounds. The security of New South Wales was at issue. Hay was at this time engaged in his first venture at out-settling the French and he consulted Barrow, who promised that the ship which was on regular station off New South Wales would 'visit occasionally the coasts of New Zealand'.[1] In 1827, however, Hay was answering inquiries about commercial openings in New Zealand with the routine answer that New Zealand was not a dependency of New South Wales 'nor in any degree a British Possession'.[2]

* * * * *

For the colonial governors, New Zealand created perpetual difficulties, but in England others saw interesting possibilities. Robert Torrens, whose hopes had not been dashed by the collapse of the Lambton scheme, pursued the shipowners' memorial with a long paper on Australian prospects. The penal colonies, he wrote, could not be continued as enormous work-houses at a 'perpetually increasing expenditure'. A governor expert in political economy, however, could make New South Wales the centre of civilization in the Southern Ocean. At the very least he could offer his own services as commander of a detachment of marines which should be sent to New Zealand to prepare the way for a major future settlement.[3]

Torrens pressed his imaginative views in season and out. In 1827, as chairman of Horton's Emigration Committee, he asked Goderich for detailed information concerning trade and commerce in the eastern colonies, and proposed an ambitious 'triangular' scheme which would be self-financing. Ships would carry poor emigrant families to New Zealand, where their healthy labours in cutting timber and cultivating flax would provide the capital and skills necessary for their successful re-settlement in Australia. Sir Byam

[1] C.O. 201/175/203, Lack–Hay, 6 June 1826; Memorial of 24 Apr. 1826 at C.O. 201/179/601 ff.; C.O. 202/18/11, Hay–Barrow, 14 June 1826; 201/175/29, Barrow–Hay, 15 June 1826. Later the same year Hay rejected overtures for a French trade with New South Wales: C.O. 201/175/205, Lack–Hay, 26 July 1826.

[2] C.O. 202/19/59, Hay–J. Chaulk, 26 Apr. 1827.

[3] C.O. 323/206/365, Memorial 1826; 201/179/469, Torrens–Horton, 4 July 1826, enc. Torrens–Horton, 27 June 1826.

Martin conceded that New Zealand timber was at least as suitable as the Russian or American for naval purposes, and colonial flax was by now a hackneyed subject. But he thought the plan Utopian and costly, and when Hay forwarded Torrens' riposte drew upon practical experience to throw cold water on this particular colonial dream.[1]

By 1828 Torrens had decided to take a personal part in the colonizing process and wrote to ask for land with a harbour in the new settlement on the Western Coast. He foresaw in Australia's development great national benefits and wanted to locate 'industrious settlers on an extensive scale' engaged in the production of a well-chosen colonial staple.[2] An ambitious venture in New Zealand which obtained the modified approval of the Colonial Office and the Board of Trade, ran into difficulties the next year, and he stood out again for some naval or military presence to protect the interest of settlers and whalers.[3] In 1830 he again requested to be given some kind of official position in New Zealand to direct the course of colonization. James Stephen, however, defended the rights of the Maoris as 'owners and sovereigns of the Soil'. A 'private Empire' was objectionable. It would mean 'extension of the British power in the South Seas'. A military occupation would 'inevitably and shortly lead to the assumption of a permanent dominion'.[4]

Pressure from New South Wales drove the Colonial Office towards some kind of action.[5] The *Sydney Gazette* was confident that New Zealand would soon 'form an integral and productive part of the immense Australian Empire'.[6] Peter Dillon's zeal to forward French interests probably played a part.[7] Early in 1831 Hay told Dumaresq that 'any increase to our Foreign Possessions is at this moment entirely out of the question'; though he shared the Colonel's high regard for New Zealand's future prosperity.[8] He also wrote to

[1] C.O. 201/189/277, Torrens–Horton, 27 May 1827; 201/186/36, Martin–Hay, 6 June 1827; /189/281, Torrens–Hay, 14 June 1827; /186/44, Martin–Hay, Private, 19 June 1827.

[2] C.O. 201/199/540, Torrens–Murray, 4 Dec. 1828; 18/1/268, Torrens–Twiss, 4 Dec. 1828; 202/23/103, Twiss–Torrens, 11 Dec. 1828.

[3] C.O. 201/207/443, Torrens–Twiss, 24 Jan. 1829; 202/24/15, Twiss–Lack, 9 Apr. 1829.

[4] C.O. 201/215/696, Minute of 25 May 1830.

[5] *H.R.A.* I/xiv/603, Darling–Murray, 4 Jan. 1829; C.O. 202/24/120, Twiss–Stephen, 19 Nov. 1829.

[6] 21 Apr. 1831.

[7] C.O. 201/228/333 ff. Dillon's correspondence; 202/24/200, Hay–Dillon, 11 May 1830; 202/24/147, Twiss–Dillon, 8 Jan. 1830; 202/26/2, Hay–Dillon, 22 June 1830.

[8] C.O. 324/87/10, Hay–Dumaresq, Private, 17 Jan. 1831.

Major Mitchell that the 'restless views of individuals' must be heard only with great caution. Expense was the key.[1] Yet when Torrens wrote in favour of a show of strength at least in New Zealand, Howick had already asked the navy to increase their formal role.[2]

Naval reports and the representations of individuals indicated the need for a government presence. Darling, moved by 'humanity and national interest', was not ready to stand by as an idle spectator. He would have liked to send Captain Sturt as British resident, and told his successor Richard Bourke that New Zealand was the outstanding question awaiting his attention. The Executive Council favoured vigorous moves.[3] At last the Treasury conceded five hundred pounds a year as salary for a British resident, and James Busby was appointed.[4] His wings were clipped by the decision not to send a military force.[5] But the Admiralty could be relied on to do what it could, though reluctant to commit itself to a firm promise of the continuous presence of a ship of war.[6] It may not have been necessary to present Busby at court, but the Colonial Office could safely count on commencing another formal file.[7]

*   *   *   *   *

By 1831 still another, and major, episode in imperial expansion had begun. Bigge had recommended that the country near Spencer's Gulf, which some had suggested as more suited for a convict outstation than Moreton Bay, should be kept for later free settlement.[8] Now Sturt's discoveries had made colonizers keen to try their hand in

---

[1] C.O. 324/87/27, Hay–Mitchell, 26 Aug. 1831.

[2] C.O. 201/224/506, Minute of Torrens–Goderich, 29 Jan. 1831; C.O. 202/26/84, Howick–Barrow, 5 Jan. 1831; 201/222/9, Elliott–Howick, 7 Jan. 1831.

[3] C.O. 201/228/404, Darling–Goderich, 21 June 1832; 201/221/99, Darling–Bourke, 12 Oct. 1831; H.R.A. I/xvi/442, Lindesay–Goderich, 4 Nov. 1831, enc. Saumarez–Lindesay, 30 Oct. 1831 and Ex. Co. Minutes, 31 Oct. 1831.

[4] 202/28/18, Howick–Stewart, 27 Sept. 1831; 201/222/366, Stewart–Howick, 3 Oct. 1831; /288/338, Stewart–Hay, 24 Mar. 1832; C.O. 202/28/126, Hay–Busby, 28 Mar. 1832; C.O. 209/1/177, Busby–Hay, 31 Mar. 1832; 202/28/162, Hay–Busby, 30 May 1832.

[5] C.O. 201/228/179, Fitzroy Somerset–Hay, 6 Feb. 1832; 202/28/47, Hay–Fitzroy Somerset, 18 Feb. 1832.

[6] C.O. 202/28/16, Howick–Barrow, 27 Sept. 1831; /33, Howick–Elliott, 19 Oct. 1831; /113, Hay–Barrow, 8 Mar. 1832; /119, Hay–Elliott, 20 Mar. 1832; /128, Hay–Barrow, 29 Mar. 1832.

[7] At C.O. 209/1 ff. New Zealand.

[8] C.O. 201/142/237, Bigge–Horton, 2 Dec. 1822.

South Australia.[1] Howick and Hay both resisted such a settlement at first, but forces were gathering over which they had no control.[2] Major Bacon, armed with references from Sir Herbert Taylor, was not satisfied with Hay's weary and entirely accurate reply that colonizing plans 'always end in becoming in some way or other a source of expense to the Revenue of the country'.[3] He was soon joined by a more formidable combination, against which Hay stood firm.[4] Although there was no hope of raising the securities which were demanded by the Colonial Office before they would give the venture a *fiat*, Bacon had the consolation of William Tooke's comment that 'the Colonial Office is too much under the influence of the *ancien régime*, and requires reform more than any other department of government'.[5] Yet even this could only stir a lukewarm response from Howick.[6]

When the project was renewed, Hay's cautious response to the 'embryo' company in endless discussions earned him more opprobrium. But his objections to the proposed charter as a daring proposal for a popular assembly, thus erecting out of time 'within the British monarchy a government purely Republican' were no idiosyncratic Conservative gloss. Nor were his attitudes accounted for merely by inertia or, far less, by unfamiliarity with grandiose visions of colonization.[7] For Hay had the support of very disparate colleagues in Howick and Goderich, who brushed aside the attacks of the *Morning Chronicle* and Gouger's 'splenetic effusion' as 'trumpery nonsense' and of fleeting interest.[8]

More important, perhaps, Hay knew that when he condemned the charter, he spoke also for James Stephen. Stephen's searing report found little but social, financial and legal shortcomings in the scheme.

---

[1] E. Hodder, *The Founding of South Australia* (London, 1898), p. 41; D. Pike, op. cit., Ch. 3; Mills, op. cit., Chs. VI, VIII; Burroughs, op. cit., Ch. VI, esp. 169–173.

[2] C.O. 202/24/179, Hay–Copland, 2 Apr. 1830; 202/26/82, Howick–Marty, 31 Dec. 1830; /90, Howick–James Dixon, 12 Jan. 1831. (For Dixon, cf. also C.O. 201/178/405, Dixon–Bathurst, 24 Feb. 1826.)

[3] C.O. 13/1/42, Taylor–Hay, 13 Feb. 1831, enc. Bacon–Taylor, 2 Feb. 1831; /49, Bacon–Hay, 20 Feb. 1831.

[4] C.O. 13/1/55, Torrens, Bacon, Gouger, Tooke, Mangles, etc.–Hay, 25 Aug. 1831.

[5] C.O. 13/1/65, Tooke–Bacon, 9 Sept. 1831; /67, 27 Oct. 1831.

[6] 13/1/69, Howick–Bacon, 31 Oct. 1831.

[7] C.O. 202/28/170, Hay–Darling, 14 June 1832; /187, Hay–Torrens, 17 July 1832; /199, Hay–Torrens, 6 Aug. 1832.

[8] C.O. 13/1/201, Goderich–Hay, 25 Sept. 1832.

As it stood, it seemed to demand the surrender of the 'sovereignty of a territory larger than Spain and Portugal'. This any government would be loth to do. When Hay looked back on what had been done to consolidate the imperial stake in Australasia over the previous ten years, the idea must have seemed little short of ridiculous.[1]

[1] C.O. 13/1/211 ff. Charter draft; /265 ff. Stephen's observations.

X

TOWARDS A FREE COMMUNITY:
THE GOVERNMENT AND SOCIAL
RECONSTRUCTION

THE government of the Australian colonies during the 1820s would
have been very different if Commissioner Bigge had not returned a
Report which was at bottom favourable to the continuation of the
convict system as an imperial asset. All plans and projects had in
effect to be considered in relation to the workings of transportation,
which cast its long shadow over every administrative decision. This
could often be frustrating to those who in growing numbers were
learning to regard 'Botany Bay' as more than a joke or a vast gaol.
The system was in many ways so successful an instrument of official
purpose that it resisted reform.

The Home Office, however, especially under Peel, was by no
means entirely a force of reaction. Even Sidmouth had been ready
when pressed to take the practical steps that seemed necessary to
prevent New South Wales from becoming an Antipodean hell of
social dereliction and human despair.[1] The friendly interest of the
Home department was a *sine qua non* of colonial development, for its
executive actions determined the very make-up of most of the colonial
community. But it was to the Colonial Office that men looked for a
constructive interest which was not merely routine and indirect. Its
local representatives, and particularly the colonial governors, were
engaged in a perpetual search for satisfactory ways to reconcile
apparently incompatible imperial and colonial ends. The official
mind, being open at a hundred places, was perplexed and divided.[2]

The Bigge Report created a great deal more work for the Colonial
department than it did for the Home Office. Henry Hobhouse, who

---

[1] e.g. *H.R.A.* I/ix/120, Bathurst–Macquarie, 11 May 1816; I/ix/484, Macquarie
Bathurst, 12 Sept. 1817; I/x/143, Bathurst–Macquarie, 12 Apr. 1819, enc. Hobhouse–Goulburn, 29 Jan. 1819; I/x/173, Macquarie–Bathurst, 17 July 1819.

[2] A. G. L. Shaw, *Convicts and the Colonies*, Ch. VI, Controversy in England
1810–1830; L. C. Robson, *The Convict Settlers of Australia* (Melbourne, 1965),
Ch. 7.

had long been acquainted with the details of the convict system, was perfectly content to let Horton arrange for the necessary legislative and administrative reorganization. But Peel naturally made comments about those parts of the Report which more closely concerned his department: and he took an interest in the clauses of the 1823 Bill which dealt with improvements in convict management. Horton fervently wished he had given more assistance especially when the Bill ran into trouble.[1]

Relations between the two departments were cordial. Peel was willing in principle to assist the colonial authorities in their attempt to build up a civil police force, but a shortage of good men was retarding his own projects for the metropolis.[2] In 1823 he supported Sir Humphrey Davy's request that Brisbane have one thousand pounds to measure the arc of the meridian, which should, he wrote, 'serve as a base line for any future interior survey of the Colony.'[3] Yet whenever he gave full attention to the subject of New South Wales, he seems to have had doubts. Transportation was, after all, for him the substitute for capital punishment, and he was puzzled how to combine deterrence and punishment with the legitimate aspirations of expanding colonies. The crime rate was rising; police reform meant increased detection of offences; and costs hung over everything like a pall. With Horton, he was always willing to consider the opinions of such people as Elizabeth Fry and Sydney Smith: and his experience taught him to place great value on the views of active administrators. But he had also, which Horton to his chagrin did not, a firm place in the innermost counsels of state. Perhaps, behind his feeling that the penal colonies were inefficient and his inability to discover satisfactory alternatives, he judged that 'Botany Bay' was, after all, one successful safety valve against social unrest and political rebellion at home which the Colonial Office could be relied upon to keep in smooth enough running order. The Whigs might have agreed. Three-fifths of the convicts sent to the Australian colonies were transported after 1830.[4]

Lack of actual experience of colonial conditions could sometimes

---

[1] C.O. 324/144/281, Horton–Hobhouse, 5 Oct. 1822; 201/144/105, Hobhouse–Horton, 21 Feb. 1823, enc. Peel's comments; /134, Hobhouse–Horton, 19 May 1823; /150, Hobhouse–Horton, 28 July 1823; B.M. Add. MSS. (Peel Papers) 40357, f. 48, Hobhouse–Peel, 5 July 1823; f. 50, Horton–Peel, 5 July 1823; /67, Horton–Peel, 7 July 1823; /73, Horton–Peel, 8 July 1823.

[2] C.O. 201/144/157, Hobhouse–Horton, 22 Aug. 1823.

[3] C.O. 201/144/165, Peel–Bathurst, Private, 20 Oct. 1823.

[4] Shaw, op. cit., pp. 131, 144–8 and Chs. 9 and 11.

cause the Home and Colonial Offices to come to odd conclusions. When Brisbane's experiment of a free Press and the spate of political controversy which burst on the colony in 1825 was reported in England, Peel and Horton seem to have imagined that trouble loomed from a dangerous concentration of 'educated convicts'. Peel told Bathurst that the subject could not be raised in Parliament. Mention of it in the House of Commons would set the colony 'into a flame'.[1] It was suggested that educated convicts be segregated in the interior. Arthur and Darling were mystified that a few odd men out, and a handful of harmless but dishonest clerks could have attracted so much attention.[2] Peel opposed the idea of a 'gentleman's gaol' but action of a sort followed. In 1831 a convict wrote that Wellington Valley had become 'the Valley of Swells'.[3]

Peel promised in 1826 to take greater care in selecting convicts for transportation, and to concentrate, for the good of the colony, on sending out able-bodied workers and mechanics. This result was doubtless gratifying to young John Macarthur, who had played a part in raising the alarm with his talk of a 'wild democracy' springing up in the colony.[4] Where the Home Office had a vested interest in the convict system, the Colonial Office tended to have a bias towards the encouragement of free settlement. Horton, volatile and enthusiastic for grand designs, turned his attention early towards free emigration both for what it could do for the colonies and the mother country; and from his activities the Australian colonies were not excluded. In this field Peel was a very cautious participant. He had co-operated with Goulburn and knew enough about Irish distress to approve the end whole-heartedly. But how to find the means eluded him, particularly after the period of Indian summer which had come to an end with the slump of 1825–6.[5]

Horton's political leaning towards the Canningites, who thought

[1] C.O. 324/75/35, Bathurst–Horton, Minutes 1824–6.

[2] H.R.A. I/xii/340, Horton–Darling, 31 May 1826; I/xiii/189, Darling–Horton, Private and Confidential, 26 Mar. 1827; III/v/235, Hay–Arthur, 21 May 1826; /487, Arthur–Bathurst, 27 Jan. 1827; /495, Arthur–Hay, 27 Jan. 1827; /665, Arthur–Hay, 23 Mar. 1827.

[3] C.O. 201/175/236, Peel–Horton, Private, 8 Feb. 1826; /228/518, J. Harte–Secretary of State, Mar. 1831.

[4] C.O. 201/164/121, Peel–Horton, 8 Feb. 1826; 201/167/302, Macarthur–Horton, 18 July 1825.

[5] Goulburn Papers, 11/13, Peel–Goulburn, 7 Feb. 1815; B.M. Add. MSS. (Peel Papers) 40329, f. 71, Peel–Goulburn, 30 Apr. 1823; 40330, f. 90, Peel–Goulburn, 4 Aug. 1824; 40356, f. 373, Horton–Peel, 20 June 1823; 40357, f. 247, Horton–Peel, 2 Aug. 1823; f. 281, Peel–Horton, 6 Aug. 1823; P.D. n.s. XVI/506, 15 Feb. 1827.

him too much of a crusader, did not serve him well. Early in 1827 in the midst of the political collapse of the long Liverpool administration, Horton's Emigration Committee alarmed Peel, Herries and Robinson by pressing for a grandiose national policy of emigration.[1] Peel, who had been bombarded by Horton with memoranda, was very uneasy about Horton's notions for financing large-scale emigration from government loans, and objected to the Colonial Office appearing to be committing the government. 'It is vain to make a distinction,' he wrote to Robinson, 'between the Chairman of a Committee and an Undersecretary of State.' Robinson replied that he had given Horton no encouragement and that any plan involving such expense would have to be a Cabinet question.[2] Bathurst, despite Horton's desperate efforts to gain his support, remained unenthusiastic, especially about Australian emigration. In the course of the Committee's proceedings Bathurst had told Hay that he had little sympathy with a policy of 'directing the stream of Emigration to New South Wales', nor did he understand how such an emigration would 'prevent the commission of transportable offences' as had been claimed.[3]

* * * * *

In April Horton begged the Secretary of State to allow his name to be used to promote emigration as a matter of prime national importance. 'It is your measure, it sprung from under your Department,' he wrote.[4] Less than a week later, despite Canning's efforts to keep him, Bathurst had resigned.[5] Bathurst thought highly enough of his former under-secretary, and considered Horton much undervalued; but he distrusted Horton's inclination to spread himself unmethodically on issues outside 'the duties of his official table'.[6] In the event Horton lost what influence he could have exercised with the High Tories

[1] P.D. n.s. XVI/475, 15 Feb. 1827; /653, 26 Feb. 1827; /653, 26 Feb. 1827; W. F. Adams, *Ireland and Irish Emigration to the New World from 1815 to the Famine* (Yale, 1932), Ch. 6, p. 241 ff., 274 ff., 289 ff.

[2] B.M. Add. MSS. 40392, f. 263, Peel–Robinson, Confidential, 12 Mar. 1827; f. 269, Robinson–Peel, 12 Mar. 1827.

[3] B.M. Loan 57 (*Bathurst Papers*) /59, Bathurst–Hay, 13 Jan. 1827 and 57/17, July 1826–Mar. 1827 *passim*.

[4] *B.M.* 57/18/2238, Horton–Bathurst, Most Confidential, 26 Apr. 1827.

[5] B.M. Loan 57/18/2232, Bathurst–Canning, 12 Apr. 1827; /2234, Bathurst–Canning, 15 Apr. 1827; /2236, Bathurst–Canning, 15 Apr. 1827.

[6] B.M. Loan 57/59, Bathurst–Hay, Confidential, 14 Aug. 1827; 24 Dec. 1828. He told Horton he should approach Robinson boldly for a high post: Bathurst–Horton, 27 Nov. 1827, q. in Jones, *Horton*, p. 86.

without obtaining any real advantage from Canning or Robinson. In 1827 he was ill and quite out of his depth among the warring Tory factions. When Robinson formed a government Horton was expected to move to a higher office, but Huskisson was unwilling or too busy to take special trouble to forward his career.[1] He wished to try his luck in practical administration as Governor of Canada, but the King had candidates and the post was denied him.[2] In the wreck of the Goderich government he lingered on at the Colonial Office waiting for an acceptable offer, perhaps at the Board of Trade or the Admiralty; and there was always Emigration, to which Lansdowne and Spring Rice seemed to be friendly. When Peel came to power again in 1828 he apologized for omitting Horton, who he thought, perhaps correctly, was tiring of the parliamentary charade. Besides, Horton supported Catholic Emancipation, which was awkward; and he carried no particular weight in party politics. On the contrary he was much criticized and a potential liability.[3] He ceased to support the Wellington government when the Canningites left it in May 1828.

At the end of 1828 he disclaimed vaulting ambition. He had really wanted Ireland from Peel and Wellington; but told the Arbuthnots that he had, 'good, easy fool, maintained that the true way was to work hard at details, and to serve a government sedulously and zealously' instead of taking Lord Ellenborough's advice to 'make yourself feared and hated by Government'.[4] Nevertheless his influence continued. In 1830 Peel, then receiving friendly advice from Bentham, who had been consulted in the affairs of the Colonization Society, wrote to Bentham's fellow theorist Horton that he would not hinder his 'most honorable labours'.[5] In the July–August election of that year he did not stand; and his seat went to Peel's brother. In September, at a time of great political confusion and economic distress, Peel sent a long letter in which he commented on Horton's suggestions

[1] B.M. Add. MSS. (*Huskisson Papers*) 38749, f. 141, Horton–Huskisson, 2 Mar. 1827; 38750, f. 22, Goderich–Huskisson, 14 Aug. 1827; f. 227, Huskisson–Stanley, 4 Sept. 1827.

[2] B.M. Add. MSS. 38751, f. 323, Horton–Huskisson, 27 Oct. 1827; 38752, f. 32, Huskisson–Horton, 7 Nov. 1827; f. 38, Huskisson–Goderich, 7 Nov. 1827.

[3] B.M. Add. MSS. (*Peel Papers*) 40395, f. 144, Horton–Peel, 28 Jan. 1828; f. 148, Peel–Horton, 29 Jan. 1828; f. 164, Horton–Peel, 29 Jan. 1828; Jones, op. cit., pp. 77–98, 253 ff.

[4] *The Correspondence of Charles Arbuthnot*, ed. A. Aspinall (Camden 3rd Series XXV, 1941), p. 111, letter 112.

[5] B.M. Add. MSS. (Peel Papers) 40400, f. 5, Bentham–Peel, 2 Jan. 1830; f. 134, Bentham–Peel, 28 Mar. 1830; 40401, f. 31, Peel–Horton, 8 July 1830.

concerning an emigration loan of thirty million pounds to be raised on the poor rates and the employment of the out-of-work on public works. Peel favoured wide measures, he wrote, but knew the Poor Laws to be too complicated for an easy decision. Above all, measures must be popular if they were to be effective.[1] Horton taxed Peel with lukewarmness, which the minister disclaimed; but he too was soon out of office.[2]

Howick's adoption of Horton's emigration Bill early the next year was a tribute to his work, but it proved unsuccessful. An Emigration Commission set up in June 1831 by Goderich, however, included Howick and Hay. It was to be temporary and exploratory, and did indeed provide the Colonial Office indirectly with much information from home and the colonies about emigration both unassisted and semi-assisted. Its efforts probably led to a reduction of fares for passages to Australia; and its secretary, T. F. Elliott, a Colonial Office employee, was to become Agent-General for Emigration and to make a distinguished career in the Colonial Lands and Emigration Commission. But results were not encouraging and as no money was available for action, Goderich wound up the original group in August 1832. By that time the principle of financing emigration from land sales had brought about an important change.[3]

The Australian colonies would have gained much had some of the more ambitious emigration schemes come to fruition. Horton's Emigration Commissioners heard evidence supporting Australian ventures, some of them very broad in scope. The lack of favourable public opinion, political influence, money, and insufficient administrative expertise brought most 'official' schemes to little. Distance, costs, and the apparent finality of proceeding to the Antipodes meant that Australia was by-passed by the growing streams of emigrants who crossed the Atlantic on their own initiative.[4] The next decade

[1] B.M. Add. MSS. (*Peel Papers*) 40401, f. 171, Peel–Horton, Private, 21 Sept. 1830.
[2] ibid., f. 279, Horton–Peel, 15 Nov. 1830; f. 281, Peel–Horton, 16 Nov. 1830.
[3] C.O. 324/146/299, Goderich–Commissioners, 30 June 1831; /326, Goderich–Commissioners, 1 July 1831; 324/87/34, Hay–Arthur, 9 Jan. 1832; /48, Hay–Arthur, 8 Mar. 1832; pp. 1831–2 XXXII (724), Goderich–Commissioners, 4 Aug. 1832; R. B. Madgwick, *Immigration into Eastern Australia 1788–1851* (London, 1937); F. H. Hitchens, *The Colonial Land and Emigration Commission* (Philadelphia, 1931) Ch. I; Mills, op. cit., pp. 177–87.
[4] e.g. pp. 1826 IV (404), 91 ff. Eagar's Evidence; *H.R.A.* I/xii/766, Darling–Hay, 16 Dec. 1826; I/xii/515, Darling–Bathurst, 1 Sept. 1826; I/xiii/213, Bathurst–Darling, 31 Mar. 1827, enc. Hobhouse–Hay, 14 Mar. 1827.

was to bring about significant migration, both assisted by government bounty, and free. Francis Place wrote to Horton that the 'increase of civilization and wealth in the colonies' was only to be considered when Britain's own permanent advantage had been consulted.[1] The Colonial Office, immersed in the complicated government of a world wide Empire, could have no such clear-cut values, for it necessarily admitted defeat when British interest and colonial development were allowed to become irreconcilable.

* * * * *

In the Australian colonies, if the overwhelming stain of convictism could not be washed out by draughts of free emigration from Britain, colonial administrators had perforce to seek out other alternatives. Among these was the encouragement of those few settlers of 'respectability and capital' who did find their way to the colonies, approval of British-based enterprises which seemed to hold out hope for the future, and the constructive fostering of those internal features of colonial life which were thought to reflect the better features of the metropolitan power. The colonies shared in many of the social and religious developments, movements, and controversies, which were taking place in Britain. It was a time when even the most time-honoured institutions were in process of rapid change, revitalization, or decay; and when few established privileges were left unquestioned.[2] Transplantation, however, had to be selective, especially in fields where there existed several important limitations of the common background which linked the mother country to her colonies. Despite the strongest ties of government, some adaptation was dictated by the absence of rooted tradition, the workings of the penal system, the physical make-up of the continent, and the presence of strong concentrations of Irish and Scots. It is by no means surprising that the Tory authorities should look to religion and education for support in their efforts to remodel the social framework of the Australian colonies.

[1] Place–Horton, 1 Aug. 1830; q. in Jones, op. cit., p. 311.
[2] G. F. A. Best, 'The Protestant Constitution and its Supporters 1800–1829', *Trans. R.H.S.* 1958, pp. 105–27; *Temporal Pillars* (Cambridge, 1964), Chs. IV and VI; R. Border, *Church and State in Australia 1788–1872*, (London, 1962), Chs. 3–5; U. Henriques, *Religious Toleration in England 1787–1883* (London, 1961), Chs. V, VII; Pike, *Paradise of Dissent*, Ch. I; G. Nadel, *Australia's Colonial Culture* (Melbourne, 1957), Ch. VI, p. 181 ff.

If Bathurst and Bigge cannot altogether be deemed the conscious 'architects' of a conservative grand design, there was certainly an earnest effort during the decade to lay down foundations of something more closely resembling the English pattern than the frail and ramshackle arrangements which had evolved during the early years of settlement.[1] Bathurst instructed Bigge to report on 'Education and Religion', two branches of the colonial establishment which 'ought in all cases to be inseparably connected',[2] and the Commissioner heard a great deal of evidence from the pioneer Anglican chaplains. He could hardly fail to be impressed by Sam Marsden, but gave greater credit to the less controversial Cowper and Cartwright.[3]

Marsden, bold and outspoken in his correspondence as in all else, had fallen out with Lachlan Macquarie on a number of private and public issues. In 1818 he had unsuccessfully applied for leave of absence to make a visit to England to recruit chaplains and schoolmasters. In his protest to Bathurst about the Governor's military brusqueness, he made substantial points which were to be raised often in the next few years. Convict schoolteachers were unsatisfactory. Clerical life in New South Wales was trying and unpleasant. No part of the Empire needed moral attention more than that colony.[4] He had also come to realize that the friendly interest of the London and the Church Missionary societies or of Evangelical friends such as William Wilberforce was insufficient to obtain the official action he thought was needed. At the same time he obviously felt no great devotion to the Colonial Office, who had by this time become a sort of administrative midwife for various clerical and missionary projects. In 1821 he demanded that it be decided under whose ecclesiastical jurisdiction the Australian colonies actually lay.[5]

Bathurst, who had a reputation for staunch churchmanship, was ready to follow up Bigge's sketchy recommendations, especially as they fitted in with wider imperial arrangements to regularize and devolve ecclesiastical administration. He was probably not unwilling also to give the benefit of government patronage and assistance to the

[1] M. Roe, *Quest for Authority in Eastern Australia 1835–1851* (Melbourne, 1965), pp. 5–6, 14, 15, 18; J. Barrett, *That Better Country. The Religious Aspect of Life in Eastern Australia 1835–1850* (Melbourne, 1965), pp. 11–15.

[2] C.O. 202/9/8, Bathurst–Bigge, 6 Jan. 1819.

[3] C.O. 201/127, Evidence Ecclesiastical etc.; C.O. 201/142/269, Confidential Report, 7 Feb. 1823.

[4] e.g. C.O. 201/93/384, Marsden–Bathurst, 20 May 1818: M.L. C/244 *Marsden Papers* and A/1998 *passim*.

[5] C.O. 201/127/553, Marsden–Bishop of London, 26 Aug. 1821.

Anglican Church which was now meeting with stiff competition from colonial dissent, both Catholic and Protestant—a dissent which, however, he had positively permitted and tolerated. The Thomas Hobbes Scott, Bigge's secretary, submitted a report on Education to Bathurst from notes he had taken in the colony and doubtless from discussions with his friend John Macarthur Junior.[1] Wilberforce wrote 'with the freedom of an old connection' to stir Bathurst to greater efforts on behalf of the church in Van Diemen's Land; and the Bishop of London endorsed Marsden's plea that the convicts, free settlers and native born of New South Wales be not denied the consolations and discipline of religion. 'It should not be forgotten,' he wrote, 'that Catholics are very numerous in these settlements and men of the same characters as those who have created so great public calamities in Ireland, and many of them had a share in executing those public evils.'[2]

Scott, consulted in the Commissioner's absence by Horton, whose friend Reginald Heber had recently gone as bishop to Calcutta, drew up supplementary reports on religion early in 1824. He supported the appointment of an archdeacon, to be his own diocesan and under instructions from the Secretary of State; the setting up of schools on the Bell system under the Archdeacon's supervision; and an elaborate scheme for the provision of the Church establishment. Clergy reserves of at least one-tenth of the Crown land should be set aside and a Board of Trustees authorized by Charter to administer the revenues arising from the reserves. The Church trustees would control a national school system with parochial primary schools, contributory if possible, a central High School, and eventually a University. In the meantime Exhibitioners should be sent to Oxford and Cambridge to 'strengthen the connexion between the colony and the parent country by implanting English habits and opinions amongst the best educated members of the community'.[3] In July Scott told Horton that arrangements were being made to place the colony under the Bishop of London, but it was in fact decided in October that an Australian archdeaconry would be erected subject to Heber at Calcutta.[4] Among

[1] C.O. 201/147/343 ff., 4 Sept. 1823.
[2] B.M. Loan 57/55/12, Wilberforce–Bathurst, 6 Dec. 1823; C.O. 201/156/189, W. London–Bathurst, 10 Mar. 1824.
[3] C.O. 201/157/150, Scott–Bathurst, 23 Feb. 1824; /156 ff.; 170 ff. Report, 30 Mar. 1824.
[4] C.O. 201/157/198, Scott–Horton, 15 July 1824; H.R.A. I/xiv/399, Darling–Huskisson, enc. Scott–Darling, 18 Sept. 1828.

his general recommendations concerning land, Scott kept the conditions of the colonial clergy in mind. To James Stephen's objections that a corporate body should not be entrusted with Crown Lands, he argued that simple reservation of two-sevenths of the land, one-seventh for the Church and one for 'Crown Reserves', would be to repeat in Australia an outmoded system known from Canadian experience to be disadvantageous.[1]

Out of these discussions came a recommendation that Bathurst should consent to the formation of an Ecclesiastical Board in London, composed of the Bishop of London and other bishops, which would 'take into their own hands the whole jurisdiction . . . of the Church throughout the Colonies generally'.[2] By 1825 this became a *fait accompli* when Archdeacon Hamilton, secretary of the Society for the Propagation of the Gospel, was appointed Secretary of a Board. But though Hamilton sent in reports and forwarded correspondence, there were difficulties about his expenses, and Bathurst seems to have enjoyed his regular personal interviews with the clergy.[3]

It was hoped particularly that the Board's help would be effective in selecting and examining suitable chaplains. Much of Hamilton's work was in fact connected with the expanding clerical establishment of the Australian colonies. He forwarded duplicates of Scott's reports to the Colonial Office, but the archdeacon naturally took care that his demands for wide increases in men and improvements in conditions came directly before the Governor and the Secretary of State. Hamilton was doubtless frustrated by being side-stepped in consultation and also by his inability in practice to carry out the expensive requests passed on to him.[4] In 1827 he was asked to prepare detailed reports on the state of education and religion in the colonies, but could do little more than draw on Scott's incessant pleas for more men and more government support.[5] This he continued to do, without obtaining many really tangible results. He felt that his office, however ineffectively maintained, could fulfil a useful purpose in representing the colonial clergy. He was particularly anxious about reports of the

[1] C.O. 201/157/238, Scott–Horton, 5 Oct. 1824.

[2] C.O. Minute at 201/157/265.

[3] C.O. 323/199/439, Memorandum, Dec. 1824; 324/145/81, Horton–Harrison, 12 Feb. 1825; 323/203/299, ff. Appointment of Hamilton, 8 Feb. 1825; cf. also, D. M. Young, op. cit., pp. 76–7, 182.

[4] e.g. C.O. 202/18/34, Hay–Hamilton, 26 July 1826; /96, Hay–Hamilton, 17 Oct. 1826.

[5] C.O. 201/186/343, ff. Reports; 323/209/231, Hamilton–Bathurst, 11 Feb. 1828.

apparent triumph of dissent in Australia and the neglect of the convicts in Van Diemen's Land. But he found it impossible at a distance
to do much to settle the constant troubles which disturbed the religious peace or the disputes which Scott seemed to attract wherever
he went.[1]

By 1831 Hamilton's Board was a natural target for the retrenchers,
and the Archbishop of Canterbury was willing to let it go. 'Very little
business' had been transacted, he agreed when Goderich approached
him; though he felt that the Board could still have performed a useful
function if its functions were revised and methods improved.[2]
Goderich tactfully replied that nothing but the extraordinary urgency
of the times would have induced the government to discontinue the
Board.[3] Hamilton, offended by the abolition of his office, complained that Bathurst had rarely consulted him, and unsuccessfully
sought compensation.[4] The Board was clearly not one of the Colonial
Office's most happy experiments.

In May 1824 James Stephen had reported on the rights and duties
of colonial archdeacons, largely with Canada in mind. This information was again put to use when at the end of the year it was formally
decided to send Hobbes Scott himself as Archdeacon to New South
Wales. He was to have wide powers, a large salary, precedence next in
order to the Lieutenant-Governor, visitatorial faculties, and a subordinate rural Dean in Van Diemen's Land. He had also a considerable but controversial asset in the long, complicated, and hopefully
definitive Charter of Incorporation for the Management of Church
and School Estates, whose draft accompanied the new land regulations of 1 January 1825.[5]

Scott's colonial experience turned out to be a nightmare of disappointment and disillusionment.[6] He had set himself out to accomplish what was, despite the most friendly influence of government,
already impossible—to establish his Church firmly in practice. He fell
out with Brisbane, became thoroughly immersed in politics, and
engaged in bitter personal disputes with his own clergy, some of

[1] C.O. 201/206/407, Hamilton–Murray, 16 Feb. 1829.
[2] C.O. 323/213/356, W. Canterbury–Goderich, 16 Jan. 1831.
[3] C.O. 324/146/285, Goderich–W. Cantuar, 20 Jan, 1831.
[4] C.O. 324/146/286, Hay–Hamilton, 20 Jan. 1831; 323/213/282, Hamilton–
Goderich, 25 Jan. 1831; /289, Hamilton–Goderich, 29 Apr. 1831.
[5] C.O. 323/198/381, Report by Stephen of 7 May 1824; *H.R.A.* I/xi/419, Bathurst–Brisbane, 21 Dec. 1824; Charter at /444, enc. in Bathurst–Brisbane, 1 Jan.
1825.
[6] C. M. H. Clark, Vol. 2, p. 56 ff.

whom had formed very independent ways.[1] He soon saw that the arrangements originally fixed upon would have to be modified. Governor Darling did his best to provide satisfactory alternatives when it became clear that the Charter would not as it stood provide for the management of religion and education. Though he had his doubts, he sent on Scott's estimates for a vastly increased establishment, amounting in 1826 to a yearly thirty thousand pounds.[2]

The Colonial Office was shocked. Darling was promptly warned of his financial responsibilities. The system laid down for clergy lands should be given further trial. Scott's demands were far too extensive. Two more chaplains, not twelve, would be sent out.[3] Soon the Governor had more complaints to report about the workings of the Corporation. Scott's zeal was indeed disrupting the good-natured amateur financial management of several government institutions such as the Orphan School. Goderich demanded far more detailed information.[4]

Scott refused to compromise, and Darling reported that difficulties connected with survey had made the implementation of the Charter impossible. He outlined his generous interim arrangements. He also forwarded reports of discussions which had taken place about the Archdeacon's proposals to ensure social 'respectability' and an adequate income for his clergy. There was doubt about certain proposals because of the prohibition of officials receiving land grants, but Darling was ready to give grants to the families of clergymen and to their daughters as a marriage portion.[5]

In February 1829 Darling reported that he had at last decided to transfer to the Church trustees 393,283 acres of land; and he forwarded

[1] B. M. Loan 57/58, Bathurst–Hay, 12 July 1826; C.O. 201/179/401, Scott–Horton, Private, 13 Jan. 1826; *Scott's Papers* at M.L. A/850 Letter books 1825–9; and *Macarthur Papers*, A/2955 Scott: 1822–44.
[2] *H.R.A.* I/xii/308, Darling–Bathurst, 22 May 1826; enc. Scott–Darling, 1 May 1826; /324, Darling–Bathurst, 24 May 1826, enc. Scott–Darling, 4 May 1826.
[3] *H.R.A.* I/xii/607, Bathurst–Darling, 6 Oct. 1826; /738, Bathurst–Darling, 11 Dec. 1826. It is strange to note that about this time the young Wilberforces and Newmans were making wry jokes about going as chaplains to 'Botany Bay' if Lord Winchilsea became Governor, as was rumoured: D. Newsom, *The Parting of Friends* (London, 1966), p. 91.
[4] *H.R.A.* I/xiii/122, Darling–Bathurst, 22 Feb. 1827; I/xiii/462, Goderich–Darling, 27 July 1827.
[5] *H.R.A.* I/xiv/47, Darling–Huskisson, 27 Mar. 1828, enc. Scott–Darling, 25 Sept. 1827; /76, Darling–Huskisson, 30 Mar. 1828; I/xiii/771, Darling–Goderich, 11 Feb. 1828, enc. Scott–Darling, 2 Aug. 1827; I/xiv/385, Darling–Huskisson, 4 Sept. 1828.

the doleful report of that official body for their first two years. The Governor assured Murray that he had done his best 'to put the Church in possession of their land, if only to relieve the colonial Revenue from the demands, to which it has been subjected on Account of the Stipends of the Clergy and the Expense of the School Establishments, which at present amount to little short of £20,000 per annum'.[1]

By May 1829, however, it was clear to the Colonial Office that the earlier plan had missed its mark. After a manful attempt to master the intricacies of the colonial administration of ecclesiastical, benevolent and educational funds, a dispatch was sent which took into account all the information Darling had sent. Provisions were to be made to allow every clergyman to support his wife and family and 'Keep up an appearance becoming his Station'; but the expense to colonial revenue forbade approval of some of the more liberal proposals put forward to meet costs. If the churches were ill-attended, as was reported, and the colony suffered from a notable 'want of a proper sense of Religion', this should not necessarily be attributed to shortage of church space or lack of clerical zeal. In Van Diemen's Land Governor Arthur was sending more encouraging news, for example, of the inhabitants voluntarily setting out to provide their own places of worship. The government could not or should not do everything, but it would permit such efforts to be subsidized from colonial funds. The British authorities were obviously uneasy about Scott's ambitious plans; and not averse, in the year of Emancipation, to the introduction of a voluntary principle. Even the former abhorrence at the idea of convict school teachers was muted. Most important of all, the Secretary of State, congratulating himself that the experience of the Corporation in New South Wales had not been repeated in Van Diemen's Land, announced that steps were being taken to withdraw the Charter. Darling was therefore instructed to see that the Church lands were disposed of, by sale or by lease, in such a way as to allow the Colonial Treasurer to provide the community with schools and churches. Whatever had been made over to, or done for, the Church Schools Estates, could be written off.[2]

The Corporation's process of dissolution proved as complicated and expensive as the rest of its career. Despite intermittent attempts

[1] *H.R.A.* I/xiv/638, Darling–Murray, 11 Feb. 1829; /659, Darling–Murray,19 Feb. 1829.
[2] *H.R.A.* I/xiv/784, Murray–Darling, 25 May 1829; C.O. 201/192/281, C.O. Précis of 1829.

to obtain well-trained and reliable teachers from home, the educational system was still rudimentary at the end of the decade.[1] Scott, thoroughly disgusted at the shipwreck of his plans and up to his ears in clerical dispute, resigned his office and left the Governor and his successor, William Broughton, the joy of refurbishing the sad and battered wreck of his vision.[2] On his way back home he was able to assist the struggling colonists at Swan River with his very welcome ministrations.[3]

William Broughton, the next archdeacon, had once been a clerk in the financial department of the East India Company, and had obtained his appointment by patronage of 'the Duke'. He soon tried to make the best out of a very difficult situation. The home government was not inclined to be generous; and the spread of settlement had greatly widened the scope of his cure.[4] He had the advantage of membership of the Council and the privileges of high station in a very limited society, and could presume the substantial support of many well-intentioned officials of the colonial government. He set himself and his clergy to take greater pains with the convicts, outcasts and aborigines; and to place religious and moral standards firmly where they belonged, at the foundation of society. Yet his supposition of establishment inevitably raised opposition and the constitution of the inhabitants doomed him to fall short of his ideal.[5]

When Darling returned to Europe at the end of 1831 he brought with him a long and gloomy report from Broughton. The dissenters were too powerful, he thought, especially the Roman Catholics. Colonial morals and intemperance were deplorable. Finance was troublesome. The strongest support of the State would be necessary to bring the people to an appreciation of education and religion.[6]

[1] *H.R.A.* I/xv/117, Darling–Murray, 17 Aug. 1829, enc. Scott–Darling, 19 Apr. 1829; /540, Murray–Darling, 7 June 1830; I/xvi/254, Darling–Goderich, 27 Apr. 1831; M.L. *C.S.I.L.* 4/3614, Church and Schools Corporation 1828–36; 4/3615, Clergy 1826–32; C.O. 201/213/161 f., Report of Trustees 1828–30; /218/ 174 f., Report 1830; /222/506, Howick–Brickwood, 5 Mar. 1831—Church lands and Aus. Ag. Co.; A. G. Austin, *Australian Education 1788–1900* (Melbourne, 1961), pp. 9–25.

[2] *H.R.A.* I/xv/212, Darling–Murray, 18 Oct. 1829, enc. Scott's report and Scott–Darling, 1 Sept. 1829.

[3] III/vi/615, Stirling–Murray, 20 Jan. 1830.

[4] *H.R.A.* I/xv/550, Murray–Darling, 12 June 1830. Clark, Vol. 2, p. 93 ff.

[5] *H.R.A.* I/xv/345, Darling–Murray, 26 Jan., enc. Broughton's Charge to the clergy; /725, Darling–Murray, 20 Sept. 1830, enc. Broughton–Darling, 19 June 1830.

[6] C.O. 201/221/189, Darling–Goderich, 12 Nov. 1831, enc. Broughton–Darling, 29 Sept. 1831.

Broughton had set much store by the King's School which he hoped to establish in the colony.[1] But John Dunmore Lang, then in England, had plans for his Australian College, which would, of course, be without Anglican links. The Archdeacon resented the friendly reception that Lang had encountered at the Colonial Office, even though his own scheme obtained the cordial approval of the Secretary of State. He thought that the prospects of the King's School would be dimmed by support which Goderich had promised to Lang's project.[2]

Goderich replied that the Colonial Office had no wish to evade its duties regarding the Church, education and the aborigines in Australia. The new Whig government, however, could take no responsibility for what had gone before November 1830. There had been an 'immense weight of business' and many complicated questions awaiting his attention at first, and Lang's personal attendance had won his plan an accidental priority of official sanction. Only subsequently had the project for the King's School come to his attention. Broughton should not be offended. No slight was meant.[3] Lang, who was an inveterate controversialist, had already been reproved for publishing the letters which had been exchanged.[4] The Archdeacon remained dissatisfied, however, particularly when neither Governor Bourke nor the Secretary of State seemed inclined to interfere on his behalf in the question of official precedence.[5]

* * * * *

In Van Diemen's Land, Scott's official visitations had led to a disagreement between Arthur and the archdeacon about the moral and political state of the colony and the administrative and financial steps which should be taken to reform it. Arthur, an Evangelical, was ready to back demands for more education and church services, but he was less jaundiced about prospects for the future. He suggested, predictably, a separate jurisdiction for the colony; and recommended that Wesleyans would be better qualified for work in the penal settlements 'than any Gentlemen who have received a liberal University educa-

[1] *H.R.A.* I/xv/356, Darling–Murray, 10 Feb. 1830; /586, Murray–Darling, 15 July 1830.
[2] *H.R.A.* I/xvi/22, Goderich–Darling, 12 Jan. 1831; /223, Goderich–Darling, 29 Mar. 1831; /449, Lindesay–Goderich, 18 Nov. 1831, enc. Broughton–Goderich, 18 Nov. 1831, enc. Broughton–Goderich, 19 Oct. 1831; /112, Goderich–Darling, 22 Mar. 1831.
[3] *H.R.A.* I/xvi/658, Goderich–Bourke, 13 June 1832.
[4] I/xvi/590, Goderich–Bourke, 3 Apr. 1832.
[5] I/xv/500, Bourke–Goderich, 2 Jan. 1832; /690, Goderich–Bourke, 5 Aug. 1832.

tion'. The expenses of churches and schools should be met liberally, he thought, by imperial rather than colonial funds, for only by them could a foundation be laid for a free and civilized community.[1]

Bathurst replied that Scott's plans were, as always, too comprehensive and unrealistic. He obviously considered Arthur's ideas much more to the point, and pressed him for his ideas concerning the administration of Church lands.[2] In London, Archdeacon Hamilton reacted strongly. Wesleyan Missionaries, he wrote, should not be afforded 'recognition . . . inconsistent with the exclusive principle inherent in the idea of an Established Church'. No religion was better than one based on unsound principles.[3] Bathurst was unconvinced and arrangements were made with the Wesleyans to send out suitable men.[4]

Arthur had no intention of adding the worry of a Church and Schools Corporation to his manifold problems, and continued to maintain that the mother country had a duty to plant the Church along with the other instruments of civilization in a new land. Religion, he thought, played a special part in a convict society, showing man his degraded state. 'Even when people are not really sincere in their religious sentiments, the profession of it has, nevertheless, the most advantageous influence upon Society,' he told Huskisson. Archdeacon Scott, whom the Governor admired, could be quoted against a Corporation. He had, in a disillusioned and confidential letter to Arthur, deplored the surrender of land to the management of persons 'scarcely qualified to look after a Cabbage garden.' Twiss was offended at this, for Scott after all had proposed the Corporation in the beginning.[5]

On his second visit the Archdeacon impenitently renewed his unrealistic demands. Arthur encountered difficulties in providing funds for religion and education, but he obtained a promise from the Colonial Office that no Corporation would be established in the colony.[6]

It was in Van Diemen's Land that the practical shortcomings of

[1] *H.R.A.* III/v/149, Arthur–Bathurst, 21 Apr. 1826, enc. Scott–Arthur, 13 Feb. 7 Mar. 1826.

[2] *H.R.A.* III/v/469, Bathurst–Arthur, 22 Dec. 1826.

[3] C.O. 280/14/378, Hamilton–Hay, Private, 20 Mar. 1827.

[4] *H.R.A.* III/vi/13, Bathurst–Arthur, 18 Apr. 1827.

[5] C.O. 280/18/219, Arthur–Huskisson, Private and Confidential, 14 Apr.1828, enc. Scott–Arthur, P. and C., 11 Apr. 1828, and C.O. Minute.

[6] C.O. 280/18/234, Arthur–Huskisson, 14 Apr. 1828, enc. Scott–Arthur, 25 Mar. 1828; 408/5/127, Murray–Arthur, 16 Feb. 1829; 280/21/371, Arthur–Murray, 30 Sept. 1829; 280/25/272, Arthur–Murray, 19 Aug. 1830.

colonial policy towards the aboriginal inhabitants became most calamitously apparent. The central authorities never deviated from their determination that the natives be conciliated and that relations with aborigines be always governed by 'amity and kindness'. But official benevolence and goodwill proved sadly deficient as time brought more drastic collisions between settlers, convicts, sealers, soldiers and the fierce, gentle, mysterious, fugitive, ever-present people of the Australian 'bush'. Neither Macquarie's sincere interest, Bigge's inquiries, nor Sorell's honest concern could avert disaster. Many of the colonial clergy tried to influence the fatal course, but few of their efforts did much more than thinly disguise a failure beside which confusion over land-titles and even the plight of the convicts appears to pale.[1]

It is doubtful whether even the activities of the powerful groups who had helped stamp out slavery throughout the Empire could have saved the situation, and the struggle for emancipation of course directed their attention elsewhere. Bathurst approved of the setting aside of land so that the missionary societies, including the Wesleyans, could work 'to improve the condition of the Aborigines of New South Wales'.[2] At the end of 1826 Darling wrote that Threlkeld, who had been a missionary in New Zealand, was at work among the natives; and Scott, conscious of his responsibilities, promised full inquiries and a report. When he did report, the Archdeacon wrote that he did not hold out much hope of effective action until he could obtain more men.[3]

Goderich wrote in vague appreciation of the missionaries' exertions to save the natives from their ignorance and 'nomad life', but insisted that expenses be kept down. Scott, he thought, should confine his activities to obtaining information.[4] The Archdeacon however had in the meantime compiled an extensive plan for 'the Civilization and Education' of the aborigines, and Darling sent it on apologetically to Huskisson. Though the objective was admirable, he wrote, effective measures would be very costly.[5] When he saw Scott's despondent

[1] C. M. H. Clark, *History of Australia*, I pp. 80, 168, 315–17; II, Chs. 6, 8, 10; G. R. Mellor, *British Imperial Trusteeship 1783–1850* (London, 1951), p. 279 ff.
[2] *H.R.A.* I/xi/512, Brisbane–Bathurst, 8 Feb. 1825; I/xii/46, Bathurst–Darling, 31 July 1825; I/xii/364, Darling–Bathurst, 19 July 1826; I/xiii/14, Bathurst–Darling, 10 Jan. 1827.
[3] *H.R.A.* I/xii/795, Darling–Bathurst, 22 Dec. 1826.
[4] *H.R.A.* I/xiii/433, Goderich–Darling, 6 July 1827.
[5] *H.R.A.* I/xiv/54, Darling–Huskisson, 27 Mar. 1828, enc. Scott–Darling, 1 Aug. 1827.

prediction that the natives would disappear within thirty years, James Stephen was indignant. He believed that zealous and enthusiastic Methodists or Moravians would be able to work wonders, and offered his services to obtain suitable men from the Missionary Societies. Murray agreed readily to this, but Twiss, who knew the susceptibilities of Anglican Archdeacons of that time, suggested that the Church Missionary Society was most suitable.[1] Dandeson Coates, Secretary of the C.M.S., was a very familiar correspondent and often unwelcome visitor of the Colonial Office. He was particularly zealous in making arrangements for the transport of missionaries and supplies to the colony and to New Zealand; and he urged the department to extend its decisions favouring aborigine land grants.[2] He sent so many stores with the two men destined for Van Diemen's Land that the navy complained.[3] But he now insisted on controlling men in the field; and this was understandable enough, for the missionaries almost always seemed to come to loggerheads with the local church authorities.[4]

Stephen made tentative arrangements with Coates to send out suitable men. The Colonial Office however was undergoing the unwelcome attentions of the Committee of Colonial Enquiry and baulked at Coates' carefully constructed estimates.[5] The question was raised again with the new government. Howick refused to concede that the mission could now be viewed as an official measure, but was ready to subsidize the Missionary Society's efforts on behalf of the natives.[6] Even the tentative patronage given by government to the Missionary Societies had its ill effects, for Threlkeld had fallen out with his society and with Broughton, who felt slighted that the aboriginal mission had been withdrawn from his care.[7] Strong assurances that the Colonial Office meant no discourtesy and that no

---

[1] C.O. 201/195/497, Stephen–Twiss, 4 Nov. 1828.

[2] C.O. 202/18/63, Hay–Coates, 31 Aug. 1826; /79, Hay–Coates, 27 Sept. 1826; 201/186/378, Coates–Bathurst, 21 Jan. 1827.

[3] C.O. 201/186/34, Martin–Hay, 6 June 1827.

[4] C.O. 201/186/380, Coates–Hay, 12 Feb. 1827; 202/19/2, Hay–Coates, 27 Feb. 1827.

[5] C.O. 201/214/467, Coates–Twiss, 1 Jan. 1830; 202/24/160, Twiss–Coates, 18 Feb. 1830; 201/214/484, Coates–Twiss, 11 Nov. 1830; /488, Coates–Twiss, 30 Nov. 1830.

[6] C.O. 201/222/463, Coates–Howick, 17 Feb. 1831; H.R.A. I/xvi/477, Goderich–Bourke, 21 Dec. 1831.

[7] H.R.A. I/xv/672, Darling–Murray, 9 Aug. 1830; I/xvi/14, Goderich–Darling, 8 Jan. 1831.

novelty was intended could not really soothe his feelings.[1] Nothing short of the clear rights of establishment could do that, and the new governor was not the man to encourage this development.[2]

In Van Diemen's Land aboriginal affairs descended into an abyss of violence and terror. Arthur, justifiably disturbed about the 'stain on his administration', appointed a remarkable protector and 'conciliator' in the Methodist schoolteacher G. A. Robinson; but Robinson's counsels did not prevail. The end of the decade witnessed a confused series of government and military measures which culminated in an attempt to collect the aborigine remnant and remove it from active and passive harm. The Colonial Office, faced with a *fait accompli* across the world, could only deplore atrocities and prepare the dispatches for parliamentary publication.[3]

* * * * *

If the progress of ecclesiastical, educational and aboriginal affairs was marred by considerable administrative failures, colonial dissenters could at the end of the decade claim a number of victories which placed them in some ways in a better position than their confrères in the British Isles. The first Presbyterian chaplain to sail for the Australian colonies left England for Van Diemen's Land in 1822, without exciting much interest from the Colonial Office.[4] But Scots interest in advancing the fortunes of their national churches, both established and free, could be taken for granted.[5] Certainly John Dunmore Lang, who arrived in Sydney in May 1823, could not and would not be overlooked. The terms of the official rejection of Lang's memorial of 4 August 1823, seeking government assistance for the Church of Scotland, caused a colonial scandal and startled Bathurst, for the Presbyterians were informed that they would receive help when they had proved as useful to the community as their deadly rivals the Roman

[1] C.O. 201/221/237, Darling–Goderich, 13 Nov. 1831, esp. Minute of James Stephen; *H.R.A.* I/xvi/658, Goderich–Bourke, 13 June, 1832.

[2] *H.R.A.* I/xvi/703, Bourke–Goderich, 17 Aug. 1832, enc. Broughton–Bourke, 5 June 1832; A. H. King, *Bourke*, pp. 268 ff., 314 ff.

[3] C.O. 280/24/596, Arthur–Murray, 15 Apr. 1830; /613, Arthur–Twiss, Private, 28 May 1830; 280/25/354, Arthur–Hay, 18 Oct. 1830; /372, Arthur–Hay, 20 Nov. 1830; 280/28/200, Arthur–Murray, 12 Feb. 1831; /416, Arthur–Murray, 4 Apr. 1831; /30/149, Arthur–Murray, 25 Oct. 1831; C. Turnbull, *Black War* (Melbourne, 1948); Mellor, op. cit., p. 297 ff.; N. J. B. Plomley, *Friendly Mission* (Sydney, 1966), pp. 21–32.

[4] C.O. 201/110/141, Rev. A. Macarthur–Bathurst, 10 July 1822.

[5] D. S. Macmillan, *Scotland and Australia 1788–1850* (Oxford, 1967), pp. 111–13.

Catholics. Sir Thomas Brisbane tried to make amends to Lang and disclaimed any ill will: he was after all a Scot. Yet the incident probably played its part in his recall, and obtained a sympathetic hearing for Lang when he returned to England to gather recruits and ensure home support.[1]

The Presbyterians of the colonies pressed Darling for equal status with the Anglicans, and while Bathurst was ready to offer government subsidies for their projects, he thought the question of their ecclesiastical status worth referring to the Law officers.[2] Continued demands and publicity, of which Lang was a past master, brought further government patronage, but of course nothing compared to that enjoyed by the Anglicans. In 1829 Murray began to refuse Lang's incessant demands, but by this time Lang had other assistance to call on and decided to return to England yet again. He saw Howick and spoke with him about Scots emigration, his hopes for the projected college which he now hoped would be clearly Presbyterian rather than the non-denominational school with which he had earlier been satisfied. He described the iniquities of the Church and Schools Corporation; and obtained the tangible results which infuriated Broughton.[3]

The Catholics, who composed perhaps a third of the population, posed very special problems for the colonial and central government. In 1817 Jeremiah O'Flynn, an Irish priest who had worked in the West Indies, approached Bathurst for permission to go to Australia, and when he failed to receive it, sailed anyway, thus cutting red tape in a way which horrified Governor Macquarie. He had met in Rome Richard Hayes, brother of Michael, a rebel of 1798 who had been transported to Australia; and had been authorized as vicar-general for

[1] *H.R.A.* I/xi/341, Brisbane–Bathurst, 14 Aug. 1824; /346, Bathurst–Brisbane, 16 Aug. 1824; B. M. Loan 57/64/22, Bathurst–Brisbane, Private, 23 Aug. 1824; *H.R.A.* I/xi/550, Brisbane–Bathurst, 24 Mar. 1825; I/xii/62, Bathurst–Darling, 1 Oct. 1825, enc. Lang–Horton, 18 Jan. 1825 and Horton–Lang, 25 Jan. 1825; C.O. 201/167/215, Lang–Bathurst, 18 Jan. 1825; A. Gilchrist, *J. D. Lang* (Melbourne, 1951), p. 65 ff.; Lang's papers are at M.L. A/2221 ff.

[2] *H.R.A.* I/xii/555, Darling–Bathurst, 9 Sept., enc. Lang–Darling, 30 June 1826; I/xiii/218, Bathurst–Darling, 1 Apr. 1827; C.O. 201/185/367, Bathurst–Law Officers, 14 Apr. 1827.

[3] *H.R.A.* I/xiv/396, Darling–Huskisson, 20 Sept. 1828; C.O. 201/198/419, Wemyss–Murray, 8 Nov. 1828; 201/198/421 ff., is Lang's *Narrative of the Settlement of the Scots Church* (Sydney, 1828), pp. 108; *H.R.A.* I/xiv/707, Murray–Darling, 16 Apr. 1829; C.O. 201/215/383, Lang–Murray, 22 Feb. 1830; *H.R.A.* I/xv/421, Darling–Murray, 22 Feb. 1830; *H.R.A.* I/xv/421, Darling–Murray, 15 Apr. 1830; /795, Murray–Darling, 14 Oct. 1830; C.O. 201/215/391, Lang–Goderich, 28 Dec. 1830; /397, Lang–Goderich, 30 Dec. 1830; C.O. 202/26/98, Howick–Lang, 19 Jan. 1831.

New South Wales. Governor Macquarie thought that the Catholics would become rebellious if worked upon by a priest, and was at first inclined to ship O'Flynn straight back home; but allowed him to remain in case Bathurst's approval should arrive belatedly. To the Governor's anger and against his express commands, the priest used his time to minister to his very much neglected co-religionists and countrymen. By the time Macquarie clapped him aboard a ship as a 'meddling, ignorant, dangerous character', he had rallied to his support a large number of Catholic inhabitants, free, military and bond.[1] Bathurst approved the Governor's conduct, but he was obviously embarrassed at O'Flynn's return as a prisoner.[2]

Michael Hayes, who had written to William Poynter, vicar-apostolic of the London District, in terms even stronger than the public memorials, could be dismissed by the Secretary of State as 'a most unpractical fellow'. But his pleas for toleration, and the consolations of his faith, and complaints against the regimentation of Catholic dissenters could not long be ignored.[3] Despite his opposition to Catholic Emancipation in England and his witty remarks at Horton's expense, Bathurst was not an intolerant man. Indeed he was impatient with any attempt by the established Church to stamp out or supplant other religious denominations of what he called in 1825 'an essentially common faith'.[4] He was ready to do whatever he could to give the Anglican Church an inside running in the remodelling of the ecclesiastical arrangements of the Empire in 1824–5, but thought it unwise to interfere, or to be thought interested in interfering with the beliefs of others. In 1819, therefore, he was quite ready to countenance the appointment of official Catholic chaplains. Macquarie, anticipating this development, had suggested that, if Popish priests were to be sent out, 'they should be English, of liberal education and sound constitutional principles'.[5] The Catholic authorities now directly concerned were Poynter and an English Benedictine Edward Bede Slater, recently appointed by Pius VII vicar-apostolic of the 'Cape of

[1] *H.R.A.* I/ix/710, Macquarie–Bathurst, 12 Dec. 1817; /799, Macquarie–Bathurst, 18 May 1818; C.O. 201/93/217 ff. Petition of Roman Catholics of N.S.W. and R.C. Soldiers of 48th Regt., C. M. H. Clark, op. cit., pp. 320–21; E. O'Brien, *The Dawn of Catholicism in Australia* (Sydney, 1928), II, Ch. XXV and *Life and Letters of Archpriest J. J. Therry* (Sydney, 1922), Ch. I.

[2] *H.R.A.* I/ix/833, Bathurst–Macquarie, 24 Aug. 1818.

[3] C.O. 201/93/468, 470, Minute of 1818; 324/140/142, Goulburn–Poynter, 24 July 1818.

[4] C.O. 324/74/56, Bathurst–Bishop of Barbadoes, 3 Nov. 1825.

[5] *H.R.A.* I/ix/799, Macquarie–Bathurst, 18 May 1818.

Good Hope, Madagascar, Mauritius, and New Holland with the adjacent islands'. But there was a good deal of interest in the subject in Ireland. Slater imagined that the Catholic population of New South Wales was nearly twenty thousand, instead of perhaps half that number. He was not able to obtain English priests, but promised that any Irishman he chose would be morally and politically acceptable to the Colonial Office. Henry Goulburn noted that Bathurst would be prepared to give the men chosen one hundred pounds per annum as a stipend. By August 1819 satisfactory references were available for two priests, Philip Conolly and John Joseph Therry. They sailed in a convict ship, authorized by both Church and State, and arrived in Sydney in May 1820.[1]

Macquarie was told that the priests had the approval of government subject to their 'good conduct'. Their exiguous salaries were to come from colonial funds.[2] The Governor's initial attitude was one of executive peremptoriness combined with abrupt, detailed regulation, but later gave way to a gruff but friendly trust when he saw that the priests were sincere and busy men.[3] Bigge was courteous and helpful. He heard conflicting evidence about the state of the Catholic inhabitants. John Youl at Launceston said that they would never attend Protestant schools or services if they could avoid it. Cowper and Cross were convinced that all dissenters, including the Catholics, did not have rooted objections to attendance at Church, for any religion seemed better than none at all. Conolly and Therry made out their own case for the removal of hindrances to their work; and the Catholics sent the Commissioner a broad, patriotic petition which asked for more priests, schools of their own, and 'to participate in religious liberty which our Protestant colonists so happily and freely enjoy'.[4]

In 1821 Conolly, an eccentric scholar temperamentally incompatible with his companion, went to Van Diemen's Land where he

[1] C.O. 201/96/296, Slater–Bathurst, 18 May 1819; 324/141/93, Goulburn–Slater, 24 May 1819; 201/96/319, Slater–Bathurst, 3 Aug. 1819, enc. Bishop of Cork–Slater, 17 July 1819; O'Brien, *Therry*, pp. 11–22. *Therry Papers* are at Canisius College, Sydney, cf. my entry on 'Therry' *A.D. Biography* (Melbourne, 1967) Vol. 2.

[2] *H.R.A.* 1/x/200, Goulburn–Macquarie, 20 Aug. 1819; /204, Bathurst–Macquarie, 20 Oct. 1819.

[3] *Therry Papers*, F. Goulburn–Therry and Conolly, 10 Oct. 1820.

[4] C.O. 201/127/105, Bigge Appendix; Macquarie's Instructions to R.C. Chaplains, 14 Oct. 1820; /122/448, Evidence of Youl; /127/25, Cowper; /19, Cross; /94, Conolly; /109, Therry–Bigge, 8 Feb. 1821; /110, Therry–Bigge, 9 Sept. 1820; /101, Petition of Catholics, 12 Feb. 1820.

received full co-operation from Sorell and Arthur. Therry was left for five years the only priest on the mainland. Articulate and thorough, pious and essentially middle-class, he set himself the task of attending to every aspect of the moral and religious life of the Catholics. His travels never seemed to falter, for he visited his scattered people wherever they were to be found. His influence with the Protestant inhabitants was quite impressive. Among the convicts it was outstanding, and his correspondence shows that they trusted him as banker, adviser, and arbitrator as well as spiritual director and community leader. On 29 October 1821 Macquarie laid the foundation stone of Therry's first church, on a site he had assigned at the edge of Hyde Park, near the convict barracks. The assistance or substantial tolerance of the leading colonists was assured. The government architect, Francis Greenway, made himself available for consultation. Colonial officials such as J. T. Campbell, John Piper and Frederick Goulburn were regularly involved in the organization of subscriptions. Government help was promised, but Therry was criticized for the elaborate design and size of the church, and the project quickly got out of hand financially. Other churches had to be built at Parramatta and the outlying townships. Demands for the priest's services came from the hospital, gaols, farms, the government establishments, his own Sunday and day schools, and from road-gangs and assigned convicts. He soon became a key figure in the small community, particularly as he resented the oppressive behaviour which officials and settlers had often grown to adopt towards convicts or soldiers. He refused to be excluded from government institutions, especially the Orphan School. Inevitably he was sucked into the political vortex.

Sir Thomas Brisbane, who was willing to support any group he considered useful to the colonial community and its social morals, gave Therry what help he could and wanted to give more. In 1824 he asked Bathurst for more priests to be sent to cope with the 'barbarous ignorance and total want of education' of the Catholic Irish. 'Had there never been a priest here,' he wrote, 'perhaps the Roman Catholic worship might have dwindled away or become ingrafted with the Protestant.' As it was, one priest could only find time to drive his flock away from other churches, without offering any real hope of satisfying their religious and educational needs in a positive way.[1] Bathurst replied that he would arrange with Poynter to have two more

[1] *H.R.A.* I/xi/382, Brisbane–Bathurst, 28 Oct. 1824.

priests sent to the colony, but warned Brisbane against giving liberal financial aid for ambitious church-buildings.[1] In 1823 Bathurst, forgetful of Therry and Conolly, had expressed qualms about giving a government salary for a priest about to sail for Van Diemen's Land, but now he called upon Poynter to present likely candidates. Poynter had friendly relations with Bathurst, Horton and Hay, and in 1826 wrote that he regretted that lack of men and resources prevented him from doing more for the colonies.[2] Again the Irish bishops were approached to supply recruits for the Australian colonies and for the Cape.[3] One of the men proposed was mistakenly rejected as politically dangerous.[4] Poynter insisted however that he had instructed chaplains in the strongest terms 'never to interfere in any political matters, but to use their influence to restrain others from every species of opposition to the civil constituted authorities in the colony.'[5]

By this time Therry, who had been held up by Brisbane and Frederick Goulburn as a model to the horrified Presbyterian Lang, had fallen out with the authorities. Along with other dissenters, he found the Church and Schools Corporation too much to swallow. It was, he thought, a Leviathan. He had been proud of his contacts with non-Catholics and irenical rather than sectarian by conviction; but had found it hard enough to cope with the demands of ten thousand Catholic Irish for assembly, instruction, marriage and burial without having to face the prospect of perpetual disputes with the privileged Anglicans over precedence, registration, fees, and access to colonial funds. Already a rallying point for religious grievance, he now became prominent in a possible opposition party. Above all, he was prepared to employ what he later termed 'a free, liberal and talented press'.[6] On 14 June 1825 the *Sydney Gazette* misquoted him as having but 'qualified'—he had written 'unqualified'—respect for the 'Reverend Gentlemen of the Establishment'. The incident was magnified at a time of tension. Scott wrote angrily home. Bathurst, already wary of Therry's pragmatic approach to those regulations he regarded as

[1] *H.R.A.* I/xi/671, Bathurst–Brisbane, 20 June 1825.
[2] C.O. 323/206/286, Poynter–Bathurst, 1 Mar. 1826.
[3] C.O. 201/147/243, Poynter–Horton, 22 Aug. 1823.
[4] C.O. 201/168/16, Poynter–Bathurst, 30 June 1825, enc. Conolly–Poynter, 12 June 1824; /179/303, Poynter–Bathurst, 2 May 1826; /305, Poynter–Hay, 26 May 1826; /307, Poynter–Hay, 16 June 1826; /309, Poynter–Hay, 17 June 1826; /317, Poynter–Hay, 15 Aug. 1826; /323, Poynter–Hay, 18 Nov. 1826.
[5] C.O. 201/179/317, Poynter–Hay, 15 Aug. 1826; /325, Poynter–Murphy and Power, 12 Aug. 1826.
[6] *Therry Papers*, 13 Mar. 1839.

unjust or petty, was not prepared to assert Scott's religious monopoly, but he decided that Therry must go.[1] Scott also protested at great length to Poynter and Slater about Therry's behaviour and lack of co-operation, especially in the field of education.[2] He failed to appreciate that he was not up against disciplined civil disobedience so much as the traditional instinct of a substantial national minority which refused to be moulded in a cast not of its own choosing.[3] The English Catholic authorities, long accustomed to cautious relations with the Establishment and anxious not to disturb the delicacy of their position in the years preceding Emancipation, were almost as incapable as Scott of grasping the historical roots and style of Irish intransigence. Slater wrote from Mauritius to reprimand Therry severely, particularly for the publication of correspondence with the local government in such a way as to render it a matter of party contest. 'I cannot approve,' he wrote 'of this itch for giving publicity to all that passes between you and the constituted authorities.'[4] To Daniel Power, the priest who Darling hoped would take Therry's place, Slater was more explicit. He was to avoid any dispute with the authorities 'and never on any account seek to acquire strength or to form a party'. Representations should be respectful and would always be attended to by the authorities 'if conveyed in the language of deference'.[5]

Bathurst consulted Poynter and instructed Darling to get rid of Therry. He could be sent home at government expense. But Therry told the governor that he would not abandon his people for five thousand pounds a year, much less a promise of three hundred pounds.[6] Darling feared the priest's influence among the convicts, and did not want to antagonize further public opinion; but he could cancel Therry's salary and remove him from his official situation as chaplain. The arrival of Daniel Power also encouraged him to ignore Therry rather than to expel him. The withdrawal of government approval involved the priest in continual disabilities and hindrances in the exercise of his priestly functions, especially in the visitation of

---

[1] C.O. 324/85/41, Hay–Poynter, 17 May 1826; /51, Hay–Poynter, 1 July 1826; 202/15/113, Hay–Scott, 5 Aug. 1826; /17/1, Bathurst–Scott, 14 Nov. 1826.
[2] M.L. A/850, Scott–Poynter, Private, 20 June 1825.
[3] cf. e.g., Roe, op cit., p. 103.
[4] *Therry Papers*, Slater–Therry, 12 Jan. 1827.
[5] ibid., Slater–Power, 1 Mar. 1827.
[6] *H.R.A.* I/xii/173, Bathurst–Darling, 1 Feb. 1826; /693, Darling–Bathurst, 18 Nov. 1826; *Therry Papers*, Memo of 18 Dec. 1826.

the sick and dying in gaols and hospitals, and in the performance of marriages. But he remained the chief influence, for Power was a delicate man who could not cope adequately with the pressures placed on him by Darling on one side and his formidable colleague on the other. Therry expostulated against the ridiculous rumours that he was about to raise a rebellion, but stood firm against any claim by the church establishment to a religious monopoly, which he maintained had never been intended by the British government.[1]

The question of Therry's marriages raised important social and legal issues, and his point of view was supported by Stephen, who drew on imperial precedents.[2] When Scott asserted a jurisdiction over the issue of marriage licences in 1828, he failed to convince either Stephen or Twiss. Stephen noted that it had always been the 'sound policy of H.M.G. to confine the colonial clergy to duties entirely and properly of a spiritual nature'.[3] The English Church authorities, despite a vague disquiet, declined to interfere.[4] Huskisson could only exhort the Governor to temper if he could the deplorable religious animosities which threatened the colony.[5]

Power died in 1830, and the Governor wrote to ask for a successor more capable of dealing with Therry, who had obtained a good deal of sympathy from opponents of the administration.[6] The news of Catholic Emancipation, the collapse of the Church and Schools Corporation, and the appointment of Roger Therry as Commissioner of the Court of Requests all offered new heart to the priest, whose work was soon to be extended by Ullathorne and the English Benedictines as well as by Irish secular priests. The arrival of Sir Richard Bourke and the appointment of J. H. Plunkett as Solicitor-General completed the basis for rapid and hopeful achievement. Henry Goulburn's small gesture in offering Therry and Conolly an official salary

---

[1] *H.R.A.* I/xii/543, Darling–Bathurst, 6 Sept. 1826, enc. Therry–MacLeay, 24 June 1826; /761, Darling–Horton, Secret and Confidential, 15 Dec. 1826; C.O. 201/189/98, Poynter–Goderich, 15 Nov. 1827; /99, Power–Poynter, 1 Mar. 1827; /105, Therry–MacLeay, 26 May 1827; *Therry Papers*, Therry–MacLeay, 26 Jan. 1828.

[2] *H.R.A.* I/xiii/372, Goderich–Darling, 28 May 1827; C.O. 201/185/386, C.O. Minute of 13 June 1827.

[3] C.O. 201/204/298, C.O. Minutes, 30 May 1829, on Darling–Huskisson, 22 Sept. 1828 (at *H.R.A.* I/xiv/399 f.).

[4] C.O. 201/186/351, Hamilton–Hay, Private, 30 Mar. 1827; /206/244, Bishop of Calcutta–Twiss, 22 June 1829.

[5] *H.R.A.* I/xiv/162, Huskisson–Darling, 29 Apr. 1828.

[6] *H.R.A.* I/xv/382, Darling–Murray, 16 Mar. 1830.

had in some ways brought about the inevitable progress of a religiously plural society in the colonies of Australia.[1]

* * * * *

If education and religion could not provide the government with the answers they sought, there had been even in defeat some advance in social maturity. Piecemeal progress with a good deal of shade as well as light was perhaps the best that could have been expected for any institution at that time and in that place. Though the Australian colonies had survived and were beginning to flourish, they had not yet formed a way of life in which more than a handful of men, and few of them officials of government, could hope to have clear success in carrying out their projects. 'All is still to be done here' was a frequent reflection of administrators 'fagged to death with business'. Yet very little appeared ever to be completed, Chief Justice Forbes remarked. He thought that some outstanding statesman with a mind 'gifted by nature and elaborated by study and experience' could frame a brilliant design for 'this young Empire' like some latter-day Solon or Lycurgus. The very structure of government had, he wrote, to be created rather than reorganized, by a government 'so encumbered with details that it has not time for the loftier objects of political economy'.[2]

Appearances could, however, be deceptive. In his speech at the second reading of the 1828 New South Wales Bill, Huskisson said his great object had been to meddle as little with details as possible, which were 'always much better arranged upon the spot.'[3] Details were important in the building up of a society which contained within it freedom and bondage in such unprecedented proportions; and single steps counted for much at a time when 'a more enlarged and liberal course', though guaranteed, was still in the future.[4]

Huskisson, and Horton before him, toyed with the idea of ceasing transportation to Australia, but there were always difficulties.[5]

[1] *H.R.A.* I/xv/818, Murray–Darling, 15 Nov. 1830; C.O. 324/86/152, Hay–Bramston, 19 Aug. 1830; C.O. 201/206/20, 'An Emigrant Catholic' (R. Therry)–Murray, 25 July 1829; C.O. 201/230/227, C.O. Minute of 3 Feb. 1832 re Plunkett and Rev. J. McEncroe; *H.R.A.* I/xvi/587, Bourke–Goderich, 2 Apr. 1832; /707, Goderich–Bourke, 20 Aug. 1832; T. L. Suttor, *Hierarchy and Democracy in Australia 1788–1870* (Melbourne, 1965), pp. 20–7, 32 ff.
[2] *H.R.A.* IV/i/679, Forbes–Horton, 6 Feb. 1827.
[3] P.D. n.s. XVIII/1565, 18 Apr. 1828.
[4] P.D. n.s. XVIII/1566, Spring Rice, 18 Apr. 1828.
[5] B.M. Add. MSS. 38756, f. 62, Huskisson–Anglesey, 15 Apr. 1828.

George Arthur, soon to become devoted to a special vision of the future, wrote in 1826 of the jarrings and general discontent which was the accompaniment of the government's efforts to 'lay the foundation of a free Colony' among convicted felons at the far side of the world. Eventually, 'when the rugged scaffolding and rubbish is removed,' he told Bathurst, a magnificent building would emerge, a monument to British patience and skill.[1]

Robert Hay and some of his colleagues clearly deplored the continued export of British criminals to 'those great and rising colonies' which gave them so much trouble, but in whose progress they took proprietary pride.[2] After the Bigge Report, Horton and later Hay carried out a long, and desultory, series of probes to see if they could compass some change; but they could obtain little purchase on the Home Office, whose support would have been a *sine quâ non*.[3]

Attempts were made to examine alternative destinations for convict transportees. In 1827 the Admiralty asked for more men to be sent to Bermuda, where convicts had been working in the dockyard since 1824. The Colonial Office was ready to oblige but unsure and perhaps divided about what opportunity this might open for changing the course of transportation away from Australia. They certainly knew there was a great demand for able-bodied men in the colonies. Melville protested that, with all deference to New South Wales and its agricultural prosperity, the naval fortifications at Bermuda were 'of much more pressing importance to this country'. There were, he thought, probably enough poachers to go round, but expressed a 'latent hope that the period is not distant when very *few* will be sent to New South Wales'. He thought the Cabinet had 'no idea of the principle on which you are now proceeding as to that country' and would be surprised at the importance which seemed to be attached to assuring the Australians of their labour supply.[4]

The Home Office was in principle willing to help the emigration of useful and free labour to Australia.[5] Lansdowne was friendly enough to particular propositions, but reluctant to interfere with what he claimed was a Colonial Office responsibility. Along with Peel,

---

[1] *H.R.A.* III/v/149, Arthur–Bathurst, 21 Apr. 1826.

[2] C.O. 280/13/287, C.O. Minute of 23 June 1828.

[3] A. H. King, op. cit., pp. 202–4; C.O. 323/202/176, C.O.–Home Office, 14 July 1825.

[4] C.O. 323/149/385, Melville–Hay, 16 Jan. 1827; cf. also 202/18/293, Hay–Dawson, 3, 4 Jan. 1827 and B.M. Add. MSS. (Peel) 40391, f. 116, Horton–Peel, Private, 18 Jan. 1827.   [5] C.O. 201/185/234, Hobhouse–Hay, 14 Mar. 1827.

Huskisson and many others, he had his doubts about the severity and salutary effect of transportation. 1827 was besides not a good year to hope for politicians to give undivided attention to concerns which seemed to be able to proceed without tampering.[1] The episode however, caused Horton to consult Edward Barnard, agent for the Australian colonies. Barnard answered forcefully and at length on the 'proposal to desist in future from sending convicts to New South Wales and Van Diemen's Land' and commented on the various criticisms which had been made about the convict system. He argued that punishment was severe indeed. There would be serious inconvenience if transportation were to cease. Ventures such as the Australian Agricultural Company should not be deprived of the work-force they had counted on and in effect been guaranteed. He had letters from Arthur and others to back his case.[2]

James Stephen was not far wrong when he confessed that the workings of convict assignment had introduced a sort of slavery to Australia. It was a point later taken up by Wakefield. The Home Office, Stephen wrote, had 'considered merely their own business, namely, in getting rid of the convict', in drawing up the law governing assignment (5 Geo. 4 cap. 84); and he was anxious that the colonial government's supervisory authority be insisted upon in future considerations on the point.[3]

All agreed that the presence of women would have helped, especially when transportation was suggested as a punishment for lesser crimes. Peel had favoured an extension of the existing system of sending out the wives of recommended convicts in 1826.[4] In 1828 Samuel March Phillipps told Twiss that the Home Office, moved by the needs of 'those settlements as Colonies, no less than the state of Society and Morals in this country' was interested in the plans of local government to 'convey the destitute unmarried women to New South Wales'. Twiss insisted that the good of the colonies demanded that only respectable women be sent. He fully supported government assistance for the emigration of some deserving convict families.[5]

[1] C.O. 280/14/87, Hobhouse–Hay, 30 July 1827.
[2] C.O. 201/185/48, Barnard–Horton, 23 Jan. 1827.
[3] C.O. 201/185/408, M. of Stephen, 8 Aug. 1827; /206/486, Gouger–Murray, 25 July 1829; /195, Memorial of 4 Mar. 1828; /441 in Stephen–Murray, 15 Aug. 1828; /204/277, M. of 17 Jan. 1830; /214/163, Stephen–Hay, 26 Mar. 1830; /215 /166, Stephen–Barrow, 18 Aug. 1830, enc. Dumaresq–Hay, Private, 16 Mar. 1830.
[4] C.O. 201/164/121, Peel–Horton, 8 Feb. 1826; cf. also 324/144/136 Horton–Hobhouse, 3 June 1822.
[5] C.O. 201/195/314, Phillipps–Twiss, 5 Nov. 1828 and Minutes.

Hay sent Arthur a private and hedged letter in 1829 about possible reaction to the ending of transportation to Australia. He had no authority to suppose a change was likely at present. It was a question, he wrote, 'founded entirely upon a speculation of my own, and is not in any degree suggested by any measure which the government may have in contemplation'. But he asked the Governor to weigh the obvious disadvantages to the colonies against the improvement they would gain in reputation.[1] He put his views tentatively to Peel who showed polite interest.[2] In February 1830 he made a similar approach to Henry Goulburn, Chancellor of the Exchequer and about to guide the Commission of Enquiry into Colonial expenses.[3] He asked Byam Martin for detailed information about the effect of changes in the system.[4]

Later in 1830, Sir Willoughby Gordon, an effective member of the Commission of Enquiry and with long experience of military administration, wrote to ask for information on Australia.[5] Gordon was fascinated by what he read and keen to do something about it. He had come to the conclusion that transportation was a 'vast mistake', not only on financial but on social and penal grounds. The Colonial Office should not be blamed for the expense of the system. Only the 'Highest Legislative and Executive power of the Kingdom could take the steps necessary to review the problem root and branch.'[6]

Hay, disillusioned by his experiences, and by the reception of his previous suggestions, replied that transportation was a difficult and important subject, but that 'its consideration more properly belongs to the Home Office than to Ours'. He had tried to interest Peel. Horton too had done his best, but was now out of Parliament. He knew that the colonial governors opposed the cessation of the system. The labour of the convicts and the money expended on their maintenance was very important to the prosperity of the colonies. This was not a conclusive objection, but it immensely complicated the question. Sir George Murray would regard Gordon's letter as confidential.[7]

[1] C.O. 324/86/122, Hay–Arthur, 7 Oct. 1829.
[2] C.O. 323/156/170, Peel–Hay, 25 May 1829.
[3] C.O. 324/93/177, Hay–Goulburn, Private and Confidential, 25 Feb. 1830.
[4] C.O. 324/93/185, Hay–Martin, Private, 24 Mar. 1830.
[5] C.O. 323/162/152, Gordon–Hay, 10 Aug. 1830; 324/93/209, Hay–Gordon, 13 Aug. 1830.
[6] C.O. 323/156/78, Gordon–Hay, Most Confidential, 18 Aug. 1830.
[7] C.O. 324/93/10, Hay–Gordon, 23 Aug. 1830.

It was most improbable that the last days of the Tory government would see much attention paid to such a subject, though Peel called it an important one worthy of the most thorough investigation.[1] The way was prepared at least for the inconclusive but seminal Select Committee on Secondary Punishments of 1831.[2]

Hay had reason enough behind his comments. The colonial response to his gentle inquiries had been loud and firm. Montagu in Van Diemen's Land read him a lesson in Australian history and proved to his own satisfaction that the colonies were nothing without the convicts. Free emigration was attracted by transportation and cheap labour, which was the only way to compete with the United States and Canada.[3] Governor Arthur was in an agony of apprehension.[4] He would have been still further disturbed had he read a Minute on Bourke's instructions which told the new governor discreetly to be ready for the abandonment of transportation.[5] Free emigration was well and good, and Arthur was ready to encourage it by every available means. Whatever might be said of New South Wales, the convicts were the *unum necessarium* for his government machine. His local advisers were unanimous: the more useful convicts that could be sent the better.[6] When Howick put forward his new land regulations in 1831, Hay told him not to 'imagine the colonists in the Australian Provinces are desirous of changing the present system of transportation'. For his own part he still favoured abolition.[7]

As Arthur's dispatches and more came to the notice of the Home Office, a change grew less and less likely. Howick approached Phillipps to see if Melbourne would consider the 'propriety of discontinuing the transportation of convicts to New South Wales'. The system was ineffective and as settlement spread might prove dangerous and unmanageable. Trinidad or Mauritius would be more suitable.[8] But 'severity' became the order of the day.[9] In 1833 Stanley, now

[1] P.D. n.s. XXIV/941–6, 21 May 1830.
[2] P.P. 1831, VII (276).
[3] C.O. 280/27/198, Montagu–Hay, 10 Apr. 1830.
[4] C.O. 280/28/129, Arthur–Hay, Private, 2 Jan. 1831.
[5] C.O. 201/225/54, M. of June 1831.
[6] C.O. 280/29/168, Arthur–Goderich, 9 July 1831; 280/33/368, Arthur–Howick, 18 Feb. 1832; /34/175, Arthur–Goderich, 28 June 1832; /338, Arthur–Goderich, 31 July 1832; /36/359, Arthur–Hay, 12 Dec. 1832.
[7] C.O. 324/93/224, Hay–Howick, 3 Jan. 1831.
[8] C.O. 202/26/125, Howick–Phillipps, 25 Mar. 1831; cf. also /188, Howick–Phillipps, 13 July 1831.
[9] Shaw, op. cit., p. 250 ff.

Secretary of State, supported Melbourne's plan to increase the numbers of convicts destined for the Antipodes.[1]

For New South Wales Colonel Dumaresq spoke with George Arthur's tongue. In a letter which suggested that the British occupy New Zealand without any nonsense, and set up a puppet King, he scouted the idea of abolishing transportation. If the convicts could no longer be counted upon 'the fate of this colony is sealed for our generation'. New South Wales would languish imperceptibly, and end up as poor as South America, 'and as unprofitable to live in'.[2]

Governor Arthur's emphasis on the responsibilities of government towards infant societies may not have been altogether acceptable to a British administration intent on retrenchment all round. The Colonial Office probably did not savour the Governor's strictures on their 'grand scheme of supplying the colony with a hardy peasantry'. Yet in the previous decade there had passed much which might have been adduced to justify Goderich's remark that 'it was the interest of the colony which was the principal object'.[3]

---

[1] C.O. 202/29/346, Hay–Phillipps, 25 June 1833.

[2] C.O. 201/223/352, Dumaresq–Hay, Private, 16 Nov. 1831.

[3] C.O. 280/29/168, Arthur–Goderich, 9 July 1831; 408/7/242, Goderich–Arthur, 27 Jan. 1832.

BIBLIOGRAPHY

MANUSCRIPT SOURCES

A   Public Record Office
- I   Colonial Office
  1. South Australia
  2. Western Australia
  3. New South Wales
  4. New Zealand
  5. Van Diemen's Land
  6. Colonies General
- II   Paymaster General's Department
- III   Treasury
- IV   Audit Office
- V   Home Office
- VI   Admiralty
- VII   Board of Trade

B   Other Manuscript Sources: England
C   Other Manuscript Sources: Australia

PRINTED SOURCES

A   Parliamentary Debates and Papers

Cobbett's Parliamentary Debates
Hansard's Parliamentary Debates
Select List of Parliamentary Papers (House of Commons)

B   Contemporary Newspapers
C   Contemporary Books and Memoirs

COLLECTIONS OF DOCUMENTS AND WORKS OF REFERENCE

LATER WORKS

A   Theses
B   Books, monographs and articles

MANUSCRIPT SOURCES

A. Public Record Office
I   *Colonial Office*

1. *South Australia*

C.O. 13/1	Original Correspondence	1831–2

2. *Western Australia*

C.O. 18/1–12	Original Correspondence	1828–33
397/1–3	Original Correspondence	1828–35

3. *New South Wales*

C.O. 201/90–230	Original Correspondence, Public Offices and Individuals	1818–32
201/237	Settlers	1831–3
201/270	J. D. Shelley's Case	1829–37
202/8–29	Entry Books	1814–33
204/1–5	Minutes of Executive Council	1825–32
206/1–54	Newspapers	
206/63/73	Blue Books	1822–33

4. *New Zealand*

C.O. 209/1	Original Correspondence	1830–5

5. *Van Diemen's Land*

C.O. 280/1–40	Original Correspondence	1824–33
280/90	Burnett's Case	1834–7
282/1–4	Executive Council Minutes	1825–32
284/44–56	Blue Books	1822–33
408/1–9	Entry Books	1825–33

6. *Colonies General*

C.O. 323/40–9	Law Officers' Opinions on Colonial Laws	1814–33
323/95	Law Officers' Opinions, Eastern Colonies	1827–9
323/117–39	Applications for Colonial Appointments	1819–30
323/146	Private Letters to R. W. Hay, Miscellaneous and Eastern Colonies	1825–6
323/147	Private Letters to R. W. Hay	1825–7

C.O.	323/149	Private Letters to R. W. Hay, Eastern Colonies	1827
	323/155	Private Letters to R. W. Hay, Eastern Colonies	1828
	323/156	Private Letters to R. W. Hay, Eastern Colonies	1828–30
	323/157	Private Letters to R. W. Hay, Eastern Colonies	1829
	323/162	Private Letters to R. W. Hay, Eastern Colonies	1830
	323/165	Private Letters, R. W. Hay, A–G	1831
	323/166	Private Letters, R. W. Hay, H–P	1831
	323/167	Private Letters, R. W. Hay, R–Z	1831
	323/168	Private Letters, R. W. Hay, A–G	1832
	323/169	Private Letters, R. W. Hay, H–Z	1832
	323/188–214	Original Correspondence: In-Letters, Public Offices and Individuals	1818–32
	324/	Entry Books of Out-Letters	
	324/73–4	Private Letters from Earl Bathurst	1821–7
	324/75	Minutes by Earl Bathurst	1823–7
	324/76–94	Private Letters from R. W. Hay	1825–36
	324/95–100	Private Letters from Wilmot Horton	1825–7
	324/100–2	Private Letters from Lord Goderich and Huskisson	1827–8
	324/103	Circulars to Governors (Colonial)	1794–1815
	324/104	Circulars to Governors, Consuls, and others (military)	1811–20
	324/105–6	Circulars to Governors	1825–41
	324/139–46	Letters from Colonial Office, Domestic	1816–32
	325/6	Memoranda on Trade	
	325/16	Return of Colonial Appointments	1817
	325/21	Register of Colonial Appointments	
	325/22	Colonial Appointments	1826–32

C.O. 325/28   New South Wales and Van Die-
                  men's Land, Clergy and
                  Memoranda
      325/33   Eastern Colonies, Private Papers 1826–7
      325/35   Wilmot Horton: Private Papers 1825–7
      325/36   Colonial Lands
      537/22   Colonial Office Establishment,
                  Minutes, Letters and Memo-
                  randa   1832–72
      854/1   Circular Dispatches, mostly
                  printed   1808–36

II   *Paymaster General's Department*
     1/1   Letters of Sir Thomas Brisbane to
                  W. Craufurd   1822–3

III *Treasury*
     1   Original Correspondence

IV   *Audit Office*
     1   Declared Accounts
     2   Declared Accounts
     6   Minutes

V   *Home Office*
     7/2   Capper
     10   Convict Papers
     11   Transportation Registers
     13/42   Convicts
     28/49   Correspondence (Admiralty)   1823–5
     29/7   Entry Books (Admiralty)   1823–36

VI   *Admiralty*
     1/191–205   East India Station   1821–32
     1/4238–44   Secretary of State: In-Letters 1819–30
     1/4362–4   Secret Letters   1816–30
     2/1694   Entry Books (secret)   1825–31

VII *Board of Trade*
     5   Minutes of the Board
     6   Original Correspondence, Trade

B. Other Manuscript Sources: England
Bathurst Papers: B.M. Add. MSS. Loan

57/11–23		1816–
57/55	Private Letters, Eastern Cols.	1824
57/56	North America Letters	1824
57/57–9	Letters, Drafts and Memoranda to Under-secretary Hay	1825–8
57/74	Private Letters, Eastern Cols.	1822–4
57/77	Family Letters	1801–50
57/82	Family Papers	
57/89	Miscellaneous & Private Letters	1813–27
57/107	Melville Papers	1788–1830

Bourke Papers: Rhodes House, Oxford, Correspondence and Entry Books 1816–45
Goulburn Papers: Surrey County Record Office
Huskisson Papers: B.M. Add. MSS.
   38742–58: Original Correspondence 1821–31
Peel Papers: B.M. Add. MSS.

40307–9	Correspondence with Wellington	1828–34
40317	Correspondence with Lord Melville	1822–30
40320	Correspondence with Croker	1828–33
40329–33	Correspondence with Goulburn	1823–41
40355–7	General Correspondence	1823
40391–40401	General Correspondence	1827–30

Ripon Papers: B.M. Add. MSS.
   4087–80 Applications for Colonial Appointments 1832

C. Other Manuscript Sources: Australia
Therry Papers: Canisius College, Pymble
In the *Mitchell Library*, Sydney:
New South Wales Archives Authority: Original Correspondence, Entry Books, Memoranda, Minutes, Miscellaneous; Governor, Private Secretary, Colonial Secretary: In-Letters, Entry Books, Departmental Records.
Bathurst Papers   A 73 (Letters to Horton)
Blaxland Family Papers A 1322; C 196

Brisbane Papers	A 1859, 1–3 (Letter Books); fm 4/1626–7
Dumaresq Papers	A 2571
Forbes Papers	A 741–50; A 820; A 1381; A 1819 Af 10; Af 23
Hall Papers	Ah 14
Harris Papers	A 1597
Hassall Papers	A 1677
King Papers	A 1976
Lang Papers	A 2221–36

Macarthur Papers

A 2897	Letters and Biography, 1806–1930
2898	John Macarthur, Letters to Mrs. Macarthur 1808–32
2899	John Macarthur, Letters to his sons, 1815–32
2900	John Macarthur, Correspondence 1800–31
2901	John Macarthur, Letters and Accounts from Hannibal Macarthur, 1810–29
2902	John Macarthur Accounts, 1806–32
2905	Legal Papers, 1818–27
2906	Mrs. John Macarthur, Journal & Correspondence, 1789–1840
2908	Mrs. John Macarthur, Extracts from Letters, 1789–1840
2910	Family History
2911	John Macarthur Jnr., Correspondence, 1810–31
2912–13	Letters of Sir E. Macarthur
2917	Sir E. Macarthur, In-Letters 1806–66
2920	James Macarthur, Correspondence, 1819
2922–6	James Macarthur, In-Letters, 1819–67
2931	James Macarthur, Letters to Relatives, 1827–55
2955	The Letters of Archdeacon Scott, 1822–44
2956	The Davidson Correspondence, 1815–46
2974	Papers relating to Dr. Bowman, 1829–55

4246   (Bowman)
4250   Land grants
4266–7   (Bowman)
4304–5   (Macleay)
4314–21   Original Correspondence, Australian Ag.
                Co. 1824–
4331   Miscellaneous Letters and Accounts Aust.
                Ag. Co. 1824–60

Mackaness Papers   A 317
Macquarie Papers   A 772–4
Marsden Papers   A 1922; A 1997–9; BT (Bonwick
                         Transcripts) Missionary C 244
James Mitchell Papers   A 2026
Oxley Papers   A 1717–19; A 1752
Piper Papers   A 254–6
Riley Papers   A 106; 107; 111
T. Hobbes Scott Papers   A 850–1, Letter Books 1825–9
Throsby Papers   A 1940 (1810–21)
Wentworth Papers   A 754–7; A 764–6; A 1440

PRINTED SOURCES

A. Parliamentary Debates and Papers
    Cobbett's Parliamentary Debates
    Hansard's Parliamentary Debates
    Select List of Parliamentary Papers (House of Commons)

Year	Vol. No.	Paper No.	Short Title
1810	IV	348	28th Report of SC on Finance etc.
1812	II	339	12th Report of C on Public Expenditure of U.K. etc.
1812	II	341	Rpt. of SC on Transportation
1816	XVIII	314	Account of deaths of Convicts since 1810
1816	XVIII	450	Papers relative to Settlements in New South Wales 1811–14
1819	I	579	Rpts. from Cs on Gaols and other places of Confinement
1819	XV	8	Army Estimates

Year	Vol. No.	Paper No.	Short Title
1819–20	IV	74	2 rpts. of J. Capper on Transportation
1819–20	IV	85	Comparative Lists of Civil Establishments
1820	III	269	1st rpt. of the SC of House of Lords on Foreign Trade
1821	XIV	557	Return of annual expenditure in New South Wales
1821	XIV	334	Treasury Establishments
1821	XXI	18	2 rpts. of J. Capper on Confinement of Offenders
1821	XXI	193–4	Land grants above 100 acres 1812–21
1821	XXI	439	Navy Office Rpts.
1822	XX	377	Names of Colonial Agents
1822	XX	477	Land grants in New South Wales 1812–21
1822	XX	448	Rpt. on the state of the Colony of New South Wales
1822	XXI	479	Exports and Imports
1823	X	33	Rept. on Judicial Est. N.S.W. and V.D.L.
		136	Rept. on State of Agric. and Trade N.S.W.
1823	XIV	438	Receipts and Expenditure of V.D.L. and N.S.W.
1823	XIV	531	Annual Expenditure of New South Wales
1823	XIV	532	Instructions to Mr. Bigge
1824	XVI	17	Estimates on Civil Establishments
		116	Colonial Income and Expenditure
		292	Dollars imported into New South Wales
	XVII	363	Excise rpts.
		274	Imports to the U.K.
		186	Value of Exports to N.S.W. and V.D.L.
1825	XV	157	1st rpt. of Inquiry into Administration of Justice in W.I.
	XIX	314	Establishment

Year	Vol. No.	Paper No.	Short Title
		215	Intended Arrangements for Canada Co.
		303	Intended Arrangements for Van Diemen's Land Co.
		236	Colonial Trade of Mauritius
		421	Grants of Powers to Judges in N.S.W. and V.D.L.
	XXI	207	Tonnage of shipping to and from N.S.W. and V.D.L.
1826	IV	404	Emigration from the U.K.
	XX	16	Navy Estimates
	XXVI	277	Conduct of Magistrates in N.S.W.
		334	Laws and Ordinances of Gvt. and Council of N.S.W.
1826–7	V	88	1st Rpt. of SC on Emigration from the U.K.
		237	2nd Rpt. of SC on Emigration from the U.K.
		550	3rd Rpt. of SC on Emigration from the U.K.
1826–7	XX	301	Commission of Inquiry of last 20 years—Expenses
1828	V	420	2nd rpt. SC on Public Income and Expenditure, Ordinance
		480	3rd rpt. SC on Public Income and Expenditure, Superannuations
		519	4th rpt. SC on Public Income and Revenue, Expenditure and Debt
1828	VII	569	Rpt. of SC on Civil Govt. of Canada
1828	XXI	477	Rpt. by Macquarie on N.S.W.
		538	2 Dispatches... Sudds and Thompson
		335	Laws and Ordinances of Gvt. and Council of N.S.W.
		109	Rpt. of Cockburn on Emigration
		477	Return to an address of the Commons by N.S.W.
		538	Sudds and Thompson
1829	VI	290	Rpt. of Inquiry into keeping of Accounts in Principal Depts.

Year	Vol. No.	Paper No.	Short Title
	XXI	212	Account of Expenses *re* Cs. of Inquiry
1830	XXIX	650	Return of number of emigrants from U.K. since 1820
		586	Papers explanatory of charges against Darling
1830–1	IV	64	Rpts. from Commissioners on Colonial Revenue
	VII	92	Colonial Audit
	IX	233	Canada Co. Lands
1830–1		241	Acts and Ordinances of Gvt. and Council of N.S.W.
		242	Acts and Ordinances of Gvt. and Council of V.D.L.
1830–1	IX	163	Laws and Ordinances of Gvt. and Council of N.S.W. 1829–30
		81	Instructions *re* Penal Settlements
		625	New South Wales Veterans Cos.
1831	VII	276	Rpt. of SC on Secondary Punishments
1831	XIX	328	Crown Lands and Emigration
		261	Instructions on Moral and Religious Instruction of aborigines
		259	Military Operations *v.* the Aborigines
		260	Returns of Population, Trade, etc. in the Colonies
1831–2	XXVI	512	Finance Accounts, Expenses of Royal Commissions
		430	Superannuation for Mr. Justice Stephen
		369	Grant of £500 p.a. to Mr. Justice Stephen
	XXXII	724	Rpt. of Commissioners on Emigration
		161	Expenses *re* Convicts in N.S.W.
		606	Alienation of Crown Lands in N.S.W. and V.D.L. in last 10 years
		394	Instructions to Darling etc. on appropriating N.S.W. lands

Year	Vol. No.	Paper No.	Short Title
1833	VII	650	Rpt. of C on Army and Navy Appointments
		646	Rpt. of SC on Civil List Charges
	XII	44	1st rpt. of SC on Public Documents
		717	2nd rpt. of SC on Public Documents
1834	XLIV	615	Returns of sale of Lands in Canada etc.
	XLVII	82	Crime: secondary punishments
1835	VI	473	Rpt. of SC on Colonial Military Expenditure
		580	Rpt. of SC on the Conduct of Darling
		278	Land grants, Canada
		87	Papers re Emigration to Colonies
1836	XI	512	Rpt. from SC on disposal of Land in Colonies
1837		539	Rpt. of SC on Communication with India
	VII	425	Rpt. of SC on Aborigines
		516	Rpt. of SC on Colonial Acts, Receipt and Expenditure
	XIX	518	Rpt. of SC on Transportation—its efficacy and effects
1837–8	XXII	669	Rpt. of SC on Transportation
1839	XXXIV	572	Returns of revenue 1827–37
1854	XXVII	1715	Rept. of Committee of Enquiry into C.O. 15 December 1849
1854–5	XX	1870	Reorganization of Civil Service

B. Contemporary Newspapers and Periodicals

Britain:

Annual Register
Eclectic Review
Edinburgh Monthly Review
Frazer's Magazine
Monthly Review
New Monthly Magazine
Quarterly Review
The Times

Blackwood
Edinburgh Magazine
Edinburgh Review
Gentleman's Magazine
Morning Chronicle
Political Register
Spectator
Westminster Review

Australia:

Sydney Gazette   Australian   Monitor

C. Contemporary Books and Memoirs
All books are published in London unless stated otherwise.

ASPINALL, A. (ed.), *The Formation of Canning's Ministry, February–August 1827*, R.H.S. (Camden Soc. 3rd Series, vol. LIX, 1937).
The Correspondence of Charles Arbuthnot, R.H.S. (Camden Soc. 3rd series, vol. LXV, 1941).
The Diary of Henry Hobhouse (1820–27), (1947).
The Letters of George IV 1812–30, 3 vols. (Cambridge, 1938).

ATKINSON, J., *An Account of the State of Agriculture and Grazing in New South Wales etc.* (1826).

BALFOUR, J. O., *A Sketch of New South Wales* (1845).

BAMFORD, F. and the DUKE OF WELLINGTON (eds.), *The Journal of Mrs. Arbuthnot 1820–32*, 2 vols. (1950).

BARROW, SIR J., *An Auto-biographical Memoir* (1847).

BENNETT, G., *Wanderings in New South Wales, Batavia etc.* 2 vols. (1834).

BENTHAM, J., *Emancipate Your Colonies. Addressed to the National Convention of France, anno 1793* (1830).

BETTS, T., *An Account of the Colony of Van Diemen's Land* (Calcutta, 1830).

BEVINGTON, M. M. (ed.), *The Memoirs of James Stephen* (1954).

BICKLEY, F. (ed.), *Report on the MSS. of Earl Bathurst Preserved at Cirencester Park.* Historical MSS. Commission (1923).

BLOSSEVILLE, E. DE, *Histoire des Colonies Pénales de L'Angleterre dans L'Australie* (Paris, 1831).

BRAIM, T. H., *A History of New South Wales from its Settlement to the Close of the Year 1844* (1846).

BRETON, LIEUT., *Excursions in New South Wales, Western Australia and van Diemen's Land During the Years 1830–33* (1833).

BUNBURY, W. ST. P. and MORELL, W. P. (eds.), *Early Days in Western Australia. Being the Letters and Journal of Lt. H. W. Bunbury, 21st Fusiliers* (Oxford, 1930).

BUSBY, J., *Authentic Information Relative to New South Wales and New Zealand* (1832).

BUXTON, C. (ed.), *Memoirs of Sir T. F. Buxton* (1848).

BYRNE, J. C., *Twelve Years' Wanderings in the British Colonies 1835–47* (1848).

CHALMERS, T., *On Political Economy in Connexion with the Moral State and Moral Prospects of Society* (Glasgow, 1832).

CLARK, C. M. H. (ed.), *Emigrant Mechanic: Settlers and Convicts* (Melbourne, 1953).

COBBET, W., *Rural Rides* (ed. 1932).

COLLINS, S. H., *Geographical Description of Australasia etc.* (1830).

COX, W., *Memoirs of William Cox, J.P.* (Sydney, 1901).

CRAMP, W. B., *Narrative of a Voyage to India etc.* (1823).

CUNNINGHAM, P., *Two Years in New South Wales*, 2 vols. (1827).

CURR, E., *An Account of the Colony of van Diemen's Land* (1824).

DAWSON, R., *The Present State of Australia* (1831).

DIXON, J., *Condition and Capabilities of van Diemen's Land etc.* (1839).

DOUGLAS, D. C. (ed.), *English Historical Documents*, Vol. XI, 1783–1832, ed. A. Aspinall and E. A. Smith (1959).

DOYLE, M. (ed.), *Extracts from the Letters and Journals of G. F. Moore, now filling a Judicial Office at the Swan River Settlement* (1834).

EAGAR, E., *Letters to the Rt. Hon. Robert Peel, M.P., Secretary of State for the Home Department, on the Advantages of New South Wales and van Diemen's Land as Penal Settlements etc.* (1824).

ENDERBY, C., *Proposal for Re-establishing the British Southern Whale Fishery* (1847).

FRY, K. and CRESSWELL, R. E. (eds.), *Memoir of the Life of Elizabeth Fry*, 2 vols. (1848).

HALL, E. S., *The State of New South Wales in December 1830* (1831).

HAMILTON, SIR R. V. (ed.), *Letters and Papers of Admiral of the Fleet Sir Thomas Byam Martin*. Navy Records Society (1898–1903).

HASLAM, J., *A Narrative of a Voyage to New South Wales in the Year 1816* (1819).

HAZLITT, W., *The Spirit of the Age* (1825).

HENDERSON, J., *Excursions and Adventures in New South Wales*, 2 vols. (1851).

Observations on the Colonies of New South Wales and van Diemen's Land (Calcutta, 1832).

HORTON, R. W., *An Enquiry into the Causes and Remedies of Pauperism* (1830).

Exposition and Defence of Earl Bathurst's Administration of the Affairs of Canada during the years 1822 to 1827 inclusive (1839).

HUGHES, E. (ed.), *The Diaries and Correspondence of James Losh*, 2 vols. (Surtees Society CLXXI and CLXXIV (1962–3).

HUSKISSON, W., *Substance of Two Speeches Delivered in the House of Commons on the 24th and 25th of March 1823 by the Rt. Hon. W. Huskisson* (1825).

The Speeches of the Rt. Hon. William Huskisson, 3 vols. (1831).

JENNINGS, L. J. (ed.), *The Correspondence and Diaries of the late Rt. Hon. J. W. Croker*, 3 vols. (1885).

KENT, T., *A Letter to Barron Field* (1824).

LANG, J. D., *The Coming Event* (Sydney, 1850).

Account of the Steps taken in England with a view to the establishment of an Academical Institution, a College, in New South Wales etc. (Sydney, 1831).

The Present Aspect and Prospects of the Church with a Plain Statement of the Case of the Church of Scotland and the British Colonies (Edinburgh, 1831).

An Historical and Statistical Account of New South Wales, 2 vols. (3rd ed. 1840).

Emigration; considered chiefly in Reference to the Practicability and expediency of imparting and settling throughout the territory of New South Wales, a numerous, industrious, and virtuous agricultural population (Sydney, 1833).

LA PILORGÉRIE, J. DE, *Histoire de Botany-Bay* (Paris, 1836).

LEWIS, G. C., *Essay on the Government of Dependencies* (1841).

MACKANESS, G. (ed.), *The Discovery and Exploration of Moreton Bay and the Brisbane River* (Sydney, 1956).

A Chronology of Momentous Events in Australian History 1788–1846 (Sydney, 1952).

Fourteen Journies over the Blue Mountains of New South Wales 1813–41 (Sydney, 1950).

MACDONNELL, A., *Colonial Commerce* (1828).

McKAY, A. (ed.), *Journals of the Land Commissioners for Van Diemen's Land, 1826–28* (Hobart, 1962).

MACKINTOSH, R. J. (ed.), *Memoirs of the Life of the Rt. Hon. Sir James Mackintosh*, 2 vols. (2nd ed. 1836).

MACLEHOSE, H., *The Picture of Sydney and Strangers' Guide in New South Wales for 1838* (Sydney, 1838).

McCULLOCH, J. R., *A Discourse on the Rise, Progress, Peculiar Objects and Importance of Political Economy* (Edinburgh, 1824).

MACQUEEN, T. P., *Australia as she is and as she may be* (1840).

MARJORIBANKS, A., *Travels in New South Wales* (1847).

MARTIN, R. M., *History of the Colonies of the British Empire* (1843).

MARTINEAU, H., *The History of England during the Thirty Years' Peace 1816–1846* (1849).

MASLEM, T. J., *The Friend of Australia, or, A Plan for Exploring the Interior, etc.* (1830).

MELVILLE, H., *The History of the Island of Van Diemen's Land from 1824–35 inclusive* (1835).

MERIVALE, H., *Lectures on Colonization and Colonies* (Oxford, 1928).

MOORE, G. F., *Diary of Ten Years Eventful Life of an Early Settler in Western Australia* (1884).

MUDIE, J., *The Felonry of New South Wales* (1837).

MUDIE, R., *The Picture of Australia* (1829).

NAPIER, C. J., *The Colonies* (1833).

NOEL, B. W., *The State of the Metropolis Considered* (1835).

ONSLOW, S. MACARTHUR (ed.), *Some Early Records of the Macarthurs of Camden* (Sydney, 1914).

PEEL, R., *The Speeches of the Late Rt. Hon. Sir Robert Peel*, 4 vols. (1853).

PELLEW, G., *The Life and Correspondence of the Rt. Hon. H. Addington, 1st Viscount Sidmouth*, 3 vols. (1847).

PORTER, G. R., *The Progress of the Nation* (1851).

SANDERSON, C. R. (ed.), *The Arthur Papers*, 3 vols. (Toronto, 1957).

SMITH, S., *The Works of Sydney Smith* (1840).
Selected Writings of Sydney Smith, ed. by W. H. Auden (New York, 1956).
The Letters of Sydney Smith, ed. by N. C. Smith, 2 vols. (Oxford, 1953).

SRAFFA, P., *The Works and Correspondence of David Ricardo*, Vol. V (Cambridge, 1952).

STAPLETON, A. G., *The Political Life of the Rt. Hon. G. Canning*, 3 vols. (1831).
George Canning and his Times (1859).

STRACHEY, L. and FULFORD, R. (eds.), *The Greville Memoirs 1814–60*, 8 vols. (1938).

TAYLOR, E. (ed.), *The Taylor Papers; Reminiscences, Letters and Journals of Sir Herbert Taylor* (1913).

TAYLOR, H., *The Statesman*, ed. H. J. Laski, (Cambridge, 1927).

THERRY, R., *An Appeal on behalf of the Roman Catholics of New South Wales* (Sydney, 1833).

TOWNSEND, J. P., *Rambles and Observations in New South Wales* (1849).

TWISS, H., *The Public and Private Life of Lord Chancellor Eldon*, 3 vols. (1844).

WAKEFIELD, E. G., *A Letter from Sydney, etc.* (ed. 1929).
Plan of a Company to be established for the purpose of founding a Colony in Southern Australia etc. (1832).
Sketch of a proposal for Colonizing Australasia.
A View of the Art of Colonization (Oxford, ed. 1914).

WENTWORTH, W. C., *A Statistical, Historical, and Political Description of the Colony of New South Wales etc.* (1820).

WHATELEY, R., *Thoughts on Secondary Punishment in a Letter to Earl Grey* (1832).

WILBERFORCE, R. I. and S., *The Life of William Wilberforce by his Sons*, 5 vols. (1818–38).

COLLECTIONS OF DOCUMENTS AND WORKS OF REFERENCE

CHISHOLM, A. H. (ed.), *Australian Encyclopaedia*, 10 vols. (Sydney, 1958).

CLARK, C. M. H. (ed.), *Select Documents in Australian History 1788–1850* (Sydney, 1950).

Dictionary of National Biography.

FERGUSON, J. A. (ed.), *Bibliography of Australia Vol. I, 1784–1830* (Sydney, 1941).

HOUGHTON, W. E. (ed.), *Wellesley Index to Victorian Periodicals 1824–1900* (Toronto, 1966).

MCLINTOCK, A. H. (ed.), *An Encyclopaedia of New Zealand*, 3 vols. (Wellington, 1966).

MCNAB, R. (ed.), *Historical Records of New Zealand* (Wellington, 1908–).

PIKE, D. (ed.), *Australian Dictionary of Biography 1788–1850* (Melbourne 1966–7).

THEAL, C. McC. (ed.), Records of the Cape Colony (1902–).

WATSON, F. (ed.), *Historical Records of Australia*, Series I, III, IV/1, (Sydney 1914).

LATER WORKS

A. Theses

BEAGLEHOLE, J. C., 'The Royal Instructions to Colonial Governors 1783–1854' (London Univ. Ph.D. thesis 1929).

BROWN, L. M., 'The Policy of the Board of Trade in Relation to British Tariffs and Foreign Trade' (London Univ. Ph.D. thesis 1955).

CASSIRER, R., 'The Irish Influence on the Liberal Movement in England 1798–1832, with Special Reference to the Period 1815–32' (London Univ. Ph.D. thesis, 1940).

CROWLEY, F. K., 'Working Class Conditions in Australia 1788–1851' (Melbourne Univ. Ph.D. thesis 1949).

DAVIDSON, J. W., 'European Penetration of the South Pacific, 1779–1842' (Cambridge Univ. Ph.D. thesis 1942).

FRASER, P., 'The Conduct of Public Business in the House of Commons 1812–27' (London Univ. Ph.D. thesis 1957).

GULLAND, J. A., Criminal Law Reforms 1822–7 (London Univ. M.A. thesis 1930).

HARDY, S. M., 'William Huskisson 1770–1830: Imperial Statesman and Economist' (London Univ. Ph.D. thesis 1943).

HARRIS, M., 'British Migration to Western Australia 1829–50' (London Univ. Ph.D. thesis 1934).

HOWARD, D., 'The English Activities on the North Coast of Australia in the first half of the 19th Century' (London Univ. M.A. thesis 1924).

JONES, E. G., 'Sir R. J. Wilmot Horton, Bart., Politician and Pamphleteer' (Bristol Univ. M.A. thesis 1936).

KING, A. H., 'Aspects of British Colonial Policy 1825–1837, with particular reference to the Administration of Major General Sir Richard Bourke in Cape Colony and New South Wales' (Oxford Univ. D.Phil. thesis 1959).

KING, S. T., 'James Silk Buckingham, 1786–1855, Social and Political Reformer' (London Univ. M.A. thesis 1932).

MCLACHLAN, N. D., 'The Role of Government in New South Wales 1788–1855' (London Univ. Ph.D. thesis 1957).

MADDEN, A. F., 'The Attitude of the Evangelicals to the Empire and Imperial Problems 1820–50' (Oxford Univ. D.Phil. thesis 1950).

MITCHELL, A., 'The Whigs in Opposition: 1815–30' (Oxford Univ. D.Phil. thesis 1963).

RAWSON, D. W., 'Factions in New South Wales Politics 1820–40' (Melbourne Univ. M.A. thesis 1951).

RIDDELL, R. G., 'A Study in Imperial Land Policy 1783–1848' (Oxford Univ. B.Litt. thesis 1934).

ROE, M., 'New South Wales under Governor King' (Melbourne Univ. M.A. thesis 1955).

TUCKER, H. F. G., 'The Press and the Colonies 1802–33' (Bristol Univ. M.A. thesis 1936).

WYNNE, W. H., 'The Development of Land Policy in Australia with Special Reference to New South Wales 1788–1922' (Cambridge Univ. Ph.D. thesis 1926).

B.   Books, articles and monographs

ABBOTT, G. C., 'Staple Theory and Australian Economic Growth 1788–1820', *Business Archives and History* V (1965).
'A note on the volume of New South Wales Treasury Bill Expenditure 1788–1821', *Business Archives and History* VI (1966).

ADAMS, W. F., *Ireland and Irish Emigration to the New World from 1815 to the Famine* (Oxford 1932).

ARNDT, E. H. D., *Banking and Currency Development in South Africa 1652–1927* (Cape Town and Johannesburg 1928).

ASHTON, T. S., *The Industrial Revolution 1760–1830* (Oxford 1948).

ASHTON, T. S. and SAYERS, R. S. (ed.), *Papers in English Monetary History* (Oxford 1953).

ASPINALL, A., 'The Canningite Party', *TRHS* XVII (1934).
'George IV and Sir William Knighton', *EHR* LV (1940).
'The Coalition Ministries of 1827', *EHR* XLII (1927)
'The Last of the Canningites', *EHR* L (1935)
Politics and the Press 1780–1850 (1949)
Lord Brougham and the Whig Party (1927)
'The Grand Cabinet', 1800–1837, *Politica* III (1938)

AUSTIN, A. G., *Australian Education 1788–1900* (Melbourne, 1961)

BADHAM, C., *The Life of J. D. Hume, Secretary of the Board of Trade* (1859).

BAGOT, J., *George Canning and his Friends*, 2 vols. (1909).

BALLHATCHET, K., *Social Policy and Social Change in Western India 1817–30* (1957).

BARNARD, M., *Macquarie's World* (Melbourne, 1941 and 1961).

BARRETT, J., *That Better Country* (Melbourne, 1966).

BARRY, J. V., *Alexander Maconochie of Norfolk Island* (Melbourne, 1958).

BARTLETT, C. J., *Great Britain and Sea Power 1815–53* (Oxford, 1963).

BASSETT, M., *The Hentys* (Oxford, 1954).

BASTER, A. S. J., *The Imperial Banks* (1929)

BATESON, C., *The Convict Ships 1787–1868* (Glasgow, 1959).

BEEVER, E. A., 'The Origin of the Wool Industry in New South Wales', *Business Archives and History* V (1965).

BELL, S. S., *Colonial Administration of Great Britian* (1859).

BEST, G. F. A., 'The Protestant Constitution and its Supporters 1800–29', *TRHS* (1958).

'The Whigs and the Church Establishment in the Age of Grey and Holland', *History* XLV (1960).

BEST, G. F. A., *Temporal Pillars* (Cambridge, 1964).

BIRT, H. N., *Benedictine Pioneers in Australia* (1911).

BLAKE, R., *Disraeli* (1966).

BORDER, R., *Church and State in Australia 1788–1872* (1962).

BOWDEN, K. N., *Captain James Kelly of Hobart Town* (Melbourne, 1964).

Democracy in the Dominions (Toronto, 1948).

BRANCH-JOHNSON, W., *The English Prison Hulks* (1957).

BRIGGS, A., *Press and Public Opinion in Early 19th cent. Birmingham* (Oxford, 1949).

The Age of Improvement (1959).

BROCK, W. R., *Lord Liverpool and Liberal Toryism 1820–27* (Cambridge, 1941).

BUER, M. C., *Health, Wealth and Population in the Early Days of the Industrial Revolution* (1926).

BURN, W. L., *Emancipation and Apprenticeship in the British West Indies* (1937).

BURROUGHS, P., *Britain and Australia, 1831–55* (Oxford, 1967).

BURTON, A., *Church Beginnings in the West* (Perth, 1941).

BUTLIN, S. J., *The Foundations of the Australian Monetary System 1788–1851* (Melbourne, 1953).

CABLE, B., *A Hundred Year History of the P & O, 1837–1937* (1937).

The Cambridge History of the British Empire.

The Cambridge History of British Foreign Policy, Vol. II: 1815–66 (Cambridge, 1923).

CAMPBELL, J. F., 'The First Decade of the Australian Agricultural Company 1824–30', *RAHS* IX (1923).

CHALMERS, R., *A History of Currency in the British Colonies* (1893).

CLAPHAM, J. H., *An Economic History of Modern Britain 1820–1850* (Cambridge, 1950).

The Bank of England, vol. 2, 1797–1914 (Cambridge, 1944).

CLARK, C. M. H., *Select Documents in Australian History*, vol. 2, 1788–1850 (Sydney, 1958).
A Short History of Australia (New York, 1963).
A History of Australia, vol. 1, From the Earliest Times to the Age of Macquarie (Melbourne, 1962).
Vol. 2, *New South Wales and Van Diemen's Land 1822–1838* (Melbourne, 1968).

COGHLAN, T. A., *Labour and Industry in Australia*, vol. 1 (Oxford, 1958).

COHEN, E., *The Growth of the British Civil Service 1780–1939* (1941).

COLLIER, J., *The Pastoral Age in Australia* (1911).

CORRIGAN, U., *Catholic Education in New South Wales* (Sydney, 1930).

COUPLAND, R., *The British Anti-Slavery Movement* (1933).
The Quebec Act (Oxford, 1925).
Raffles (Oxford, 1926).
Wilberforce (Oxford, 1933).

COWHERD, R. G., *The Politics of English Dissent* (1959).

CRAIG, J., *A History of Red Tape* (1955).

CRAMP, K. R. and MACKANESS, G., *A History of the United Grand Lodges of Ancient, Free and Accepted Masons of New South Wales*, 2 vols. (Sydney, 1938).

CRAWFORD, R. M., *Australia* (1952).

CREIGHTON, D. G., 'The Struggle for Financial Control in Lower Canada 1818–31', *Canadian History Review* XII (1931).

CURREY, C. H., *British Colonial Policy 1783–1915* (Oxford, 1916).

DARVALL, F. O., *Popular Disturbances and Public Order in Regency England* (Oxford, 1934).

DALEY, L. T., *Men and a River. A History of the Richmond River District 1828–95* (Melbourne, 1966).

DALLAS, K., 'Transportation and Colonial Income', *HSANZ* III (1949).

DAVIDSON, W. L., *Political Thought in England. The Utilitarians* (1915).

DAVIS, H. W. C., 'Brougham, Lord Grey and Canning, 1815–30', *EHR* XXXVIII (1923).
The Age of Grey and Peel (Oxford, 1929).

DE KIEWET, C. W., *A History of South Africa* (Oxford, 1941).
British Colonial Policy and the South African Republics 1848–72 (1929).

308 BIBLIOGRAPHY

The Imperial Factor in South Africa (Oxford, 1937).

DICEY, A. V., *Lectures on the Relationship between Law and Public Opinion in England during the 19th Century* (1914).

DOWDEN, E., (ed.), *Correspondence of Henry Taylor* (1888).

DUNHAM, A., *Political Unrest in Upper Canada 1815–36* (1927).

DUNSDORFS, E., *The Australian Wheat Growing Industry 1788–1948* (Melbourne, 1956).

EDWARDS, I. E., *The 1820 Settlers in South Africa* (1934).

EGERTON, H. E., *The Origin and Growth of the English Colonies and of their system of Government* (Oxford, 1904).

A Short History of British Colonial Policy (5th ed. 1918).

ELDER, J. R., *The Letters and Journals of Samuel Marsden 1765–1838* (Otago, 1932).

ELDERSHAW, M. B., *The Life and Times of Captain John Piper* (Sydney, 1939).

ELLIS, M. H., *Lachlan Macquarie, His Life, Adventures and Times* (Sydney, 1952).

John Macarthur (Sydney, 1955).

EMBREE, A. T., *Charles Grant and British Rule in India* (1962).

FAY, C. R., *The Corn Laws and Social England* (Cambridge, 1932).

Life and Labour in Newfoundland (Cambridge, 1956).

Great Britain from Adam Smith to the Present Day (5th ed. 1957).

Huskisson and his Age (1951).

FEILING, K. G., *The Second Tory Party* (1938).

FERGUSON J. A., et al., *The Howes and their Press* (Sydney, 1936).

FITZPATRICK, B., *British Imperialism and Australia 1783–1833* (1939).

FLANAGAN, R., *The History of New South Wales etc.* 2 vols. (1862).

FOGARTY, J. P., 'The Staple Approach and the Role of the Government in Australian Economic Development: the Wheat Industry' *Business Archives and History*, VI (1966).

FOGARTY, R., *Catholic Education in Australia 1806–1950* (Melbourne, 1959).

FORSYTH, W. D., *Governor Arthur's Convict System* (1935).

FRASER, P., 'Public Petitioning and Parliament before 1832', *History* XLVI (1961).

GALBRAITH, J. S., *Reluctant Empire. British Policy on the South African Frontier 1834–54* (Los Angeles, 1963).

The Hudson's Bay Company as an Imperial Factor 1821–69 (Los Angeles, 1957).

GASH, N., *Mr. Secretary Peel* (1961).
Politics in the Age of Peel (1953).
GAYE, A. D., ROSTOW, W. W. and SCHWARTZ, A. J., *The Growth and Fluctuation of the British Economy 1790–1850*, 2 vols. (Oxford, 1953).
GIBLIN, R. W., *The Early History of Tasmania* (Melbourne, 1939).
GILCHRIST, A., *J. Dunmore Lang*, 2 vols. (Melbourne, 1951).
GILROY, M., 'Customs Fees in Nova Scotia', *CHR* XVII (1936).
'The Imperial Customs Establishment in Nova Scotia', *CHR* XIX (1938).
GHOSH, R. M., 'The Colonization Controversy: R. J. Wilmot-Horton and the Classical Economists', *Economica* n.s. XXXI (1964).
'Malthus on Emigration and Colonization: Letters to Wilmot-Horton', *Economica* n.s. XXX (1963).
GOODWIN, C. D., 'Political Economy in Australia: the Growth of a Discipline', *Business Archives and History* VI (1966).
Economic Enquiry in Australia (Durham, 1966).
GRAHAM, G. S., *Sea Power and British North America 1783–1820* (Cambridge, 1941).
GRATTAN, C. H., *The South West Pacific to 1900* (Anne Arbor, 1963).
GRATTAN, C. H., (ed.), *Australia* (Los Angeles, 1947).
GRAY, D., *Spencer Percival: The Evangelical Prime Minister 1762–1812* (Manchester, 1965).
GREENWOOD, G. (ed.), *Australia: A Social and Political History* (Sydney, 1955).
Early American-Australia Relations (Melbourne, 1944).
GREGSON, J., *The Australian Agricultural Company 1824–75* (Sydney, 1907).
GRIFFITHS, G. N., *Some Houses and People of New South Wales* (Sydney, 1949).
HALÉVY, E., *The Growth of Philosophical Radicalism* (1928).
HANCOCK, W. K., *Australia* (Brisbane, 1961 and 1930).
HARLOW, V. and MADDEN, F. (eds.), *British Colonial Developments 1774–1834* (Oxford, 1953).
HARTWELL, R. M., 'Australia's First Trade Cycle: 1820–32', *RAHS* XLII (1956).
The Economic Development of Van Diemen's Land 1820–50 (Melbourne, 1954).

HARVEY, D. C., 'The Civil List and Responsible Government in Nova Scotia', *CHR* XXVIII (1947).

HASLUCK, A., *Thomas Peel of Swan River* (Melbourne, 1965).

HAWTREY, C. L. M., *The Availing Struggle: A Record of the Planting and Development of the Church of England in Western Australia* (Perth, 1949).

HERRIES, E., *Memoir of the Public Life of the Rt. Hon. J. C. Herries*, 2 vols. (1880).

HINDE, R. S., *The British Penal System 1773–1950* (1951).

HITCHENS, F. H., *The Colonial Land and Emigration Commission* (Philadelphia, 1931).

HOGAN, J. F., *The Irish in Australia* (Melbourne, 1888).

HOSKINS, H. L., *British Routes to India* (New York, 1928).

JEANS, D. N., 'Crown Land Sales and the Accommodation of the Small Settler in New South Wales' 1825–1842', *HSANZ* XII (1966).

JENKS, L. H., *The Migration of British Capital up to 1875* (1938).

JEPHSON, H., *The Platform: Its Rise and Progress* (1892).

JOHNSON, S. C., *A History of Emigration from the United Kingdom to North America* (1913).

JONES, W. D., *Prosperity Robinson: The Life of Viscount Goderich 1782–1859* (1967).

JUDD, G. P. (IV), *Members of Parliament 1734–1832* (New Haven, 1955).

JUDD, W. J., 'Governor Arthur and the Gellibrand Affair', *RAHS* XXXIV (1948).

KENNY, DEAN, *A History of the Commencement and Progress of Catholicity in Australia up to the Year 1840* (Sydney, 1886).

KER, J., 'The Wool Industry in New South Wales 1803–30', *Business Archives and History* I (1956).

KIERNAN, T. J., *The Irish Exiles in Australia* (1954).

Transportation from Ireland to Sydney 1791–1816 (Canberra, 1954).

KING, C. J., *The First Fifty Years of Agriculture in New South Wales* (Sydney, 1950).

KITTRELL, E. R., '"Laissez Faire" in English Classical Economics', *Journal of the History of Ideas* XXVII (1966).

KLINGSBERG, F. S., *The Anti-Slavery Movement in England* (New Haven, 1926).

KNAPLUND, P., 'James Stephen on Canadian Banking Laws 1821–46', *CHR* XXXI (1950).

'Sir James Stephen and B N A Problems: 1840–1847', *CHR* V (1924).

'Mr. Oversecretary Stephen', *Journal of Modern History* I (1929).

James Stephen and the British Colonial System 1813–47 (Madison, 1953).

KNIGHT, F. H., 'Theory of Economic Policy and the History of Doctrine', *Ethics* LXIII (1952).

KNORR, K. E., *British Colonial Theories 1570–1850* (Toronto, 1944).

KNOWLES, L. C. A., *The Industrial and Commercial Revolution in Great Britain during the 19th Century* (1927).

The Economic Development of the British Overseas Empire (1924).

LA NAUZE, J. A., 'The Collection of Customs in Australia: a Note on Administration', *HSANZ* IV (1949.

'Australian Tariffs and Imperial Control', *The Economic Record* XXIV (1948).

LEIGHTON-BOYCE, J. A. S., *Smiths the Bankers 1658–1958* (1958).

LEROY-BEAULIEU, P., *De la Colonizazion chez les Peuples Modernes*, 2 vols. (Paris, 1902).

LEVY, M. C. I., *Governor George Arthur: A Colonial Benevolent Despot* (Melbourne, 1953).

LEWIS, Sir G. C., *Essay on the Administration of Great Britain from 1783–1830* (1864).

LEWIS, M., *The Navy in Transition 1814–64, a Social History* (1965).

LINGELBACH, A. L., 'William Huskisson as President of the Board of Trade', *AHR* XLIII (1938).

'The Inception of the British Board of Trade', *AHR* XXX (1925).

MCCARTY, J. W., 'The Staple Approach in Australian Economic History', *Business Archives and History* IV (1964).

MCCULLOCH, S. C. (ed.), *British Humanitarianism: Essays Honouring Frank J. Klingberg* (Philadelphia, 1950).

MACDONALD, N., *Canada 1763–1841: Immigration and Settlement* (1939).

MCDOWELL, R. B., *Public Opinion and Government Policy in Ireland 1801–46* (1952).

MACKANESS, G., *Blue Bloods of Botany Bay* (1953).

MACKAY, A. L., *The Australian Banking and Credit System* (1931).

MCLACHLAN, N., 'Edward Eager (1787–1866): A Colonial Spokesman in Sydney and London', *HSANZ* X (1963).

MACMILLAN, D. S., 'The Beginning of Scottish Enterprise in Australia; the Contribution of the Commercial Whigs', *Business Archives and History* II (1962).

Scotland and Australia 1788–1850 (Oxford, 1967).

MADGWICK, R. B., *Immigration to Eastern Australia 1788–1851* (1937).

MANNING, H. T., 'Who Ran the British Empire 1830–50?', *The Journal of British Studies* V (1965).

'Colonial Crises before the Cabinet, 1829–35', *BIHR* XXX (1957).

British Colonial Government after the American Revolution, 1782–1820 (New Haven, 1933).

'The Civil List of Lower Canada', *CHR* XXIV (1943).

The Revolt of French Canada 1800–35 (1962).

'The Colonial Policy of the Whig Ministers 1800–37', *CHR* XXIII (1952).

MARAIS, J. S., *The Colonisation of New Zealand* (Oxford, 1927).

MARSDEN, J. B., *Life and Work of Samuel Marsden* (Christchurch, 1913).

MEENAI, S. A., 'Robert Torrens, 1780–1864', *Economica* XXIII (1956).

MELBOURNE, A. C. V., *W. C. Wentworth* (Brisbane, 1934).

Early Constitutional Development in Australia 1788–1856 (Oxford, 1934) (Brisbane, 1963).

MILLER, E. M., *Pressmen and Governors* (Sydney, 1952).

Australian Literature from its Beginnings to 1935, 2 vols. (Melbourne, 1940).

MILLER, E. M. (ed. F. T. MACARTNEY), *Australian Literature* (Sydney, 1956).

MILLER, J., *Early Victorian New Zealand* (1958).

MILLS, R. C., *The Colonization of Australia 1829–42* (1915).

MURRAY, D. J., *The West Indies and the Development of Colonial Government 1801–34* (Oxford, 1965).

NADEL, G., *Australia's Colonial Culture* (Melbourne, 1957).

NAPIER, MACVEY, *Selections from the Correspondence of the Late MacVey Napier* (1879).

NEWMAN, C. E. T., *The Spirit of Wharf House 1788–1930* (Sydney, 1961).

O'BRIEN, E., *The Foundation of Australia* (1937).

Life and Letters of Archpriest John Joseph Therry (Sydney, 1922).

The Dawn of Catholicism in Australia, 2 vols. (Sydney, 1928).

ORMSBY, W., 'The Problem of Canadian Union, 1822–28', *CHR* XXIX (1958).

PARRY, A., *Parry of the Arctic*, (1963).

PATTERSON, G. C., *Land Settlement in Upper Canada 1783–1840* (Toronto, 1921).

PERRY, T. M., *Australia's First Frontier: The Spread of Settlement in New South Wales 1788–1829* (Melbourne, 1963).

PHILIPS, C. H., *The East India Company 1784–1834* (Manchester, 1940).

PHILLIPS, M., *A Colonial Autocracy. New South Wales under Governor Macquarie* (1909).

PIKE, D., *Australia: the Quiet Continent* (Cambridge, 1962).
    'Wilmot Horton and the National Colonization Society', *HSANZ* VII (1956).
    Paradise of Dissent: South Australia 1829–70 (Melbourne, 1957).

PLOMLEY, N. J. B. (ed.), *Friendly Mission: The Tasmanian Journals and Papers of G. A. Robinson 1829–34* (Sydney, 1966).

PORTUS, G. V., *Australia: an Economic Interpretation* (Sydney, 1933).

PRICE, A. G., *Founders and Pioneers of South Australia* (Adelaide, 1929).

RADZINOWICZ, L., *A History of English Criminal Law and its Administration from 1750*, 3 vols. (1948).

RAMSDEN, E., *Busby of Waitangi: H.M.'s Resident at New Zealand 1833–40* (Sydney, 1942).

RIDDELL, R. G., 'A Study in the Land Policy of the Colonial Office 1763–1855', *CHR* XVIII (1937).

ROBBINS, L., *Robert Torrens and the Evolution of Classical Economics* (1958).

ROBBINS, L., *The Theory of Economic Policy in English Classical Political Economy* (1961).

ROBERTS, S. H., *History of Australian Land Settlement 1788–1920* (Melbourne, 1924).
    The Squatting Age in Australia 1835–47 (Melbourne, 1935).

ROBSON, L. L., *The Convict Settlers of Australia* (Melbourne, 1965).

ROE, M., *Quest for Authority in Eastern Australia 1835–51* (Melbourne, 1965).

ROSE, L. N., 'The Administration of Governor Darling', *RAHS* VIII (1922).

RUDÉ, G., *The Crowd in History, 1730–1848* (New York, 1964).

RUSDEN, G. W., *History of Australia in 3 Volumes* (1883).
    History of New Zealand (Melbourne, 1859).

SCHENK, H. G., *The Aftermath of the Napoleonic Wars* (1947).

SCHUYLER, R. L., *Parliament and the British Empire* (New York, 1929).

The Fall of the Old Colonial System (Oxford, 1945).

SCOTT, E., *Australian Discovery by Land* (1929).

SEELEY, J. R., *The Expansion of England* (1883).

SHANN, E. O. G., *An Economic History of Australia* (Cambridge, 1948).

SHARP, A., *The Discovery of Australia* (Oxford, 1963).

SHAW, A. G. L., *The Story of Australia* (1955).

Convicts and the Colonies (1966).

The Economic Development of Australia (1950).

SINCLAIR, K., *A History of New Zealand* (Oxford, 1961).

SMART, W., *Economic Annals of the 19th Century*, 2 vols. (1910).

SMITH, W., 'Canada and Constitutional Development in New South Wales', *CHR* VII (1926).

'Side-Lights on the Attempted Union of 1822', *CHR* II (1921).

STAUNTON, SIR G. T., *Memoir of Sir John Barrow Bart. etc.* (1853).

STEPHEN, C. E., *The Rt. Hon. James Stephen. Letters with Biographical Notes* (Cambridge, 1906).

STEPHEN, L., *The English Utilitarians*, 3 vols. (1900).

STEVEN, M., 'The Changing Pattern of Commerce in New South Wales 1810–21', *Business Archives and History* III (1963).

Merchant Campbell 1796–1846. A Study of Colonial Trade (Melbourne, 1965).

SUTTOR, T. L., *Hierarchy and Democracy in Australia 1788–1870* (Melbourne, 1965).

SWEETMAN, E., *Australian Constitutional Development* (Melbourne, 1925).

TAPP, E. J., *Early New Zealand. A Dependency of New South Wales 1788–1841* (Melbourne, 1958).

TASKER, REV. N. (ed.), *Reminiscences of Sir Thomas MackDougall Brisbane* (Edinburgh, 1860).

TAYLOR, H., *Autobiography 1800–75*, 2 vols. (1885).

THEAL, G. M., *History of South Africa 1795–1872*, 5 vols. (1892).

THERRY, R., *Reminiscences of Thirty Years' Residence in New South Wales and Victoria* (1863).

TURBERVILLE, A. S., *The House of Lords in the Age of Reform 1784–1837* (1958).

TURNBULL, C., *Black War: The Extermination of the Tasmanian Aborigines* (Melbourne, 1848).

UREN, M., *Land Looking West* (Oxford, 1948).

VEITCH, G. S., *The Genesis of Parliamentary Reform* (1913).

VINER, J., *The Long View and the Short. Studies in Economic Theory. and Policy* (1958).

WADHAM, S., WILSON, R. K., and WOOD, J., *Land Utilization in Australia* (Melbourne, 3rd ed. 1957).

WALKER, R. B., *Old New England. A History of the Northern Tablelands of New South Wales 1818–1900.*

WALPOLE, S., *A History of England from the Conclusion of the Great War in 1815*, 5 vols. (1878).

WALSH, G. P., 'The Geography of Manufacturing in Sydney 1788–1851', *Business Archives and History* III (1963).

WARD, B., *The Eve of Catholic Emancipation*, 3 vols. (1911–12).

WARD, J. M., *British Policy in the South Pacific 1786–1893* (Sydney, 1948).
Empire in the Antipodes. The British in Australasia 1840–60 (1966).

WARD, R., *The Australian Legend* (Melbourne, 1958).
Australia (New Jersey, 1965).

WEST, J., *The History of Tasmania* (Launceston, 1852).

WHITE, C., *Convict Life in New South Wales and Van Diemen's Land* (1889).

WHITINGTON, F. T., *William Grant Broughton* (Sydney, 1936).

WICKWAR, W. H., *The Struggle for the Freedom of the Press 1819–32* (1928).

WIGHT, M., *The Development of the Legislative Council 1606–1945* (1946).

WILLIAMS, E. T., 'The Colonial Office in the Thirties', *HSANZ* II II (1943).
'James Stephen and the British Intervention in New Zealand 1838–40', *JMH* (1941).

WINCH, D., *Classical Political Economy and Colonies* (London, 1965).

WOOD, F. L. W., 'Jeremy Bentham vs New South Wales', *RAHS* XIX (1933).
The Constitutional Development of Australia (1933).

WRIGHT, H. R. C., *East-Indian Economic Problems of the Age of Cornwallis and Raffles* (1961).

WURTZBURG, C. E., *Raffles of the Eastern Isles* (1954).

WYATT, R. T., *The History of Goulburn, New South Wales* (Goulburn, 1941).

YONGE, C. D. (ed.), *The Life and Administration of Robert Banks, 2nd Earl of Liverpool*, 3 vols. (1868).

YOUNG, D. M., *The Colonial Office in the Early 19th Century* (1961).

YOUNG, G. M., *Victorian England—Portrait of an Age* (Oxford, ed. ed. 1957).

ZIEGLER, P., *Addington* (1965).

INDEX